AREA 1

SOUTH WEST ENGLAND – Isles of Scilly to Anvil Point

The Reeds Nautical Almanac 2026 available as an eBook

www.adlardcoles.com

Key to Marina Plans symbols

	Bottled gas	P	Parking
	Chandler		Pub/Restaurant
	Disabled facilities		Pump out
	Electrical supply		Rigging service
	Electrical repairs		Sail repairs
	Engine repairs		Shipwright
	First Aid		Shop/Supermarket
	Fresh Water		Showers
D	Fuel - Diesel		Slipway
P	Fuel - Petrol	WC	Toilets
	Hardstanding/boatyard		Telephone
@	Internet Café		Trolleys
	Laundry facilities	V	Visitors berths
	Lift-out facilities		Wi-Fi

Area 1 - South West England

MARINAS
Telephone Numbers
VHF Channel
Access Times

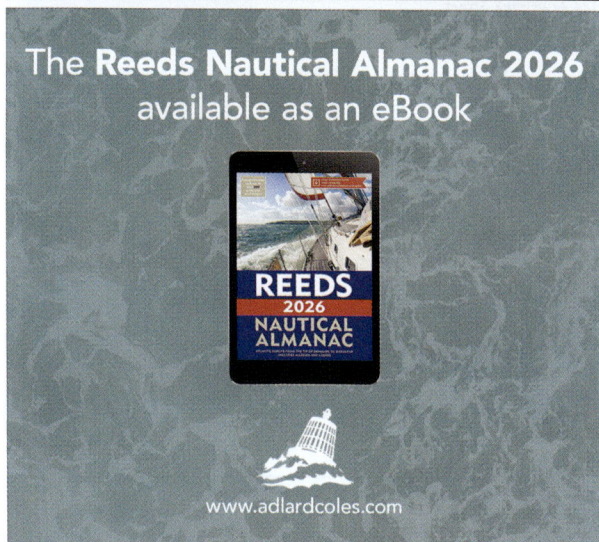

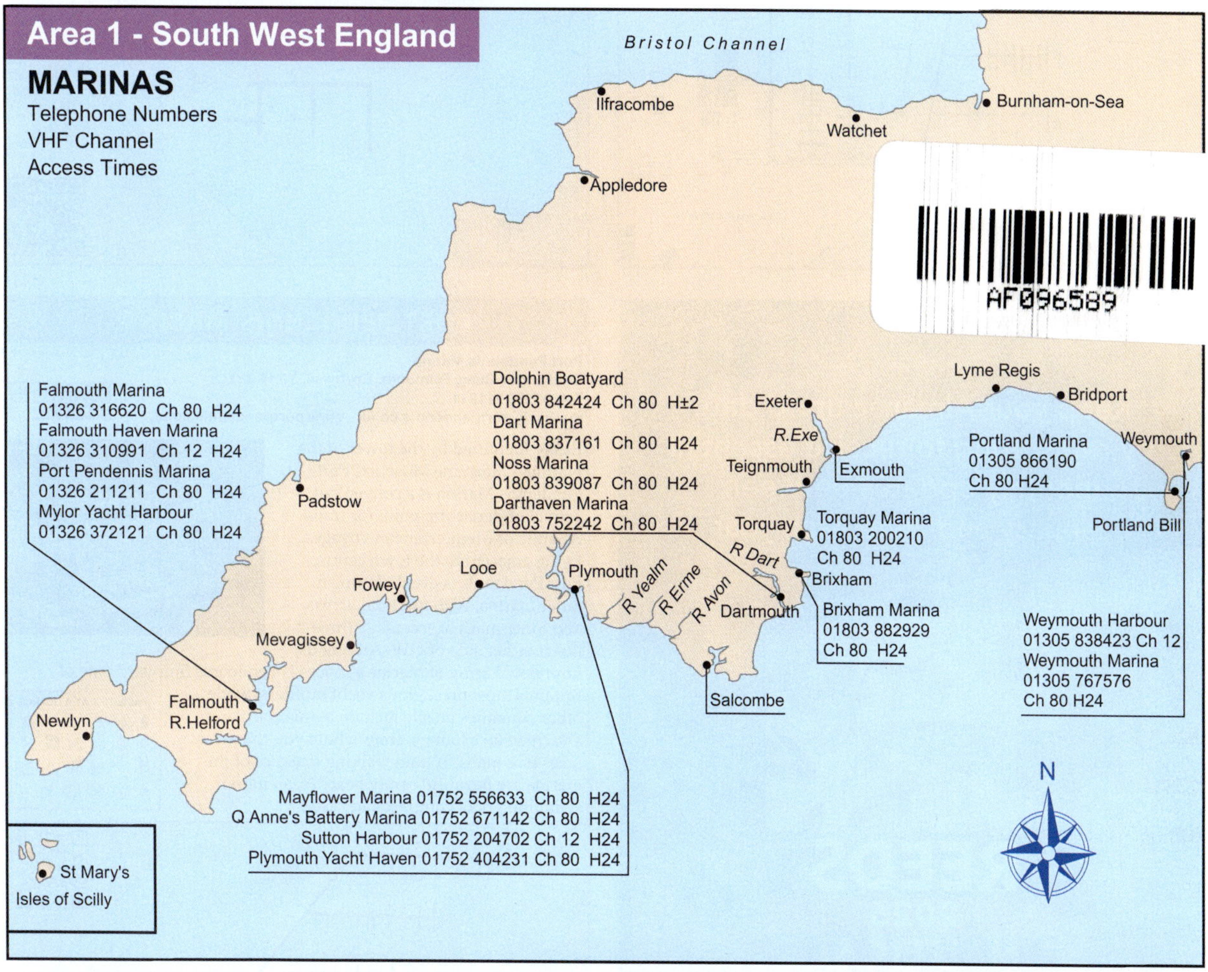

Bristol Channel

Ilfracombe • Watchet • Burnham-on-Sea
• Appledore

Falmouth Marina 01326 316620 Ch 80 H24
Falmouth Haven Marina 01326 310991 Ch 12 H24
Port Pendennis Marina 01326 211211 Ch 80 H24
Mylor Yacht Harbour 01326 372121 Ch 80 H24

Dolphin Boatyard 01803 842424 Ch 80 H±2
Dart Marina 01803 837161 Ch 80 H24
Noss Marina 01803 839087 Ch 80 H24
Darthaven Marina 01803 752242 Ch 80 H24

Lyme Regis • Bridport
Exeter • R.Exe • Weymouth
Teignmouth • Exmouth
Portland Marina 01305 866190 Ch 80 H24
Portland Bill
Torquay • Torquay Marina 01803 200210 Ch 80 H24
Brixham
Padstow
Fowey • Looe • Plymouth • R Yealm • R Erme • R Avon • R Dart • Dartmouth
Brixham Marina 01803 882929 Ch 80 H24
Weymouth Harbour 01305 838423 Ch 12
Weymouth Marina 01305 767576 Ch 80 H24
Mevagissey •
Salcombe
Newlyn • Falmouth R.Helford

Mayflower Marina 01752 556633 Ch 80 H24
Q Anne's Battery Marina 01752 671142 Ch 80 H24
Sutton Harbour 01752 204702 Ch 12 H24
Plymouth Yacht Haven 01752 404231 Ch 80 H24

St Mary's Isles of Scilly

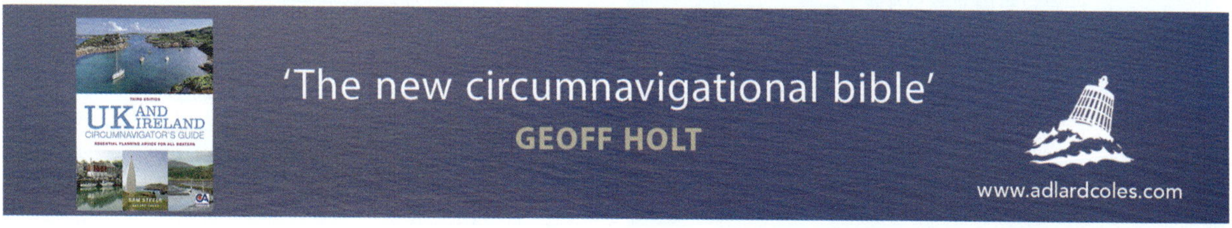

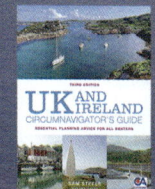

'The new circumnavigational bible'
GEOFF HOLT

www.adlardcoles.com

MARINA GUIDE 2026

MARINAS & SERVICES

FALMOUTH MARINA

Falmouth Marina
North Parade, Falmouth, Cornwall, TR11 2TD
Tel: 01326 316620
Email: falmouth@premiermarinas.com
www.premiermarinas.com

VHF Ch 80
ACCESS H24

Falmouth Marina sits within the safe and sheltered waters and outstanding natural beauty of the Fal Estuary, with 24/7 access to the glorious cruising grounds and countryside of Cornwall.

The marina full-service, family-friendly facility, ideal for boaters of all abilities, with both secure wet and dry stack berthing options. Falmouth provides first-class facilities, along with an array of marine and hospitality services, including a chandlery, brokerage, fully serviced boatyard, bar/restaurant and an onsite hairdresser.

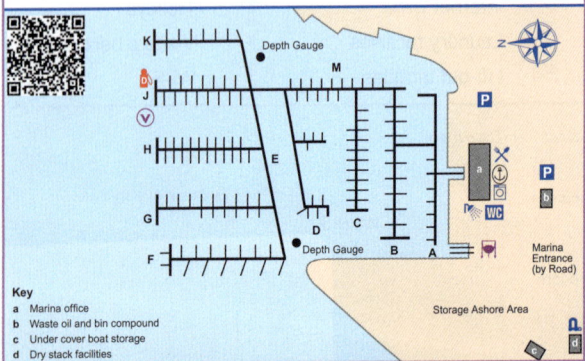

FALMOUTH HAVEN MARINA

Falmouth Haven Marina
44 Arwenack Street
Tel: 01326 310991
Email: welcome@falmouthhaven.co.uk

VHF Ch 12
ACCESS H24

Run by Falmouth Harbour Commissioners (FHC), Falmouth Haven Marina has become increasingly popular since its opening in 1982, enjoying close proximity to the amenities and entertainments of Falmouth town centre. Sheltered by a breakwater, Falmouth Haven caters for 50 boats and offers petrol and diesel supplies as well as good shower and laundry facilities.

Falmouth Harbour is considered by some to be the cruising capital of Cornwall and its deep water combined with easily navigable entrance – even in the severest conditions – makes it a favoured destination for visiting yachtsmen.

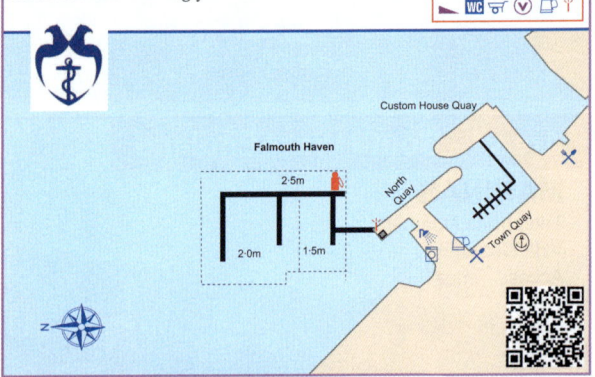

PORT PENDENNIS MARINA

Port Pendennis Marina
Challenger Quay, Falmouth, Cornwall, TR11 3YL
Tel: 01326 211211
marina@portpendennis.co.uk   www.portpendennis.co.uk

VHF Ch 80
ACCESS H24

Easily identified by the tower of the National Maritime Museum, Port Pendennis Marina is a convenient arrival or departure point for trans-Atlantic or Mediterranean voyages. Lying adjacent to the town centre, Port Pendennis is divided into an outer marina, with full tidal access, and inner marina, accessible three hours either side of HW. Among its impressive array of marine services is Pendennis Shipyard, one of Britain's most prestigious yacht builders, while other amenities on site include tennis court and a yachtsman's lounge, from where you can send faxes or e-mails. Within walking distance of the marina are beautiful sandy beaches, an indoor swimming pool complex and castle.

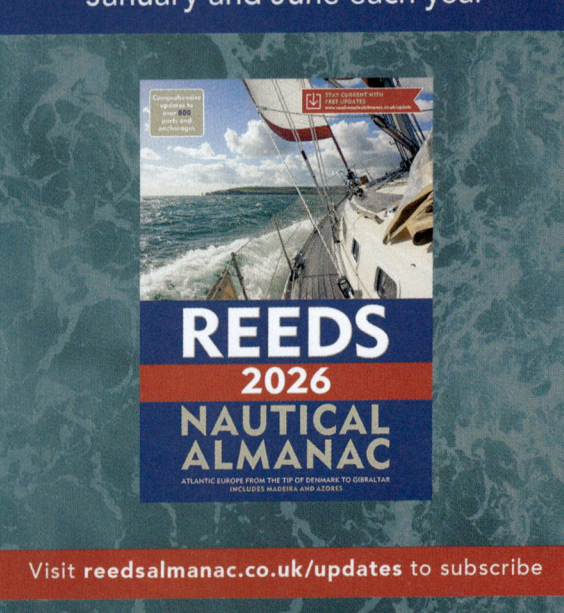

Keep your Almanac up to date by registering to receive essential monthly updates between January and June each year

REEDS 2026 NAUTICAL ALMANAC

Visit reedsalmanac.co.uk/updates to subscribe

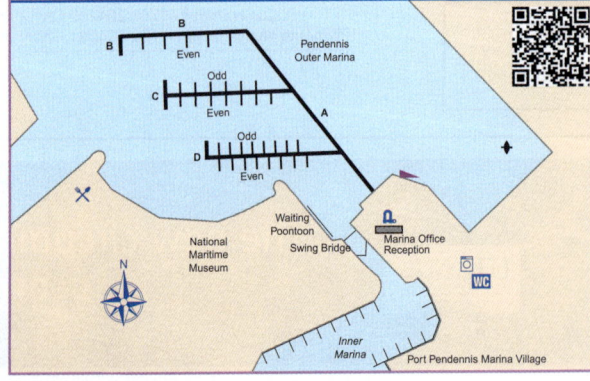

MARINA GUIDE 2026

REEDS MARINA GUIDE 2026

The source directory for all sail & power boat owners

© Adlard Coles Nautical 2025

Adlard Coles Nautical,
50 Bedford Square, London, WC1B 3DP

29 Earlsfort Terrace, Dublin 2, Ireland

Tel: +44 (0)20 7631 5600

e-mail: info@reedsalmanacs.co.uk
www.reedsalmanacs.co.uk

Cover photo:
Poole Quay Boat Haven
Tel: 01202 649488
www.poolequayboathaven.co.uk

Section 1

The Marinas and Services Section has been fully updated for the 2026 season. These useful pages provide chartlets and facility details for some 200 marinas around the shores of the UK and Ireland, including the Channel Islands, the perfect complement to any Reeds Nautical Almanac.

Section 2

The Marine Supplies & Services section lists more than 1000 services at coastal and other locations around the British Isles. It provides a quick and easy reference to manufacturers and retailers of equipment, services and supplies both nationally and locally together with emergency services.

Advertisement Sales
Enquiries about advertising space should be addressed to:
adlardcoles@bloomsbury.com

Printed and bound in Italy by
L.E.G.O. S.p.A.

MIX
Paper | Supporting responsible forestry
FSC® C023419

Section 1
Marinas and Services Section 2–98

Area Guide Chart 2

Area 1 - SW England
Area 1 Marina Chart 3
Falmouth Marina 4
Falmouth Haven Marina 4
Port Pendennis Marina 4
Mylor Yacht Harbour 7
Mayflower Marina 7
Queen Anne's Battery 7
Plymouth Yacht Haven 9
Sutton Harbour 9
Darthaven Marina 11
Dart Marina Yacht Harbour 11
Noss Marina 11
Dolphin Boatyard 12
Brixham Marina 12
Torquay Marina 12
Portland Marina 12
Weymouth Marina 13
Weymouth Harbour 13

Area 2 - Central S England
Area 2 Marina Chart 15
Ridge Wharf 16
Lake Yard Marina 16
Cobb's Quay Marina 16
Poole Quay Boat Haven 16
Port of Poole Marina 17
Parkstone Yacht Haven 17
Salterns Marina 17
Yarmouth Harbour 17
Lymington Yacht Haven 18
Berthon Lymington Marina 18
Lymington Town Quay 18
Lymington - Dan Bran Visitor 19
Bucklers Hard 19
Hythe Marina Village 21
Cowes Yacht Haven 21
Island Harbour Marina 21
Cowes Hbr Shepards Marina 22
E Cowes Marina 22
Town Quay 23
Ocean Village Marina 23
Shamrock Quay 23
Kemps Quay 23
Saxon Wharf 25
Hamble Point Marina 25
Port Hamble Marina 25
Mercury Yacht Harbour 25
Universal Marina 26
Swanwick Marina 26
Deacons Marina 26
Ryde Marina 26
Bembridge Marina 27
Haslar Marina 27
Gosport Marina 28
Royal Clarence Marina 28
Port Solent Marina 29
WicorMarine YH 29
Southsea Marina 29
Sparkes Marina 29
Northney Marina 30
Emsworth Yacht Harbour 30
Chichester Marina 31
Birdham Pool 31

Area 3 - SE England
Area 3 Marina Chart 33
Littlehampton Marina 34
Lady Bee Marina 34
Brighton Marina 34
Newhaven Marina 34
Sovereign Harbour 35
Harbour of Rye 35
Dover Marina 35
Ramsgate Royal Hbr 35

Area 4 - E England
Area 4 Marina Chart 37
Gillingham Marina 38
Port Werburgh 38
Chatham Maritime Marina 39
Limehouse Waterside & Marina 39
South Dock Marina 40
Chelsea Harbour 40
St Katharine Docks 40
Brentford Dock Marina 41
Penton Hook Marina 41
Windsor Marina 41
Bray Marina 41
Burnham Yacht Harbour 42
Essex Marina 42
Bridgemarsh Marina 42
Heybridge Basin 43
Bradwell Marina 43
Fambridge Yacht Station 43
Fambridge Yacht Haven 44
Blackwater Marina 44
Tollesbury Marina 44
Titchmarsh Marina 45
Walton Yacht Basin 45
Suffolk Yacht Harbour 45
Shotley Marina 46
Royal Harwich YC 46
Fox's Marina 47
Woolverstone Marina 47
Ipswich Beacon Marina (Neptune) 48
Ipswich Beacon Marina 48
Lowestoft Haven Marina 49
Royal Norfolk & Suffolk YC 49
Lowestoft CC 49

Area 5 - NE England
Area 5 Marina Chart 51
Wisbech Yacht Harbour 52
Boston Gateway Marina 52
Humber Cruising Association 52
Hull Waterside & Marina 53
South Ferriby Marina 54
Whitby Marina 54
Hartlepool Marina 54
Sunderland Marina 54
Royal Quays Marina 55
St Peters Marina 55
Royal Northumberland YC 55
Amble Marina 55

Area 6 - SE Scotland
Area 6 Marina Chart 56
Port Edgar Marina 57
Arbroath Harbour 57

Area 7 - NE Scotland
Area 7 Marina Chart 58
Peterhead Bay Marina 59
Banff Harbour Marina 59
Nairn Marina 59
Whitehills Marina 60
Lossiemouth Marina 60
Inverness Marina 61
Seaport Marina 61
Caley Marina 61
Wick Marina 61
Kirkwall Marina 62
Stromness Marina 62

Area 8 - NW Scotland
Area 8 Marina Chart 63
Stornoway Marina 64
Mallaig Marina 64
Tobermory Marina 64
Dunstaffnage Marina 64
Kerrera Marina 65
Melfort Pier and Hbr 65
Craobh Marina 65
Ardfern Yacht Centre 65

Area 9 - SW Scotland
Area 9 Marina Chart 67
Port Ellen Marina 68
Crinan Boatyard 68
Tarbert Harbour 69
Port Bannatyne Marina 69
Portavadie Marina 69
Campbeltown Marina 70
Holy Loch Marina 70
Rhu Marina 70
Sandpoint Marina 70
Kip Marina 71
James Watt Dock Marina 71
Largs Yacht Haven 72
Clyde Marina 72
Troon Yacht Haven 73
Stranraer Marina 73
Kirkcudbright Marina 73
Maryport Marina 73

Area 10 - NW England
Area 10 Marina Chart 74
Whitehaven Marina 75
Glasson Waterside & Marina 75
Douglas Marina 76
Peel Marina 76
Fleetwood Harbour Marina 76
Preston Marina 77
Liverpool Marina 77
Conwy Marina 77
Deganwy Marina 78
Holyhead Marina 78
Pwllheli Marina 78

Area 11 - South Wales
Area 11 Marina Chart 79
Aberystwyth Marina 80
Milford Marina 80
Neyland Yacht Haven 81
Swansea Marina 81
Cardiff Marina 81
Penarth Marina 82
Bristol Marina 82
Portishead Quays Marina 83
Padstow Harbour 83

Area 12 - S Ireland
Area 12 Marina Chart 84
Malahide Marina 85
Howth Marina 85
Dun Laoghaire Marina 85
Arklow Marina 85
New Ross Marina 86
Kilmore Quay 86
Waterford City Marina 86
Crosshaven BY Marina 86
Salve Marine 87
Cork Harbour Marina 87
Royal Cork YC Marina 87
Kinsale YC Marina 88
Bantry Harbour Marina 88
Castlepark Marina 88
Lawrence Cove Marina 88
Cahersiveen Marina 89
Dingle Marina 89
Fenit Harbour 89
Kilrush Creek Marina 89

Area 13 - N Ireland
Area 13 Marina Chart 91
Galway City Marina 92
Rossaveel Marina 92
Foyle Port Marina 92
Coleraine Marina 92
Seatons Marina 93
Coleraine Harbour Marina 93
Ballycastle Marina 93
Carrickfergus Marina 93
Bangor Marina 94
Carlingford Marina 94
Ardglass Marina 94
Portaferry Marina 94

Area 14 - Channel Islands
Area 14 Marina Chart 95
Beaucette Marina 96
St Peter Port 96
St Peter Port Victoria Marina 96
St Helier Harbour 98

Section 2
Marine Supplies and Services Section 99–128

AREA GUIDE COASTAL DIVISIONS

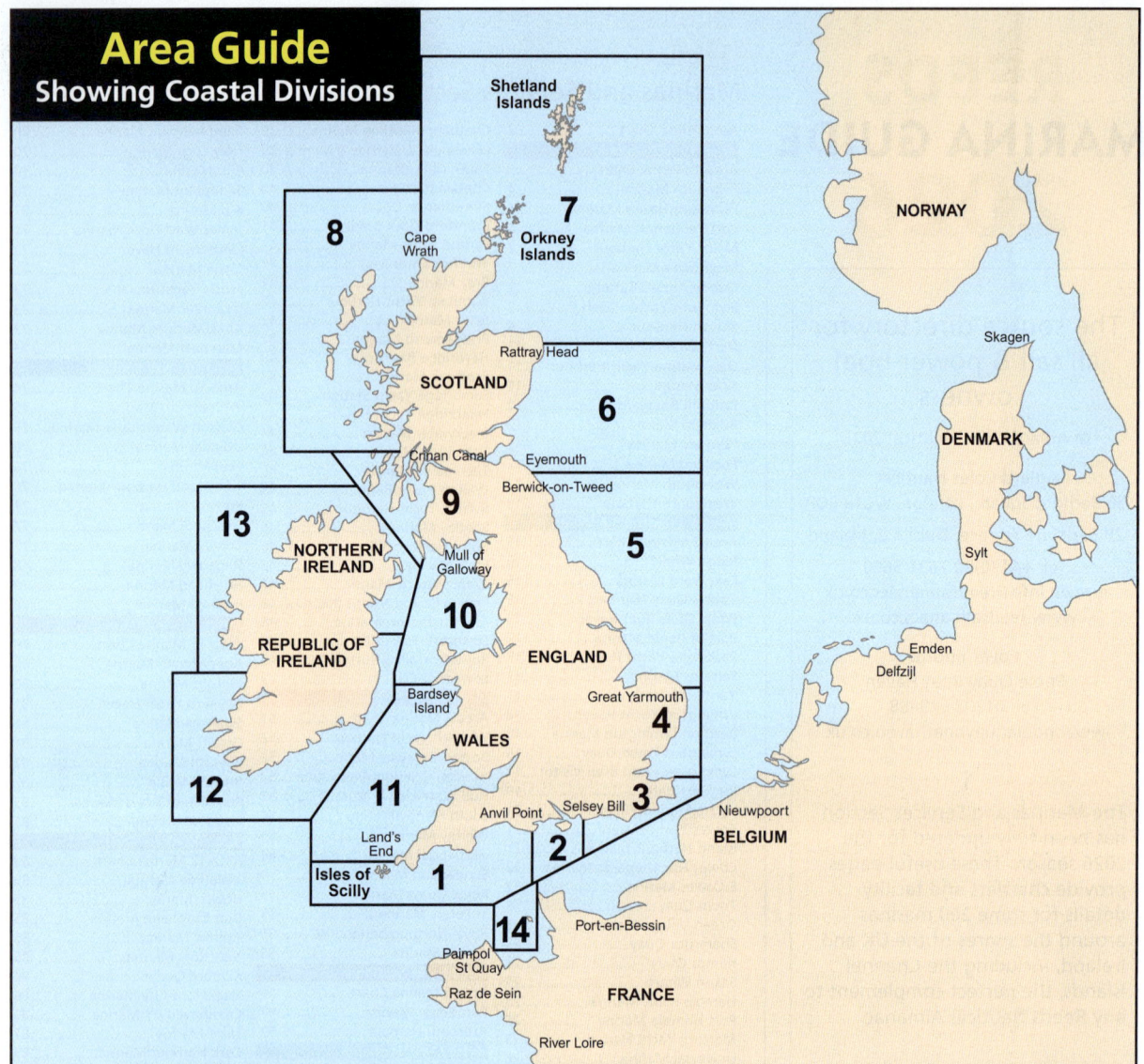

Area Guide
Showing Coastal Divisions

Area 1	South West England	Isles of Scilly to Anvil Point
Area 2	Central Southern England	Anvil Point to Selsey Bill
Area 3	South East England	Selsey Bill to North Foreland
Area 4	East England	North Foreland to Great Yarmouth
Area 5	North East England	Great Yarmouth to Berwick-upon-Tweed
Area 6	South East Scotland	Eyemouth to Rattray Head
Area 7	North East Scotland	Rattray Head to Cape Wrath including Orkney & Shetland Is
Area 8	North West Scotland	Cape Wrath to Crinan Canal
Area 9	South West Scotland	Crinan Canal to Mull of Galloway
Area 10	North West England	Isle of Man & N Wales, Mull of Galloway to Bardsey Is
Area 11	South Wales & Bristol Channel	Bardsey Island to Land's End
Area 12	South Ireland	Malahide, clockwise to Liscannor Bay
Area 13	North Ireland	Liscannor Bay, clockwise to Lambay Island
Area 14	Channel Islands	Guernsey and Jersey

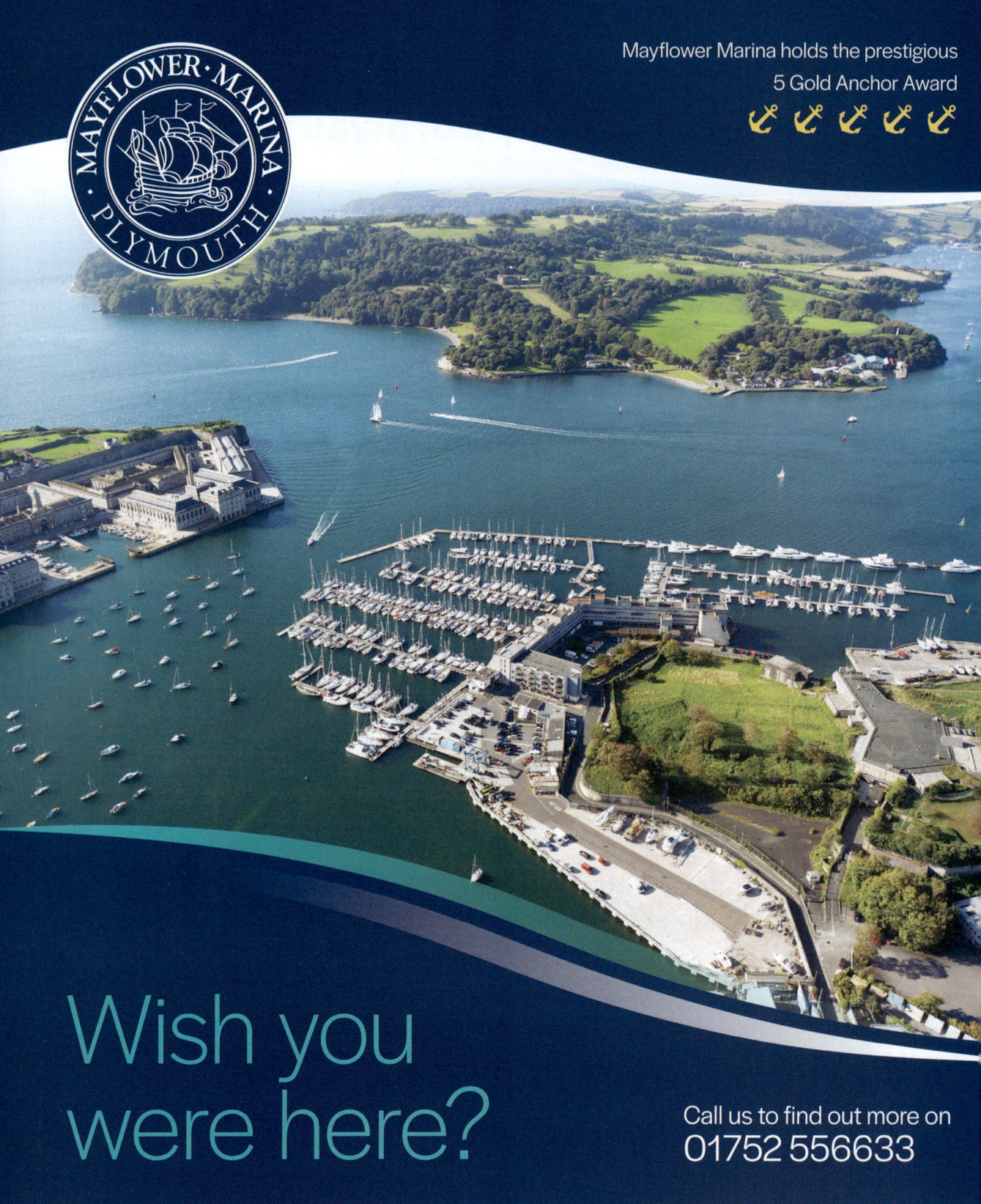

SOUTH WEST ENGLAND | AREA 1

MYLOR YACHT HARBOUR

Mylor Yacht Harbour Marina
Wylor, Falmouth, Cornwall, TR11 5UF
Tel: 01326 372121
Email: enquiries@mylor.com

VHF Ch M, 80
ACCESS H24

Nestled on the western shore of the beautiful Fal Estuary, Mylor Yacht Harbour's stunning marina has 180 berths and is surrounded by 240 swinging moorings. A large dedicated visitor pontoon, easy H24 access and excellent shoreside facilities set within an Area of Outstanding Natural Beauty combine to make Mylor a must-visit cruising destination.

The historic site was founded in 1805 as the Navy's smallest dockyard but is now a thriving yacht harbour and full service boatyard. Superb on site café, restaurant and yacht club all overlook the harbour and scenic coastal footpaths run from the top of the gangway. Falmouth is just 10 minutes away.

FACILITIES AT A GLANCE

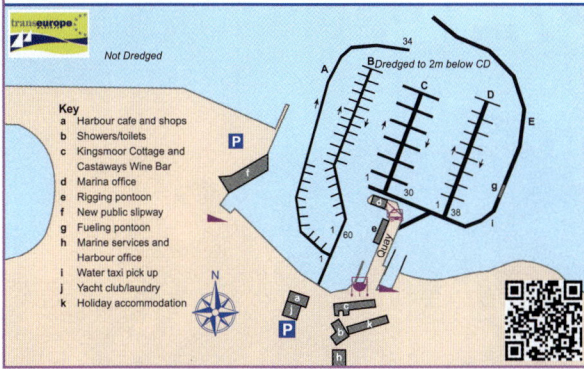

Destination Mylor

A welcoming yacht harbour anchored by the country's finest sailing waters.

Image © Aerial Cornwall

- Contemporary marina & safe moorings
- One of the largest visitor pontoons in the south west
- Full service boatyard
- Boat lifting & shore storage
- 1st class shore side facilities
- All tides access & prime sailing location

VHF ch. 37/80

Mylor Yacht Harbour
mylor.com
01326 372 121
enquiries@mylor.com

MAYFLOWER MARINA

Mayflower Marina
Richmond Walk, Plymouth, PL1 4LS
Tel: 01752 556633
Email: info@mayflowermarina.co.uk

⚓⚓⚓⚓⚓
VHF Ch 80
ACCESS H24

Sitting on the famous Plymouth Hoe, with the Devon coast to the left and the Cornish coast to the right, Mayflower Marina is a friendly, well-run marina. Facilities include 24 hour access to fuel, gas and a launderette, full repair and maintenance services as well as an on site bar and brasserie. The marina is located only a short distance from Plymouth's town centre, where there are regular train services to and from several major towns and cities.

FACILITIES AT A GLANCE

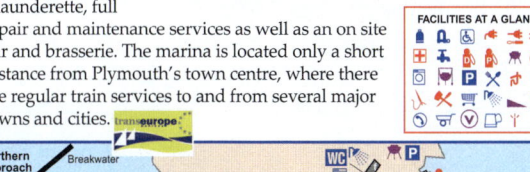

QUEEN ANNE'S BATTERY

Queen Anne's Battery
Plymouth, Devon, PL4 0LP
Tel: 01752 671142
Email: qab@mdlmarinas.co.uk www.queenannesbattery.co.uk

VHF Ch 80
ACCESS H24

Plymouth, a vibrant and fast growing city, is home to Queen Anne's Battery, a 235 resident berth marina with outstanding facilities for yachtsmen and motor cruisers alike. Located just south of Sutton Harbour, QAB promises a welcoming stay with alongside pontoon berthing protected by the surrounding breakwater. While on the city's doorstep, the marina is a short walk away from the historical Barbican, providing peace and tranquility to visitors.

The marina is often frequented by crowds of people marveling the many prestigious international yacht and powerboat races Plymouth Sound facilitates.

QAB is an exposed treasure along a beautiful historic coastline, at times resembling a mini 'Cowes' with its vibrancy.

FACILITIES AT A GLANCE

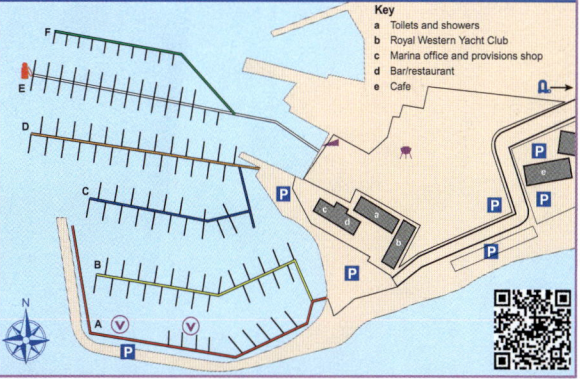

MARINA GUIDE 2026

SOUTH WEST ENGLAND

AREA 1

PLYMOUTH YACHT HAVEN

Plymouth Yacht Haven Ltd
Shaw Way, Mount Batten, Plymouth, PL9 9XH
Tel: 01752 404231   www.yachthavens.com
Email: enquiries@plymouthyachthaven.com

VHF Ch 80
ACCESS H24

Situated minutes from Plymouth Sound, Plymouth Yacht Haven enjoys a tranquil setting, yet is just a five minute water taxi ride from the bustling Barbican with all its restaurants and attractions. The Yacht Haven offers excellent protection from the prevailing SW winds and is within easy reach of some of the most fantastic cruising grounds.

This 450-berth marina can accommodate vessels up to 45m in length and 7m in draught. Members of staff are on site 24/7 to welcome you as a visitor and to serve diesel. With an on site 75T travel hoist and storage, a restaurant, chandlery, and extensive range of marine service, Plymouth Yacht Haven has plenty to offer both on and off the water.

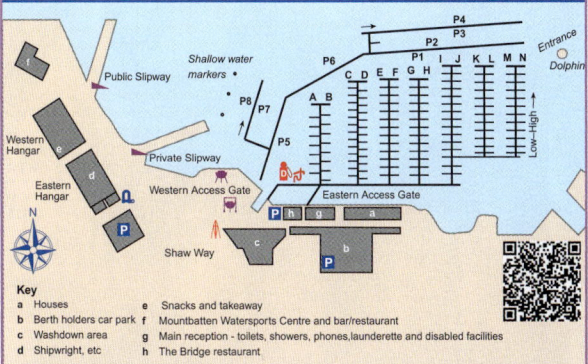

Key
- a Houses
- b Berth holders car park
- c Washdown area
- d Shipwright, etc
- e Snacks and takeaway
- f Mountbatten Watersports Centre and bar/restaurant
- g Main reception - toilets, showers, phones, launderette and disabled facilities
- h The Bridge restaurant

SUTTON HARBOUR

Sutton Harbour
The Jetty, Sutton Harbour, Plymouth, PL4 0DW
Tel: 01752 204702 Fax: 01752 204693
Email: marina@sutton-harbour.co.uk
www.suttonharbourmarina.com

VHF Ch 12
ACCESS H24

Sutton Harbour Marina, located in the heart of Plymouth's historic Barbican area and a short stroll from the city centre, offers 5-star facilities in a sheltered location, surrounded by boutique waterfront bars and restaurants. Offering 490 pontoon berths with a minimum 3.5m depth, the harbour has 24hr lock access on request with free flow approx 3hrs either side of high tide. The marina of choice for international yacht races such as The Transat and Fastnet. Visitors are invited to come and enjoy the unrivalled shelter, facilities, atmosphere and location that Sutton harbour offers.

Key
- a Fish market
- b National Marine Aquarium
- c Customs House
- d The Cove
- e Marina office
- f Lock tower

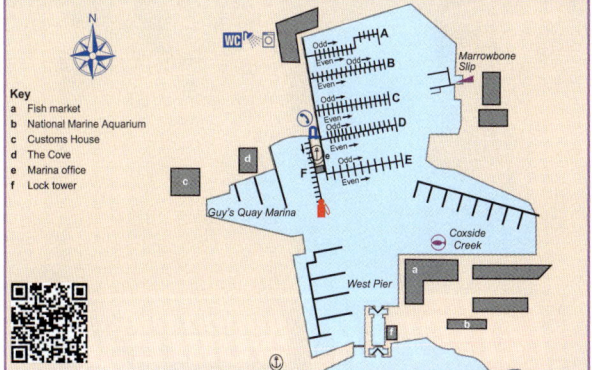

The perfect at-a-glance handbooks for all skippers and crew

SKIPPER'S COCKPIT NAVIGATION GUIDE — RENÉ WESTERHUIS

- Charts 2
- Buoys, Marks & Lights 5
- Using a Compass 8
- Tides & Currents 12
- Log & Depth Gauge 14
- Passage Planning 21

ADLARD COLES

SKIPPER'S COCKPIT WEATHER GUIDE — FRANK SINGLETON

- Air Masses & Their Clouds 5
- Large-scale Weather 8
- GMDSS Information 10
- Computer Forecasts 14
- Using Forecasts & DIY 17
- Small-scale Weather 23
- Visibility 27
- Sea State & Water Level 29

ADLARD COLES

www.adlardcoles.com

MARINA GUIDE 2026

WORLD CLASS SKIPPERS WANTED

NO PRESSURE

Sir Robin Knox-Johnston
Founder of the Clipper Round the World Yacht Race

Join the elite and take on the world's longest yacht race, crewed exclusively by novice crew embarking on the race of their lives.

Clipper Race Skippers are exceptional. These men and women have the fortitude to take on the toughest of mental challenges, and the physical endurance to successfully lead a team through Mother Nature's extreme environments on a 40,000 mile lap around the globe.

We are recruiting experienced professional Skippers for the next edition of the Clipper Race. To qualify you must hold a valid Yachtmaster Ocean certificate [commercial endorsed] or International Yacht Training Master of Yachts.

⤓ APPLY NOW

clipperroundtheworld.com/careers
raceskipper@clipper-ventures.com
+44 (0) 2392 526000

SOUTH WEST ENGLAND

AREA 1

DARTHAVEN MARINA

Darthaven Marina
Brixham Road, Kingswear, Devon, TQ6 0SG
Tel: 01803 752242
Email: admin@darthaven.co.uk
www.darthaven.co.uk

VHF Ch 80
ACCESS H24

Darthaven Marina is a family run business situated in the village of Kingswear on the east side of the River Dart. Within half a mile from Start Bay and the mouth of the river, it is the first marina you come to from seaward and is accessible at all states of the tide. Darthaven prides itself on being more than just a marina, offering a high standard of marine services with both electronic and engineering experts plus wood and GRP repairs on site. A shop, post office and three pubs are within a walking distance of the marina, while a frequent ferry service takes passengers across the river to Dartmouth.

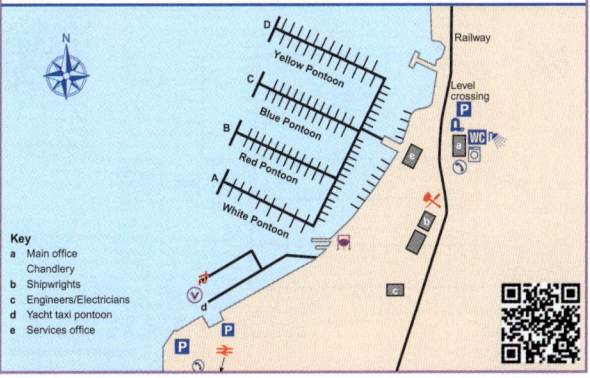

DART MARINA YACHT HARBOUR

Dart Marina Yacht Harbour
Sandquay Road, Dartmouth, Devon, TQ6 9PH
Tel: 01803 837161
Email: yachtharbour@dartmarina.com
www.dartmarinayachtharbour.com

VHF Ch 80
ACCESS H24

Dart Marina Yacht Harbour, in one of the most stunning locations on the UK coastline, is a peaceful spot for simply sitting on deck relaxing and perfectly positioned for day sailing or more ambitious cruising. With visitor berths, 116 annual berths, all accessible at any tide, the Yacht Harbour is sought after for its intimate atmosphere and stylish setting.

Professional, knowledgeable and helpful, the marina team is on-site all year round and there are impeccable facilities including showers, bathrooms and laundry.

In Dartmouth there are restaurants, bistros, cafes, delis, independent shops, galleries, a cinema, chandlers, antique and lifestyle shops in abundance.

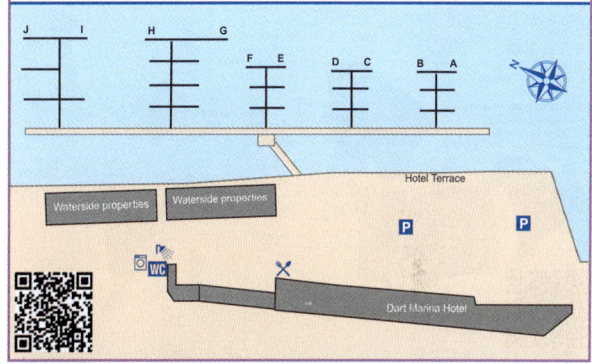

NOSS ON DART MARINA

Noss on Dart Marina
Bridge Road, Kingswear, Devon, TQ6 0EA
Tel: 01803 839087
Email: noss@premiermarinas.com
www.premiermarinas.com

VHF Ch 80
ACCESS H24

Set on the eastern bank of the River Dart, in a secluded area of outstanding natural beauty, Noss on Dart Marina offers easy access to some of the most beautiful anchorages and ports in Devon. Located close to astounding woodland walks along the Dart Valley Trail, for wildlife spotting and a hotspot for local festivals and regattas.

Phase one of the Noss on Dart £75m redevelopment is now complete with the 232-berth floating marina, full-service boatyard, dry stack, Premier Self Store and two commercial buildings to accommodate marine tenants. Phase two of the redevelopment started in 2023 and includes the construction of a hotel, restaurant and residential apartments.

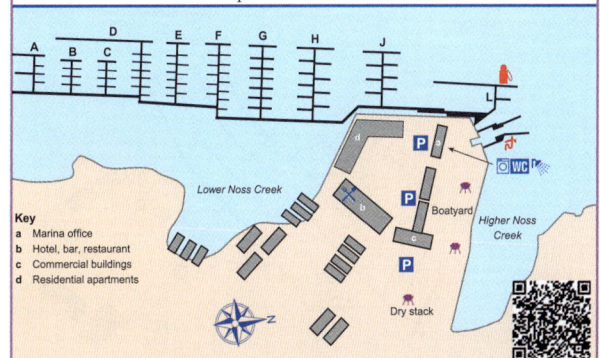

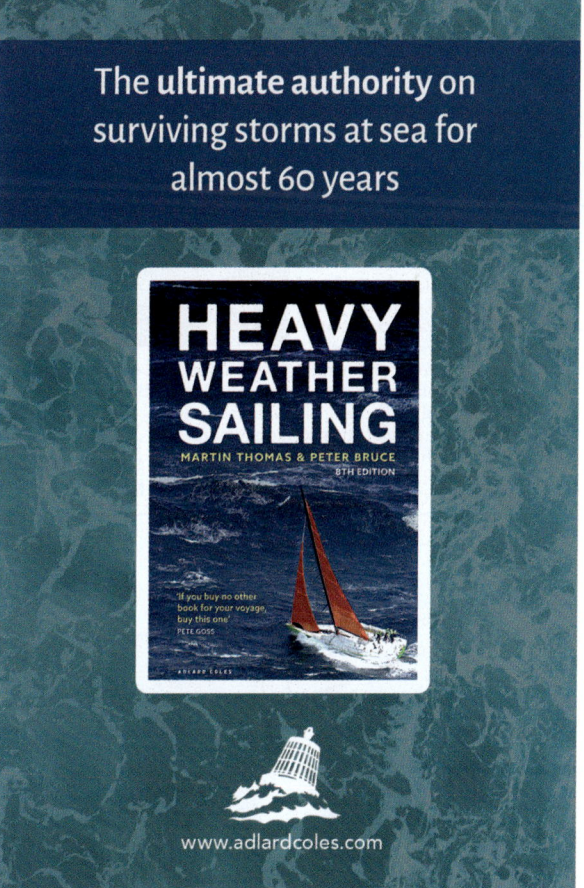

MARINA GUIDE 2026

MARINAS & SERVICES

DOLPHIN BOATYARD

Dolphin Boatyard
Galmpton Creek, Brixham, Devon, TQ5 0EH
Tel: 01803 842424
Email: ahoy@dolphinboatyard.co.uk
www.dolphinboatyard.co.uk

VHF Ch 80
ACCESS HW±2

Located at the head of Galmpton Creek, Dolphin Boatyard lies three miles upriver from Dartmouth. In a sheltered position and with beautiful views across to Dittisham, it offers extensive boatyard facilities. The seven-acre dry boat storage area has space for over 300 boats and is serviced by a 65-ton hoist operating from a purpose-built dock, plus a 20-ton trailer hoist operating on a slipway. There are also a number of overnight/ monthly moorings available (dry out) in the summer months. You will also find various specialist marine tenants on site able to assist with boat repairs and maintenance.

FACILITIES AT A GLANCE

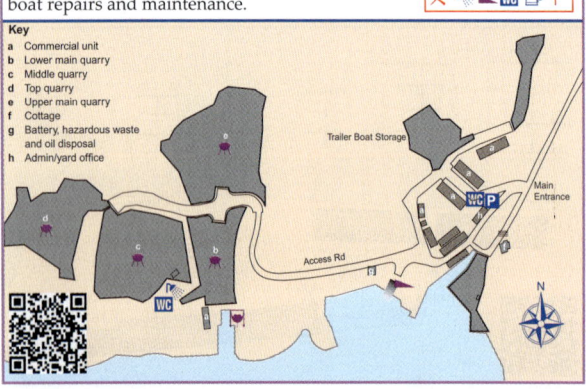

BRIXHAM MARINA

Brixham Marina
Berry Head Road, Brixham, Devon, TQ5 9BW
Tel: 01803 882929
Email: brixham@mdlmarinas.co.uk
www.brixhammarina.co.uk

VHF Ch 80
ACCESS H24

Home to one of Britain's largest fishing fleets, Brixham Harbour is located on the southern shore of Torbay, which is well sheltered from westerly winds and where tidal streams are weak. Brixham Marina, housed in a separate basin to the work boats, provides easy access in all weather conditions and at all states of the tide. Provisions and diesel are available and there is a bar and restaurant, ideal for when you've worked up an appetite out on the water. Local attractions include Berry Head Nature Reserve and a visit to the replica of Francis Drake's *Golden Hind*.

FACILITIES AT A GLANCE

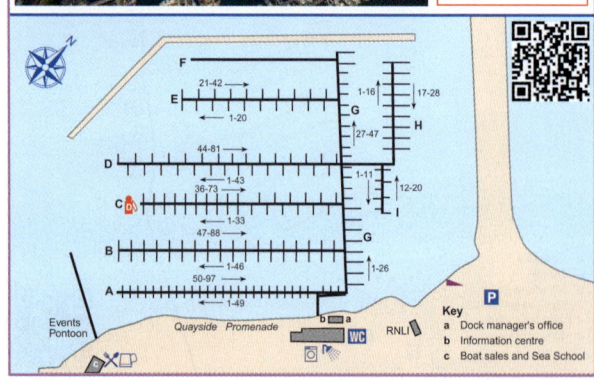

TORQUAY MARINA

Torquay Marina
Torquay, Devon, TQ2 5EQ
Tel: 01803 200210
Email: torquaymarina@mdlmarinas.co.uk
www.torquaymarina.co.uk

VHF Ch 80
ACCESS H24

Tucked away in the north east corner of Torbay, Torquay Marina is well sheltered from the prevailing SW'ly winds, providing safe entry in all conditions and at any state of the tide. Located in the centre of Torquay, the marina boasts a sea school, stand-up paddleboarding/watersports centre and artisan café, and also offers easy access to the town's numerous stores, bars and restaurants.

Torquay is ideally situated for either exploring Tor Bay itself, with its many delightful anchorages, or else for heading west to experience several other scenic harbours such as Dartmouth and Salcombe. It also provides a good starting point for crossing to Brittany, Normandy or the Channel Islands.

FACILITIES AT A GLANCE

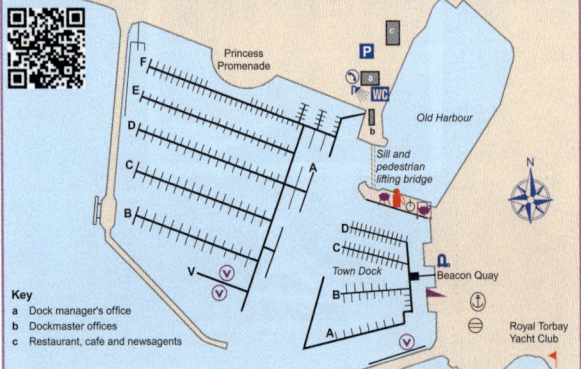

PORTLAND MARINA

Portland Marina
Osprey Quay, Portland, Dorset, DT5 1DX
Tel: 01305 866190
Email: portland@boatfolk.co.uk
www.boatfolk.co.uk/portlandmarina

VHF Ch 80
ACCESS H24

Portland Marina is an ideal location for both annual berthing and weekend stopovers. The marina offers first class facilities including washrooms, on-site bar and restaurant, lift out and storage up to 50T, dry stacking up to 9m, 24-hour manned security, fuel berth, sewage pump out, extensive car parking and a full range of marine services including a chandlery.

The marina is within walking distance of local pubs and restaurants on Portland with Weymouth's bustling town centre and mainline railway station just a short bus or ferry ride away.

FACILITIES AT A GLANCE

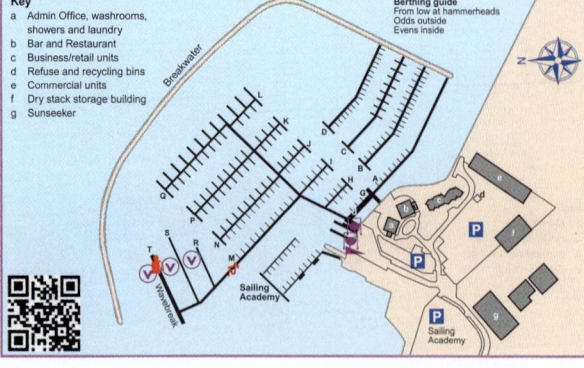

SOUTH WEST ENGLAND

AREA 1

WEYMOUTH HARBOUR

Harbour Office
13 Custom House Quay, Weymouth, Dorset, DT4 8BG
Tel: 01305 838423
Email: weymouthharbour@dorsetcouncil.gov.uk
www.weymouth-harbour.co.uk

VHF	Ch 12
ACCESS	H24

Weymouth Harbour, situated on the Jurassic Coast, lays N of Portland in the protected waters of Weymouth Bay. Located in the heart of the old town and accessible at any state of tide, the Georgian harbour has numerous overnight berths. Pontoons on both quays have electricity and fresh water, as well as modern shower facilities. Restaurants and shops abound within walking distance and visitors are also welcome in the Royal Dorset YC and Weymouth SC, both situated on the quayside.

Vessels are advised to call *Weymouth Harbour* on Ch12 on approach, and vessels over 15m are recommended to give prior notification of intended arrival.

FACILITIES AT A GLANCE

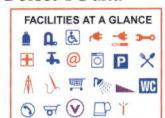

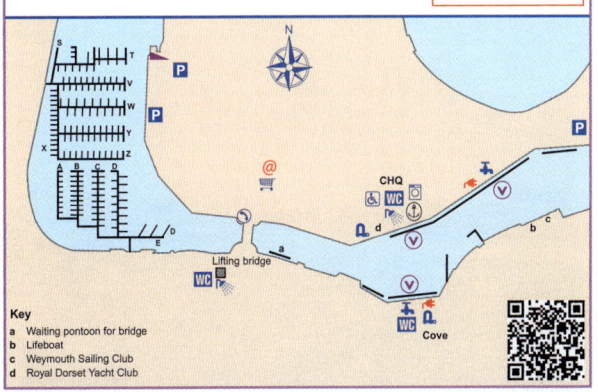

Key
- a Waiting pontoon for bridge
- b Lifeboat
- c Weymouth Sailing Club
- d Royal Dorset Yacht Club

WEYMOUTH MARINA

Weymouth Marina
70 Commercial Road, Dorset, DT4 8NA
Tel: 01305 767576 Fax: 01305 767575
Email: weymouth@boatfolk.co.uk
www.boatfolk.co.uk/weymouthmarina

VHF	Ch 80
ACCESS	H24

With more than 280 permanent and visitors' berths, Weymouth is a modern, purpose-built marina ideally situated for yachtsmen cruising between the West Country and the Solent. It is also conveniently placed for sailing to France or the Channel Islands. Accessed via the town's historic lifting bridge, which opens every even hour 0800–2000 (plus 2100 Jun–Aug), the marina is dredged to 2.5m below chart datum. It provides easy access to the town centre, with its abundance of shops, pubs and restaurants, as well as to the traditional seafront where an impressive sandy beach is overlooked by an esplanade of hotels.

FACILITIES AT A GLANCE

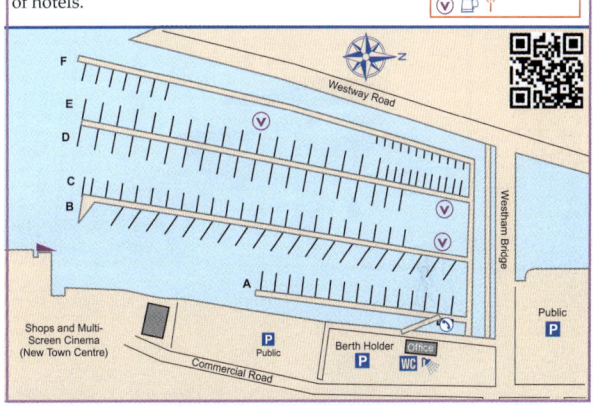

A fresh view...

Experience Dorset's dramatic coastline at your own pace. Choose a berth at Weymouth Marina or Portland Marina and set out to discover the Jurassic Coast's sights, scenes, and breathtaking seascapes.

To discover more visit boatfolk.co.uk

WEYMOUTH MARINA

PORTLAND MARINA

boatcare   boatpoint   Beyonder.   by boatfolk

More than just a berth

Chichester Marina

With Premier you'll enjoy more than just stunning marinas, first-class facilities, quality boatyards and exceptional service. Annual berthing customers also have the Premier Advantage - our unrivalled package of rewards and benefits.

PREMIER AD>ANTAGE

Premier Advantage is the package of rewards and benefits for annual customers to help them make the most of time on the water.

> REWARD
- Berthing Loyalty Reward
- Annual Boatyard Reward
- Refer a Friend Reward
- Online contract renewal discount
- Fuel at cost
- Free storage ashore
- Premier Self Store discount

> RELAX
- MyPremier online account
- Dedicated free parking
- Free WiFi
- Sea Start breakdown support
- Easy contract transfer to new boat owner

> ROAM
- 42 marina visitor nights
- Unlimited marina day visits
- Premier App with on the go tools
- Easy contract transfers between our marinas

Call **01489 884 060**
Visit **premiermarinas.com/premieradvantage**

PREMIER MARINAS

Falmouth | Noss on Dart | Swanwick | Universal (Hamble) | Gosport | Trafalgar Wharf (Portsmouth Harbour) | Port Solent | Southsea | Chichester | Brighton | Eastbourne

CENTRAL SOUTHERN ENGLAND – Anvil Point to Selsey Bill

AREA 2

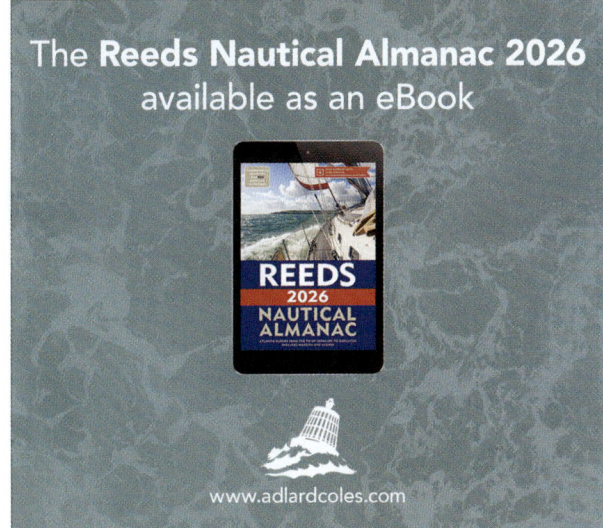

Key to Marina Plans symbols

Bottled gas		Parking	
Chandler		Pub/Restaurant	
Disabled facilities		Pump out	
Electrical supply		Rigging service	
Electrical repairs		Sail repairs	
Engine repairs		Shipwright	
First Aid		Shop/Supermarket	
Fresh Water		Showers	
Fuel - Diesel		Slipway	
Fuel - Petrol		Toilets	
Hardstanding/boatyard		Telephone	
Internet Café		Trolleys	
Laundry facilities		Visitors berths	
Lift-out facilities		Wi-Fi	

Area 2 - Central Southern England

MARINAS
Telephone Numbers
VHF Channel
Access Times

Port Hamble Marina 023 8045 2741 Ch 80 H24
Hamble Point Marina 023 8045 2464 Ch 80 H24
WicorMarine 01329 237112 H24
Emsworth Yacht Harbour 01243 377727 Ch 80 HW±2
Shamrock Quay 023 8022 9461 Ch 80 H24
Saxon Wharf Marina 023 8033 9490 Ch 80 H24
Deacons Mna 023 8040 2253 Ch 80 H24
Mercury Yt Hbr 023 8045 5994 Ch 80 H24
Northney Marina 023 9246 6321 Ch 80 H24
Town Quay Marina 023 8023 4397 Ch 80 H24
Ocean Village Marina 023 8022 9385 Ch 80 H24
Kemps Quay 023 8063 2323 HW±3½
Swanwick Mna 01489 884081 Ch 80 H24
Gosport Marina 023 9252 4811 Ch 80 H24
Port Solent Marina 023 9221 0765 Ch 80 H24
Chichester Marina 01243 512731 Ch 80 HW±5
Lake Yard Marina 01202 674531 Ch M H24
Poole Quay Boathaven 01202 649488 Ch 80 H24
Hythe Marina 023 8020 7073 Ch 80 H24
Bucklers Hard 01590 616200 Ch 68 H24
Universal Mna 01489 574272 Ch 80 H24
Lymington Yt Haven 01590 677071 Ch 80 H24
Parkstone YC Haven 01202 738824 Ch M H24
Royal Clarence 023 9252 3523 Ch 80 H24
Cobb's Quay Marina 01202 674299 Ch 80 HW±5
Berthon Lymington Marina 01590 647405 Ch 80 H24
Haslar Marina 023 9260 1201 Ch 80 H24
Southsea Marina 023 9282 2719 Ch 80 HW±3
Birdham Pool 01243 512310 Ch 80 HW±3
Salterns Marina 01202 709971 Ch M, 80 H24
Sparkes Yacht Harbour 023 9246 3572 Ch 80 H24
Ridge Wharf 01929 552650 HW±2
Yarmouth Harbour 01983 760321 Ch 68 H24
Ryde Leisure Hbr 01983 613879 Ch 80 HW±2
Cowes Yacht Haven 01983 299975 Ch 80 H24
Shepards Wharf Marina 01983 297821 Ch 80 H24
East Cowes Marina 01983 293983 Ch 80 H24
Bembridge Harbour 01983 872828 Ch 80 HW±2.5
Island Hbr Marina 01983 539994 Ch 80 HW±4

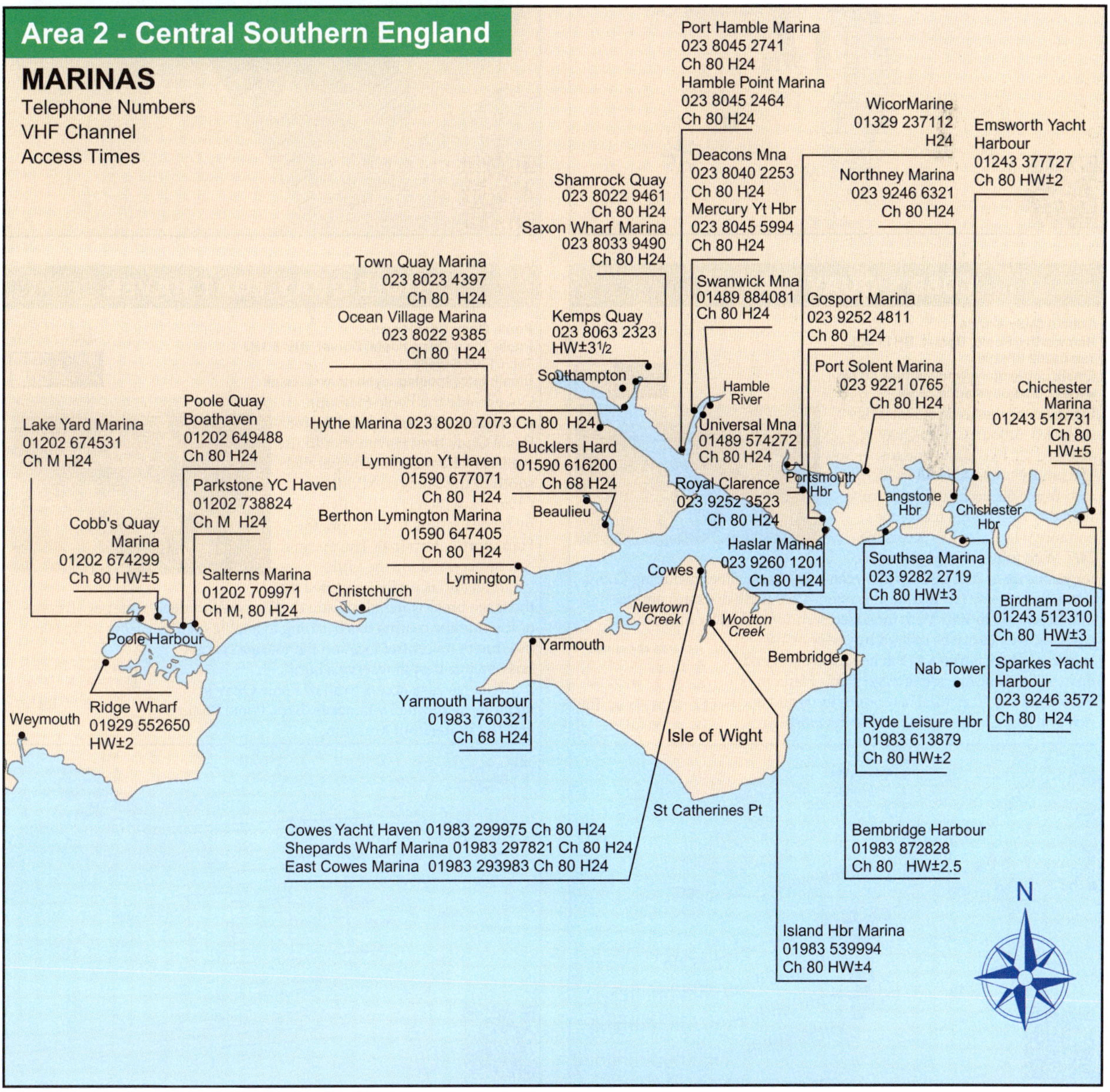

MARINAS & SERVICES

RIDGE WHARF YACHT CENTRE

Ridge Wharf Yacht Centre
Ridge, Wareham, Dorset, BH20 5BG
Tel: 01929 552650   Fax: 01929 554334
Email: office@ridgewharf.co.uk   www.ridgewharf.co.uk

VHF
ACCESS HW±2

On the south bank of the River Frome, which acts as the boundary to the North of the Isle of Purbeck, is Ridge Wharf Yacht Centre. Access for a 1.5m draught is between one and two hours either side of HW, with berths drying out to soft mud. The Yacht Centre cannot be contacted on VHF, so it is best to phone up ahead of time to inquire about berthing availability.

A trip upstream to the ancient market town of Wareham is well worth while, although owners of deep-draughted yachts may prefer to go by dinghy. Tucked between the Rivers Frome and Trent, it is packed full of cafés, restaurants and shops.

FACILITIES AT A GLANCE

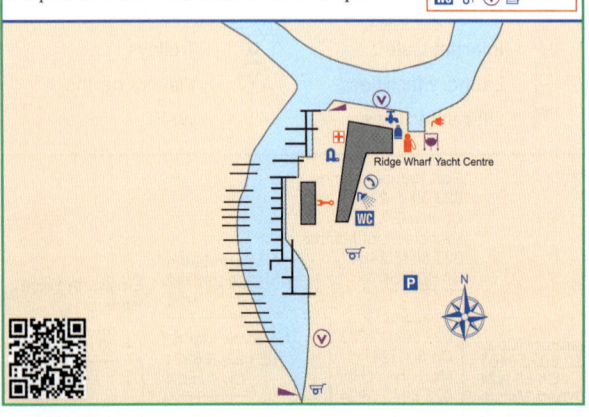

LAKE YARD MARINA

Lake Yard Marina
Lake Drive, Hamworthy, Poole, Dorset BH15 4DT
Tel: 01202 674531
Email: office@lakeyard.com   www.lakeyard.com

VHF
ACCESS H24

Lake Yard is situated towards the NW end of Poole Harbour, just beyond channel markers WH3 and WH4. The entrance can be easily identified by 2FR (vert) and 2FG (vert) lights. The marina enjoys 24/7 access, but visitors must call ahead to secure safe entry. The marina has only a short stay visitors' berth, but swing moorings are available for overnight stay. On-site facilities include maintenance and repair services as well as hard standing and a 50t boat hoist (no fuel available). Lake Yard's Clubhouse offers spectacular views across the harbour and opens 7/7 for drinks and dining, but visitors are by arrangement only.

FACILITIES AT A GLANCE

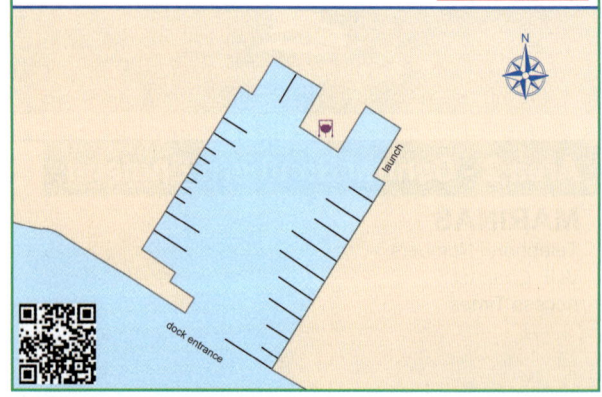

COBB'S QUAY MARINA

Cobb's Quay Marina
Hamworthy, Poole, Dorset, BH15 4EL
Tel: 01202 674299
Email: cobbsquay@mdlmarinas.co.uk
www.cobbsquaymarina.co.uk

VHF Ch 80
ACCESS H24

Lying on the west side of Holes Bay in Poole Harbour, Cobb's Quay is accessed via two lifting bridges. The hourly lifting schedule which runs from 0530 to 2330 (except for weekday rush hours) makes the entrance into Holes Bay accessible 24/7. With fully serviced pontoons for yachts up to 20m LOA, visitors can enjoy the facilities including Cobbs Bar & Restaurant. The marina also offers a 280-berth dry stack area for motorboats up to 10m. With increased security and lower maintenance costs, the service can be utilised by pre-booking launches. There is also a 40-ton hoist, fully serviced boatyard, and on-site self-storage. Poole Harbour is the second largest natural harbour in the world and is rich in wildlife, water sports and secret hideaways.

FACILITIES AT A GLANCE

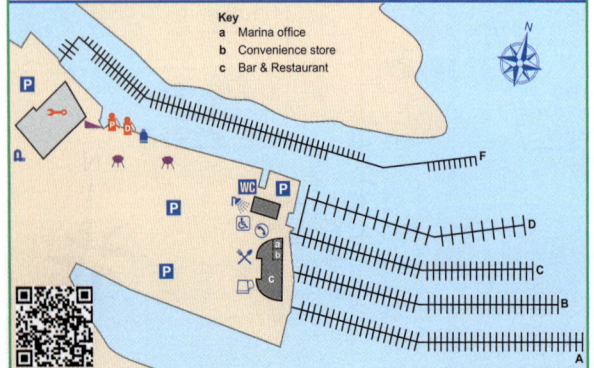

POOLE QUAY BOAT HAVEN

Poole Quay Boat Haven
Poole Town Quay, Poole, Dorset, BH15 1HJ
Tel: 01202 649488
Email: info@poolequayboathaven.co.uk

VHF Ch 80
ACCESS H24

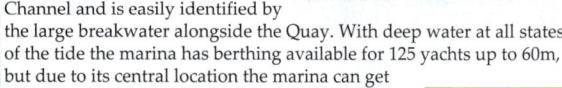

Once inside the Poole Harbour entrance small yachts heading for Poole Quay Boat Haven should use the Boat Channel running parallel south of the dredged Middle Ship Channel, which is primarily used by ferries sailing to and from the Hamworthy terminal. The marina can be accessed via the Little Channel and is easily identified by the large breakwater alongside the Quay. With deep water at all states of the tide the marina has berthing available for 125 yachts up to 60m, but due to its central location the marina can get busy so it is best to reserve a berth.

There is easy access to all of Poole Quay's facilities including restaurants, bars, Poole Pottery and the Waterfront Museum.

FACILITIES AT A GLANCE
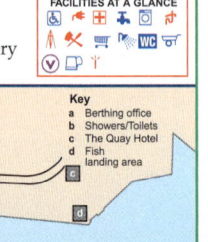

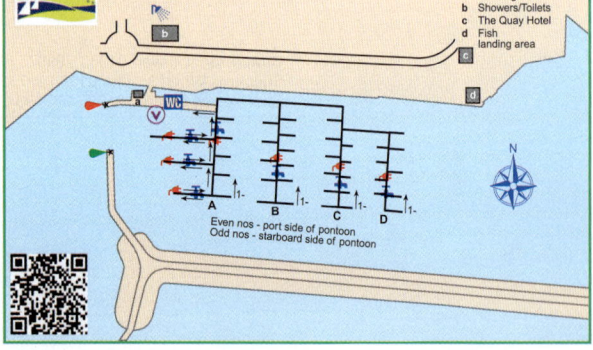

CENTRAL SOUTHERN ENGLAND   AREA 2

PORT OF POOLE MARINA

Port of Poole Marina
Poole Town Quay, Poole, Dorset, BH15 1HJ
Tel: 01202 649488
Email: info@poolequayboathaven.co.uk

VHF Ch 80 ACCESS H24

Beware of the chain ferry operating at the entrance to Poole harbour. Once inside small yachts heading for the marina should use the Boat Channel running parallel south of the Middle Ship Channel. The marina is to the east of the main ferry terminals and can be identified by a large floating breakwater at the entrance.

The marina has deep water at all tides and berthing for 60 permanent vessels. It is also used as an overflow for visitors from Poole Quay Boat Haven, subject to availability.

A water taxi is available during daylight hours to access the quay for restaurants and shops, also accessible with a 10–15min walk round the quays.

FACILITIES AT A GLANCE

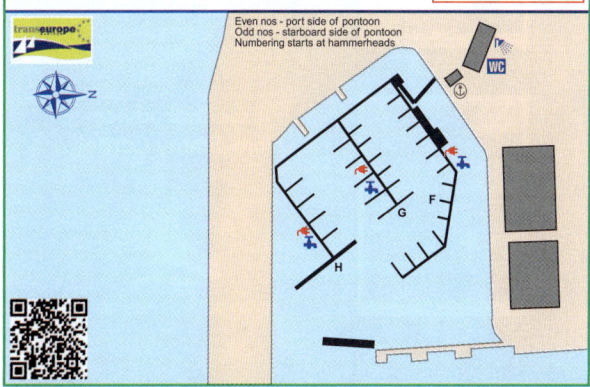

PARKSTONE YACHT HAVEN

Parkstone Yacht Club
Pearce Avenue, Parkstone, Poole, Dorset, BH14 8EH
Tel: 01202 738824 Fax: 01202 716394
Email: office@parkstoneyc.co.uk

VHF Ch M ACCESS H24

Situated on the north side of Poole Harbour between Salterns Marina and Poole Quay Boat Haven, Parkstone Yacht Haven can be entered at all states of the tides. Its approach channel has been dredged to 2.0m and is clearly marked by buoys. Run by the Parkstone Yacht Club, the Haven provides 200 deep water berths for members and visitors' berths. Other services include a new office facility with laundry and WCs, bar, restaurant, shower/changing rooms and wi-fi. With a busy sailing programme for over 2,500 members, the Yacht Club plays host to a variety of events including Poole Week, which is held towards the end of August. Please phone for availability.

FACILITIES AT A GLANCE

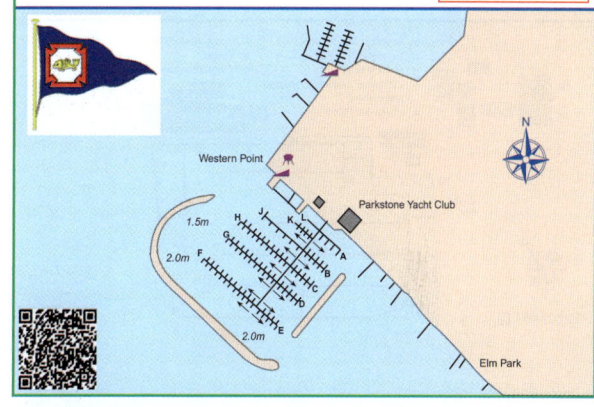

SALTERNS MARINA

Salterns Marina
40 Salterns Way, Lilliput, Poole
Dorset, BH14 8JR
Tel: 01202 709971
Email: marina@salterns.co.uk www.salterns.co.uk

VHF Ch M, 80 ACCESS H24

Salterns Marina provides a service which is second to none. Located off the North Channel, it is approached from the No 31 SHM and benefits from deep water at all states of the tide. Facilities include 275 alongside pontoon berths as well as 75 swinging moorings with a free launch service. However, with very few designated visitors' berths, it is best to contact the marina ahead of time for availability.

Fuel, diesel and gas can all be obtained 24/7 and the well-stocked chandlery, incorporating a coffee shop, stays open seven days a week.

FACILITIES AT A GLANCE

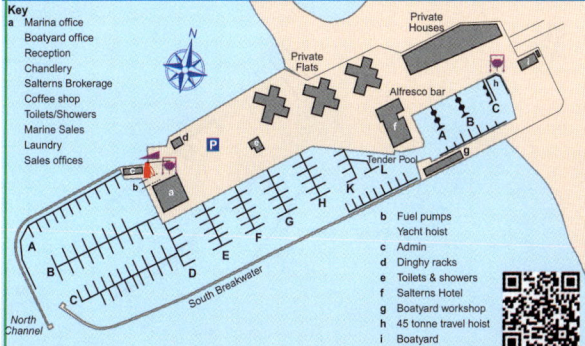

YARMOUTH HARBOUR

Yarmouth Harbour
Yarmouth, Isle of Wight, PO41 0NT
Tel: 01983 760321
info@yarmouth-harbour.co.uk
www.yarmouth-harbour.co.uk

VHF Ch 68 ACCESS H24

Yarmouth is the most westerly harbour on the Isle of Wight's NW coastline, a convenient passage stopover with all tide access, as well as a key tourism destination and gateway to West Wight's Area of Outstanding Natural Beauty. The harbour and town offer plenty of amenities, cafés, restaurants and pubs. There are two boatyards, the River Yar, and Harold Hayles.

The harbour has 150+ visitor moorings available daily from walk ashore pontoons providing direct access to Yarmouth town to non-walk ashore pontoons and moorings buoys just outside the harbour. Call *Yarmouth Harbour* on Ch68 prior to entering the harbour. Berthing masters patrol the entrance and will direct vessels for overnight and short stay berths, fuel and loading/unloading.

FACILITIES AT A GLANCE

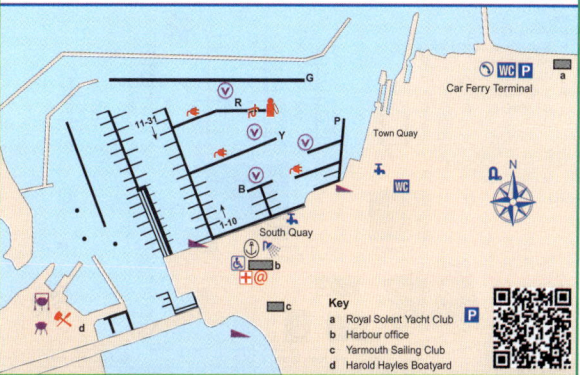

MARINA GUIDE 2026

MARINAS & SERVICES

LYMINGTON YACHT HAVEN

Lymington Yacht Haven
King's Saltern Road, Lymington, SO41 3QD
Tel: 01590 677071   www.yachthavens.com
Email: havenmasters@lymingtonyachthaven.com

VHF Ch 80
ACCESS H24

Lymington Yacht Haven has the enviable position of being the first marina that comes into sight on your port hand side as you make your way up the well-marked Lymington river channel. Nestled between the 500 acre Lymington to Keyhaven nature reserve and the famous Georgian market town of Lymington, there is something for everyone.

Lymington Yacht Haven is manned 24/7 for fuel and berthing and boasts the most modern luxury shore side facilities you will find in the UK. Bike and electric bike hire are available through the marina office to explore the beautiful New Forest.

FACILITIES AT A GLANCE

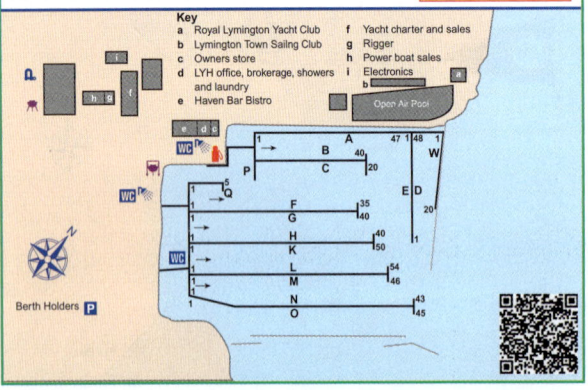

Key
a Royal Lymington Yacht Club
b Lymington Town Sailing Club
c Owners store
d LYH office, brokerage, showers and laundry
e Haven Bar Bistro
f Yacht charter and sales
g Rigger
h Power boat sales
i Electronics

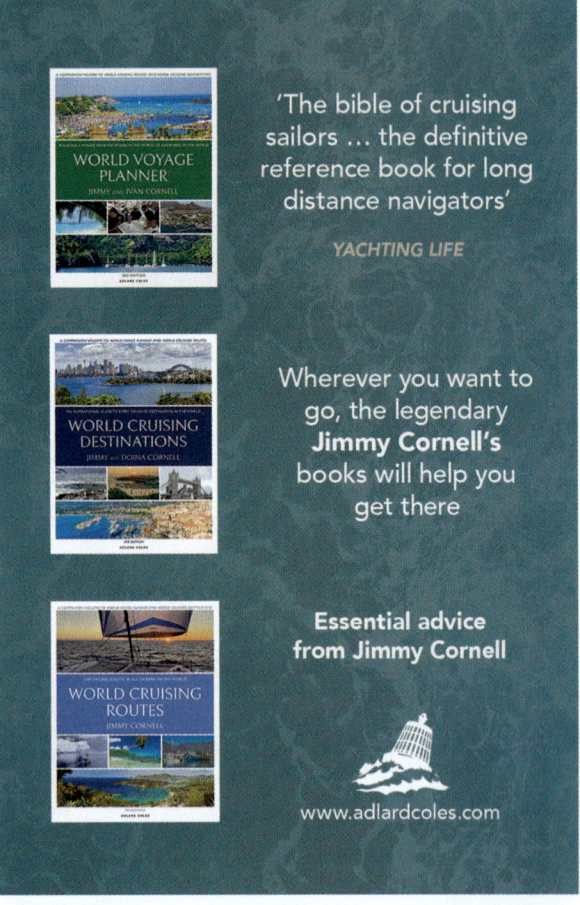

'The bible of cruising sailors … the definitive reference book for long distance navigators'

YACHTING LIFE

Wherever you want to go, the legendary **Jimmy Cornell's** books will help you get there

Essential advice from Jimmy Cornell

www.adlardcoles.com

BERTHON LYMINGTON MARINA

Berthon Lymington Marina Ltd
The Shipyard, Lymington, Hampshire, SO41 3YL
Tel: 01590 647405
www.berthon.co.uk   Email: marina@berthon.co.uk

VHF Ch 80
ACCESS H24

Situated approximately half a mile up river of Lymington Yacht Haven, on the port hand side, is Lymington Marina. Easily accessible at all states of the tide, it offers between 60 to 70 visitors' berths, with probably the best washrooms in the Solent. Its close proximity to the town centre and first rate services mean that booking is essential on busy weekends. Lymington Marina's parent, Berthon Boat Co, has state of the art facilities and a highly skilled work force of 100+ to deal with any repair, maintenance or refit.

Lymington benefits from having the New Forest on its doorstep and the Solent Way footpath provides an invigorating walk to and from Hurst Castle.

FACILITIES AT A GLANCE

Key
a Marina office
b Brokerage & boatyard offices
c Disabled parking
d Electric car charging
e BHG Marine
g Refueller

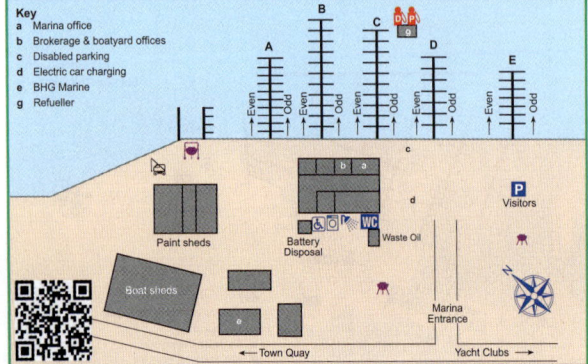

LYMINGTON TOWN QUAY

Lymington Harbour Commissioners
Bath Road, Lymington, SO41 3SE
Tel: 01590 672014
Email: info@lymingtonharbour.co.uk

VHF Ch 66
ACCESS H24

The Town Quay pontoon provides 46 walk ashore berths for visiting boats, including 26 finger berths. All have power, water and free wi-fi. The Town Quay also has 4 fore and aft visitor moorings. The washrooms are located on the quay.

The Quay provides easy access to the historic cobbles and the attractive Georgian high street with its bars, restaurants and shops. The facilities of the town are close by with the historic Saturday market in the High Street. The New Forest is easily accessible by bus, train and bicycle.

FACILITIES AT A GLANCE

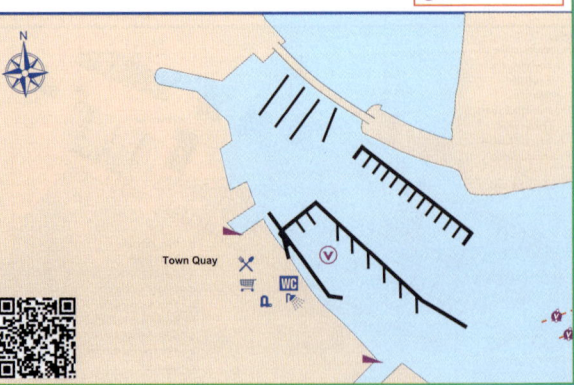

MARINA GUIDE 2026

CENTRAL SOUTHERN ENGLAND — AREA 2

LYMINGTON – DAN BRAN VISITOR PONTOON

Lymington Harbour Commissioners
Bath Road, Lymington, SO41 3SE
Tel: 01590 672014
Email: info@lymingtonharbour.co.uk

VHF Ch 66
ACCESS H24

Lymington Harbour Commission provides dedicated walk ashore visitor berths at the Lymington Town Quay and at the Dan Bran pontoon which comes ashore adjacent to the Royal Lymington YC and Lymington Town SC. Dan Bran is accessible at all states of the tide inside the wave screen. Power is available along its 650' length with use of the facilities at Lymington Town SC and walk ashore access to the town and nearby nature reserves on the salt marsh. Sited between the marinas a short walk from Town Quay, it is ideal for club rallies/events and can accommodate up to 50 boats together. The sea water swimming bath adjacent to the pontoon is a popular venue for children and families.

FACILITIES AT A GLANCE

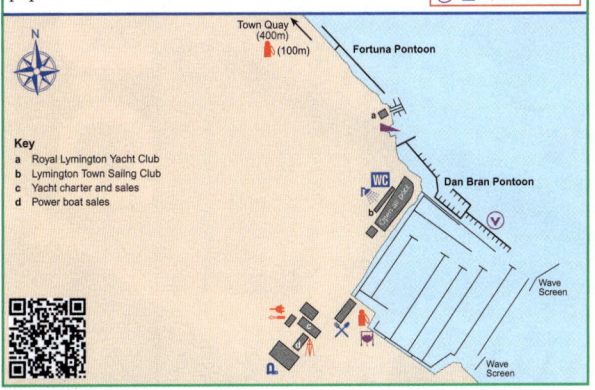

Key
a Royal Lymington Yacht Club
b Lymington Town Sailing Club
c Yacht charter and sales
d Power boat sales

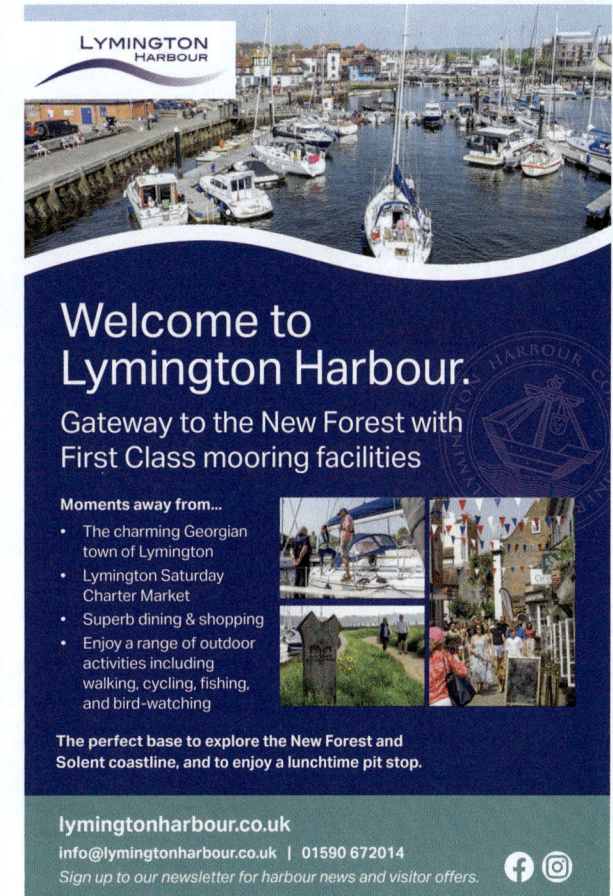

Welcome to Lymington Harbour.
Gateway to the New Forest with First Class mooring facilities

Moments away from...
- The charming Georgian town of Lymington
- Lymington Saturday Charter Market
- Superb dining & shopping
- Enjoy a range of outdoor activities including walking, cycling, fishing, and bird-watching

The perfect base to explore the New Forest and Solent coastline, and to enjoy a lunchtime pit stop.

lymingtonharbour.co.uk
info@lymingtonharbour.co.uk | 01590 672014
Sign up to our newsletter for harbour news and visitor offers.

BUCKLER'S HARD MARINA

Bucklers Hard
Beaulieu, New Forest, Hampshire, SO42 7XB
Tel: 01590 616200
www.beaulieuriver.co.uk   harbour.office@beaulieu.co.uk

VHF Ch 68
ACCESS H24

Situated on the Beaulieu River, Buckler's Hard Yacht Harbour is the ideal location from which to sail in the Solent or visit for a short stay to explore the surrounding New Forest. Recent investment in the TYHA 5 Gold Anchor marina offers improved facilities and technology to keep pace with modern demands, while preserving the unique character and charm of the unspoilt natural haven.

Both permanent marina berths and river moorings are available. Visiting boats are welcome and advised to book in advance or radio Beaulieu River Radio on CH68 before entering the river

FACILITIES AT A GLANCE

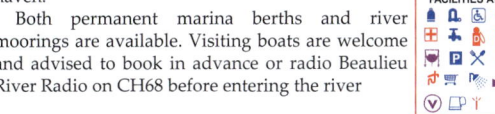

NB
Pontoon numbering runs from low inside with even numbers on the north side of pontoons and odd on the south.

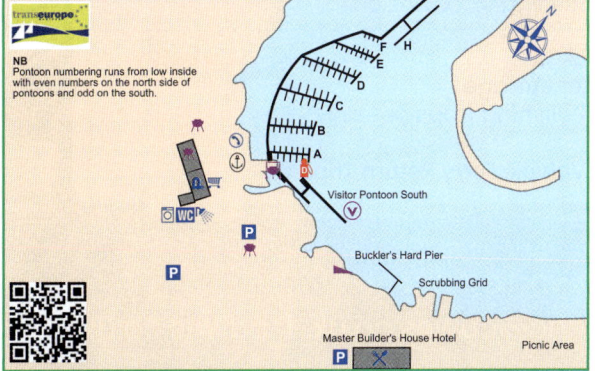

RELAX ON THE BEAULIEU RIVER

Discover your perfect berth today

beaulieuriver.co.uk
BEAULIEU RIVER
BUCKLER'S HARD YACHT HARBOUR

MARINA GUIDE 2026

SHEPARDS MARINA COWES

VISITOR AND RESIDENT BERTHS
RIBS, YACHTS AND MOTORBOATS
DRY SAILING
RALLIES AND REGATTAS

01983 297821 | shepards.chc@cowes.co.uk
cowes.co.uk | app.cowes.co.uk

KINGSTON BOATYARD EAST COWES
SMART SERVICE PACKAGES

NEW PACKAGE PRICING FOR 2025

SERVICE PACKAGE	DISCOUNT
Lift and Launch + 7 days ashore Anti-foul Treatment	Up to 19%
Lift and Launch + 7 days ashore Polishing (topsides only)	Up to 23%
Lift and Launch + 7 days ashore Anti-foul and Polishing (topsides only)	Up to 16%
PLATINUM PACKAGE - 5 months winter storage - Anti-foul and Polishing (topsides only) - Boat Valet - 3x Red Funnel Vehicle Ferry Return Trips	Up to 18%

FOR FURTHER INFORMATION AND TO SIGN UP:
01983 299385 | boatyard.chc@cowes.co.uk | cowes.co.uk/news

CENTRAL SOUTHERN ENGLAND   AREA 2

HYTHE MARINA VILLAGE

Hythe Marina Village
Shamrock Way, Hythe, Southampton, SO45 6DY
Tel: 023 8020 7073
Email: hythe@mdlmarinas.co.uk
www.hythemarinavillage.co.uk

VHF Ch 80
ACCESS H24

Situated on the western shores of Southampton Water, Hythe Marina Village is approached by a dredged channel leading to a lock basin. The lock gates are controlled H24 throughout the year with a waiting pontoon south of the approach basin.

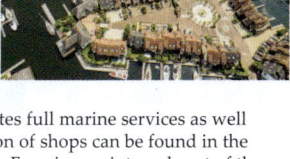

Hythe Marina Village incorporates full marine services as well as on-site restaurants and a selection of shops can be found in the town centre, a 5 minute walk away. Forming an integral part of the New Forest Waterside, Hythe is the perfect base from which to explore Hampshire's pretty inland villages and towns, or alternatively you can catch the ferry to Southampton's Town Quay.

FACILITIES AT A GLANCE

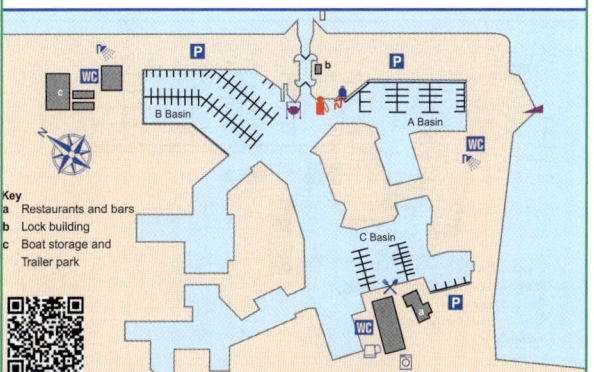

COWES YACHT HAVEN

Cowes Yacht Haven
Vectis Yard, Cowes, Isle of Wight, PO31 7BD
Tel: 01983 299975
www.cowesyachthaven.com
Email: info@cowesyachthaven.com

VHF Ch 80
ACCESS H24

Cowes is the spiritual home of yachting and Cowes Yacht Haven is located right in the middle offering unrivalled access to the shops, bars, restaurants and all that the town has

to offer. The marina, accessed H24, can be found just past the Red Jet terminal on the W bank and has two separate entrances giving access to the N and S Basins. The seasonally operating Pontoon View Bar is located below the marina offices and is open to all.

Please call VHF Ch 80 for berthing instructions. Booking is recommended (especially around big events such as Cowes Week and Round the Island race). Always phone to check availability.

FACILITIES AT A GLANCE

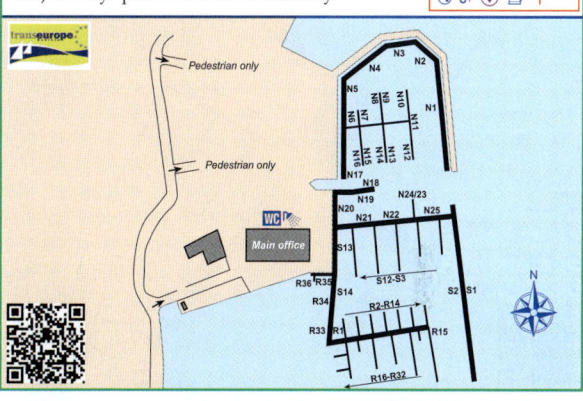

ISLAND HARBOUR MARINA

Island Harbour Marina
Mill Lane, Binfield, Newport, Isle of Wight, PO30 2LA
Tel: 01983 539994 Fax: 01983 523401
Email: info@island-harbour.co.uk

VHF Ch 80
ACCESS HW±4

Situated in beautiful rolling farmland about half a mile south of Folly Inn, Island Harbour Marina provides around 200 visitors' berths. Protected by a lock that is operated daily from 0800 – 2100 during the summer and from 0800 – 1730 during the winter, the marina is accessible for about three hours either side of HW for draughts of 1.5m.

Due to its secluded setting, the marina's on site chandlery also sells essential provisions and newspapers. A half hour walk along the river brings you to Newport, the capital and county town of the Isle of Wight.

FACILITIES AT A GLANCE

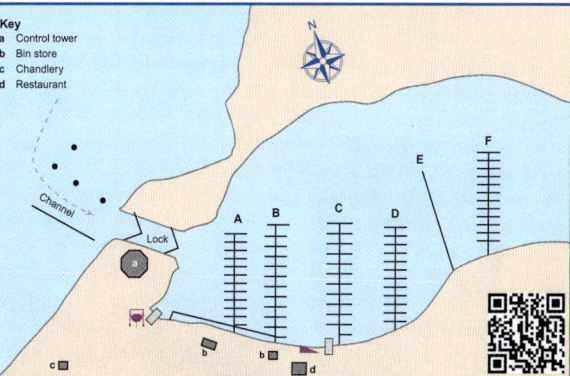

Richardsons

EST 1988

**TRAVELIFT • REPAIRS • REFITS • ENGINEERING
CHANDLERY • INSTALLATIONS • PAINTING
ELECTRICAL**

Agents for *Beta, Vetus, Mermaid & Lombardini* Inboards

Tohatsu Outboards & *Epropulsion* Electric Outboards

LEWMAR
APPROVED GOLD INSTALLER

NEW – MARINE ENGINEERING and CHANDLERY NOW OPEN in Thetis Wharf, Medina Road, Cowes. This will enable us to offer our services to a wider range of customers. Pop along and check out our new premises!

01983 821095 • info@richardsonsyacht.co.uk

www.richardsonsyacht.co.uk

Newport Site:
Island Harbour
Marina, Mill Lane,
Newport, PO30 2LA

Cowes Site:
Thetis Wharf,
Medina Road,
Cowes, PO31 7BX

MARINA GUIDE 2026

MARINAS & SERVICES

COWES HARBOUR SHEPARDS MARINA

Cowes Harbour Shepards Marina
Medina Road, Cowes, Isle of Wight, PO31 7HT
Tel: 01983 297821   Email: shepards.chc@cowes.co.uk
www.cowesharbourshepardsmarina.co.uk

VHF Ch 80
ACCESS H24

Shepards Marina is one of Cowes Harbour's main marina facilities offering services and amenities for yacht racing events, rallies, and catering also to the cruising sailor and powerboater. The marina has capacity for 130 visiting boats, and 40 resident berth holders.

Visitor berths can be booked in advance, subject to availability. All berths benefit from water and electricity, free Wi-Fi, inclusive showers, and site-wide CCTV. Discounted rates are available for rallies of six or more boats, sailing schools, and winter berthing.

On site are The Basque Kitchen, Salty Sailing, Island Divers, and Solent Sails.

Fuel can be obtained from the Cowes Harbour Services Fuel Berth, 200m south of the Chain Ferry.

FACILITIES AT A GLANCE

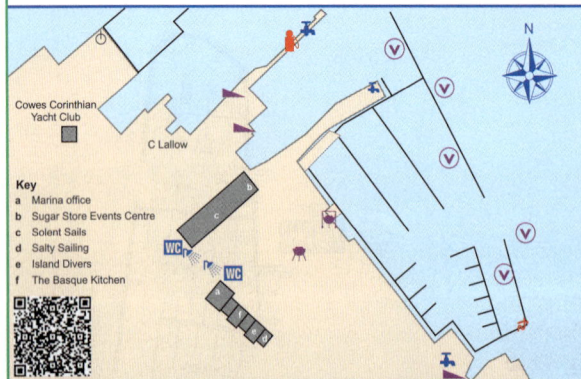

Key
a Marina office
b Sugar Store Events Centre
c Solent Sails
d Salty Sailing
e Island Divers
f The Basque Kitchen

EAST COWES MARINA

East Cowes Marina
Britannia Way, East Cowes, Isle of Wight, PO32 6UB
Tel: 01983 293983
Email: eastcowes@boatfolk.co.uk
www.boatfolk.co.uk/eastcowesmarina

VHF Ch 80
ACCESS H24

Accommodating around 235 residential yachts and 150 visiting boats at all states of the tide, East Cowes Marina is situated on the quiet and protected east bank of the Medina River, about a quarter mile above the chain ferry. A small convenience store is just five minutes walk away. The new centrally heated shower and toilet facilities ensure the visitor a warm welcome at any time of the year, as does the on-site pub and restaurant.

Several water taxis provide a return service to Cowes, ensuring a quick and easy way of getting to West Cowes.

FACILITIES AT A GLANCE

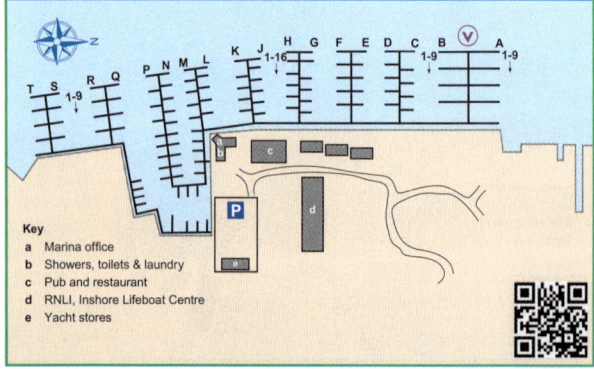

Key
a Marina office
b Showers, toilets & laundry
c Pub and restaurant
d RNLI, Inshore Lifeboat Centre
e Yacht stores

SHEPARDS MARINA COWES

HOME OF

the sugar store

EST. 1949

01983 297821 | shepards.chc@cowes.co.uk
cowes.co.uk | app.cowes.co.uk

Bar | venue

COWES HARBOUR SHEPARDS MARINA

22   MARINA GUIDE 2026

CENTRAL SOUTHERN ENGLAND

AREA 2

TOWN QUAY

Associated British Ports
Town Quay, Southampton, SO14 2AQ
Tel: 02380 234397 Mobile: 07764 293588
Email: info@townquay.com www.townquay.com

VHF Ch 80
ACCESS H24

In the heart of Southampton, Town Quay is walking distance from the City's cultural quarter, West Quay Shopping Centre and a variety of restaurants, bars and theatres making the marina a vibrant place to stay all year round.

The marina is accessible at all states of the tide and the reception is open 0700-1900 daily. There is a marina lounge, free wi-fi, cycle hire and use of a gas BBQ on the 'chill out' deck is available.

Located on the eastern shores of Southampton Water, Town Quay offers unrivalled views of Southampton's busy maritime activity and direct access to the world famous cruising and racing waters of the Solent. Town Quay no longer accepts cash payments.

FACILITIES AT A GLANCE

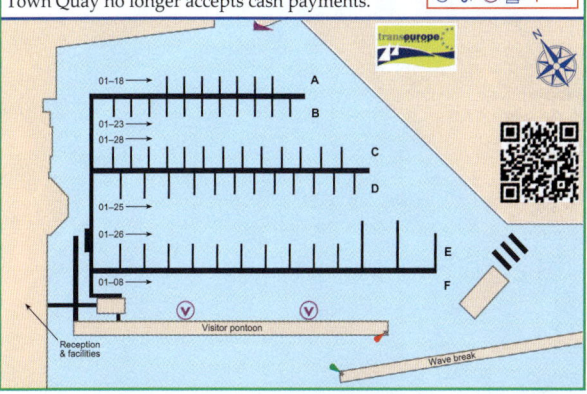

OCEAN VILLAGE MARINA

Ocean Village Marina
1 Channel Way, Southampton, SO14 3QF
Tel: 023 8022 9385
Email: oceanvillage@mdlmarinas.co.uk
www.oceanvillagemarina.co.uk

VHF Ch 80
ACCESS H24

The entrance to Ocean Village Marina lies on the port side of the River Itchen, just before the Itchen Bridge. With the capacity to accommodate large yachts and tall ships, the marina, accessible 24 hours a day, is a renowned home for international yacht races.

Situated at the heart of an exciting new waterside development incorporating shops, a cinema, restaurants, a multi-storey car park and a £50m luxury spa hotel complex, Ocean Village offers a vibrant atmosphere for all visitors.

FACILITIES AT A GLANCE

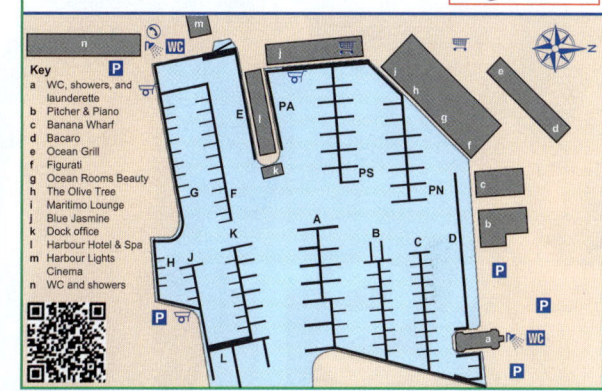

Key
a WC, showers, and launderette
b Pitcher & Piano
c Banana Wharf
d Bacaro
e Ocean Grill
f Figurati
g Ocean Rooms Beauty
h The Olive Tree
i Maritimo Lounge
j Blue Jasmine
k Dock office
l Harbour Hotel & Spa
m Harbour Lights Cinema
n WC and showers

SHAMROCK QUAY

Shamrock Quay
William Street, Northam, Southampton, Hants, SO14 5QL
Tel: 023 8022 9461
Email: shamrockquay@mdlmarinas.co.uk
www.shamrockquay.co.uk

VHF Ch 80
ACCESS H24

Shamrock Quay, lying upstream of the Itchen Bridge on the port hand side, offers excellent facilities to yachtsmen. It also benefits from being accessible and manned 24/7 a day. On-site there is a 75-ton travel hoist and a 25-ton boat mover, and for dining out a fully licenced restaurant/bar and a café.

The city centre is about two miles away, where among the numerous attractions are the Medieval Merchant's House in French Street, the Southampton City Art Gallery and the SeaCity Museum in the Civic Centre.

FACILITIES AT A GLANCE

Key
a Offices and shops
b Marina office
c Café

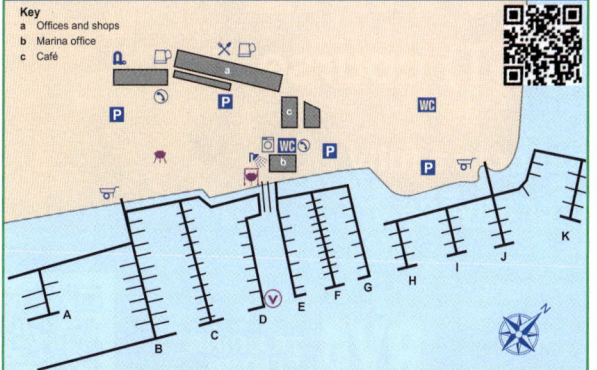

KEMPS QUAY

Kemp's Shipyard Ltd
Quayside Road, Southampton, SO18 1BZ
Tel: 023 8063 2323 Fax: 023 8022 6002
Email: enquiries@kempsquay.com

VHF
ACCESS HW±3.5

At the head of the River Itchen on the starboard side is Kemps Quay, a family-run marina with a friendly, old-fashioned feel. Accessible only 3½ hrs either side of HW, it has a limited number of deep water berths,

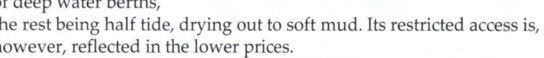

the rest being half tide, drying out to soft mud. Its restricted access is, however, reflected in the lower prices.

Although situated on the outskirts of Southampton, a short bus or taxi ride will soon get you to the city centre. Besides a nearby BP Garage selling bread and milk, the closest supermarkets can be found in Bitterne Shopping Centre, which is five minutes away by bus.

FACILITIES AT A GLANCE

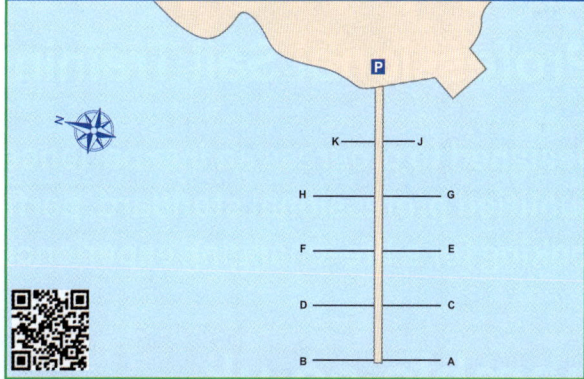

MARINA GUIDE 2026

HAMBLE
SCHOOL OF YACHTING

Hannah Brewis
Race Skipper
Clipper 2023-24 Race

Fast Track training skipper
Professional Sail Training

FAST TRACK SAIL TRAINING

GO PROFESSIONAL
Professional Sail Training (PST) course

Designed to progress an inexperienced sailor to a fully qualified professional standard, perfect for anyone looking for a life-changing experience.

hamble.co.uk

RYA TRAINING CENTRE

CENTRAL SOUTHERN ENGLAND — AREA 2

SAXON WHARF

Saxon Wharf
Lower York Street, Northam, Southampton, SO14 5QF
Tel: 023 8033 9490
Email: saxonwharf@mdlmarinas.co.uk
www.saxonwharfmarina.co.uk

VHF Ch 80
ACCESS H24

Placed on the River Itchen in Southampton, Saxon Wharf is a marine service centre specifically designed for the superyacht market. With a 200-ton boat hoist and heavy duty pontoons, Saxon Wharf is the ideal location for large vessels in need of secure, quick turnaround lift-outs, repair work or even full-scale refits.

With a Dry Stack facility boasting the largest capacity forklift truck in the UK, Saxon Wharf can now dry stack boats of up to 13m LOA. There is also ample storage ashore and 24-hour security. Shamrock Quay, where there are bars and restaurants, is within 300 metres of this location.

FACILITIES AT A GLANCE

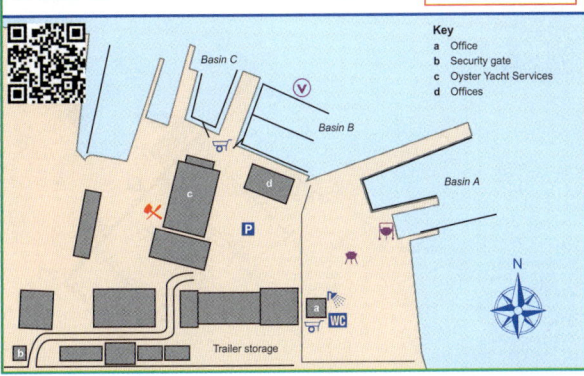

Key
a Office
b Security gate
c Oyster Yacht Services
d Offices

HAMBLE POINT MARINA

Hamble Point Marina
School Lane, Hamble, Southampton, SO31 4NB
Tel: 023 8045 2464
Email: hamblepoint@mdlmarinas.co.uk
www.hamblepointmarina.co.uk

VHF Ch 80
ACCESS H24

Situated virtually opposite Warsash, this is the first marina you will come to on the western bank of the Hamble. Accommodating yachts and power boats up to 30m in length, it offers easy access to the Solent.

The marina boasts extensive facilities including 137 dry stack berths for motorboats up to 10m and over 50 tenants who provide boat-owners with a wide range of marine services from boat repairs to electrical work. Hamble Point is within a 20-minute walk of Hamble Village, where there are a plethora of pubs and restaurants on offer.

FACILITIES AT A GLANCE

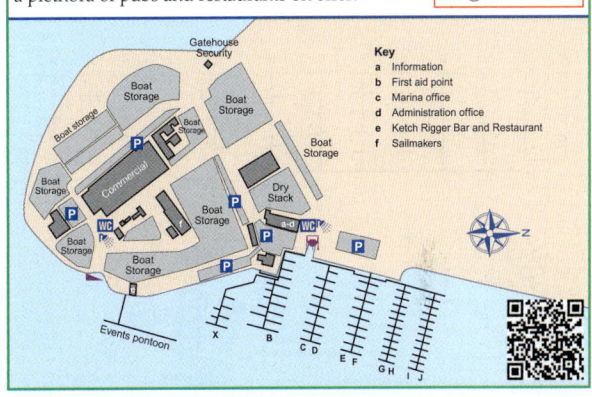

Key
a Information
b First aid point
c Marina office
d Administration office
e Ketch Rigger Bar and Restaurant
f Sailmakers

PORT HAMBLE MARINA

Port Hamble Marina
Satchell Lane, Hamble, Southampton, SO31 4QD
Tel: 023 8045 2741
Email: porthamble@mdlmarinas.co.uk
www.porthamblemarina.co.uk

VHF Ch 80
ACCESS H24

Port Hamble Marina is situated on the River Hamble right in the heart of the South Coast's sailing scene. With thousands of visitors every year, this busy marina is popular with racing enthusiasts and cruising vessels looking for a vibrant atmosphere. The picturesque Hamble village, with its inviting pubs and restaurants, is only a few minutes walk away.

On site, Port Hamble also offers excellent amenities including luxurious male and female facilities and boutique style shower rooms for members. Banana Wharf bar and restaurant provides the perfect spot to socialise by the water, whilst petrol and diesel is available 7/7. Locally there are several companies catering for every boating need.

FACILITIES AT A GLANCE

Key
a Dock manager's office
b Boat sales
c Royal Air Force YC
d Banana Wharf Bar & Restaurant

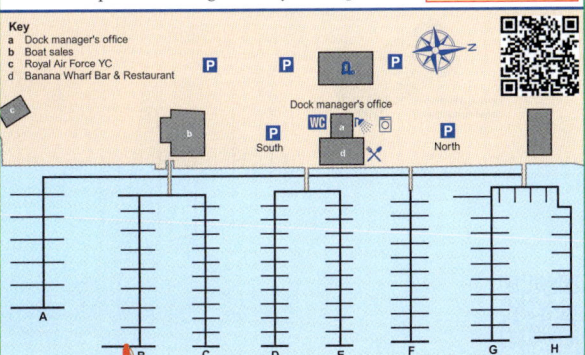

MERCURY YACHT HARBOUR

Mercury Yacht Harbour and Holiday Park
Satchell Lane, Hamble, Southampton, SO31 4HQ
Tel: 023 8045 5994
Email: mercury@mdlmarinas.co.uk
www.mercuryyachtharbour.co.uk

VHF Ch 80
ACCESS H24

Mercury Yacht Harbour is set in a picturesque and sheltered wooded site where the shallow waters of Badnam Creek join the River Hamble. Enjoying deep water at all states of the tide, it accommodates yachts up to 20m LOA and boasts an array of facilities.

For a good meal look no further than the Gaff Rigger bar and restaurant, whose roof terrace offers striking views over the water. The adjoining holiday park offers self-catering accommodation, a campsite, touring pitches and floating marine lodges in the marina itself. Hamble Village, with plenty of pubs, restaurants and shops, is only a 20-minute walk away.

FACILITIES AT A GLANCE

Key
a Toilets and showers
b Launderette
c TBS Boats
d Gaff Rigger Bar & Restaurant
e Dockmaster, marina manager's office
f Waste disposal
g Recycling area

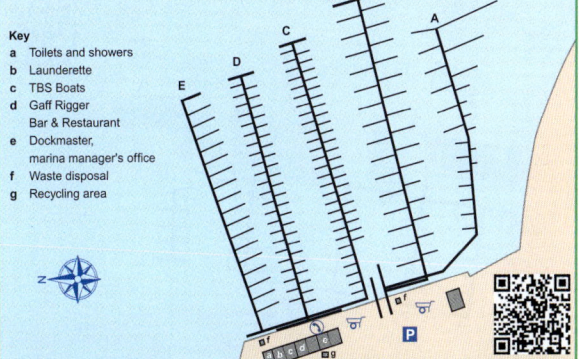

MARINA GUIDE 2026

MARINAS & SERVICES

UNIVERSAL MARINA

Universal Marina
Crableck Lane, Sarisbury Green, Southampton, SO31 7ZN
Tel: 01489 574272
Email: universal@premiermarinas.co.uk

VHF Ch 80
ACCESS H24

Beautifully located on the east bank of the River Hamble and surrounded by natural wildlife and marshlands. Universal Marina offers 24/7 access to explore the cruising grounds of the Solent, the visitor can enjoy tranquil riverside walks or simply relax and soak up the vibrant, friendly marina atmosphere.

A full-service boatyard and the river's largest drystack facility are onsite, together with a restaurant, café, and an array of marine service tenants including a chandlery.

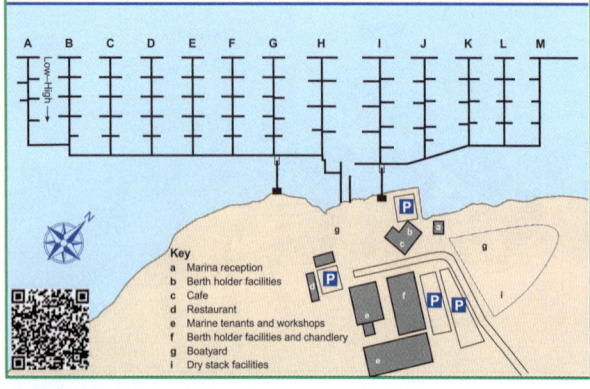

Key
a Marina reception
b Berth holder facilities
c Cafe
d Restaurant
e Marine tenants and workshops
f Berth holder facilities and chandlery
g Boatyard
i Dry stack facilities

SWANWICK MARINA

Swanwick Marina
Swanwick, Southampton, Hampshire, SO31 1ZL
Tel: 01489 884081
Email: swanwick@premiermarinas.com
www.premiermarinas.com

VHF Ch 80
ACCESS H24

Nestling on the picturesque eastern bank of the River Hamble, Swanwick Marina offers 24/7 access to the Solent, with excellent access by road and a variety of walks, pubs and restaurants to explore close by.

Welcoming to boats of all sizes, Swanwick has over 320 berths with a choice of water-berthing and dry-stack. There is a café, secure berth holder parking and The Saltings, Sales Pavilion, which houses boat sales and marine businesses. Swanwick also boasts a quality full-service boatyard, a Premier Self-Store and an outstanding mix of tenant marine services, including a chandlery.

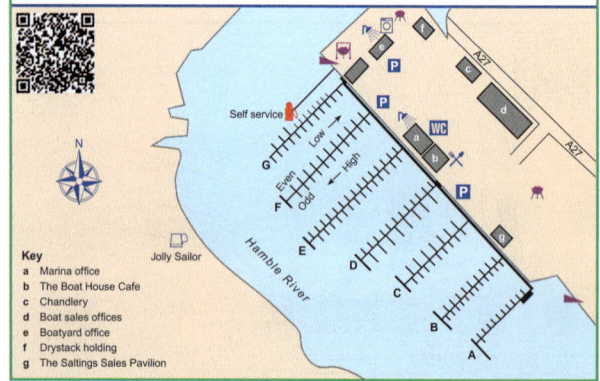

Key
a Marina office
b The Boat House Cafe
c Chandlery
d Boat sales offices
e Boatyard office
f Drystack holding
g The Saltings Sales Pavilion

DEACONS MARINA

Deacons Marina
Bridge Road, Bursledon, Hampshire, SO31 8AZ
Tel: 02380 402253
Email: deacons@boatfolk.co.uk
www.boatfolk.co.uk/deaconsmarina

VHF Ch 80
ACCESS H24

Deacons Marina and Boatyard is situated on a sheltered bank on the western side of the Hamble River, a stones throw from Bursledon, with 130 berths afloat and space for 160 boats ashore.

The marina boasts friendly and knowledgeable staff, skilled in boat repair and maintenance and offers craneage facilities for lifting boats up to 20t and 45ft in length. All supported by marine on-site businesses to provide a fully serviced one stop facility for boat owners.

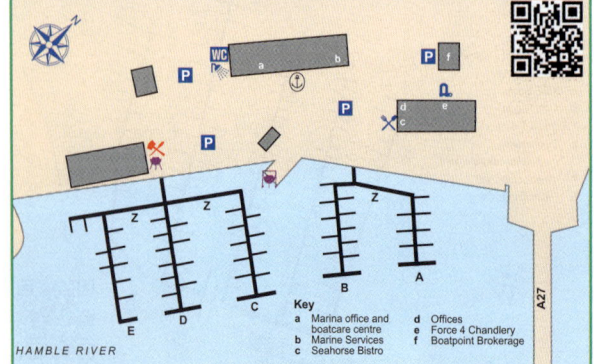

Key
a Marina office and boatcare centre
b Marine Services
c Seahorse Bistro
d Offices
e Force 4 Chandlery
f Boatpoint Brokerage

RYDE MARINA

Ryde Marina
The Esplanade, Ryde, Isle of Wight, PO33 1JA
Tel: 01983 613879   www.ryde-marina.co.uk
Email: rydemarina@rydetowncouncil.gov.uk

VHF Ch 80
ACCESS HW±2

Known as the 'gateway to the Island', Ryde, with its elegant houses and abundant shops, is among the Isle of Wight's most popular resorts. Its well-protected harbour is conveniently close to the exceptional beaches as well as to the town's restaurants and amusements.

The marina dries and is only accessible to vessels approximately HW±2 Portsmouth for a boat drawing 1.5M. There is pontoon berthing for vessels for up to about 14m and fin keel yachts may dry out on the harbour wall.

Ideal for family cruising, Ryde offers a wealth of activities, ranging from ten pin bowling and ice skating to crazy golf and tennis.

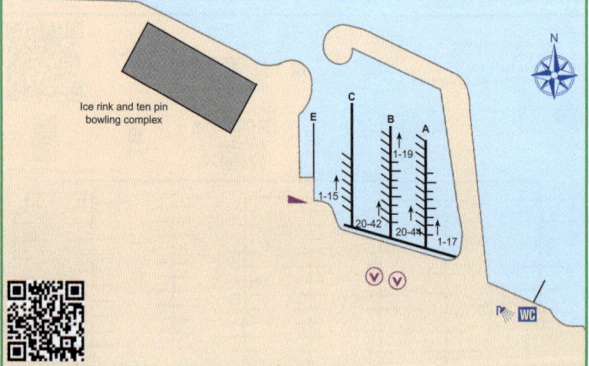

MARINA GUIDE 2026

CENTRAL SOUTHERN ENGLAND — AREA 2

BEMBRIDGE HARBOUR

Bembridge Harbour
Harbour Office, The Duver, St Helens, Ryde
Isle of Wight, PO33 1YB
Tel: 01983 872828 Fax: 01983 872922
Email: thorpemalcolm@btconnect.com
www.bembridgeharbour.co.uk

VHF Ch 80
ACCESS HW±2.5

Bembridge is a compact, pretty harbour whose entrance, although restricted by the tides (recommended entry for a 1.5m draught is 2½hrs before HW), is well sheltered in all but north north easterly gales. Offering excellent sailing clubs, beautiful beaches and fine restaurants, this Isle of Wight port is a first class haven with plenty of charm. With approximately 120 new visitors' berths on the Duver Marina pontoons, which can now be booked online, the marina at St Helen's Quay at the western end of the harbour is now allocated to annual berth holders only.

FACILITIES AT A GLANCE

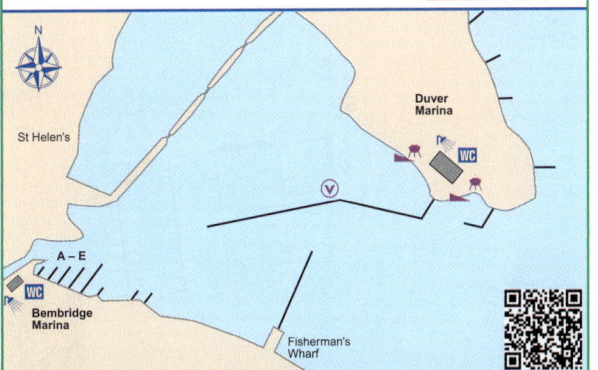

HASLAR MARINA

Haslar Marina
Haslar Road, Gosport, Hampshire, PO12 1NU
Tel: 023 9260 1201
Email: haslar@boatfolk.co.uk
www.boatfolk.co.uk/haslarmarina

VHF Ch 80
ACCESS H24

This purpose-built marina lies to port on the western side of Portsmouth Harbour entrance and is easily recognised by its prominent lightship incorporating a bar and restaurant. Accessible at all states of the tide, Haslar's extensive facilities do not however include fuel, the nearest is at the Gosport Marina only a few cables north. Within close proximity is the Royal Navy Submarine Museum and the Museum of Naval Firepower 'Explosion' both worth a visit.

FACILITIES AT A GLANCE

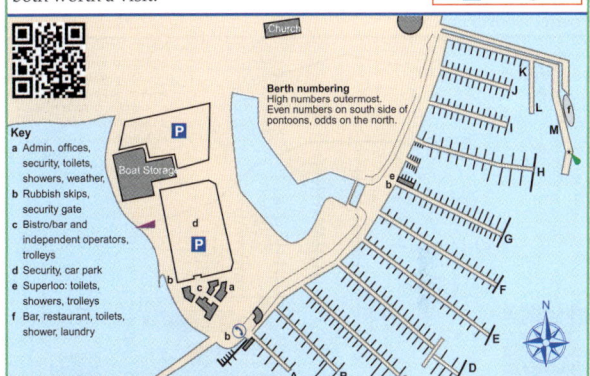

Key
a Admin. offices, security, toilets, showers, weather
b Rubbish skips, security gate
c Bistro/bar and independent operators, trolleys
d Security, car park
e Superloo: toilets, showers, trolleys
f Bar, restaurant, toilets, shower, laundry

Berth numbering
High numbers outermost.
Even numbers on south side of pontoons, odds on the north.

The glorious Solent...

Enjoy nature's playground on the Solent. From Deacons, Haslar and East Cowes marinas, the options are endless – discover hidden creeks, sandy beaches and beautiful sheltered bays.

DEACONS MARINA

HASLAR MARINA

EAST COWES MARINA

To discover more visit boatfolk.co.uk

boatcare · boatpoint · Beyonder · by boatfolk

MARINA GUIDE 2026

MARINAS & SERVICES

GOSPORT MARINA

Gosport Marina
Mumby Road, Gosport, Hampshire, PO12 1AH
Tel: 023 9252 4811
Email: gosport@premiermarinas.com
www.premiermarinas.com

⚓⚓⚓⚓⚓

VHF Ch 80
ACCESS H24

Gosport Marina is located at the mouth of Portsmouth Harbour, just minutes from the eastern edge of the cruising grounds of the Solent. Family-friendly and popular with cruisers and racers alike, Gosport offers 24/7 access to open water and a choice of both traditional wet-berth and dry-stack, and a Premier Self-Store. Gosport Marina's specialist boatyard, Endeavour Quay, is fully-equipped to lift and service boats up to 40m, with three large boatsheds and a wide variety of marine service tenants, including a dedicated chandlery. When it is time to relax, The Boat House is the perfect spot to unwind.

FACILITIES AT A GLANCE

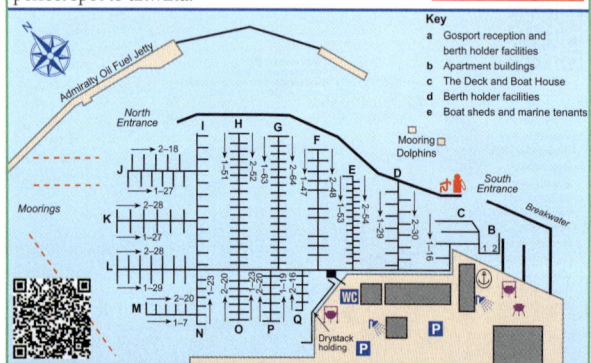

ROYAL CLARENCE MARINA

Royal Clarence Marina, Royal Clarence Yard
Weevil Lane, Gosport, Hampshire PO12 1AX
Tel: 02392 523523
Email: royalclarence@aquavista.com
www.aquavista.com/royalclarence

VHF Ch 80
ACCESS H24

Royal Clarence Marina enjoys a unique setting, with the former Royal Navy victualling yard as its backdrop. Only five minutes from the entrance of Portsmouth Harbour, this Transeurope marina lies within a deep-water basin giving 24/7 access for a draft of up to 4.5m. This remarkably peaceful and calm marina has wide pontoon spacing, little tidal flow, and exceptional protection from the swell produced in Portsmouth Harbour. The new facilities, now just opposite the marina, have been described as the best on the South Coast and with two popular restaurants onsite, makes a great location for visitors.

FACILITIES AT A GLANCE

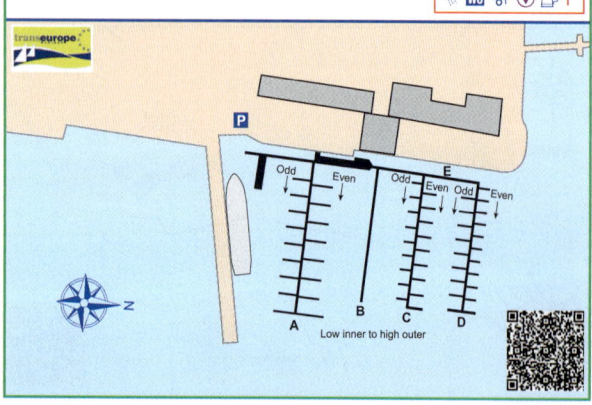

MARINA GUIDE 2026

CENTRAL SOUTHERN ENGLAND

AREA 2

PORT SOLENT MARINA

Port Solent Marina
South Lockside, Portsmouth, PO6 4TJ
Tel: 023 9221 0765
Email: portsolent@premiermarinas.com
www.premiermarinas.com

VHF Ch 80
ACCESS H24

Port Solent Marina is located to the northeast of Portsmouth Harbour, just minutes away from the cruising grounds of the Solent. Accessible via a 24/7 lock, this purpose-built marina offers a secure and sheltered berthing for yachts and motorboats alike, with a complete range of facilities including a fully serviced boatyard with a sizable boatshed, a Premier Self-Store, friendly yacht club and a array of onsite marine tenants. Onsite leisure complex, The Boardwalk offers shops, bars and restaurants, with a David Lloyd gym and a large cinema multiplex.

Key
a Laundry, berth holders showers, toilets and baby change
b Mariner's Table at the Port House
c Chandlery, marine engineers
d Boat shed and self-store
e Berth holders showers, toilets and public toilets, baby change
f David Lloyd Health and Fitness Club
g The Boardwalk - bars/restaurants
h Odeon cinema
i Marina control and Port Solent reception
j Residential building

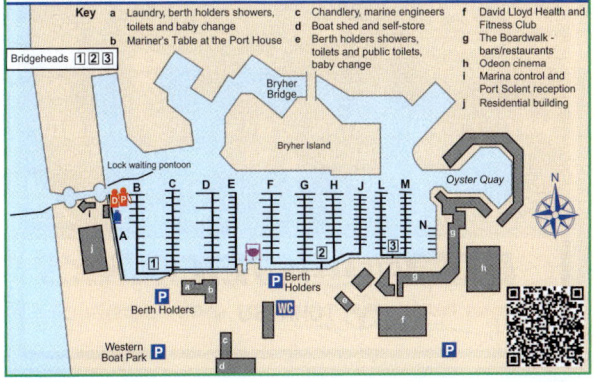

WICORMARINE YACHT HAVEN

WicorMarine Yacht Haven
Cranleigh Road, Portchester, Hampshire, PO16 9DR
Tel: 01329 237112
Email: inbox@wicormarine.co.uk   www.wicormarine.co.uk

VHF
ACCESS H24

WicorMarine Yacht Haven is situated in the picturesque upper reaches of Portsmouth Harbour away from the hustle and bustle. The walk-ashore pontoons and traditional mid-river berths offer an affordable alternative to busy marinas and are only 30 mins from the harbour entrance.

An excellent range of boatyard facilities including a 12T boat hoist, undercover storage, H24 showers and toilets, diesel, fresh water, on site repair services and a chandlery complete with Calor Gas and Campingaz exchange.

The popular, licensed Salt Cafe is open to visitors all year round where you can take in the stunning views of the harbour from the waterfront deck.

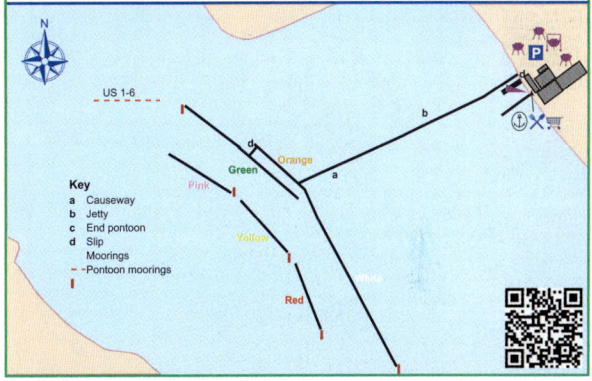

Key
a Causeway
b Jetty
c End pontoon
d Slip
   Moorings
-- Pontoon moorings

SOUTHSEA MARINA

Southsea Marina
Fort Cumberland Road, PO4 9RJ
Tel: 02392 822719
Email: southsea@premiermarinas.com
www.premiermarinas.com

VHF Ch 80
ACCESS HW±3

Nestling on the Eastney Peninsula, in the quieter reaches of Langstone Harbour, Southsea Marina is perfectly located for exploring the Solent. A family-friendly, working marina, ideal for sailing and motor cruisers alike; Southsea offers outstanding value, first-class facilities and a personal service that includes a 24/7 manned reception. Access to and from the marina is gained via a tidal cill gate. With a quality full-service boatyard, ample storage ashore and a great mix of onsite tenant marine services. When it's time to relax, the marina's two onsite restaurants offer a choice of delicious Indian and home-style cuisine.

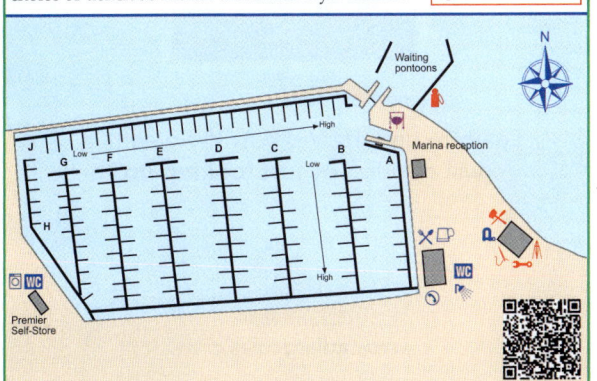

SPARKES MARINA

Sparkes Marina
38 Wittering Road, Hayling Island, Hampshire, PO11 9SR
Tel: 023 9246 3572
Email: sparkes@mdlmarinas.co.uk   www.sparkesmarina.co.uk

VHF Ch 80
ACCESS H24

Just inside the entrance to Chichester Harbour, on the eastern shores of Hayling Island, lies Sparkes Marina. Its facilities include 24-hour showers and toilets, a laundry room, an office/reception, and The Square Rigger bar and restaurant.

In addition to its berthing and marina services, Sparkes has many skilled professionals on site, including specialists in engineering, outboard engines, glass fibre repairs, rigging, sails and covers. There is a dedicated dry berthing area, 24/7 staff cover, a 7/7 working boatyard with a drystack forklift that can lift out motorboats up to 10m and yachts up to 9m, wi-fi, plus petrol and diesel are also available.

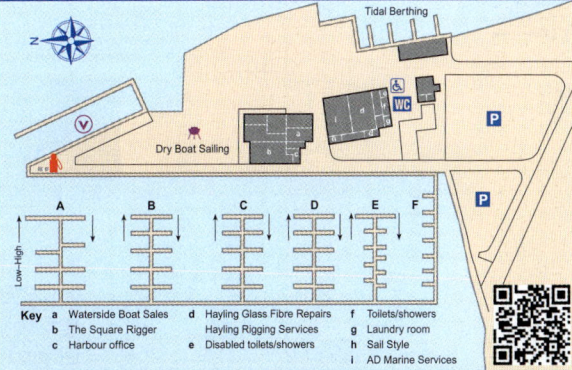

Key
a Waterside Boat Sales
b The Square Rigger
c Harbour office
d Hayling Glass Fibre Repairs
e Hayling Rigging Services
f Disabled toilets/showers
g Toilets/showers
h Laundry room
i Sail Style
j AD Marine Services

MARINA GUIDE 2026

MARINAS & SERVICES

NORTHNEY MARINA

Northney Marina
Northney Road, Hayling Island, Hampshire, PO11 0NH
Tel: 023 9246 6321
Email: northney@mdlmarinas.co.uk
www.northneymarina.co.uk

VHF Ch 80
ACCESS H24

Situated in Chichester Harbour, Northney Marina is set on the northern shore of Hayling Island in the well-marked Sweare Deep Channel, which branches off to port almost at the end of Emsworth Channel. This 228-berth marina offers excellent boatyard facilities and laundry area, diesel, a slipway, Salt Shack Café, wi-fi and 24/7 staff cover. Access is available at all states of the tide.

FACILITIES AT A GLANCE

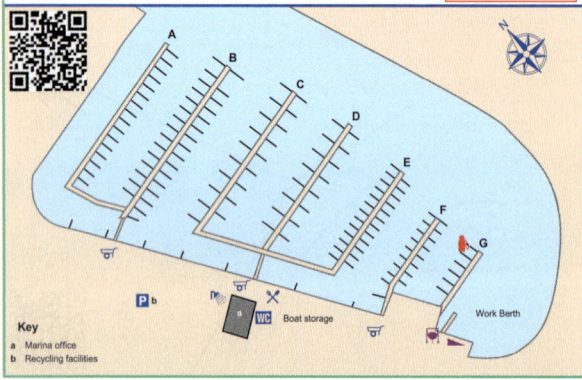

EMSWORTH YACHT HARBOUR

Emsworth Yacht Harbour Ltd
Thorney Road, Emsworth, Hants, PO10 8BP
Tel: 01243 377727
Email: info@emsworth-marina.co.uk
www.emsworth-marina.co.uk

VHF
ACCESS HW±2

Accessible about one and a half to two hours either side of high water, Emsworth Yacht Harbour is a sheltered site, offering good facilities to yachtsmen.

Created in 1964 from a log pond, the marina is within easy walking distance of the pretty little town of Emsworth, which boasts at least 10 pubs, several high quality restaurants and two well-stocked convenience stores.

FACILITIES AT A GLANCE

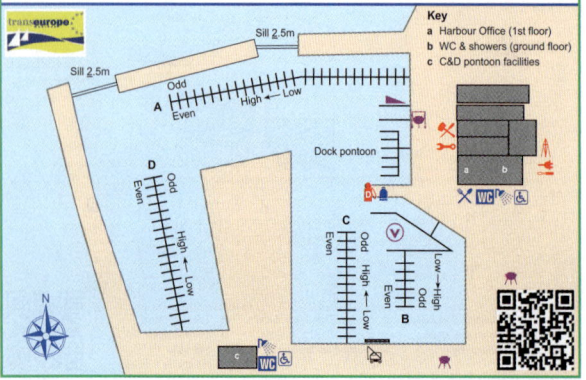

CENTRAL SOUTHERN ENGLAND | AREA 2

CHICHESTER MARINA

Chichester Marina
Birdham, Chichester, West Sussex, PO20 7EJ
Tel: 01243 512731
Email: chichester@premiermarinas.com
www.premiermarinas.com

VHF Ch 80
ACCESS HW±5

A first-class marina set in the beauty of a natural harbour and picturesque countryside makes Chichester Marina a wonderful destination and ideal to explore on foot or by boat.

This locked, family-friendly, marina is home to over 1000 berths and combines luxury facilities with serene surroundings. It is also home to a friendly yacht club and The Boat House Café, which offers bistro dining. The marina also boasts a full-service boatyard, which includes two boat hoists, a slipway and ample boat storage, plus a wide variety of tenant marine services and a Premier Self-Store.

FACILITIES AT A GLANCE

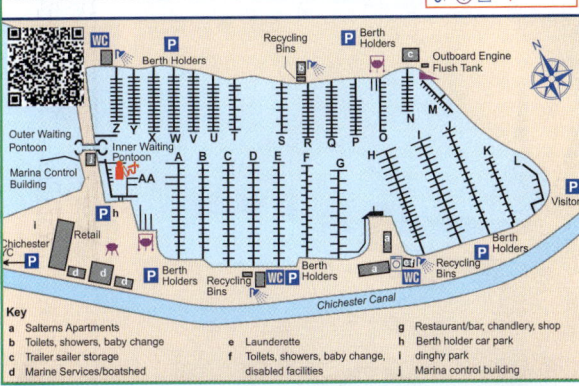

Key
a Salterns Apartments
b Toilets, showers, baby change
c Trailer sailer storage
d Marine Services/boatshed
e Launderette
f Toilets, showers, baby change, disabled facilities
g Restaurant/bar, chandlery, shop
h Berth holder car park
i dinghy park
j Marina control building

BIRDHAM POOL MARINA

Birdham Pool Marina
Birdham Pool, Chichester, Sussex
Tel: 01243 512310 Lock: 07831 466815 / 01243 511482
Email: birdhampool@aquavista.com

VHF Ch 80
ACCESS HW±3·5

Birdham Pool is the UK's oldest marina, with a charm not found elsewhere. The marina can accommodate boats of up to 14.5m in length, 4.5m beam and 1.9m draft on a mix of bow/stern to and finger pontoons. Facilities include a shipyard with 30T crane and boat mover, storage ashore and a Marine Trades Centre showcasing traditional skilled craftsmen.

Visitors will not be disappointed by the unique and picturesque setting, with views across the South Downs as well as Chichester Harbour.

Lock access is 3hrs before and 4hrs after Portsmouth HW (01243 511482/07831 466815).

FACILITIES AT A GLANCE

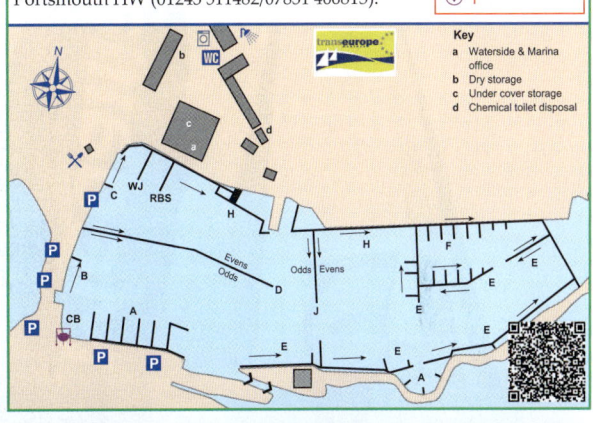

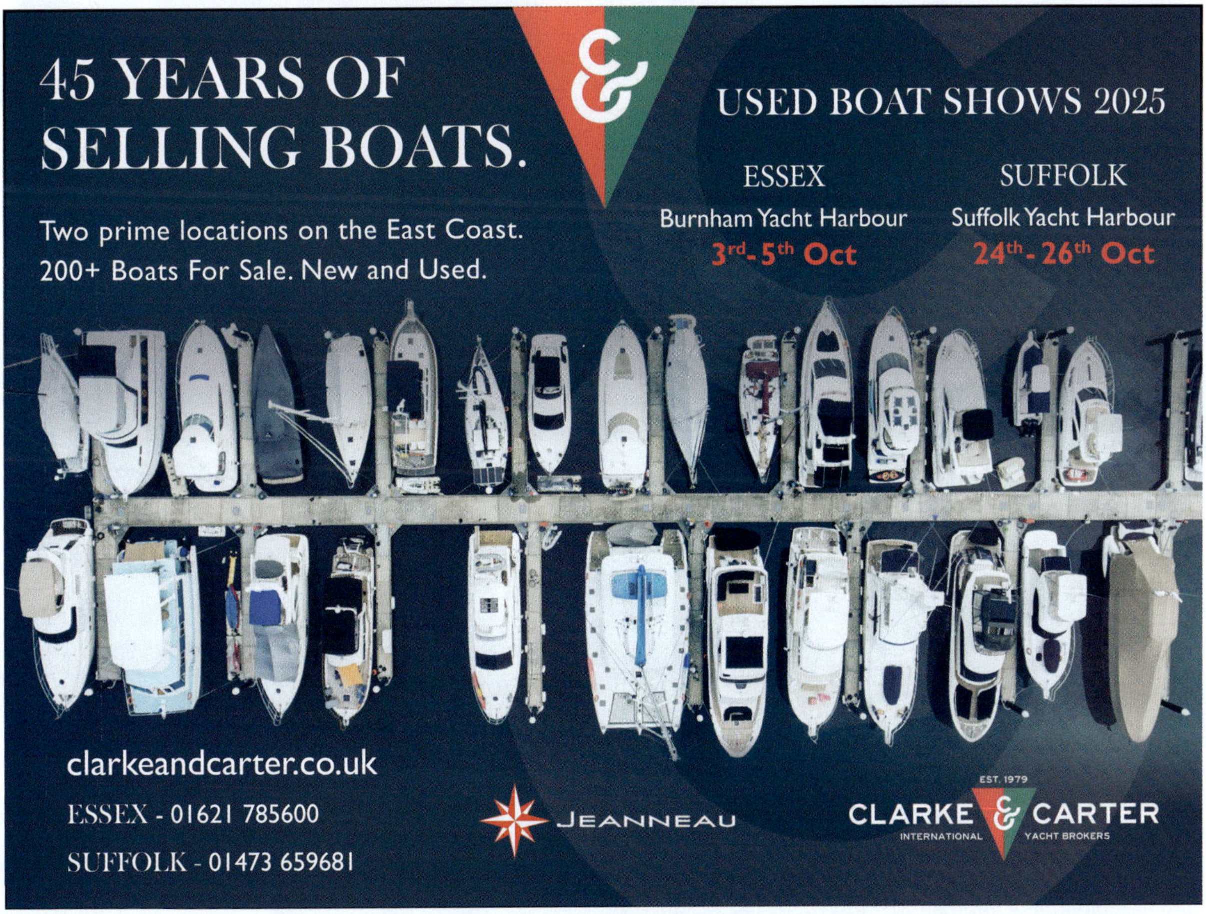

Key
a Waterside & Marina office
b Dry storage
c Under cover storage
d Chemical toilet disposal

---

45 YEARS OF SELLING BOATS.

Two prime locations on the East Coast.
200+ Boats For Sale. New and Used.

USED BOAT SHOWS 2025

ESSEX
Burnham Yacht Harbour
3rd - 5th Oct

SUFFOLK
Suffolk Yacht Harbour
24th - 26th Oct

clarkeandcarter.co.uk
ESSEX - 01621 785600
SUFFOLK - 01473 659681

JEANNEAU

CLARKE & CARTER
INTERNATIONAL YACHT BROKERS
EST. 1979

MARINA GUIDE 2026

POOLE
A SEA OF DISCOVERY AWAITS
THE SOUTH COAST'S PREMIER MARINA

POOLE QUAY BOAT HAVEN
PORT OF POOLE MARINA

GOLD ANCHOR

HOME OF Pip Hare OCEAN RACING

MARINA OF THE YEAR
2016 · 2017 · 2019 · 2020 · 2024

SUPERYACHT READY

SWINGING MOORINGS

Relax with a glass of wine, on a sunny afternoon, on your own swinging mooring in Poole Harbour overlooking Brownsea Island. Away from the madding crowd, these offer you ultimate privacy, peace & tranquillity.

VISITOR MARINA

125 visitor berths all year for vessels up to 75m in length and up to 4.8m draft

On the Port estate we can accommodate vessels up to 210m in length with a maximum draft of 9m.

Poole Town Quay, Poole, Dorset BH15 1HJ
t: 01202 649488 | poolequayboathaven.co.uk

VHF Channel 80 call sign "Poole Quay Boat Haven"

SOUTH EAST ENGLAND – Selsey Bill to North Foreland

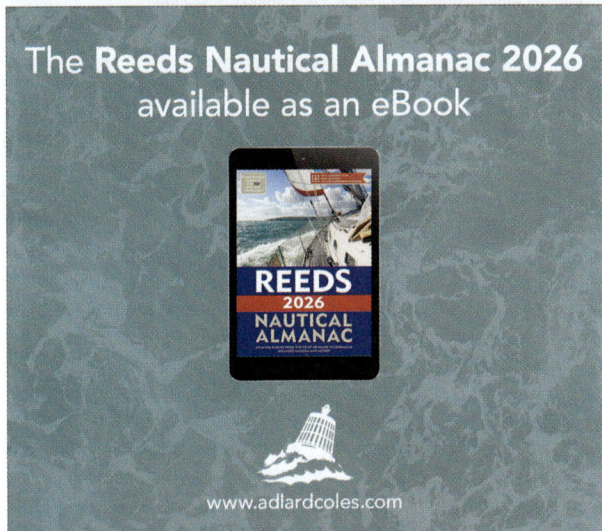

Key to Marina Plans symbols

	Bottled gas	P	Parking
	Chandler		Pub/Restaurant
	Disabled facilities		Pump out
	Electrical supply		Rigging service
	Electrical repairs		Sail repairs
	Engine repairs		Shipwright
	First Aid		Shop/Supermarket
	Fresh Water		Showers
D	Fuel - Diesel		Slipway
P	Fuel - Petrol	WC	Toilets
	Hardstanding/boatyard		Telephone
@	Internet Café		Trolleys
	Laundry facilities	V	Visitors berths
	Lift-out facilities		Wi-Fi

Area 3 - South East England

MARINAS
Telephone Numbers
VHF Channel
Access Times

Marinas shown on map:

- **Ramsgate Royal Harbour Marina** 01843 572100 Ch 14, 80 H24
- **Dover Marina** 01304 241663 Ch 80 H24
- **Harbour of Rye** 01797 225225 Ch 14 HW±2
- **Sovereign Harbour Marina** 01323 470099 Ch 17 H24
- **Newhaven Marina** 01273 513881 Ch 80 H24
- **Brighton Marina** 01273 819919 Ch M, 80 H24
- **Lady Bee Marina** 01273 593801 Ch 14 H24
- **Littlehampton Marina** 01903 713553 Ch 80 HW-3 to +2.5
- **Hillyards** 01903 713327 HW-3 to +2.5

Your essential pocket reference to all lights, shapes and marks

www.adlardcoles.com

MARINAS & SERVICES

LITTLEHAMPTON MARINA

Littlehampton Marina
Ferry Road, Littlehampton, W Sussex
Tel: 01903 713553   Fax: 01903 732264
Email: sales@littlehamptonmarina.co.uk

VHF	Ch 80
ACCESS	HW-3 to +2.5

Littlehampton is a beautiful seaside town located directly between Brighton Marina and Chichester Harbour. It has a bustling promenade and boasts wonderful sandy beaches. Situated to the East side of the town is the well-known fishing and leisure port of Littlehampton, which is fed by the renowned River Arun. Littlehampton Marina itself lies just 1.5km up river and can accept both small and large motor boats (up to 15m) as well as jet skis. Littlehampton Marina has its own concrete slipway and great onsite facilities.

FACILITIES AT A GLANCE

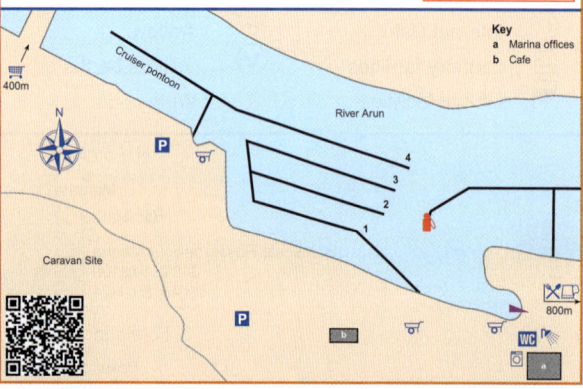

LADY BEE MARINA

Lady Bee Marina
138-140 Albion Street, Southwick, West Sussex, BN42 4EG
Tel: 01273 5591705
Email: lbchandlery@shoreham-port.co.uk

VHF	Ch 14
ACCESS	H24

Shoreham, only 5 miles W of Brighton, is one of the South Coast's major commercial ports handling, among other products steel, grain, tarmac and timber. On first impressions it may seem that Shoreham has little to offer the visiting yachtsman, but once through the lock and into the eastern arm of the R Adur, the quiet Lady Bee Marina, immediately on your left, with the waterside New Port Arms Pub and Restaurant, and the Port Kitchen Cafe, can make an interesting alternative to the lively atmosphere of Brighton Marina. Run by the harbour office, the marina meets all the usual requirements. Visitors are assured a warm welcome from the team based in the large chandlery. Pre-booking for visitors is essential.

FACILITIES AT A GLANCE

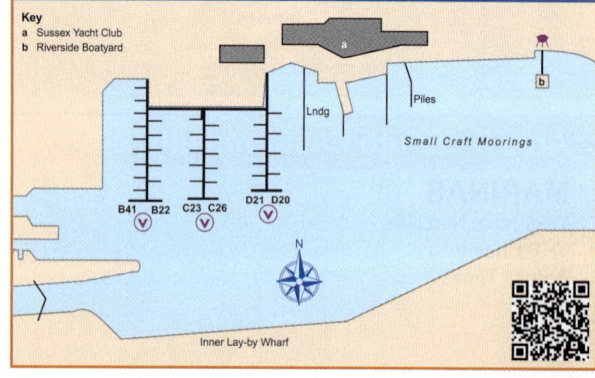

BRIGHTON MARINA

Brighton Marina
West Jetty, Brighton, East Sussex, BN2 5UP
Tel: 01273 819919
Email: brighton@premiermarinas.com
www.premiermarinas.com

⚓⚓⚓⚓

VHF	Ch M, 80
ACCESS	H24

Perfect for yachts and motorboats alike, Brighton is the UK's largest marina with over 1300 berths and offers easy access to open water and a great starting point for exploring the South Coast or a trip to France. The marina also boasts a friendly yacht club that welcomes members and visiting yachtsman, alongside local onshore leisure services including a cinema, bowling, indoor mini golf, gym, bars and restaurants. With a full-service boatyard, storage ashore, luxury facilities, a Premier Self Store and a comprehensive mix of marine tenants including a chandlery, Brighton is a great place to berth, relax and carry out boat repairs on the South Coast.

FACILITIES AT A GLANCE

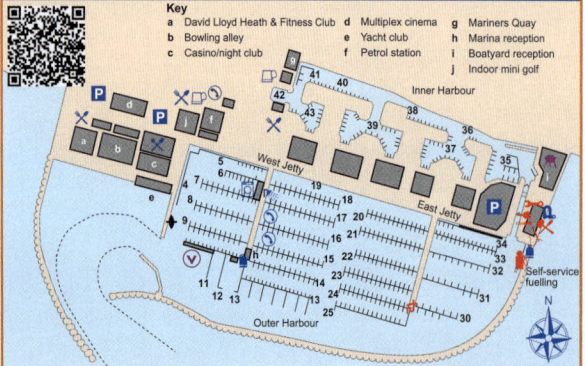

NEWHAVEN MARINA

Newhaven Marina
The Yacht Harbour, Fort Road, Newhaven
East Sussex, BN9 9BY
Tel: 01273 513881
Email: john.stirling@newhavenmarina.co.uk

VHF	Ch 80
ACCESS	H24

Some seven miles from Brighton, Newhaven lies at the mouth of the River Ouse. With its large fishing fleet and regular ferry services to Dieppe, the harbour has over the years become progressively commercial, therefore care is needed to keep clear of large vessels under manoeuvre.
The marina lies approximately quarter of a mile from the harbour entrance on the west bank and was recently dredged to allow full tidal access except on LWS.

FACILITIES AT A GLANCE

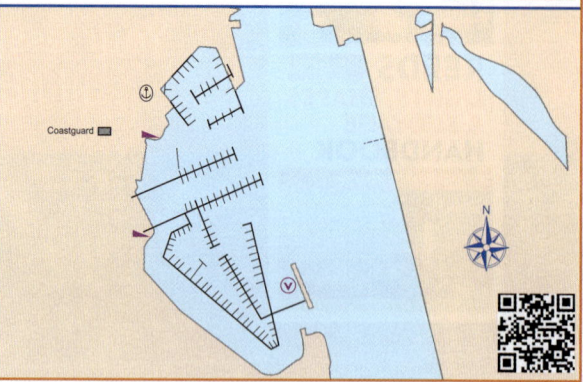

MARINA GUIDE 2026

SOUTH EAST ENGLAND — AREA 3

SOVEREIGN HARBOUR

Sovereign Harbour Marina
Pacific Drive, Eastbourne, East Sussex, BN23 5BJ
Tel: 01323 470099
Email: eastbourne@premiermarinas.com
www.premiermarinas.com

VHF Ch 17
ACCESS H24

Sovereign Harbour is Eastbourne's best kept secret, made up of four private and tranquil berthing harbours that offer over 800 quality berths. The marina is entered via one of two 24/7 high-capacity locks that are safe and easy to navigate. Sovereign Harbour offers outstanding facilities, including a full-service boatyard, chandlery and a Premier Self Store, plus a friendly Yacht Club and Berth Holder's Association. Onshore, The Waterfront leisure area boasts a mix of restaurants, bars and cafes, a hairdressers, indoor mini golf and a rich annual events programme to relax, enjoy and explore.

Key
a The Waterfront leisure area including hairdressers, bars, restaurants, shops and indoor mini golf
b Harbour office - weather information and visitor's information
c Retail park - supermarket and post office
d 24 hr fuel pontoon (diesel, petrol and holding tank pump out)
e Boatyard, boatpark, marine engineers, riggers and electricians
NB Berth numbering runs from low outer to high inner

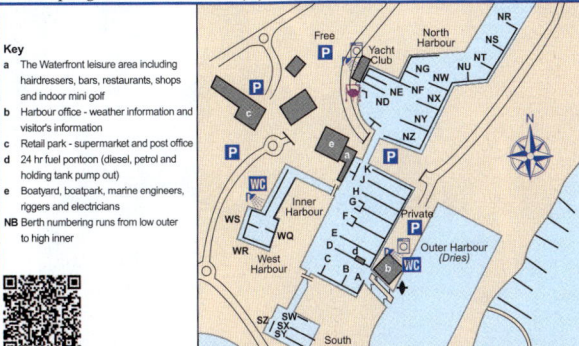

HARBOUR OF RYE

Harbour of Rye
New Lydd Road, Camber, E Sussex, TN31 7QS
Tel: 01797 225225
Email: rye.harbour@environment-agency.gov.uk
www.environment-agency.gov.uk/harbourofrye

VHF Ch 14
ACCESS HW±2

The Strand Quay Moorings in the centre of the historic of Rye with all of its short walk away. The town caters wide variety of interest with the nearby Rye Harbour Nature Reserve, town museum and numerous antique shops and plentiful pubs, bars and restaurants. Vessels with fin keel or draught greater than 1.5m should use the ladders on the west quay. Other vessels may use the pontoon on the east quay. We advise you arrive at HW but no later than HW+1. Please phone the harbour office prior to arrival. Fresh water, electricity and toilet/shower facilities are available.

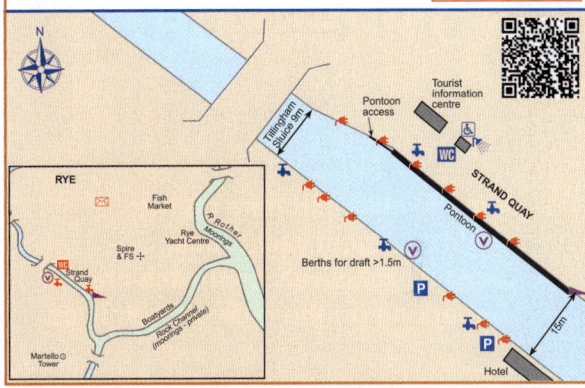

DOVER MARINA

Dover Harbour Board
Harbour House, Dover, Kent, CT17 9TF
Tel: 01304 241663 Fax: 01304 242549
Email: marina@doverport.co.uk www.doverport.co.uk/marina

VHF Ch 80
ACCESS H24

The re-developed Wellington Dock provides 135 berths alongside the new state-of-the-art Outer Marina, which opened in 2023 and sits pride of place on the picturesque waterfront with 250 berths.

From this year, the complete Dover Marina site can service up to 400 permanent or visiting berth holders, with tidal and non-tidal options, plus a boatyard and dedicated fuel berth supplying red and white diesel and petrol. The Marina Curve and Clocktower Square provide the perfect place to soak up the Kent coast, with a vibrant events and entertainment programme and local food and drink.

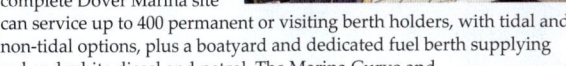
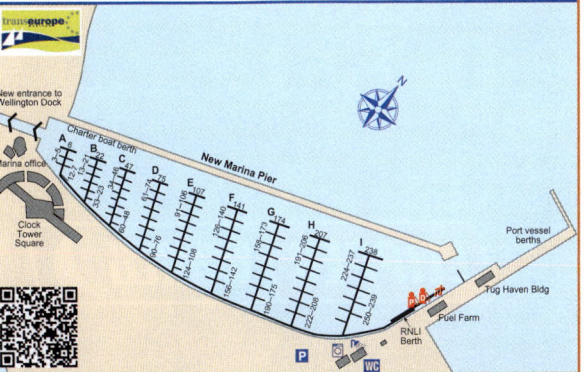

ROYAL HARBOUR MARINA

Royal Harbour Marina, Ramsgate
Harbour Office, Military Road, Ramsgate, Kent, CT11 9LQ
Tel: 01843 572100
Email: portoframsgate@thanet.gov.uk
www.portoframsgate.co.uk

VHF Ch 14, 80
ACCESS H24

Steeped in maritime history, Ramsgate was awarded 'Royal' status in 1821 by George IV in recognition of the warm welcome he received when sailing from Ramsgate. Offering good shelter and modern facilities, including both red and white diesel, the Royal Harbour comprises an outer marina accessible H24 and an inner marina, entered approximately HW±2. Permission to enter or leave the Royal Harbour must be obtained from Port Control on channel 14 and berthing instructions can be obtained from the Dockmaster on channel 80. Full information may be found on the website.

Key
a Harbour office
b Port Control (VHF 14)
c Dock office
d Showers/toilets laundry
e RNLI
f Dockmasters office
g Fuel barge (VHF 14)
h Museum

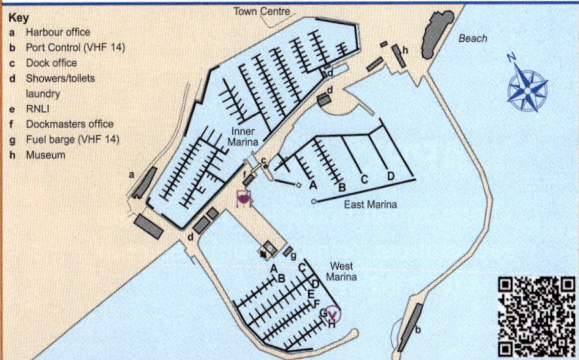

MARINA GUIDE 2026

WORLD CLASS SKIPPERS WANTED
NO PRESSURE

Sir Robin Knox-Johnston
Founder of the Clipper Round the World Yacht Race

Join the elite and take on the world's longest yacht race, crewed exclusively by novice crew embarking on the race of their lives.

Clipper Race Skippers are exceptional. These men and women have the fortitude to take on the toughest of mental challenges, and the physical endurance to successfully lead a team through Mother Nature's extreme environments on a 40,000 mile lap around the globe.

We are recruiting experienced professional Skippers for the next edition of the Clipper Race. To qualify you must hold a valid Yachtmaster Ocean certificate [commercial endorsed] or International Yacht Training Master of Yachts.

⬇ APPLY NOW

clipperroundtheworld.com/careers
raceskipper@clipper-ventures.com
+44 (0) 2392 526000

AREA 4

EAST ENGLAND – North Foreland to Great Yarmouth

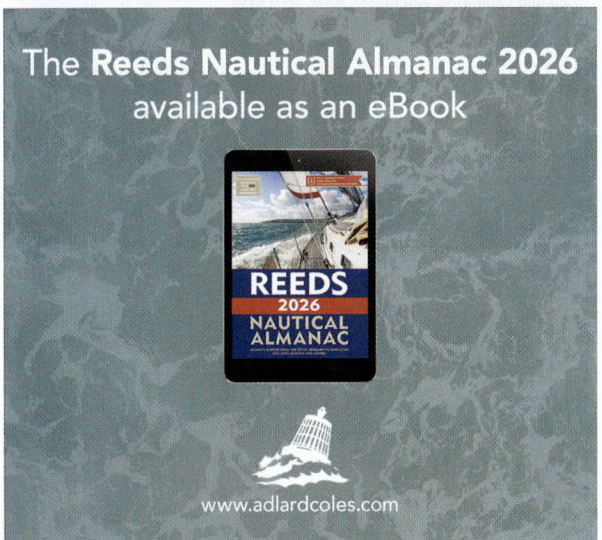

Key to Marina Plans symbols

🛢	Bottled gas	P	Parking
	Chandler		Pub/Restaurant
	Disabled facilities		Pump out
	Electrical supply		Rigging service
	Electrical repairs		Sail repairs
	Engine repairs		Shipwright
	First Aid		Shop/Supermarket
	Fresh Water		Showers
	Fuel - Diesel		Slipway
	Fuel - Petrol	WC	Toilets
	Hardstanding/boatyard		Telephone
@	Internet Café		Trolleys
	Laundry facilities	V	Visitors berths
	Lift-out facilities		Wi-Fi

Area 4 - East England

MARINAS
Telephone Numbers, VHF Channel, Access Times

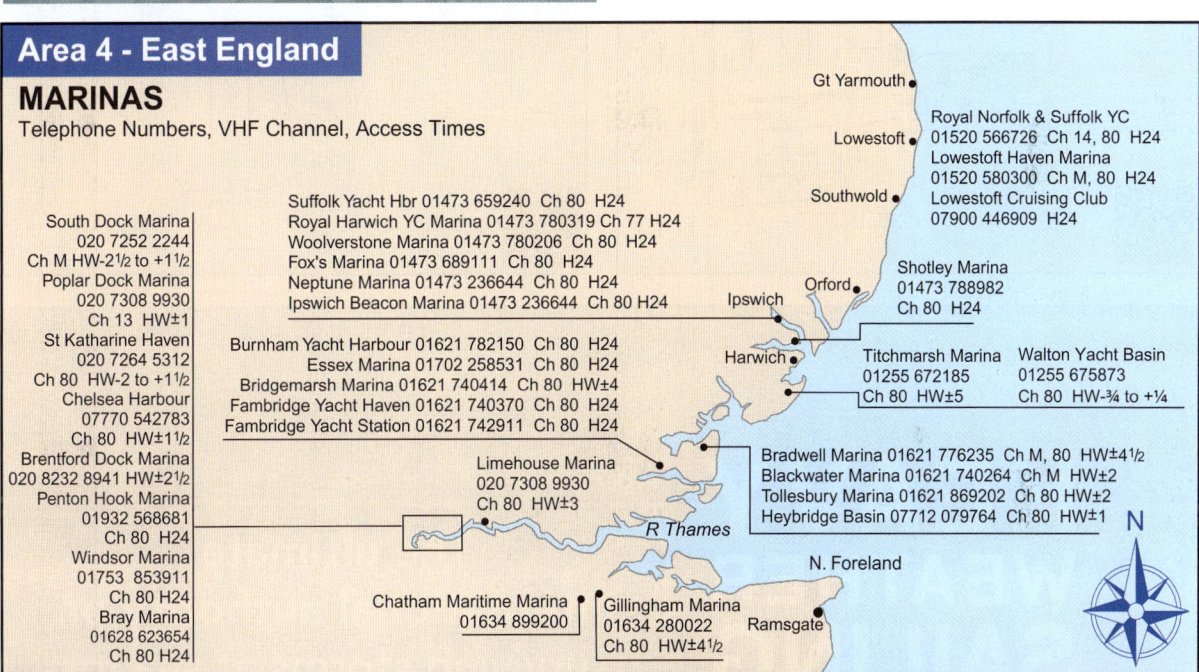

South Dock Marina 020 7252 2244 Ch M HW-2½ to +1½
Poplar Dock Marina 020 7308 9930 Ch 13 HW±1
St Katharine Haven 020 7264 5312 Ch 80 HW-2 to +1½
Chelsea Harbour 07770 542783 Ch 80 HW±1½
Brentford Dock Marina 020 8232 8941 HW±2½
Penton Hook Marina 01932 568681 Ch 80 H24
Windsor Marina 01753 853911 Ch 80 H24
Bray Marina 01628 623654 Ch 80 H24

Suffolk Yacht Hbr 01473 659240 Ch 80 H24
Royal Harwich YC Marina 01473 780319 Ch 77 H24
Woolverstone Marina 01473 780206 Ch 80 H24
Fox's Marina 01473 689111 Ch 80 H24
Neptune Marina 01473 236644 Ch 80 H24
Ipswich Beacon Marina 01473 236644 Ch 80 H24

Burnham Yacht Harbour 01621 782150 Ch 80 H24
Essex Marina 01702 258531 Ch 80 H24
Bridgemarsh Marina 01621 740414 Ch 80 HW±4
Fambridge Yacht Haven 01621 740370 Ch 80 H24
Fambridge Yacht Station 01621 742911 Ch 80 H24

Limehouse Marina 020 7308 9930 Ch 80 HW±3

Chatham Maritime Marina 01634 899200
Gillingham Marina 01634 280022 Ch 80 HW±4½

Royal Norfolk & Suffolk YC 01520 566726 Ch 14, 80 H24
Lowestoft Haven Marina 01520 580300 Ch M, 80 H24
Lowestoft Cruising Club 07900 446909 H24

Shotley Marina 01473 788982 Ch 80 H24

Titchmarsh Marina 01255 672185 Ch 80 HW±5
Walton Yacht Basin 01255 675873 Ch 80 HW-¾ to +¼

Bradwell Marina 01621 776235 Ch M, 80 HW±4½
Blackwater Marina 01621 740264 Ch M HW±2
Tollesbury Marina 01621 869202 Ch 80 HW±2
Heybridge Basin 07712 079764 Ch 80 HW±1

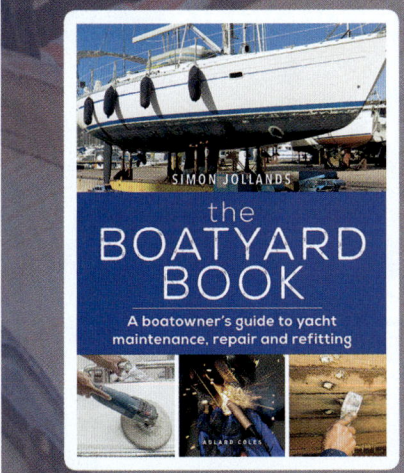

Maintenance, repairs, upgrades and refits

All the information owners need to care for their boat

www.adlardcoles.com

MARINA GUIDE 2026

MARINAS & SERVICES

GILLINGHAM MARINA

Gillingham Marina
173 Pier Road, Gillingham, Kent, ME7 1UB
Tel: 01634 280022 Fax: 01634 280164
Email: berthing@gillingham-marina.co.uk
www.gillingham-marina.co.uk

VHF Ch 80
ACCESS HW±4.5

Gillingham Marina comprises a locked basin, accessible four and a half hours either side of high water, and a tidal basin upstream which can be entered approximately two hours either side of high water. Deep water moorings in the river cater for yachts arriving at other times.

Visiting yachts are usually accommodated in the locked basin, although it is best to contact the marina ahead of time. Lying on the south bank of the River Medway, the marina is approximately eight miles from Sheerness, at the mouth of the river, and five miles downstream of Rochester Bridge. Facilities include a well-stocked chandlery, brokerage and an extensive workshop.

FACILITIES AT A GLANCE

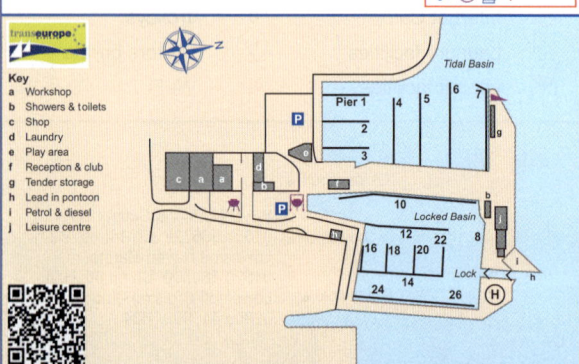

PORT WERBURGH

Port Werburgh
Vicarage Lane, Hoo, Rochester, Kent, ME3 9TW
Tel: 01634 252107 Fax: 01634 253477
Email: jillswann@wanttoliveafloat.com

VHF Ch 80
ACCESS HW±3

Hoo Marina has been purchased by Residential Marine Ltd and is now incorporated into Port Werburgh. The port, some eight miles upriver from Sheerness, can be approached either straight across the mud flats at HW or via the creek, which has access HW±3 for shallow draught boats. The path of the creek is marked by withies, which must be kept to port.

The port accommodates residential and leisure boats from 20–200ft and has a lifting service available for craft up to 17 tons; a dry dock is available for larger boats. There are no workshop facilities but boat owners are encouraged to work on their own boats. Security is provided by H24 CCTV coverage.

All berths are supplied with water and electricity and the onsite amenity block has showers, toilets and a laundry room. There is a grocery store adjacent and shops in Hoo village approximately half a mile distant. There is a frequent bus service to nearby Rochester.

FACILITIES AT A GLANCE

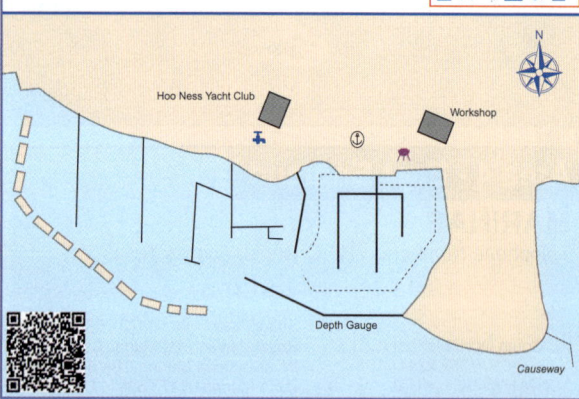

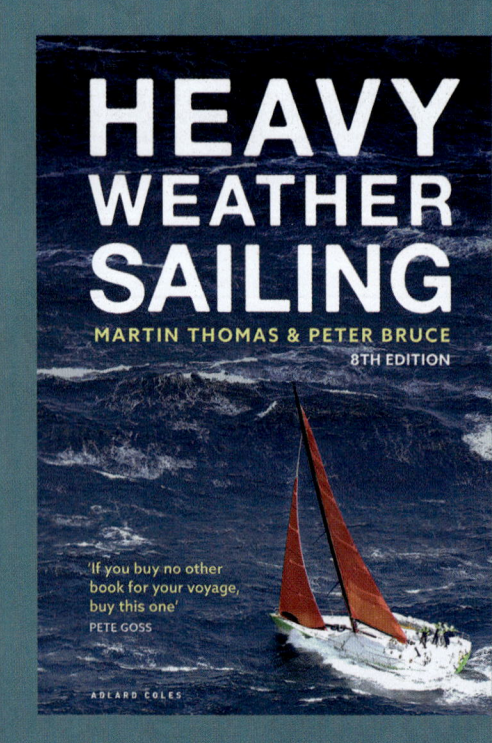

HEAVY WEATHER SAILING
MARTIN THOMAS & PETER BRUCE
8TH EDITION

'If you buy no other book for your voyage, buy this one'
PETE GOSS

ADLARD COLES

The **ultimate international authority** on surviving storms at sea for almost 60 years

www.adlardcoles.com

EAST ENGLAND — AREA 4

CHATHAM MARITIME MARINA

Chatham Maritime Marina, The Lock Building,
Leviathan Way, Chatham Maritime, Chatham, Medway, ME4 4LP
Tel: 01634 899200
Email: chatham@mdlmarinas.co.uk
www.chathammaritimemarina.co.uk

VHF Ch 80
ACCESS H24

Chatham Maritime Marina is situated on the banks of the River Medway in Kent, providing an ideal location from which to explore the surrounding area. There are plenty of secluded anchorages in the lower reaches of the Medway Estuary, while the river is navigable for some 13 miles from its mouth at Sheerness right up to Rochester, and even beyond for those yachts drawing less than 2m. Only 45 minutes from London by road, the marina is part of a multi-million pound leisure and retail development, accommodating 412 boats up to 24m LOA.

FACILITIES AT A GLANCE

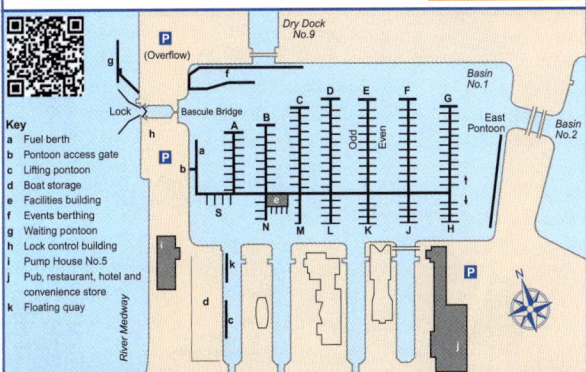

LIMEHOUSE WATERSIDE & MARINA

Limehouse Waterside & Marina
46 Goodhart Place, London, E14 8EG
Tel: 020 7308 9930
Email: limehouse@aquavista.com   www.aquavista.com

VHF Ch 80
ACCESS HW±3

Limehouse Marina, situated where the canal system meets the Thames, is now considered the 'Jewel in the Crown' of the British inland waterways network. With complete access to 2,000 miles of inland waterway systems and with access to the Thames at most stages of the tide except around low water, the marina provides a superb location for river, canal and sea-going pleasure craft alike. Boasting a wide range of facilities and 137 berths, Limehouse Marina is housed in the old Regent's Canal Dock.

FACILITIES AT A GLANCE

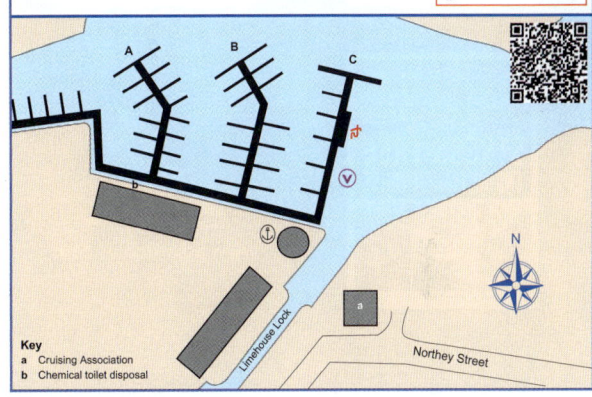

MARINA GUIDE 2026 39

MARINAS & SERVICES

SOUTH DOCK MARINA

South Dock Marina
Rope Street, Off Plough Way
London, SE16 7SZ
Tel: 020 7252 2244   Fax: 020 7237 3806
Email: christopher.magro@southwark.gov.uk

VHF	Ch M
ACCESS	HW-2.5 to +1.5

South Dock Marina is housed in part of the old Surrey Dock complex on the south bank of the River Thames. Its locked entrance is immediately downstream of Greenland Pier, just a few miles down river of Tower Bridge. For yachts with a 2m draught, the lock can be entered HW-2½ to HW+1½ London Bridge, although if you arrive early there is a holding pontoon on the pier. The marina can be easily identified by the conspicuous arched rooftops of Baltic Quay, a luxury waterside apartment block. Once inside this secure, 200-berth marina, you can take full advantage of all its facilities as well as enjoy a range of restaurants and bars close by or visit historic maritime Greenwich.

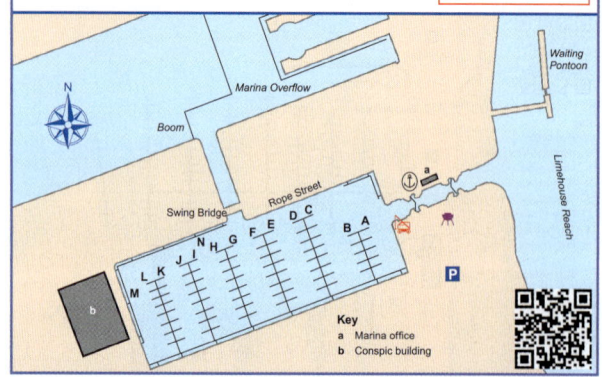

CHELSEA HARBOUR MARINA

Chelsea Harbour Marina
Estate Managements Office
C2-3 The Chambers, London, SW10 0XF
Tel: 07770 542783   Fax: 020 7352 7868
Email: harbourmaster@chelsea-harbour.co.uk

VHF	
ACCESS	HW±1.5

Chelsea Harbour is widely thought of as one of London's most significant maritime sites. It is located in the heart of SW London, therefore enjoying easy access to the amenities of Chelsea and the West End. On site is the Chelsea Harbour Design Centre, where 80 showrooms exhibit the best in British and International interior design, offering superb waterside views along with excellent cuisine in the Wyndham Grand.

The harbour lies approximately 48 miles up river from Sea Reach No 1 buoy in the Thames Estuary and is accessed via the Thames Flood Barrier in Woolwich Reach. With its basin gate operating one and a half hours either side of HW (+ 20 minutes at London Bridge), the marina welcomes visiting yachtsmen.

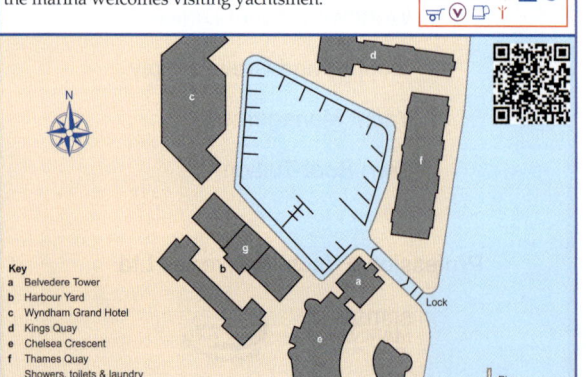

ST KATHARINE DOCKS

St Katharine Docks Marina
50 St Katharine's Way, London, E1W 1LA
Tel: 020 7264 5312
Email: ptetlow@skdocks.co.uk
www.skdocks.co.uk/marina

VHF	Ch 80
ACCESS	HW -2 to +1.5

IGY Destination, St Katharine Docks Marina offers 185 berths equipped for boats up to 40m in three separate, secure and calm basins. The historic docks are located next to Tower Bridge.

This is a unique marina benefiting from waterside dining, boutique shops and excellent transport links to the West End. Visitors are welcomed all year round and the marina provides its own calendar of events details of which can be found on the website and social media pages.

The marina is ideally situated for visiting the Tower of London, Tower Bridge, *HMS Belfast* and the City of London all of which can be reached on foot. A short river bus service away is Greenwich and the Cutty Sark and to the west the Shard and London Eye.

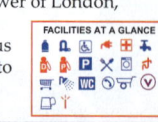

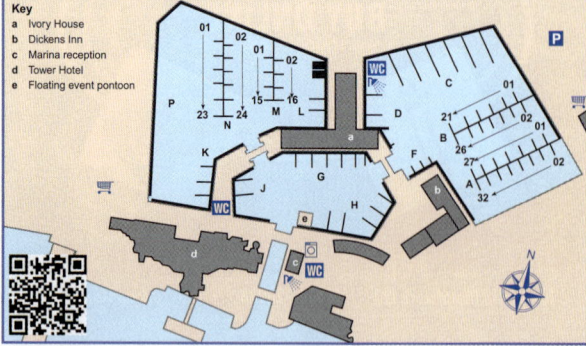

MARINA GUIDE 2026

EAST ENGLAND — AREA 4

BRENTFORD DOCK MARINA

Brentford Dock Marina
2 Justin Close, Brentford, Middlesex, TW8 8QE
Tel: 0208 568 5096
E-mail: managementoffice@brentford-dock.co.uk

VHF
ACCESS HW±2.5

Brentford Dock Marina is situated on the River Thames at the junction with the Grand Union Canal. Its hydraulic lock is accessible for up to two and a half hours either side of high water, although boats over 9.5m LOA enter on high water by prior arrangement. There is a grocery store on site. The main attractions within the area are the Royal Botanic Gardens at Kew and the Kew Bridge Steam Museum at Brentford.

FACILITIES AT A GLANCE

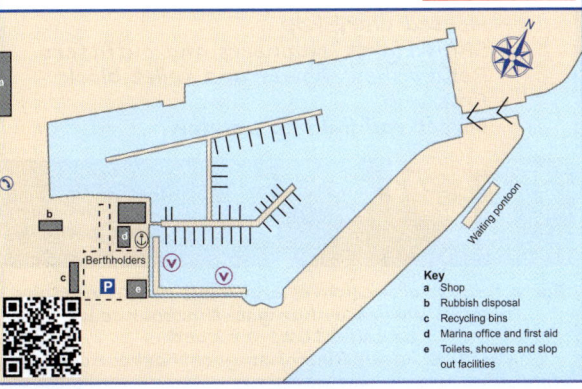

Key
a Shop
b Rubbish disposal
c Recycling bins
d Marina office and first aid
e Toilets, showers and slop out facilities

PENTON HOOK MARINA

Penton Hook Marina
Staines Road, Chertsey, Surrey, KT16 8PY
Tel: 01932 568681
Email: pentonhook@mdlmarinas.co.uk
www.pentonhookmarina.co.uk

VHF
ACCESS H24

Penton Hook, the largest inland marina in Europe, is situated on what is considered to be one of the most attractive reaches of the River Thames; close to the vibrant town of Staines-on-Thames and about a mile downstream from Runnymede.

Providing unrestricted access to the River Thames through a deep water channel below Penton Hook Lock, the marina can accommodate ocean-going craft of up to 30m LOA and is ideally placed for a visit to Thorpe Park, reputedly one of the country's most popular family leisure attractions.

FACILITIES AT A GLANCE

Key
a Information point
b Dock manager's office
c Yacht club
d Repairs and engineering
e Boat sales office

WINDSOR MARINA

Windsor Marina
Maidenhead Road, Windsor
Berkshire, SL4 5TZ
Tel: 01753 853911
Email: windsor@mdlmarinas.co.uk www.windsormarina.co.uk

VHF
ACCESS H24

Situated on the outskirts of Windsor town on the south bank of the River Thames, Windsor Marina enjoys a peaceful garden setting. On site is the Windsor Yacht Club, a small chandlery and fuel (diesel and petrol), enabling you to fill up as and when you need.

A trip to the town of Windsor, comprising beautiful Georgian and Victorian buildings, would not be complete without a visit to Windsor Castle. With its construction inaugurated over 900 years ago by William the Conqueror, it is the oldest inhabited castle in the world and accommodates a priceless art and furniture collection.

FACILITIES AT A GLANCE

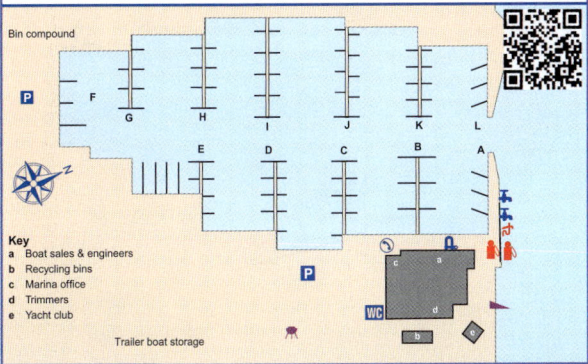

Key
a Boat sales & engineers
b Recycling bins
c Marina office
d Trimmers
e Yacht club

BRAY MARINA

Bray Marina
Monkey Island Lane, Bray
Berkshire, SL6 2EB
Tel: 01628 623654
Email: bray@mdlmarinas.co.uk www.braymarina.co.uk

VHF
ACCESS H24

Bray Marina is situated in a country park setting among shady trees, providing berth holders with a tranquil mooring. From the marina there is direct access to the Thames and there are extensive well-maintained facilities available for all boat owners. The 400-berth marina boasts a Mediterranean-themed bar and restaurant, an active club, which holds social functions and boat training lessons, a small chandlery, fuel (diesel and petrol), and engineering services. Pumpout facilities are available in the nearby Windsor Marina.

Upstream is Cliveden House, with its extensive gardens and woodlands. Cookham is home of the Queen's Swan Keeper, who can sometimes be seen in traditional costume. Farther on is Hambledon Mill; the river is navigable as far as Lechlade.

FACILITIES AT A GLANCE

Key
a Boat storage
b Boat sales office
c Marina office, toilets/showers restaurant
d Battery, hazardous waste, oil and fuel disposal
e Repairs and engineering

MARINA GUIDE 2026

MARINAS & SERVICES

BURNHAM YACHT HARBOUR MARINA

Burnham Yacht Harbour Marina Ltd
Burnham-on-Crouch, Essex, CM0 8BL
Tel: 01621 782150 HM: 01621 786832
Email: admin@burnhamyachtharbour.co.uk

VHF Ch 80
ACCESS H24

Burnham Yacht Harbour is situated in the pretty town of Burnham-on-Crouch with its quaint shops, elegant quayside and riverside walks. The train station, with direct train links to London Liverpool Street Station, is within walking. There is provision of all facilities you would expect to find from a modern secure marina with H24 tidal access, 350 fully serviced berths, the popular Swallowtail Restaurant and Bar, engineers, shipwrights, workshop, friendly staff and yacht brokerage. The entrance is easily identified by a yellow pillar buoy with an 'X' topmark.

FACILITIES AT A GLANCE

Key
a Workshop
b Yacht sales
c Marina office
d Shower block
e The Swallowtail
f RNLI shore station
g Country park

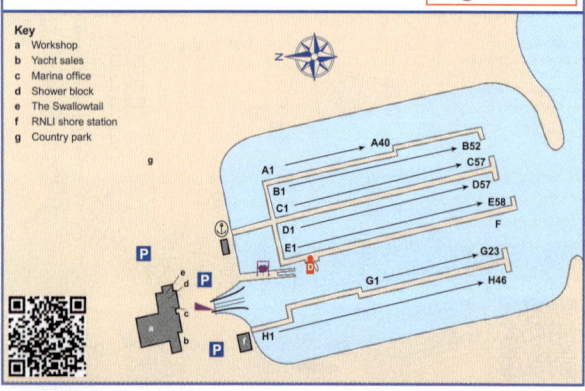

Visiting Burnham Yacht Harbour?
Please call our Harbourmaster on
01621 786832
or call up on VHF Channel 80
for visitor berth allocation.

- 350 fully serviced berths
- Safe and secure moorings
- 24 hour tidal access
- Restaurant, bar and conference room
- Heated workshop
- Shipwrights, engineers and outfitters
- Refurbished shower and toilet block
- Free Wifi
- Direct rail links to London

For a full list of incentives and deals please visit our
website www.burnhamyachtharbour.co.uk
or call 01621 782150
or email us admin@burnhamyachtharbour.co.uk

ESSEX MARINA

Essex Marina
Wallasea Island, Essex, SS4 2HF
Tel: 01702 258531 Fax: 01702 258227
Email: info@essexmarina.co.uk
www.essexmarina.co.uk

VHF Ch 80
ACCESS H24

Surrounded by beautiful countryside, Essex Marina is situated in Wallasea Bay, about half a mile up river of Burnham on Crouch. Boasting 500 deep water berths, including 50 swinging moorings, the marina can be accessed at all states of the tide. On site are a 70 ton boat hoist, a chandlery and brokerage service as well as the Essex Marina Yacht Club.

Essex Marina is the home of Boats.co.uk. There is a ferry service which runs from Easter until the end of September, taking passengers across the river 6 days a week to Burnham, where you will find numerous shops and restaurants.

FACILITIES AT A GLANCE

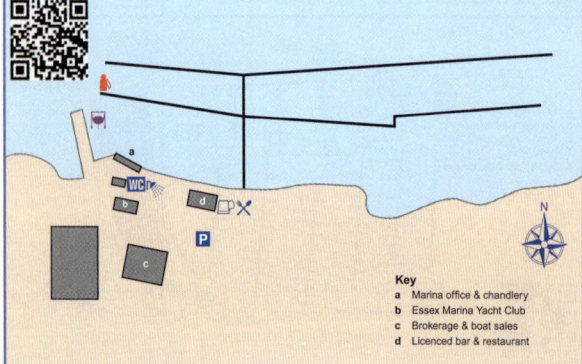

Key
a Marina office & chandlery
b Essex Marina Yacht Club
c Brokerage & boat sales
d Licenced bar & restaurant

BRIDGEMARSH MARINA

Bridgemarsh Marine
Fairholme, Bridge Marsh Lane, Althorne, Essex
Tel: 01621 740414 Mobile: 07968 696815 Fax: 01621 742216

VHF Ch 80
ACCESS HW±4

On the north side of Bridgemarsh Island, just beyond Essex Marina on the River Crouch, lies Althorne Creek. Here Bridgemarsh Marine accommodates over 100 boats berthed alongside pontoons supplied with water and electricity. A red beacon marks the entrance to the creek, with red can buoys identifying the approach channel into the marina. Accessible four hours either side of high water, the marina has an on site yard with two docks, a slipway and crane. The village of Althorne is just a short walk away, from where there are direct train services (taking approximately one hour) to London.

FACILITIES AT A GLANCE

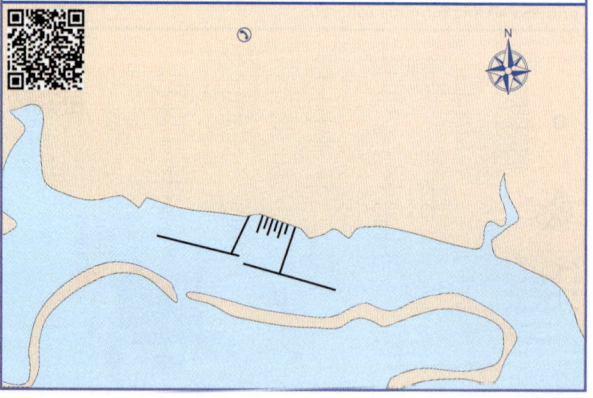

42   MARINA GUIDE 2026

EAST ENGLAND — AREA 4

HEYBRIDGE BASIN

Heybridge Basin
Lock Hill, Heybridge Basin, Maldon, Essex, CM9 4RY
Tel: 07712 079764
Email: paul.hindley@waterways.org.uk
www.essexwaterways.com

VHF Ch 80
ACCESS HW±1

Towards the head of the River Blackwater and not far from Maldon, lies Heybridge Basin sea lock. It is situated at the lower end of the 14M Chelmer and Blackwater Navigation Canal and can be entered approximately 1-1.5hrs before HW for vessels drawing up to 2m. There is good holding ground in the river just outside the lock. There are in excess of 300 permanent moorings along the navigation and room for up to 20 rafting visiting vessels in the Basin, which has a range of facilities, including shower and laundry. Please book at least 24hrs in advance especially during the summer months. The manned lock is operational for tides between 0600 and 2000 during summer months (0800–1700 Oct–Apr).

FACILITIES AT A GLANCE

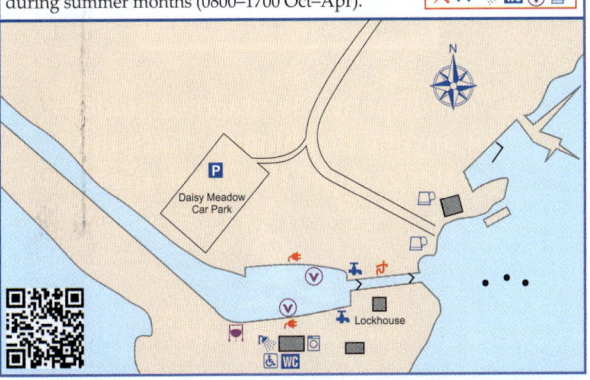

BRADWELL MARINA

Bradwell Marina, Port Flair Ltd, Waterside
Bradwell-on-Sea, Essex, CM0 7RB
Tel: 01621 776235
Email: info@bradwellmarina.com
www.bradwellmarina.com

VHF Ch M, 80
ACCESS HW±4.5

Opened in 1984, Bradwell is a privately-owned marina situated in the mouth of the River Blackwater, serving as a convenient base from which to explore the Essex coastline or as a departure point for cruising further afield to Holland and Belgium.

The yacht basin can be accessed four and a half hours either side of HW and offers plenty of protection from all wind directions. With a total of 350 fully serviced berths, generous space has been allocated for manoeuvring between pontoons. Overlooking the marina is Bradwell Club House, incorporating a bar, restaurant, launderette and ablution facilities.

FACILITIES AT A GLANCE

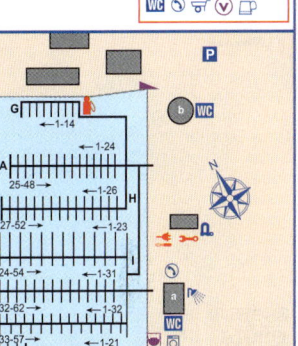

FAMBRIDGE YACHT STATION

Fambridge Yacht Station
Church Road, North Fambridge, Essex, CM3 6LU
Tel: 01621 742911   www.yachthavens.com
Email: fambridge@yachthavens.com

VHF Ch 80
ACCESS H24

The Yacht Station is located just under a mile downstream of Fambridge Yacht Haven and is set within the sheltered River Crouch directly between the rural villages of North and South Fambridge. Home to the North Fambridge Yacht Club, the Yacht Station has a 120m visitor pontoon providing deep water berthing alongside and foot access to mud berths and the North Fambridge. There are also 120 deep water swinging moorings in 4 straight E/W trots just off the visitor pontoon. A launch service operates 7 days a week during the summer, call in advance for times. As with the marina, excellent repair facilities can be found ashore for vessels with a maximum weight of 25t.

FACILITIES AT A GLANCE

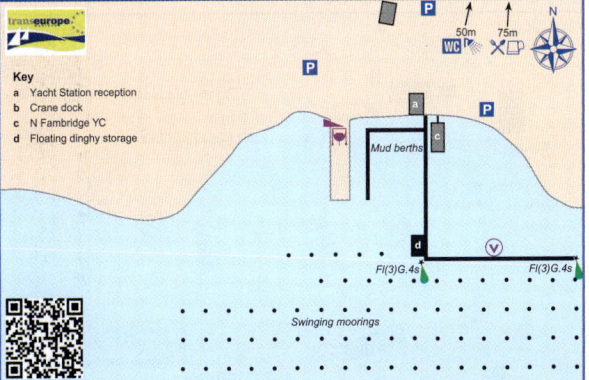

Bradwell Marina

- 350 Pontoon Berths in Rural Setting
- Access 4.5hrs either side H.W.
- VHF monitoring (CH 80)
- Water/electricity to all Pontoons
- Fuel jetty - petrol & diesel
- Bottled Calor gas
- Hot Showers
- 1st class workshop/repairs
- Day Launch Slipway
- Boat Hoistage to 45 tons
- Winter Storage
- Licensed Club (membership free)
- Free Wireless Internet

Port Flair Ltd., Waterside, Bradwell-on-Sea, Essex CM0 7RB
01621 776235/776391
www.bradwellmarina.com

MARINA GUIDE 2026

MARINAS & SERVICES

FAMBRIDGE YACHT HAVEN

Fambridge Yacht Haven
Church Road, North Fambridge, Essex, CM3 6LU
Tel: 01621 740370   www.yachthavens.com
Email: fambridge@yachthavens.com

VHF	Ch 80
ACCESS	H24

The Haven is split over two sites in the village of North Fambridge. The marina is located just under a mile upstream of its 'Yacht Station' facility with access via Stow Creek, which branches N off the R Crouch. The channel is straight and clearly marked to the ent of the Yacht Haven. Home to the West Wick Yacht Club, the marina has 220 berths to accommodate vessels up to 20m LOA. North Fambridge features the 500 year-old Ferry Boat Inn, a favourite haunt with the sailing fraternity. Burnham-on-Crouch is six miles down river, while the Essex and Kent coasts are within easy sailing distance. Excellent repair facilities can be found ashore together with undercover storage for vessels up to 19m LOA with a maximum weight of 40 tons.

FACILITIES AT A GLANCE

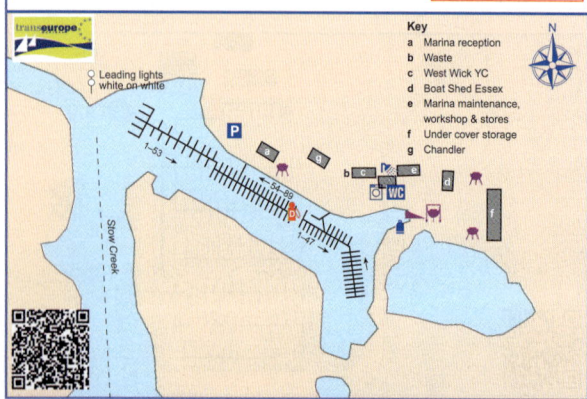

Key
a Marina reception
b Waste
c West Wick YC
d Boat Shed Essex
e Marina maintenance, workshop & stores
f Under cover storage
g Chandler

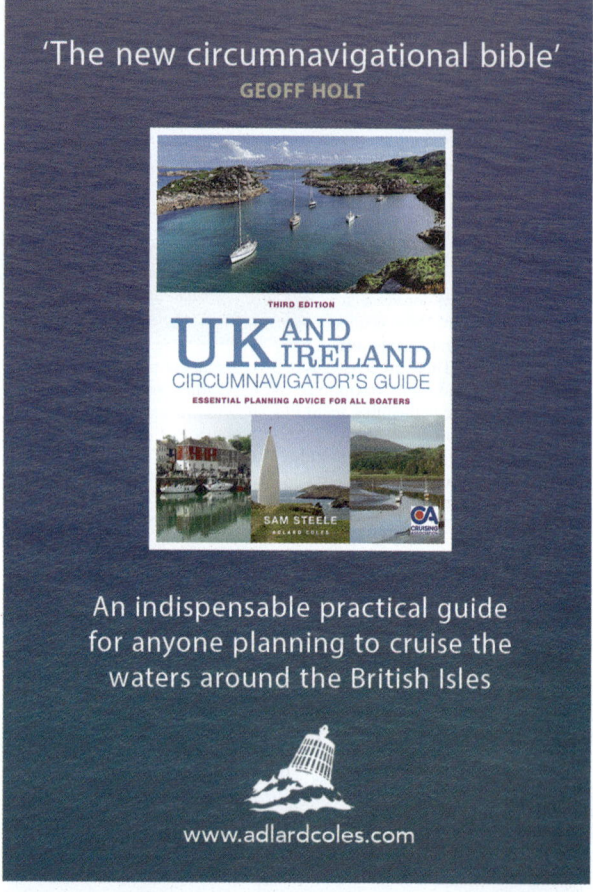

'The new circumnavigational bible'
GEOFF HOLT

UK AND IRELAND CIRCUMNAVIGATOR'S GUIDE
ESSENTIAL PLANNING ADVICE FOR ALL BOATERS
THIRD EDITION
SAM STEELE

An indispensable practical guide for anyone planning to cruise the waters around the British Isles

www.adlardcoles.com

BLACKWATER MARINA

Blackwater Marina
Marine Parade, Maylandsea, Essex
Tel: 01621 740264
Email: info@blackwater-marina.co.uk

VHF	Ch M
ACCESS	HW±2

Blackwater Marina is a place where families in day boats mix with Smack owners and yacht crews; here seals, avocets and porpoises roam beneath the big, sheltering East Coast skies and here the area's rich heritage of working Thames Barges and Smacks remains part of daily life today.
But it isn't just classic sailing boats that thrive on the Blackwater. An eclectic mix of motor cruisers, open boats and modern yachts enjoy the advantages of a marina sheltered by its natural habitat, where the absence of harbour walls allows uninterrupted views of some of Britain's rarest wildlife and where the 21st century shoreside facilities are looked after by experienced professionals, who are often found sailing on their days off.

FACILITIES AT A GLANCE

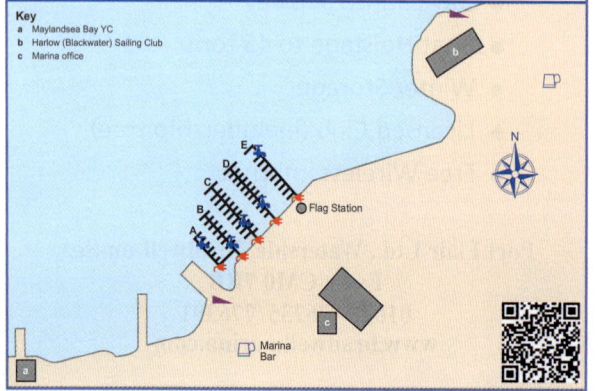

Key
a Maylandsea Bay YC
b Harlow (Blackwater) Sailing Club
c Marina office

TOLLESBURY MARINA

Tollesbury Marina
The Yacht Harbour, Tollesbury, Essex, CM9 8SE
Tel: 01621 869202
email: hm@tollesburymarina.com

VHF	Ch 80
ACCESS	HW±2

Tollesbury Marina lies at the mouth of the River Blackwater in the heart of the Essex countryside. Within easy access from London and the Home Counties, it has been designed as a leisure centre for the whole family, with on-site activities comprising tennis courts and a covered heated swimming pool as well as a convivial bar and restaurant. Accommodating over 240 boats, the marina can be accessed two hours either side of HW and is ideally situated for those wishing to explore the River Crouch to the south and the Rivers Colne, Orwell and Deben to the north.

FACILITIES AT A GLANCE

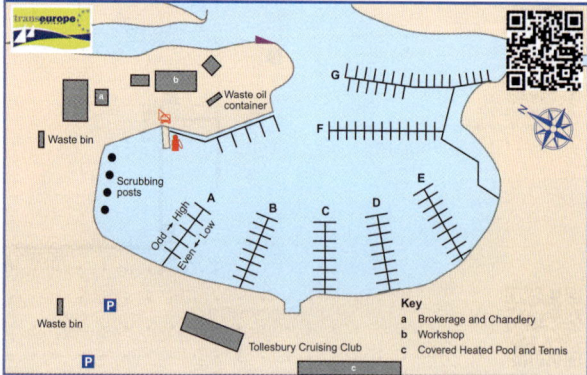

Key
a Brokerage and Chandlery
b Workshop
c Covered Heated Pool and Tennis

MARINA GUIDE 2026

EAST ENGLAND AREA 4

TITCHMARSH MARINA

Titchmarsh Marina Ltd
Coles Lane, Walton on the Naze, Essex, CO14 8SL
Tel: 01255 672185 Fax: 01255 851901
Email: info@titchmarshmarina.co.uk
www.titchmarshmarina.co.uk

VHF Ch 80
ACCESS HW±5

Titchmarsh Marina sits on the south side of The Twizzle in the heart of the Walton Backwaters. As the area is designated a 'wetland of international importance', the marina has been designed and developed to function as a natural harbour. The 420 berths are well-sheltered by the high-grassed clay banks, offering good protection in all conditions. The marina entrance has a depth of 1.3m at LWS but once inside the basin this increases to around 2m; there is a tide gauge at the fuel berth. Among the excellent facilities onsite are the well-stocked chandlery and the Harbour Lights restaurant and bar serving food daily.

Key
a Harbour master, chandlery (+ cycle hire) marine engineers, marine electronics
b Hardstanding
c Harbour Lights - restaurant and bar

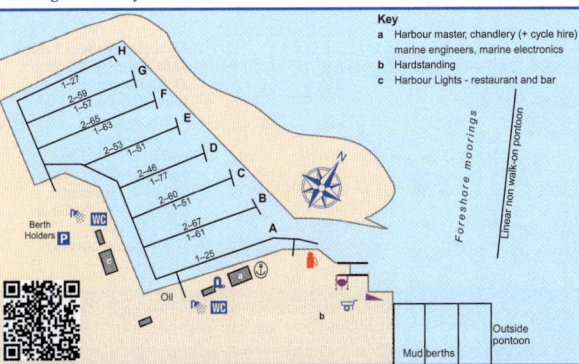

Friendly service in the beautiful Walton Backwaters
www.titchmarshmarina.co.uk
Tel: 01255 672 185   VHF: Channel 80
Email: info@titchmarshmarina.co.uk
Berthing Available - Various Options & Rates
Winter - Special Rates Ashore or Afloat
Storage Ashore - Long/ Short Term
Full Marina Facilities
Walton-on-the-Naze, Essex CO14 8SL

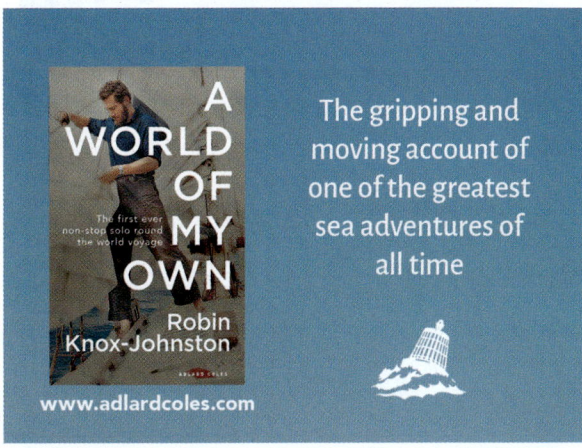

A WORLD OF MY OWN — Robin Knox-Johnston
The gripping and moving account of one of the greatest sea adventures of all time
www.adlardcoles.com

WALTON YACHT BASIN

Walton and Frinton Yacht Trust
Mill Lane, Walton on the Naze, CO14 8PF
Managed by Bedwell & Co Tel: 01255 675873
Mobile: 07957 848031

VHF Ch 80
ACCESS HW-0.75, HW+0.25

Walton Yacht Basin lies at the head of Walton Creek, an area made famous in Arthur Ransome's *Swallows & Amazons* and *Secret Waters*. The creek can only be navigated HW±2, although yachts heading for the Yacht Basin should arrive on a rising tide as the entrance gate is kept shut once the tide turns in order to retain the water inside. Before entering the gate, moor up against the Club Quay to enquire about berthing availability.

A short walk away is the popular seaside town of Walton, full of shops, pubs and restaurants. Its focal point is the pier which, overlooking superb sandy beaches, offers various attractions. Slightly further out of town, the Naze affords pleasant coastal walks with striking panoramic views.

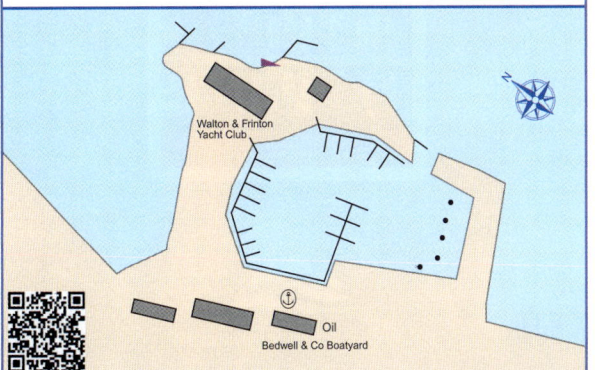

SUFFOLK YACHT HARBOUR

Suffolk Yacht Harbour Ltd
Levington, Ipswich, Suffolk, IP10 0LN
Tel: 01473 659240
Email: enquiries@syharbour.co.uk
www.syharbour.co.uk

VHF Ch 80
ACCESS H24

A friendly, independently-run marina on the East Coast of England, Suffolk Yacht Harbour enjoys a beautiful rural setting on the River Orwell, yet is within easy access of Ipswich, Woodbridge and Felixstowe. With approximately 550 berths, the marina offers extensive facilities while the Haven Ports Yacht Club provides a bar and restaurant.

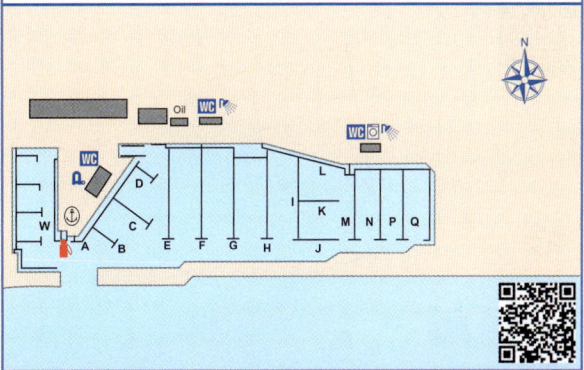

MARINA GUIDE 2026   45

MARINAS & SERVICES

SHOTLEY MARINA

Shotley Marina Ltd
Shotley Gate, Ipswich, Suffolk, IP9 1QJ
Tel: 01473 788982
Email: reception@shotleymarina.co.uk
www.shotleymarina.co.uk

VHF Ch 80
ACCESS H24

Based in the well protected Harwich Harbour where the River Stour joins the River Orwell, Shotley Marina is only eight miles from the county town of Ipswich. Entered via a lock at all states of the tide, its first class facilities include extensive boat repair and maintenance services as well as a chandlery and on site bar and restaurant plus bed and breakfast rooms. The marina is strategically placed for sailing up the Stour to Manningtree, up the Orwell to Pin Mill or exploring the Rivers Deben, Crouch and Blackwater as well as the Walton Backwaters.

FACILITIES AT A GLANCE

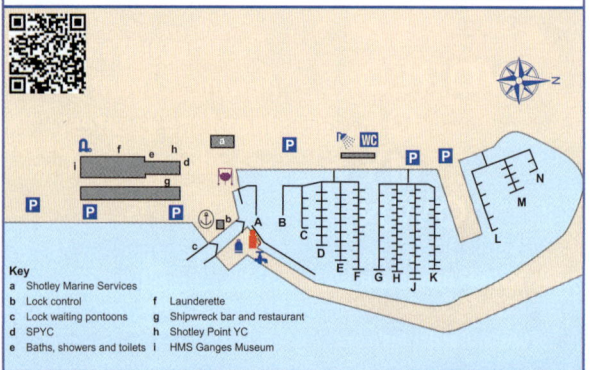

Key
a Shotley Marine Services
b Lock control
c Lock waiting pontoons
d SPYC
e Baths, showers and toilets
f Launderette
g Shipwreck bar and restaurant
h Shotley Point YC
i HMS Ganges Museum

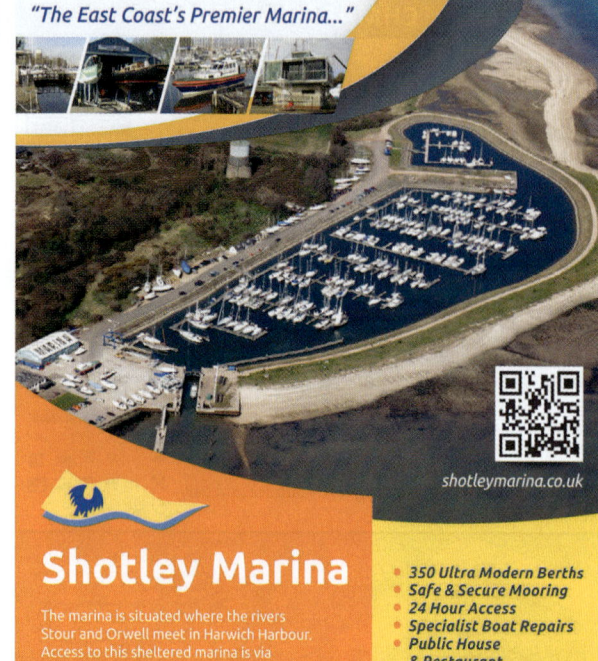

"The East Coast's Premier Marina..."

Shotley Marina

The marina is situated where the rivers Stour and Orwell meet in Harwich Harbour. Access to this sheltered marina is via a hydraulically operated lock, manned continually throughout the year, 24 hours a day. The lockmaster listens on VHF CH80. The entrance to the lock is floodlit at night and the outer end of the access channel has lit piles. An "Inogon" guidance light system assists on entering the lock.

- 350 Ultra Modern Berths
- Safe & Secure Mooring
- 24 Hour Access
- Specialist Boat Repairs
- Public House & Restaurant
- Water, Electricity, Modern Toilets, Showers, Laundry and Disabled Facilities
- Ships Stores
- WiFi Internet Access

shotleymarina.co.uk

Shotley Marina Ltd. Shotley Gate, Ipswich, Suffolk IP9 1QJ
T: 01473 788982 F: 01473 788868 E: sales@shotleymarina.co.uk

ROYAL HARWICH YACHT CLUB MARINA

Royal Harwich Yacht Club Marina
Marina Road, Woolverstone, Suffolk, IP9 1AT
Tel: 01473 780319 Fax: 01473 780919 Berths: 07742 145994
www.royalharwichyachtclub.co.uk
Email: office.manager@royalharwich.co.uk

VHF Ch 77
ACCESS H24

This 54 berth marina is ideally situated at a mid point on the Orwell between Levington and Ipswich. The facility is owned and run by the Royal Harwich Yacht Club and enjoys a full catering and bar service in the Clubhouse. The marina benefits from full tidal access, and can accommodate yachts up to 14.5m on the hammerhead. Within the immediate surrounds, there are boat repair services, and a well stocked chandlery. The marina is situated a mile's walk from the world famous Pin Mill and is a favoured destination with visitors from Holland, Belgium and Germany. The marina welcomes racing yachts and cruisers, and is able to accommodate multiple bookings.

FACILITIES AT A GLANCE

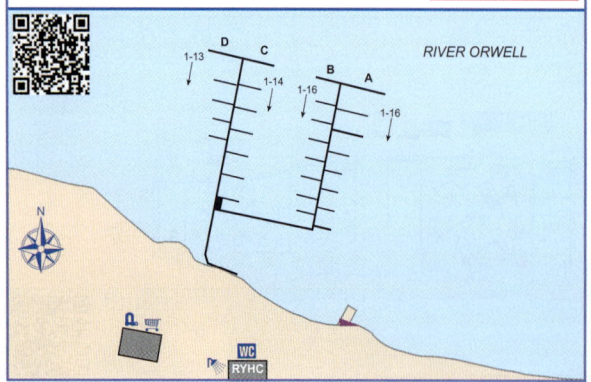

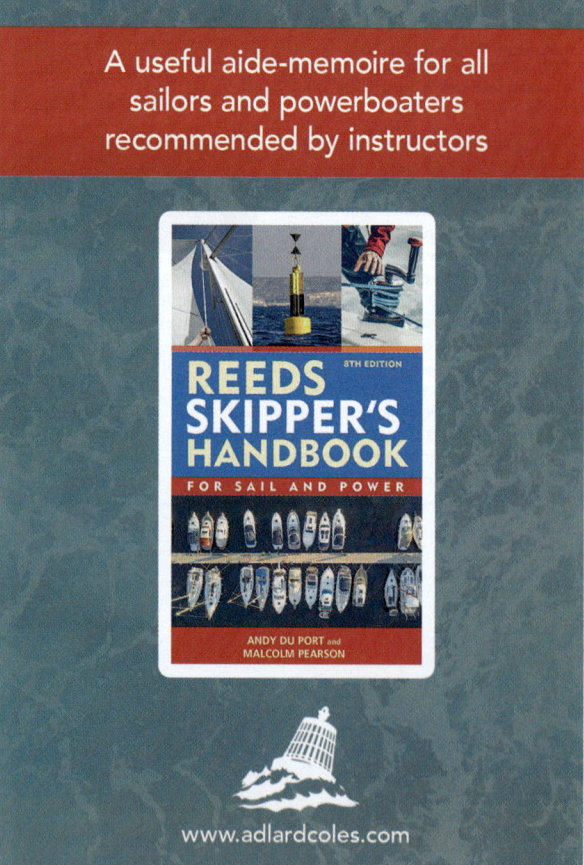

A useful aide-memoire for all sailors and powerboaters recommended by instructors

REEDS SKIPPER'S HANDBOOK
8TH EDITION
FOR SAIL AND POWER
ANDY DU PORT and MALCOLM PEARSON

www.adlardcoles.com

MARINA GUIDE 2026

EAST ENGLAND — AREA 4

The complete refit & repair service for all sailing & motor yachts

Yacht refit, repair & joinery
Sprayshop & hull finishing
Marine engineering & electronics
Spars, rigging, ropes & splicing
GRP & composite repairs
Stainless repair & fabrication
Bluewater cruising & race preparation

Ipswich, Suffolk, IP2 8SA
+44 (0) 1473 689111 foxs@foxsmarina.com
foxsmarina.com

Everything you need for you & your boat online & in-store

Above & below deck chandlery
Clothing, footwear & accessories
Maintenance & repair
Marine electronics & electricals
Safety equipment
Inflatable kayaks, SUPs & tenders
Books & charts

Ipswich, Suffolk, IP2 8NJ
+44 (0) 1473 688431 sales@foxschandlery.com
foxschandlery.com

FOX'S MARINA

Fox's Marina & Boatyard
The Strand, Ipswich, Suffolk, IP2 8SA
Tel: 01473 689111
Email: foxs@foxsmarina.com   www.foxsmarina.com

VHF Ch 80
ACCESS H24

Located on the picturesque River Orwell, Fox's provides good shelter in all conditions and access at all states of tide with 100 pontoon berths and ashore storage for 200 vessels. A 70T hoist is able to handle boats up to 80ft in length.
Fox's Marina & Boatyard offers a full range of in-house services and, with 10,000 sq ft of heated workshop space, are specialists in repairs and refits of sailing/motor yachts and commercial craft. Specific services include coppercoat and osmosis treatment, specialist GRP and gelcoat repairs, spray painting and varnishing, and custom stainless fabrication. Also on-site, Fox's Chandlery and Marine Store, is the largest stockist of marine chandlery and equipment, sailing, leisure and country clothing in East Anglia.

FACILITIES AT A GLANCE

Key
a Workshops, rigging and electronics
b Harbourmaster office
c Yacht Club
d Outlook Cafe, Bar & Bistro

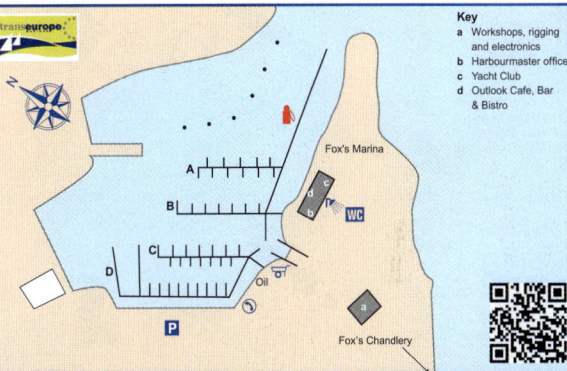

WOOLVERSTONE MARINA

Woolverstone Marina and Lodge Park
Woolverstone, Ipswich, Suffolk, IP9 1AS
Tel: 01473 780206
Email: woolverstone@mdlmarinas.co.uk
www.woolverstonemarina.co.uk

VHF Ch 80
ACCESS H24

Woolverstone Marina is set in 22 acres of glorious parkland on the picturesque River Orwell. Within easy reach of the sea and a multitude of scenic destinations, this is a great base to start cruising. Walton Backwaters and the River Deben are only a short distance away. The 235-berth marina boasts the MoniMar restaurant and bar, wi-fi, 24/7 staff cover, diesel, and slipway. There is also a berth-holders association, engineering services, a detailer, and broker. The marina also incorporates a luxury lodge park with 29 luxury lodges and the Grade II listed Cat House available for holiday rental.

FACILITIES AT A GLANCE

Key
a Marina office, toilets, showers, and launderette
b Restaurant and Bar

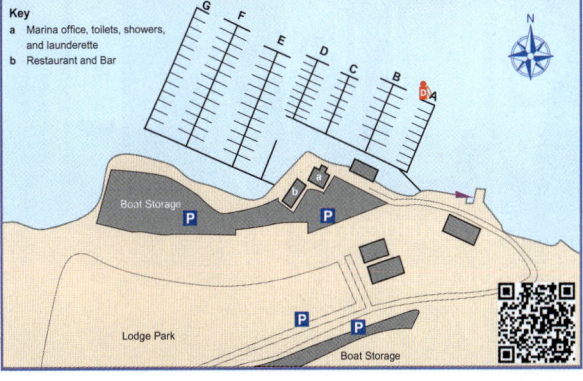

MARINAS & SERVICES

IPSWICH BEACON MARINA

Ipswich Beacon Marina
New Cut East, Ipswich, IP3 0EA
Tel: 01473 236644
Email: ipswichbeacon@abports.co.uk

VHF	Ch 80
ACCESS	H24

The old Neptune complex, now part of the Ipswich Beacon Marina, is situated at Neptune Quay on the historic waterfront, and ever-increasing shoreside developments. This 26-acre dock is accessible through a H24 lock gate, with a waiting pontoon outside. Onsite facilities include boatyard and lift-out facilities plus wifi for boat owners.

The marina building occupies an imposing position in the NE corner of the dock with quality coffee shop and associated retail units. There are a number of excellent restaurants along the quayside and adjacent to the marina. The modern town centre catering for all needs is just a 10-minute walk away.

FACILITIES AT A GLANCE

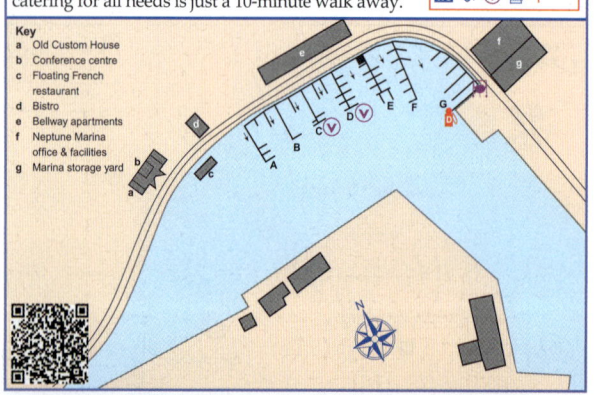

Key
a Old Custom House
b Conference centre
c Floating French restaurant
d Bistro
e Bellway apartments
f Neptune Marina office & facilities
g Marina storage yard

IPSWICH BEACON MARINA

Ipswich Beacon Marina
Associated British Ports
New Cut East, Ipswich, Suffolk, IP3 0EA
Tel: 01473 236644
Email: ipswichbeacon@abports.co.uk

VHF	Ch M, 80
ACCESS	H24

Lying at the heart of Ipswich, the Ipswich Beacon Marina enjoys close proximity to all the bustling shopping centres, restaurants, cinemas and museums that this County Town of Suffolk has to offer. The main railway station is only a 10-minute walk away, where there are regular connections to London, Cambridge and Norwich, all taking just over an hour to get to.

Within easy reach of Holland, Belgium and Germany, East Anglia is proving an increasingly popular cruising ground. The River Orwell, displaying breathtaking scenery, was voted one of the most beautiful rivers in Britain by the RYA.

FACILITIES AT A GLANCE

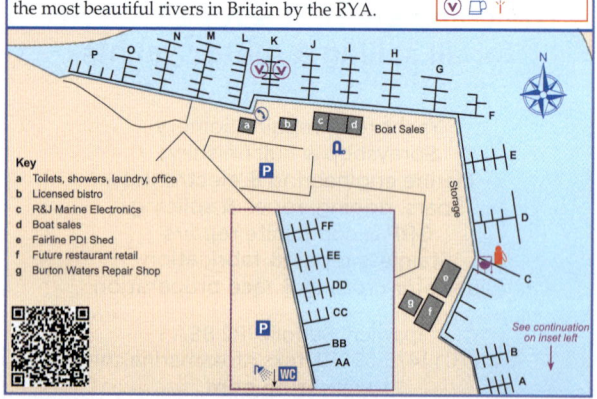

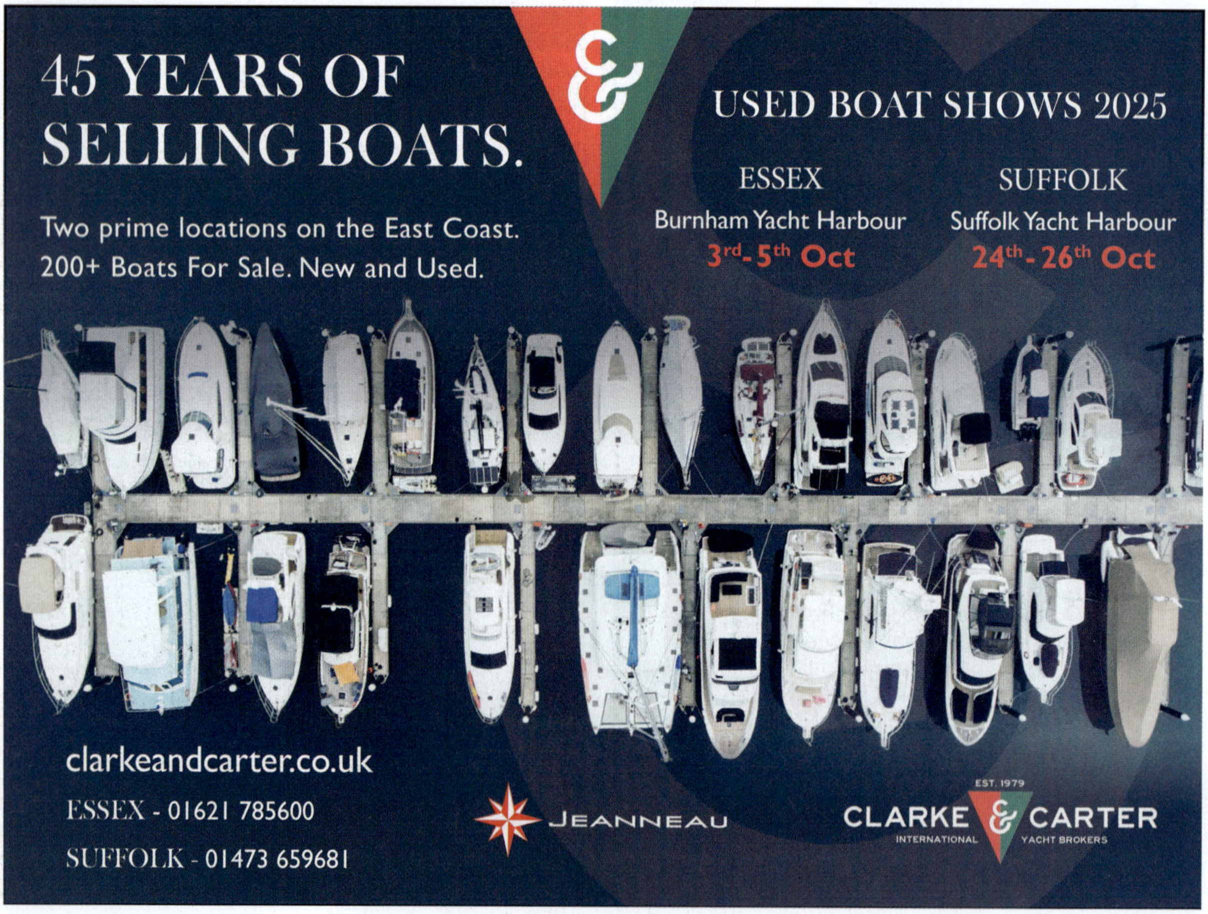

Key
a Toilets, showers, laundry, office
b Licensed bistro
c R&J Marine Electronics
d Boat sales
e Fairline PDI Shed
f Future restaurant retail
g Burton Waters Repair Shop

---

45 YEARS OF SELLING BOATS.

Two prime locations on the East Coast.
200+ Boats For Sale. New and Used.

USED BOAT SHOWS 2025

ESSEX
Burnham Yacht Harbour
3rd - 5th Oct

SUFFOLK
Suffolk Yacht Harbour
24th - 26th Oct

clarkeandcarter.co.uk
ESSEX - 01621 785600
SUFFOLK - 01473 659681

JEANNEAU

CLARKE & CARTER
INTERNATIONAL YACHT BROKERS
EST. 1979

EAST ENGLAND — AREA 4

LOWESTOFT BEACON MARINA

Lowestoft Beacon Marina
School Road, Lowestoft, Suffolk, NR33 9NB
Tel: 01502 580300
Email: lowestoftbeacon@abports.co.uk
www.beaconmarinas.co.uk

⚓⚓⚓⚓
VHF Ch M, 80
ACCESS H24

Lowestoft Beacon Marina is based on Lake Lothing with easy access to both the open sea and the Norfolk Broads. The town centres of both Lowestoft and Oulton Broad are within a short distance of the marina.

The marina's 140 berths can accommodate vessels from 7–20m. Offering a full range of modern facilities the marina welcomes all visitors.

FACILITIES AT A GLANCE

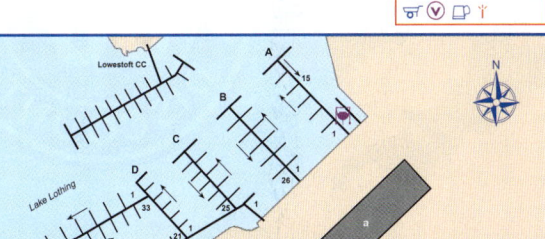

Key
a Boat storage
b Marina office

ROYAL NORFOLK & SUFFOLK YACHT CLUB

Royal Norfolk and Suffolk Yacht Club
Royal Plain, Lowestoft, Suffolk, NR33 0AQ
Tel: 01502 566726
Email: admin@rnsyc.org.uk   www.rnsyc.net

VHF Ch 14, 80
ACCESS H24

With its entrance at the inner end of the South Pier, opposite the Trawl Basin on the north bank, the Royal Norfolk and Suffolk Yacht Club marina occupies a sheltered position in Lowestoft Harbour. Lowestoft has always been an appealing destination to yachtsmen due to the fact that it can be accessed at any state of the tide, 24 hours a day. Note, however, that conditions just outside the entrance can get pretty lively when the wind is against tide. The clubhouse is enclosed in an impressive Grade 2 listed building overlooking the marina and its facilities include a bar and restaurant as well as a formal dining room.

FACILITIES AT A GLANCE

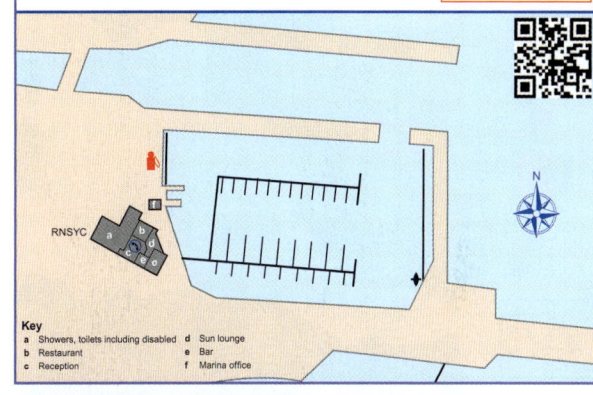

Key
a Showers, toilets including disabled   d Sun lounge
b Restaurant   e Bar
c Reception   f Marina office

LOWESTOFT CRUISING CLUB

Lowestoft Cruising Club
Off Harbour Road, Oulton Broad, Lowestoft, Suffolk, NR32 3LY
Tel: 07900 446909
www.lowestoftcruisingclub.co.uk

VHF
ACCESS H24

Lowestoft Cruising Club welcomes visitors and can offer a friendly atmosphere, some of the finest moorings and at very competitive rates. Whatever the weather, these moorings provide a calm, safe haven for visiting yachts and with the Mutford lock only 250 metres away, easy access onto the Norfolk and Suffolk Broads. Facilities include electricity and water, plus excellent showers, toilets and secure car parking. These moorings are the nearest ones to the railway stations (to Norwich and Ipswich), bus routes, shops, banks, pubs and restaurants in Oulton Broad.

FACILITIES AT A GLANCE

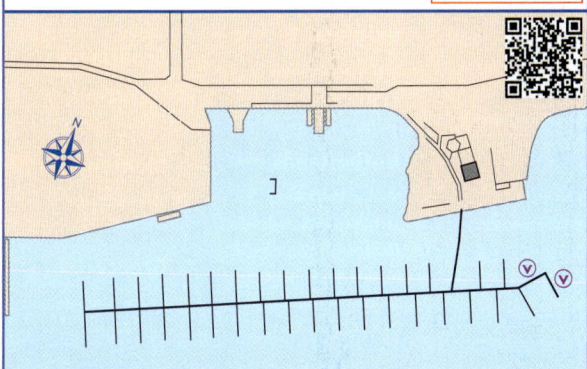

CROSSKEYS MARINA

**Safe secure pontoon berths on the tidal River Nene at West Bank, Sutton Bridge, PE12 9QH.
3 miles to the open waters of The Wash.**

- Fully serviced marina berths.
- Operated by Wisbech Yacht Harbour.
- Berths up to 20m LOA, 2m draft.
- 3 miles from The Wash, 6 miles to Wisbech Yacht Harbour, then 15 miles to the inland waterways.
- Excellent base for regular day's out in The Wash, Fishing, Sailing, Cruising, Diving, or observing wildlife.
- Gives good access to the East and West of The Wash.
- 75t boat travel hoist at Wisbech Yacht Harbour's Crab Marsh Boatyard with trailer storage facilities.
- Good road links, shops, and social facilities.

**The Boathouse, Harbour Square
WISBECH, Cambridgeshire, PE13 3BH
Tel: 01945 588059 • 07872 420497
www.fenland.gov.uk/wisbechyachtharbour
email: yachtharbour@fenland.gov.uk**

MARINA GUIDE 2026

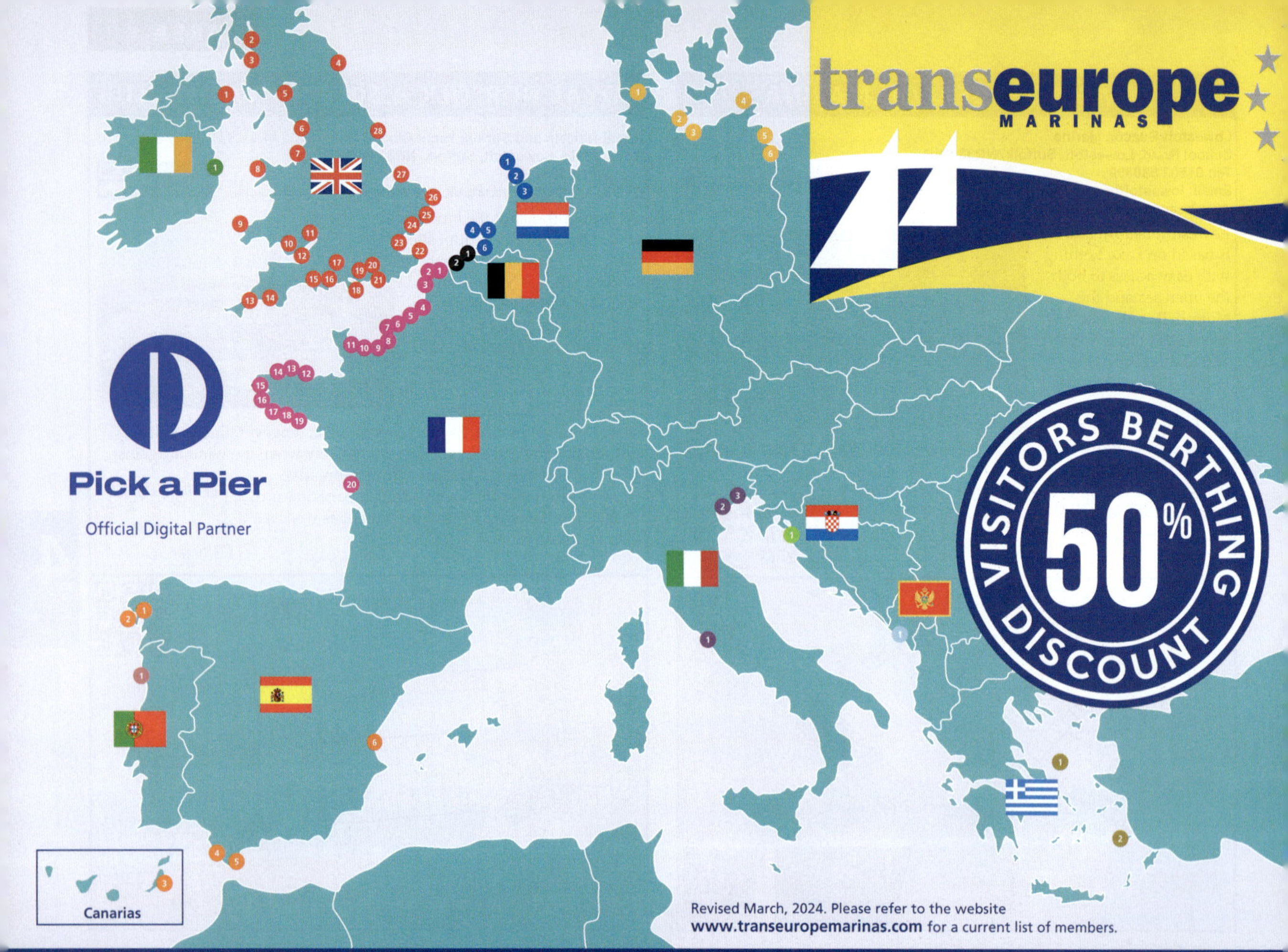

Cruise between a network of marinas across Europe

TransEurope Marinas cardholders benefit from a 50% visitor's berthing discount in each associated marina for up to five days a year.

UK
1. Bangor Marina
2. Rhu Marina
3. Troon Yacht Haven
4. Royal Quays Marina
5. Whitehaven Marina
6. Fleetwood Haven Marina
7. Liverpool Marina
8. Conwy Marina
9. Neyland Yacht Haven
10. Penarth Marina
11. Upton Marina
12. Portishead Marina
13. Mylor Yacht Harbour
14. Mayflower Marina
15. Poole Quay Boat Haven
16. Buckler's Hard Yacht Harbour
17. Town Quay Marina
18. Cowes Yacht Haven
19. Royal Clarence Marina
20. Emsworth Yacht Harbour
21. Birdham Pool Marina
22. Dover Marina
23. Gillingham Marina
24. Fambridge Yacht Haven
25. Tollesbury Marina
26. Fox's Marina
27. Brundall Bay Marina
28. Hull Marina

Portugal
1. Douro Marina

Germany
1. Sonwik Marina
2. Ancora Marina
3. Marina Boltenhagen
4. Marina Wiek auf Rügen
5. Naturhafen Krummin
6. Lagunenstadt Ueckermünde

France
1. Dunkerque
2. Calais
3. Boulogne-sur-mer
4. Saint Valery sur Somme
5. Dieppe
6. Saint Valery en Caux
7. Fécamp
8. Le Havre Plaisance
9. Port-Deauville
10. Dives-Cabourg-Houlgate
11. Ouistreham/Caen
12. Saint-Quay Port d'Armor
13. Perros-Guirec
14. Roscoff
15. Marinas de Brest
16. Douarnenez-Tréboul
17. Loctudy
18. Port la Forêt
19. Concarneau
20. La Rochelle

Spain
1. Marina Combarro
2. Nauta Sanxenxo
3. Puerto Calero
4. Puerto Sherry
5. Alcaidesa Marina
6. Pobla Marina

Belgium
1. VNZ Blankenberge
2. VY Nieuwpoort

Netherlands
1. Marina Den Oever
2. Jachthaven Waterland
3. Jachthaven Wetterwille
4. Marina Port Zélande
5. Jachthaven Biesbosch
6. Delta Marina Kortgene

Italy
1. Porto Romano
2. Venezia Certosa Marina
3. Marina del Cavallino

Ireland
1. Malahide Marina

Croatia
1. Marina Punat

Montenegro
1. Marina Lazure

Greece
1. Lineriá Marina
2. Kos Marina

For a current list of members and further information, please visit - www.transeuropemarinas.com

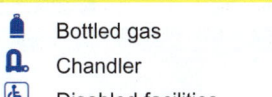

NORTH EAST ENGLAND - Great Yarmouth to Berwick-upon-Tweed

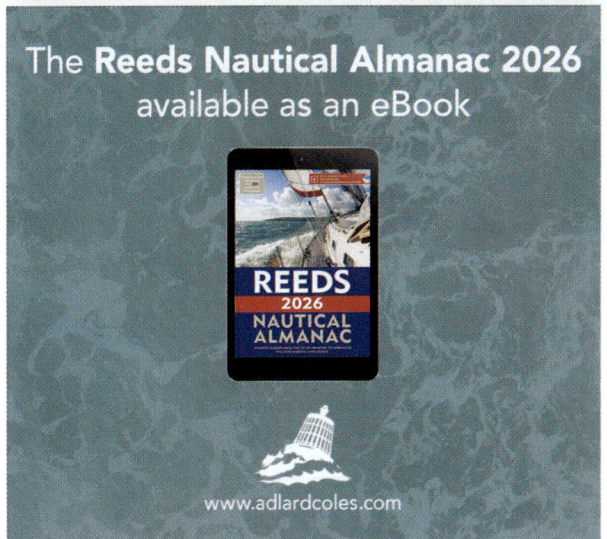

Key to Marina Plans symbols

	Bottled gas	P	Parking
	Chandler		Pub/Restaurant
	Disabled facilities		Pump out
	Electrical supply		Rigging service
	Electrical repairs		Sail repairs
	Engine repairs		Shipwright
	First Aid		Shop/Supermarket
	Fresh Water		Showers
D	Fuel - Diesel		Slipway
P	Fuel - Petrol	WC	Toilets
	Hardstanding/boatyard		Telephone
@	Internet Café		Trolleys
	Laundry facilities	V	Visitors berths
	Lift-out facilities		Wi-Fi

Area 5 - North East England

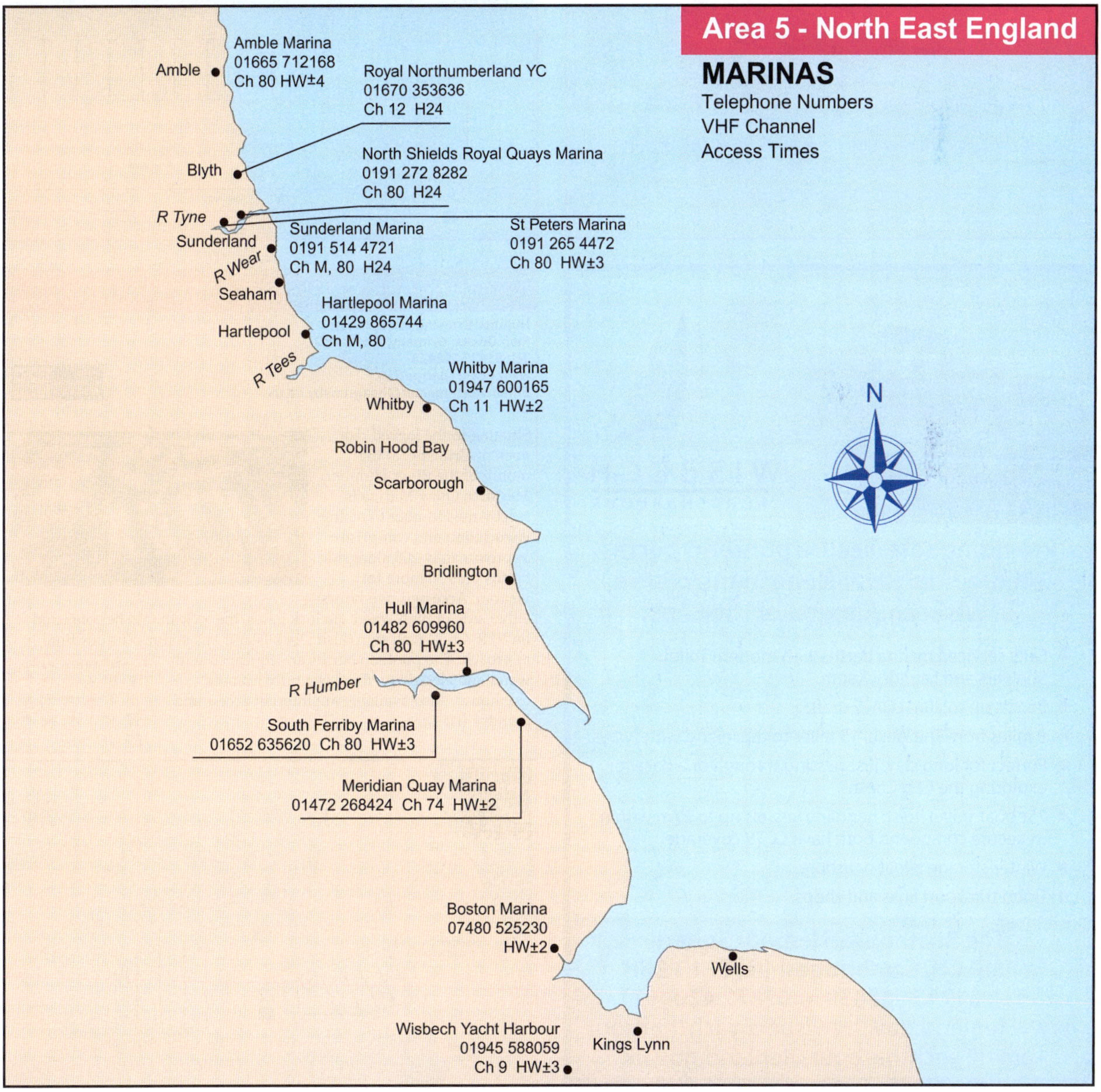

MARINAS
Telephone Numbers
VHF Channel
Access Times

Amble — Amble Marina 01665 712168 Ch 80 HW±4

Royal Northumberland YC 01670 353636 Ch 12 H24

Blyth

North Shields Royal Quays Marina 0191 272 8282 Ch 80 H24

R Tyne

Sunderland — Sunderland Marina 0191 514 4721 Ch M, 80 H24

St Peters Marina 0191 265 4472 Ch 80 HW±3

R Wear

Seaham

Hartlepool — Hartlepool Marina 01429 865744 Ch M, 80

R Tees

Whitby — Whitby Marina 01947 600165 Ch 11 HW±2

Robin Hood Bay

Scarborough

Bridlington

Hull Marina 01482 609960 Ch 80 HW±3

R Humber

South Ferriby Marina 01652 635620 Ch 80 HW±3

Meridian Quay Marina 01472 268424 Ch 74 HW±2

Boston Marina 07480 525230 HW±2

Wells

Wisbech Yacht Harbour 01945 588059 Ch 9 HW±3

Kings Lynn

MARINA GUIDE 2026

MARINAS & SERVICES

WISBECH YACHT HARBOUR

Wisbech Yacht Harbour
Harbour Master, Harbour Office, The Boathouse,
Harbour Square, Wisbech, Cambridgeshire PE13 3BH
Tel: 01945 588059   Fax: 01945 580589
Email: afoster@fenland.gov.uk   www.fenland.gov.uk

VHF Ch 9
ACCESS HW±3

Regarded as the capital of the English Fens, Wisbech is situated about 25 miles north east of Peterborough and is a market town of considerable character and historical significance. Rows of elegant houses line the banks of the River Nene, with the North and South Brink still deemed two of the finest Georgian streets in England.

Wisbech Yacht Harbour, linking Cambridgeshire with the sea, is proving increasingly popular as a haven for small craft, despite the busy commercial shipping. In recent years the facilities have been developed and improved upon and the HM is always on hand to help with passage planning both up or downstream.

FACILITIES AT A GLANCE

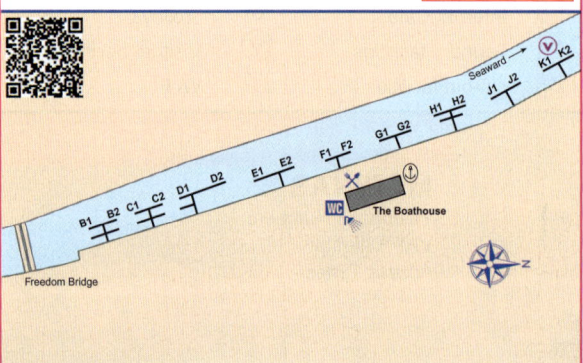

BOSTON GATEWAY MARINA

Boston Gateway Marina
Witham Bank East, Boston, Lincs, PE21 9JU
Tel: 07480 525230
Email: enquiries@bostongatewaymarina.co.uk

VHF
ACCESS H±2

Located near Boston Grand Sluice Lock on the sunny side of the River Witham, the marina is ideally situated for easy access to The Wash and is suitable for both sea-going and river boats. It is a short walk to the centre of the historic town of Boston, Lincolnshire, but retains a tranquil feel. The marina offers visitor, short-term and longer-term moorings to suit each individual customer. Power and water are available for all boats.

The town centre offers the normal variety of facilities within easy walking distance. Local tourist attractions include the 14th century St Botolph's Church – 'The Stump' – the 1390s Boston Guildhall Musuem and a 450-year old market to name but a few.

FACILITIES AT A GLANCE

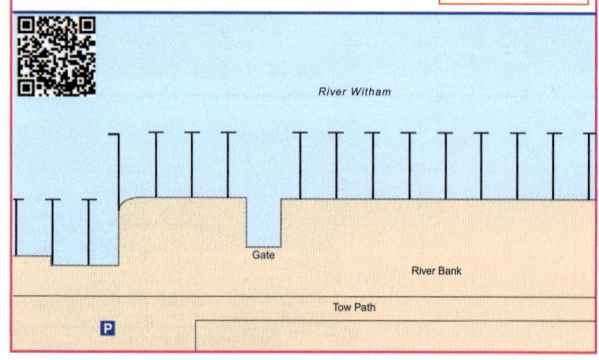

- Fully serviced marina berths with modern Toilets, Showers and Laundry Room.
- Berths up to 20m LOA, 2 draft.
- 8 miles from The Wash, 15 miles to the inland waterways.
- Perfect for long stay, just passing through or a base for exploring the East Coast.
- 75t boat travel hoist: handling vessels up to 27m within its secure compound both have CCTV coverage.
- Winter storage afloat or ashore.
- Good transport links and shops.

**The Boathouse, Harbour Square
WISBECH, Cambridgeshire, PE13 3BH
Tel: 01945 588059 • 07872 420497
www.fenland.gov.uk/wisbechyachtharbour
email: yachtharbour@fenland.gov.uk**

HUMBER CRUISING ASSOCIATION

Humber Cruising Association
Fish Docks, Grimsby, DN31 3SD
Tel: 01472 268424
www.hcagrimsby.co.uk
Email: berthmaster@hcagrimsby.co.uk

VHF Ch 74
ACCESS HW±2

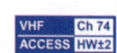

Situated in the locked fish dock of Grimsby, at the mouth of the River Humber, Meridian Quay Marina is run by the Humber Cruising Association and comprises approximately 200 alongside berths plus 30 more for visitors. Accessed two hours either side of high water via lock gates, the lock should be contacted on VHF Ch 74 (call sign 'Fish Dock Island') as you make your final approach. The pontoon berths are equipped with water and electricity; there is a fully licensed clubhouse. Also available are internet access and laundry facilities.

FACILITIES AT A GLANCE

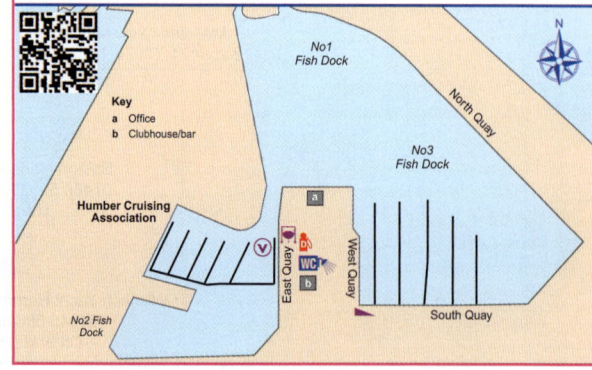

52   MARINA GUIDE 2026

NORTH EAST ENGLAND — AREA 5

HULL WATERSIDE & MARINA

Hull Waterside & Marina
W 13, Kingston Street, Hull, HU1 2DQ
Tel: 01482 609960 Fax: 01482 224148
Email: hull@aquavista.com
www.aquavista.com

VHF Ch 80
ACCESS HW±3

Situated on the River Humber, Hull Marina is literally a stone's throw from the bustling city centre with its array of arts and entertainments. Besides the numerous historic bars and cafés surrounding the marina, there are plenty of traditional taverns to be sampled in the Old Town, while also found here is the Street Life Museum, vividly depicting the history of the city.

Yachtsmen enter the marina via a tidal lock, operating HW±3, and should try to give 15 minutes' notice of arrival via VHF Ch 80. Hull is perfectly positioned for exploring the Trent, Ouse and the Yorkshire coast as well as across the North Sea to Holland or Belgium.

FACILITIES AT A GLANCE

Key
a Reception
b Boatshed
c Kildale Marine
d Lock control & lock keeper's cottage
NB Berth numbers low outer to high inner.

THE NORTH'S LARGEST CHANDLERY

KILDALE MARINE

The largest stock in the region.
Great technical knowledge.
Full rigging service.

Supplying everything for:
- Yachts
- Cruisers
- Dinghies
- Books & Charts
- Clothing & Footwear

MUSTO · Gill · HENRI LLOYD · HARKEN · LOWRANCE
spinlock · Raymarine · ICOM · International

kildalemarine.co.uk
01482 227464

Kildale Marine Ltd,
Hull Marina, Hull HU1 2DQ
Opening hours
6-days a week, closed Tuesday.

pyd — PROFESSIONAL YACHT DELIVERIES

+44 (0) 151 342 1001
pyd@pydww.com
www.pydww.com

Further Faster Safer... Since 1995

- Worldwide Yacht Delivery
- Skipper and Crew Supply
- Yacht Management
- Own Boat Tuition

Professional Yacht Deliveries Ltd

BRITISH MARINE — LEADING THE INDUSTRY
World Cruising Club — Corporate Member

MARINA GUIDE 2026

MARINAS & SERVICES

SOUTH FERRIBY MARINA

South Ferriby Marina
Red Lane, South Ferriby, Barton on Humber, Lincs, DN18 6JH
Tel: 01652 635620 (Lock 635219) Mobile: 07828 312071
Email: enquiries@southferribymarina.com

VHF Ch 74
ACCESS HW±3

Situated at the entrance to the non-tidal River Ancholme the existing marina has been established since 1966 and is well placed to provide easy access to the River Humber and North Sea. This is a family run business providing a range of services including a boatyard and chandlery. Access is by way of lock at HW±3.

The marina has excellent road and rail services within easy reach, while South Ferriby village has two pubs and a Post Office/Spar Shop just a short walk away.

The picturesque River Ancholme is navigable for about 17 miles; the maximum headroom under bridges is 4.42 metres (14ft 6ins).

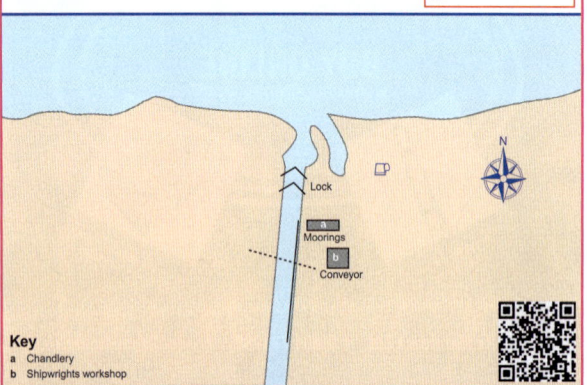

WHITBY MARINA

Whitby Marina
Whitby Harbour Office, Endeavour Wharf
Whitby, North Yorkshire YO21 1DN
Harbour Office: 01947 602354 Marina: 01947 600165
Email: port.services@northyorks.gov.uk

VHF Ch 11
ACCESS HW±2

The only natural harbour between the Tees and the Humber, Whitby lies some 20 miles north of Scarborough on the River Esk. The historic town is said to date back as far as the Roman times, although it is better known for its abbey, which was founded over 1,300 years ago by King Oswy of Northumberland. Another place of interest is the Captain Cook Memorial Museum, a tribute to Whitby's greatest seaman.

A swing bridge divides the harbour into upper and lower sections, with the marina being in the Upper Harbour. The bridge opens on request (VHF Ch 11) each half hour for two hours either side of high water.

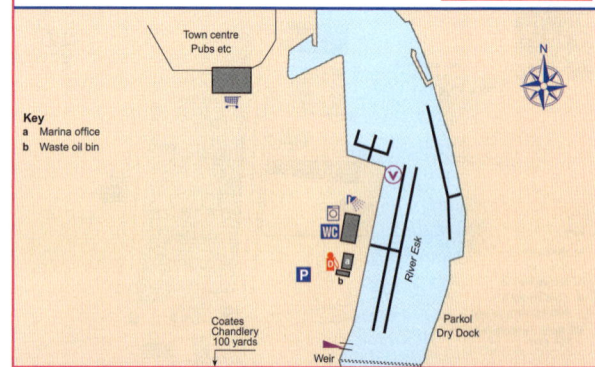

HARTLEPOOL MARINA

Hartlepool Marina
Lock Office, Slake Terrace, Hartlepool, TS24 0RU
Tel: 01429 865744 www.hartlepool-marina.com
Email: enquiries@hartlepool-marina.com

VHF Ch M, 80
ACCESS

Hartlepool Marina is a modern boating facility on the NE coast now boasting an extensively refurbished North amenity block. Nestling on the Tees Valley the multi award winning marina promotes up to 500 pontoon berths alongside a variety of reputable services all surrounded by an exciting array of on water activities, a cosmopolitan mix of bistros, bars, restaurants, shopping, hotels and entertainment options.

Beautiful cruising waters and golden sands to the North and South of the marina approach which is channel dredged to CD and accessible via a lock: vessels wishing to enter should contact the Marina Lock Office on VHF Ch M/80 before arrival.

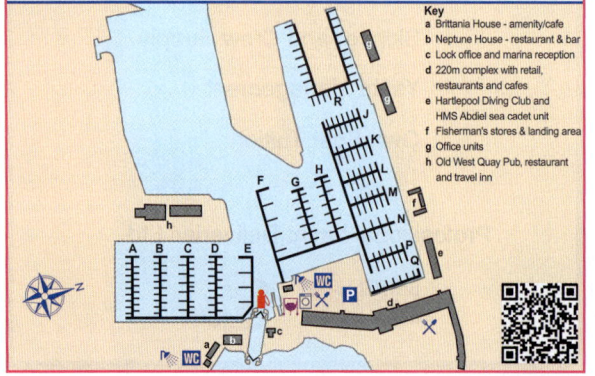

SUNDERLAND MARINA

The Marine Activities Centre
Sunderland Marina, Sunderland, SR6 0PW
Tel: 0191 514 4721
Email: info@sunmac.org.uk

VHF Ch M
ACCESS H24

Sunderland Marina sits on the the River Wear and is easily accessible through the outer breakwater at all states of tide. A short walk away from the city centre and beautiful beaches, facilities on site include the Snowgoose café and the Marina Vista Italian restaurant. Other pubs, restaurants, hotels and cafes are located nearby on the waterfront.

Sunderland Yacht Club is also located nearby and welcomes visiting yachtsman to its clubhouse.

MARINA GUIDE 2026

NORTH EAST ENGLAND — AREA 5

ROYAL QUAYS MARINA

Royal Quays Marina
Coble Dene Road, North Shields, NE29 6DU
Tel: 0191 272 8282
Email: royalquays@boatfolk.co.uk
www.boatfolk.co.uk/royalquays

VHF Ch 80 — ACCESS H24

Royal Quays Marina is ideally located near the entrance to the River Tyne, providing quick and convenient access to the open sea while serving as a well-equipped base for all vessels. Just over an hour's sail upstream brings you to the heart of Newcastle. The marina features 400 fully serviced pontoon berths and operates 24/7 via double-sector lock gates, ensuring access at all states of tide. As a TYHA 5 Gold Anchor Marina, it is known for high standards of service catering to both leisure and commercial vessels. On-site facilities include a café, bar, and restaurant. A boatyard with a 40T hoist is available for maintenance and storage ashore.

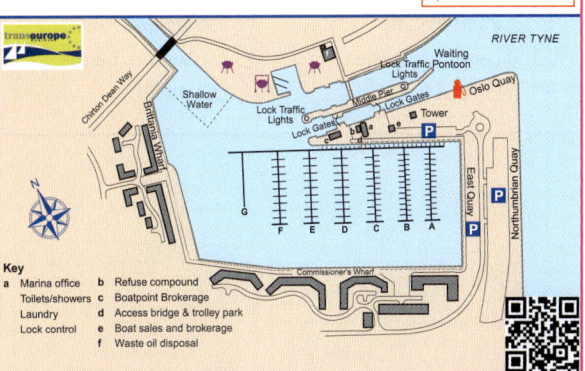

ST PETERS MARINA

St Peters Marina, St Peters Basin
Newcastle upon Tyne, NE6 1HX
Tel: 0191 2654472 Fax: 0191 2762618
Email: info@stpetersmarina.co.uk
www.stpetersmarina.co.uk

VHF Ch 80 — ACCESS HW±3

Nestling on the north bank of the River Tyne, some eight miles upstream of the river entrance, St Peters Marina is a fully serviced, 150-berth marina with the capacity to accommodate large vessels of up to 37m LOA. Situated on site is the Bascule Bar and Bistro, while a few minutes away is the centre of Newcastle. This city, along with its surrounding area, offers an array of interesting sites, among which are Hadrian's Wall, the award winning Gateshead Millennium Bridge and the Baltic Art Centre.

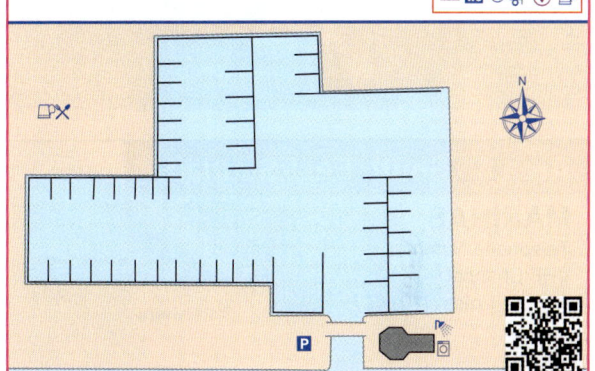

ROYAL NORTHUMBERLAND YACHT CLUB

Royal Northumberland Yacht Club
South Harbour, Blyth, Northumberland, NE24 3PB
Tel: 01670 353636

VHF Ch 12 — ACCESS H24

The Royal Northumberland Yacht Club is based at Blyth, a well-sheltered port that is accessible H24 and in all weathers except for when there is a combination of low water and strong SWly winds. This is a private club with some 113 pontoon berths.

Visitors usually berth on the north side of the most northerly pontoon and are welcome to use the clubship, HY *Tyne* – a wooden lightship built in 1880 which incorporates a bar, showers and toilet facilities. The club also controls its own boatyard, providing under cover and outside storage space plus a 20 ton boat hoist for members and emergencies only.

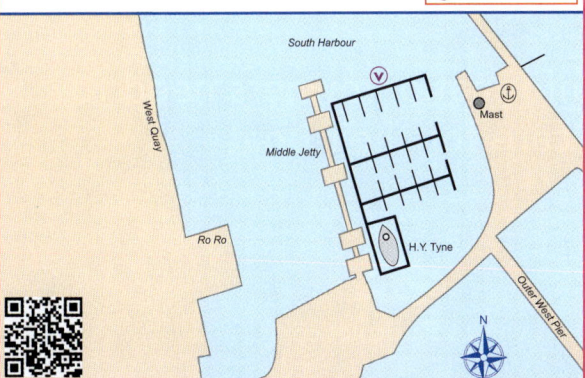

AMBLE MARINA

Amble Marina Ltd
Amble, Northumberland, NE65 0YP
Tel: 01665 712168
www.amble.co.uk

VHF Ch 80 — ACCESS HW±4

Amble Marina is a small family run business offering peace, security and a countryside setting at the heart of the small town of Amble. It is located on the banks of the beautiful River Coquet and at the start of the Northumberland coast's area of outstanding natural beauty. Amble Marina has 250 fully serviced berths for residential and visiting yachts. Cafés, bars, restaurants and shops are all within a short walk.

From your berth watch the sun rise at the harbour entrance and set behind Warkworth Castle or walk on wide, empty beaches. There is so much to do or if you prefer simply enjoy the peace, tranquillity and friendliness at Amble Marina.

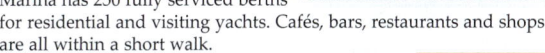

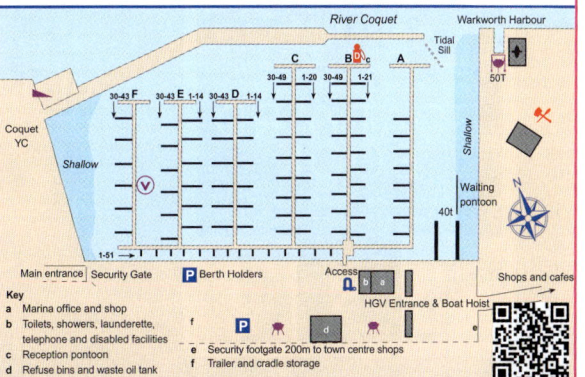

MARINAS & SERVICES

SOUTH EAST SCOTLAND – Eyemouth to Rattray Head

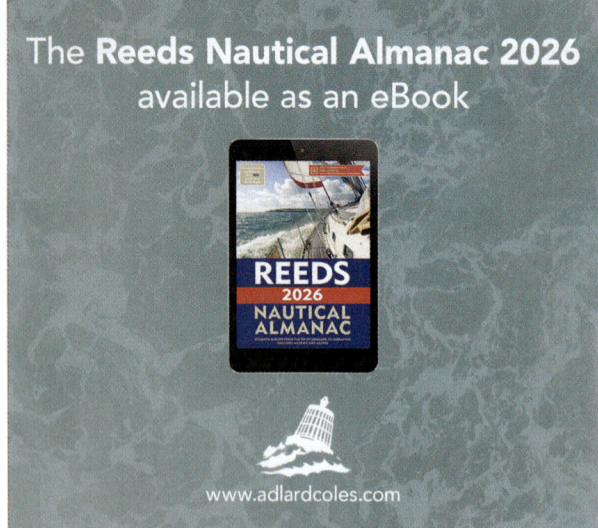

Key to Marina Plans symbols

🛢	Bottled gas	P	Parking
	Chandler		Pub/Restaurant
♿	Disabled facilities		Pump out
	Electrical supply		Rigging service
	Electrical repairs		Sail repairs
🔧	Engine repairs		Shipwright
✚	First Aid	🛒	Shop/Supermarket
	Fresh Water	🚿	Showers
D	Fuel - Diesel		Slipway
P	Fuel - Petrol	WC	Toilets
	Hardstanding/boatyard	☏	Telephone
@	Internet Café		Trolleys
	Laundry facilities	V	Visitors berths
	Lift-out facilities		Wi-Fi

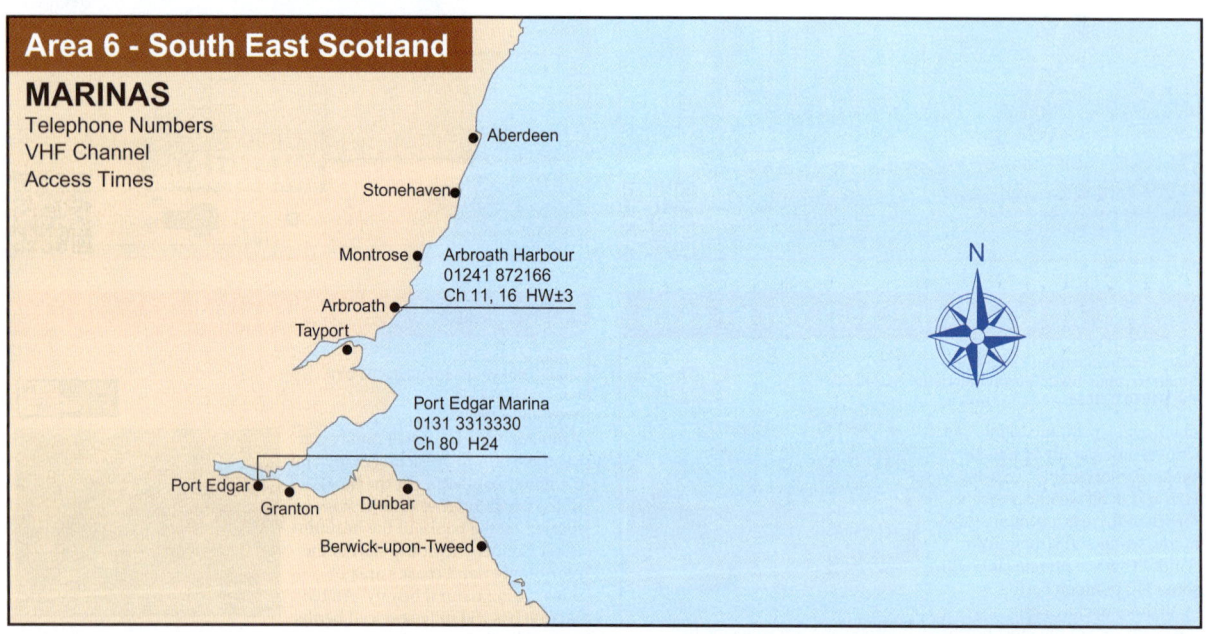

Area 6 - South East Scotland

MARINAS
Telephone Numbers
VHF Channel
Access Times

- Aberdeen
- Stonehaven
- Montrose
- Arbroath Harbour
  01241 872166
  Ch 11, 16 HW±3
- Arbroath
- Tayport
- Port Edgar Marina
  0131 3313330
  Ch 80 H24
- Port Edgar
- Granton
- Dunbar
- Berwick-upon-Tweed

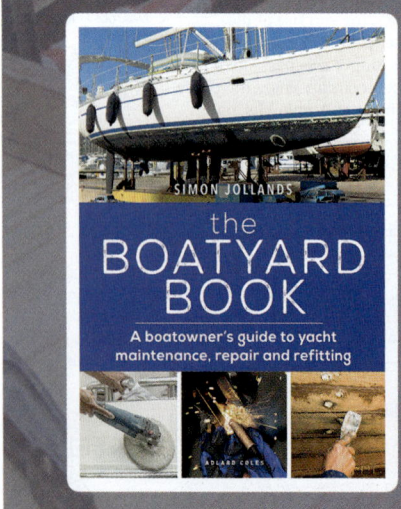

Maintenance, repairs, upgrades and refits

All the information owners need to care for their boat

www.adlardcoles.com

MARINA GUIDE 2026

PORT EDGAR MARINA

Port Edgar Marina
Shore Road, South Queensferry
West Lothian, EH30 9SQ
Tel: 0131 331 3330 Fax: 0131 331 4878
Email: info@portedgar.co.uk

VHF Ch 80
ACCESS H24

Nestled between the iconic Forth Bridges, Edinburgh's 300 berth marina is the ideal base for exploring the Capital and the Forth coastline.

A short walk away is the historic High Street of Queensferry with a great selection of bars and restaurants. Situated 15 minutes away from Edinburgh Airport with easy road access, the secure site provides full boatyard facilities including a 25T slipway hoist, chandlery and café.

FACILITIES AT A GLANCE

Key
a Changing rooms and toilets
b Landing and trolleys
c Port Edgar Yacht Club
d Cafe
e Marina office
f Blue V
g Bosuns Locker

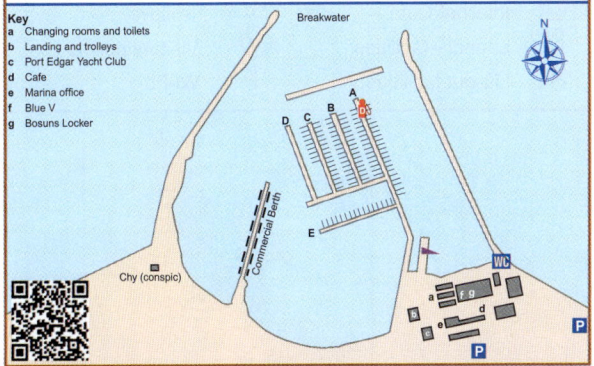

Arbroath Harbour

"Arbroath Harbour has 59 floating pontoon berths with security entrance which are serviced with electricity and fresh water to accommodate all types of leisure craft. Half height dock gates with a walkway are located between the inner and outer harbours, which open and close at half tide, maintaining a minimum of 2.5m of water in the inner harbour.

Other facilities in the harbour include free parking, toilets and showers, a crew room, fueling facilities, on site laundry facilities and boat builders' yard.

The town of Arbroath also offers a variety of social and sporting amenities to visiting crews and a number of quality pubs, restaurants, the famous twelfth century Abbey and Signal Tower Museum are located close to the harbour. The railway and bus stations are only 1km from the harbour with direct north and south connections."

Arbroath Harbour
Harbour Office • Arbroath • DD11 1PD
Harbour Master: Bruce Fleming
Tel: 01241 872166
Email: harbourmaster@angus.gov.uk

ARBROATH HARBOUR

Arbroath Harbour
Harbour Office, Arbroath, DD11 1PD
Tel: 01241 872166 Fax: 01241 878472
Email: harbourmaster@angus.gov.uk

VHF Ch 11
ACCESS HW±3

Arbroath harbour has 59 floating pontoon berths with security entrance which are serviced with electricity and fresh water to accommodate all types of leisure craft. Half height dock gates with walkway are located between the inner and outer harbours, which open and close at half tide, maintaining a minimum of 2.5m of water in the inner harbour.

The town of Arbroath offers a variety of social and sporting amenities to visiting crews and a number of quality pubs, restaurants, the famous twelfth century Abbey and Signal Tower Museum are located close to the harbour. Railway and bus stations are only 1km from the harbour with direct north and south connections.

FACILITIES AT A GLANCE

Key
a Signal Tower Museum
b Tourist Information
c RNLI
d Harbourmaster
e Harbour gates & walkway

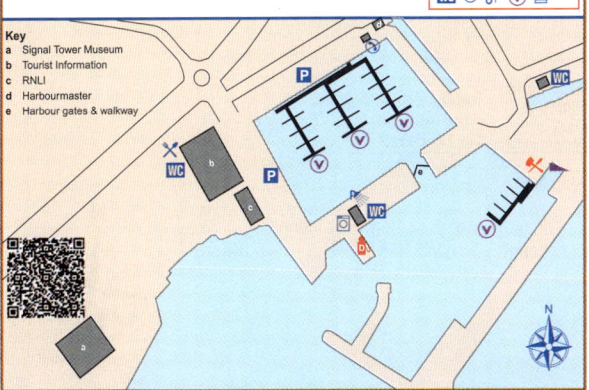

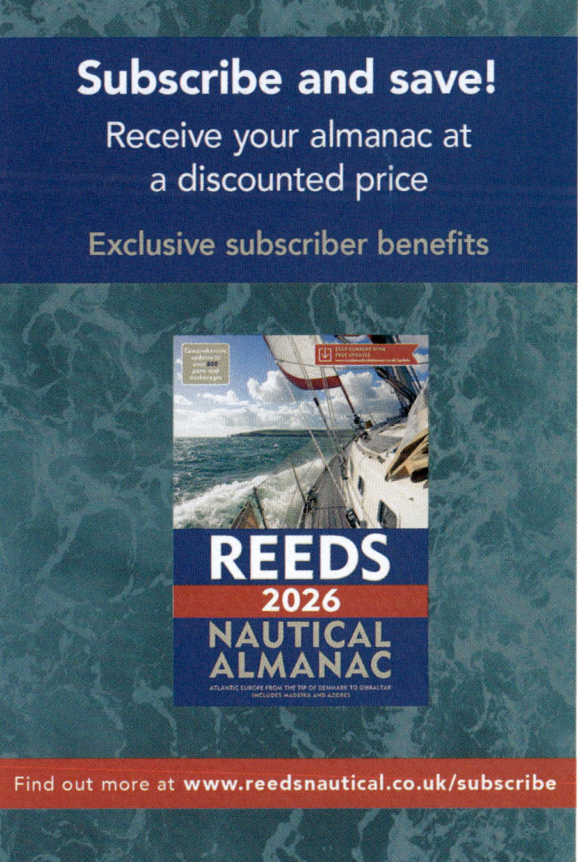

Subscribe and save!
Receive your almanac at a discounted price

Exclusive subscriber benefits

REEDS 2026 NAUTICAL ALMANAC

Find out more at www.reedsnautical.co.uk/subscribe

NORTH EAST SCOTLAND – Peterhead to Cape Wrath & Orkney & Shetland Is

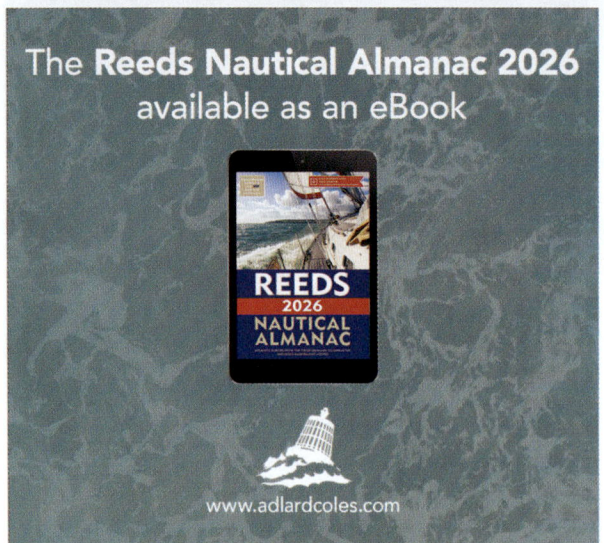

Key to Marina Plans symbols

	Bottled gas	P	Parking
	Chandler		Pub/Restaurant
	Disabled facilities		Pump out
	Electrical supply		Rigging service
	Electrical repairs		Sail repairs
	Engine repairs		Shipwright
	First Aid		Shop/Supermarket
	Fresh Water		Showers
	Fuel – Diesel		Slipway
	Fuel – Petrol	WC	Toilets
	Hardstanding/boatyard		Telephone
@	Internet Café		Trolleys
	Laundry facilities	V	Visitors berths
	Lift-out facilities		Wi-Fi

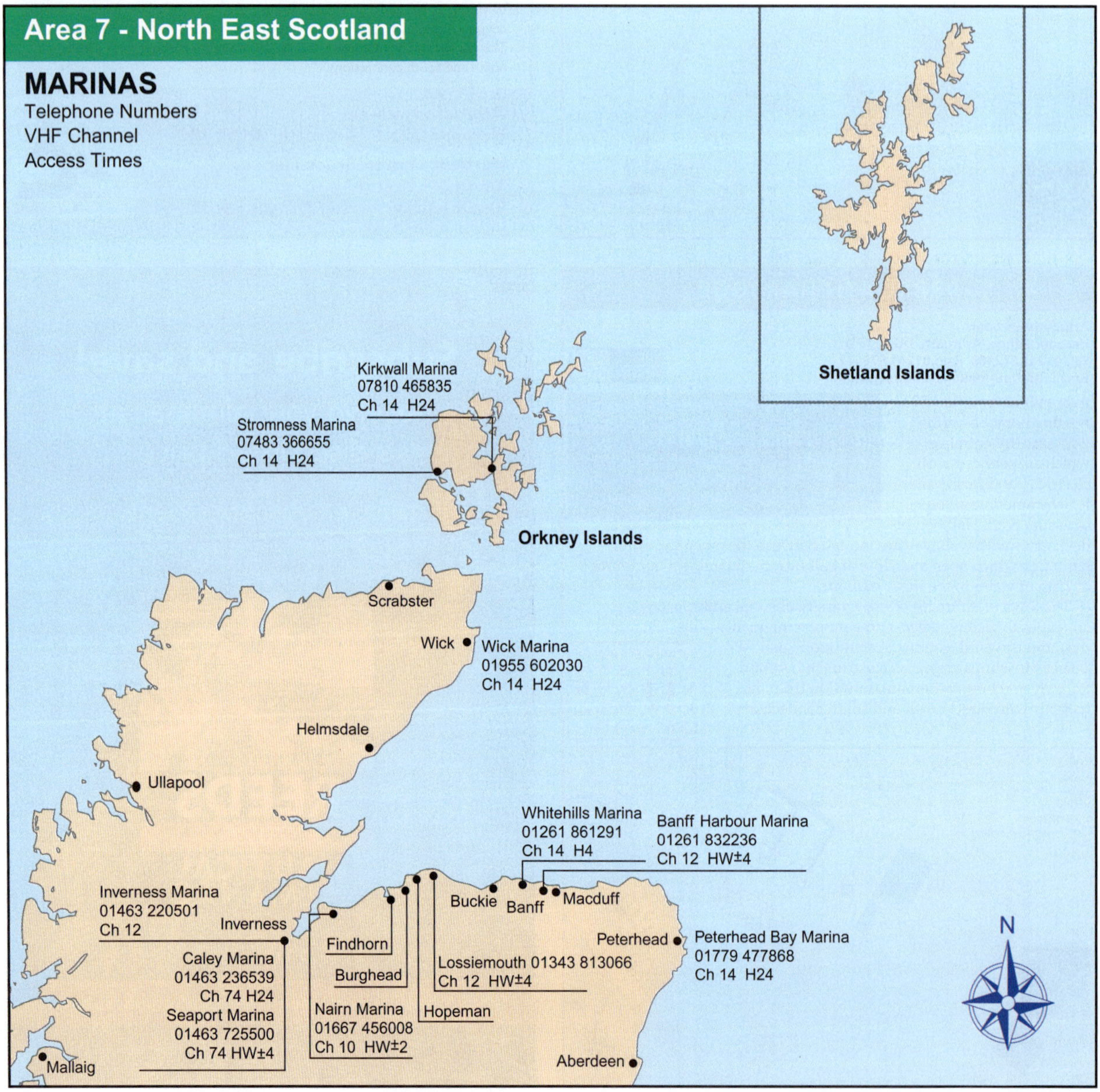

Area 7 - North East Scotland

MARINAS
Telephone Numbers
VHF Channel
Access Times

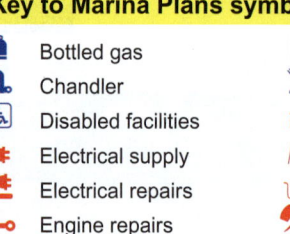

Shetland Islands

Kirkwall Marina
07810 465835
Ch 14 H24

Stromness Marina
07483 366655
Ch 14 H24

Orkney Islands

Scrabster

Wick
Wick Marina
01955 602030
Ch 14 H24

Helmsdale

Ullapool

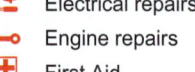

Whitehills Marina
01261 861291
Ch 14 H4

Banff Harbour Marina
01261 832236
Ch 12 HW±4

Buckie Banff Macduff

Inverness Marina
01463 220501
Ch 12   Inverness

Peterhead
Peterhead Bay Marina
01779 477868
Ch 14 H24

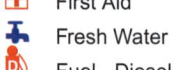

Caley Marina
01463 236539
Ch 74 H24

Findhorn
Burghead

Lossiemouth 01343 813066
Ch 12 HW±4

Seaport Marina
01463 725500
Ch 74 HW±4

Nairn Marina
01667 456008
Ch 10 HW±2

Hopeman

Mallaig

Aberdeen

MARINA GUIDE 2026

NORTH EAST SCOTLAND — AREA 7

PETERHEAD BAY MARINA

Peterhead Port Authority
Harbour Office, West Pier, Peterhead, AB42 1DW
Tel: 01779 477868/483600
Email: marina@peterheadport.co.uk
www.peterheadport.co.uk

VHF Ch 14
ACCESS H24

Based in the south west corner of Peterhead Bay Harbour, the marina provides one of the finest marine leisure facilities in the east of Scotland. In addition to the services on site, there are plenty of nautical businesses in the vicinity, ranging from ship chandlers and electrical servicing to boat repairs and surveying.

Due to its easterly location, Peterhead affords an ideal stopover for those yachts heading to or from Scandinavia as well as for vessels making for the Caledonian Canal.

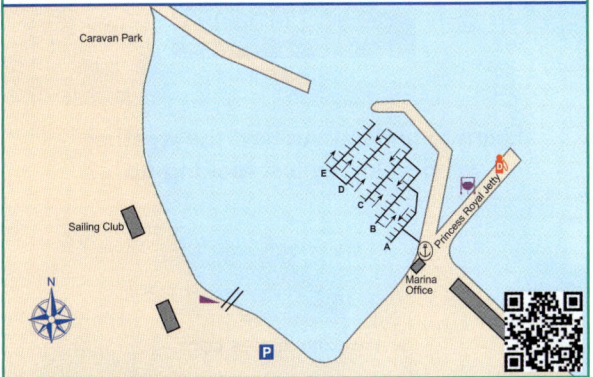

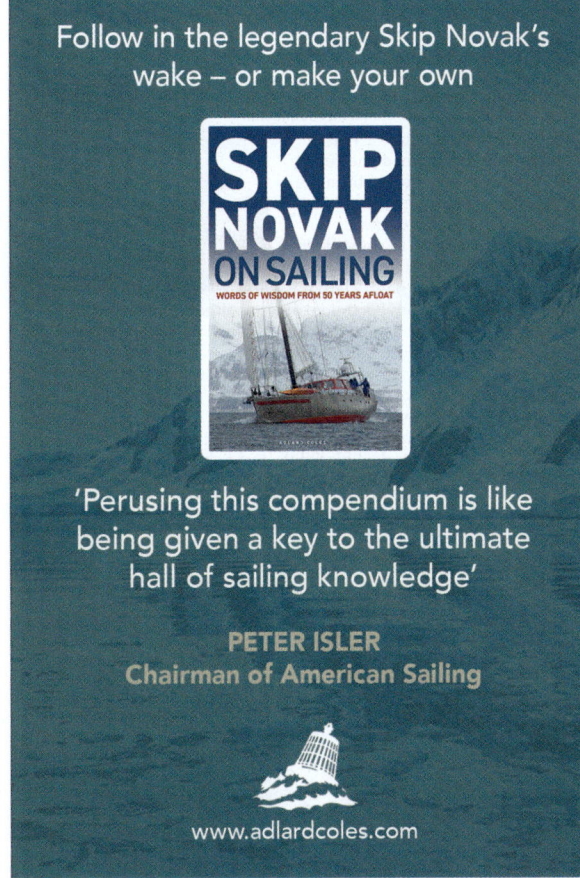

Follow in the legendary Skip Novak's wake – or make your own

SKIP NOVAK ON SAILING
WORDS OF WISDOM FROM 50 YEARS AFLOAT

'Perusing this compendium is like being given a key to the ultimate hall of sailing knowledge'

PETER ISLER
Chairman of American Sailing

www.adlardcoles.com

BANFF HARBOUR MARINA

Banff Harbour Marina
Harbour Office, Quayside, Banff, Aberdeenshire, AB45 1HQ
Tel: 01261 832236   Mobile: 07920 270360
Email: duncan.mackie@aberdeenshire.gov.uk

VHF Ch 12
ACCESS HW±4

A former fishing and cargo port located in the pretty and historic town of Banff. Banff offers excellent facilities to both regular and visiting users. The marina now provides 92 berths, of which 76 are serviced pontoon berths and 16 unserviced moorings, in one of the safest harbours on the NE coast of Scotland. There are local shops, restaurants, supermarkets, and a petrol station within easy walking distance.

Caution should be taken attempting entry in a NEly swell. Movement during LW neaps is no problem for shallow drafted boats. Deep keel boat over 10m can be accommodated at the adjacent harbour at Macduff by arrangement in advance.

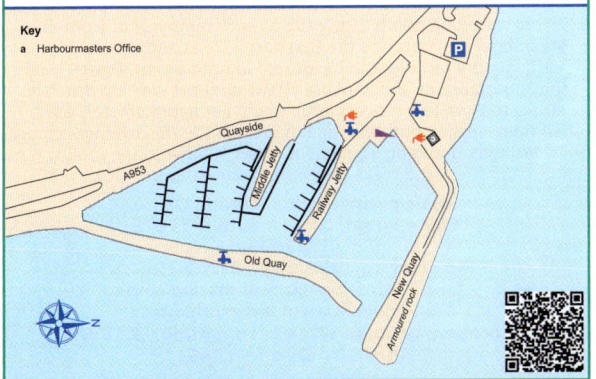

NAIRN MARINA

Nairn Marina
Nairn Harbour, Nairnshire, Scotland
Tel: 01667 456008   Fax: 01667 452877
Email: nairn.harbourmaster@virgin.net

VHF Ch 10
ACCESS HW±2

Nairn is a small town on the coast of the Moray Firth. Formerly renowned both as a fishing port and as a holiday resort dating back to Victorian times, it boasts miles of award-winning, sandy beaches, famous castles such as Cawdor, Brodie and Castle Stuart, and two championship golf courses. Other recreational activities include horse riding or walking through spectacular countryside.

The marina lies at the mouth of the River Nairn, entry to which should be avoided in strong N to NE winds. The approach is made from the NW at or around high water as the entrance is badly silted and dries out.

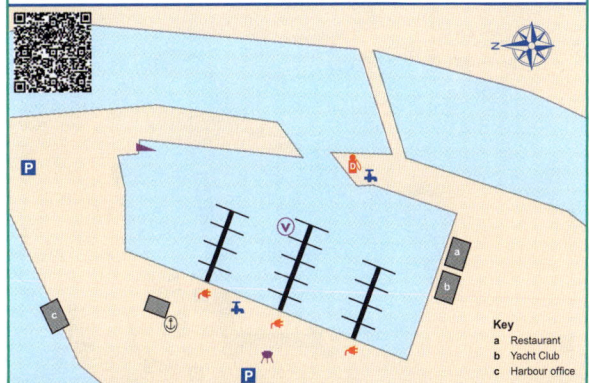

MARINA GUIDE 2026

MARINAS & SERVICES

WHITEHILLS MARINA

Whitehills Harbour Commissioners
Whitehills, Banffshire AB45 2NQ
Tel: 01261 861291
www.whitehillsharbour.co.uk
Email: harbourmaster@whitehillsharbour.co.uk

VHF Ch 14
ACCESS H24

Built in 1900, Whitehills is a Trust Harbour fully maintained and run by nine commissioners elected from the village. It was a thriving fishing port up until 1999, but due to changes in the fishing industry, was converted into a marina during 2000.

Photo by Colin Heggie

Three miles west of Banff Harbour the marina benefits from good tidal access – although there is just 1.5m at springs – comprising 38 serviced berths, with electricity, as well as eight non-serviced berths.

Whitehills village has a wide range of facilities including a convenience store, a cafe/fish & chip shop, two pubs, a fresh fish shop as well as two good restaurants. It is also a great base for families, with an excellent playpark at Blackpots, just a short walk from the harbour.

FACILITIES AT A GLANCE

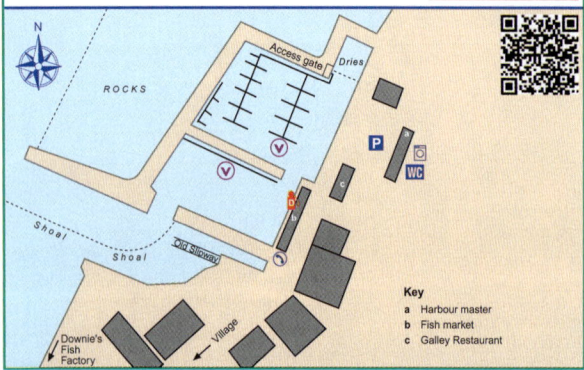

You don't need an app to forecast the weather

Reading the Clouds
HOW YOU CAN FORECAST THE WEATHER
Second Edition
Oliver Perkins
Foreword by Tom Cunliffe

Learn to understand how the weather will develop by just **looking up**

www.adlardcoles.com

LOSSIEMOUTH MARINA

Marina Office
Lossiemouth, Moray, IV31 6PB
Tel: 01343 813066
Email: info@lossiemouthmarina.com

VHF Ch 12
ACCESS HW±3

Approximately halfway between Inverness and Peterhead, the marina provides over 115 berths. Access for vessels over 1.8m draft is HW±2, this can be extended to HW±3 for those under 1.8m. Visitor berths area lie just inside the E Basin, providing free water and electricity. Visitor packs are available at marina office (Mon–Fri 9am-4pm), the blue box at the top of the ramp or the Steamboat Inn. Toilet and shower blocks with laundry facilities are located in both basins. Diesel, local shops, restaurants and ATM are all within walking distance. The marina has undercover workshop facilities, dredging equipment, a 25T sublift, and crane for masting/demasting.

FACILITIES AT A GLANCE

Elgin & Lossiemouth Harbour Company

Lossiemouth Marina lies approximately halfway between Inverness and Peterhead, providing over 125 berths. Dedicated visitor finger pontoons lie just inside the East basin, providing free water and electricity. Complimentary wi-fi is also available in the East and West basins. Visitor packs can be collected from the Marina Office (Monday to Friday 9am-4pm), from collection points at the top of each rampway or from the Steamboat Inn, opposite the East basin. Toilet and shower blocks with laundry facilities can be located in both basins. Diesel, local shops, restaurants and ATM are all within short walking distance. Buses to Elgin (the nearest large town) are approximately every half hour. Lossiemouth Marina has excellent undercover workshop facilities, dredging equipment, a twenty-five tonne sublift, and crane for masting/demasting.

Lossiemouth Marina, Marina Office,
Shore Street, Lossiemouth IV31 6PB
Tel: 01343 813066
Mob (emergencies only): 07969 213521
Email: info@lossiemouthmarina.com
Web: www.lossiemouthmarina.com
Location: Latitude 57°43′N, Longitude 03°17′W
Admiralty Chart: No.1462

NORTH EAST SCOTLAND — AREA 7

INVERNESS MARINA

Inverness Marina
Longman Drive, Inverness, IV1 1SU
Tel: 01463 220501
Email: info@invernessmarina.com
www.invernessmarina.com

VHF Ch 12
ACCESS H24

The marina is situated in the Inverness firth just one mile from the city centre and half a mile from the entrance to the Caledonian Canal. It has a minimum depth of 3m, 24hr access and 150 fully serviced berths. On site are services including rigging, engineering, electronics and boat repair. There is a chandlery off site.

Inverness has excellent transport networks to the rest of the UK and Europe and, as the gateway to the Highlands is a great location as a base for a touring golf courses, historic sites and the Whisky Trail. The marina is a perfect base for cruising Orkney, Shetland and Scandinavia.

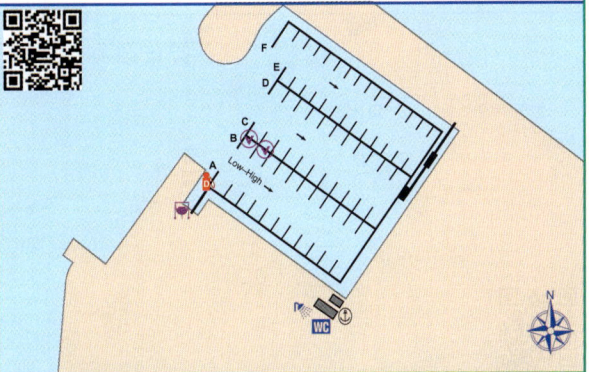

SEAPORT MARINA

Seaport Marina
Muirtown Wharf, Inverness, IV3 5LE
Tel: 01463 725500
Email: caledonian@scottishcanals.co.uk
www.scottishcanals.co.uk

VHF Ch 74
ACCESS HW±4

Seaport Marina is based at Muirtown Basin at the eastern entrance of the Caledonian Canal; a 60 mile coast-to-coast channel slicing through the majestic Great Glen. Only a 15 minute walk from the centre of Inverness, the Marina is an ideal base for visiting the Highlands.

There are shops and amenities nearby, as well as chandlers, boat repair services and a slipway. The marina also offers a variety of winter mooring packages and details of transit and short term licences, including the use of the Caledonian Canal can be found on the above website.

Photo courtesy of D Edes

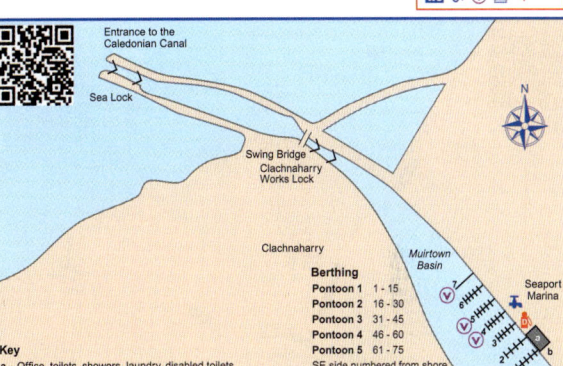

CALEY MARINA

Caley Marina
Canal Road, Inverness, IV3 8NF
Tel: 01463 236539 Fax: 01463 238323
Email: info@caleymarina.com
www.caleymarina.com

VHF Ch 74
ACCESS H24

Caley Marina is a family run business based near Inverness. With the four flight Muirtown locks and the Kessock Bridge providing a dramatic backdrop, the marina runs alongside the Caledonian Canal which, opened in 1822, is regarded as one of the most spectacular waterways in Europe. Built as a short cut between the North Sea and the Atlantic Ocean, thus avoiding the potentially dangerous Pentland Firth on the north coast of Scotland, the canal is around 60 miles long and takes about three days to cruise from east to west. With the prevailing winds behind you, it takes slightly less time to cruise in the other direction.

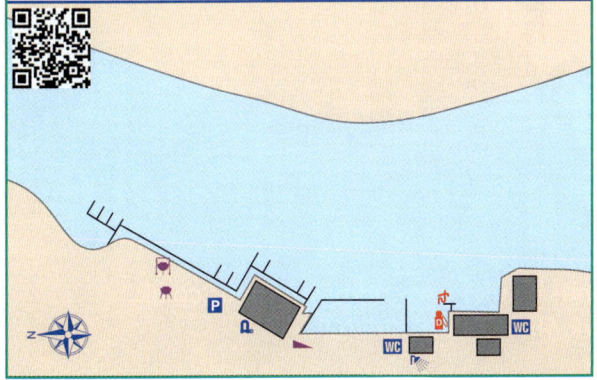

WICK MARINA

Wick Marina
Harbour Office, Wick, Caithness, KW1 5HA
Tel: 01955 602030
Email: office@wickharbour.co.uk

VHF Ch 14, 16
ACCESS H24

This is the most northerly marina on the British mainland and the last stop before the Orkney and Shetland Islands. Situated an easy five minutes walk from the town centre Wick Marina accommodates 80 fully serviced berths with all the support facilities expected in a modern marina.

This part of Scotland with its rugged coastline and rich history is easily accessible by air and a great starting point for cruising in the northern isles, Moray Firth, Caledonian Canal and Scandinavia, a comfortable 280-mile sail.

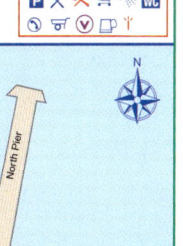

MARINA GUIDE 2026

MARINAS & SERVICES

KIRKWALL MARINA

Kirkwall Marina
Harbour Street, Kirkwall, Orkney, KW15
Tel: 07810 465835
Email: info@orkneymarinas.co.uk   www.orkneymarinas.co.uk

VHF Ch 14
ACCESS H24

The Orkney Isles, comprising 70 islands in total, provides some of the finest cruising grounds in Northern Europe. The Main Island, incorporating the ancient port of Kirkwall, is the largest, although 16 others have lively communities and are rich in archaeological sites as well as spectacular scenery and wildlife.

Kirkwall Marina, an all year facility, is located within the harbour and just yards from the visitor attractions of this ancient port. Local shops, hotels and restaurants are all within walking distance.

FACILITIES AT A GLANCE

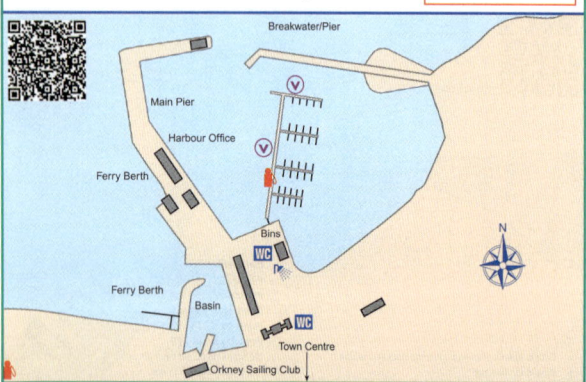

STROMNESS MARINA

Stromness Marina
Stromness, Orkney, KW16
Tel: 07483 366655
Email: info@orkneymarinas.co.uk
www.orkneymarinas.co.uk

VHF Ch 14
ACCESS H24

Stromness lies on the south-western tip of the Orkney Isles' Mainland. Sitting beneath the rocky ridge known as Brinkie's Brae, it is considered one of Orkney's major seaports, with sailors first attracted to the fine anchorage provided by the bay of Hamnavoe.

Stromness offers comprehensive facilities including a chandlery and repair services. Also on hand are an internet café, a fitness suite and swimming pool as well as car and bike hire.

FACILITIES AT A GLANCE

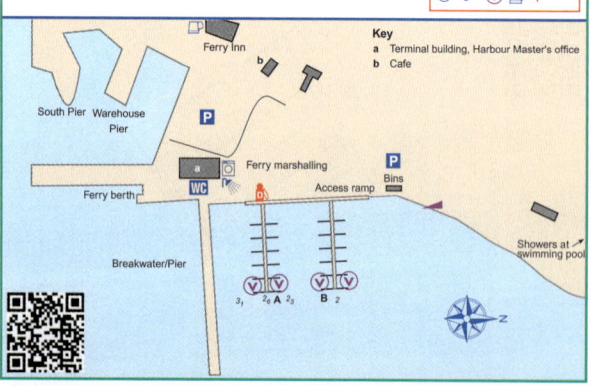

Key
a   Terminal building, Harbour Master's office
b   Cafe

SAIL TO ORKNEY

ORKNEY MARINAS

The Orkney islands are an exciting cruising destination with an abundance of wildlife, history and outstanding coastal scenery.

+44 (0)1856 871313 | info@orkneymarinas.co.uk | www.orkneymarinas.co.uk
Orkney Marinas Ltd, Dunkirk, Shore Street, Kirkwall.

AREA 8

NORTH WEST SCOTLAND – Cape Wrath to Crinan Canal

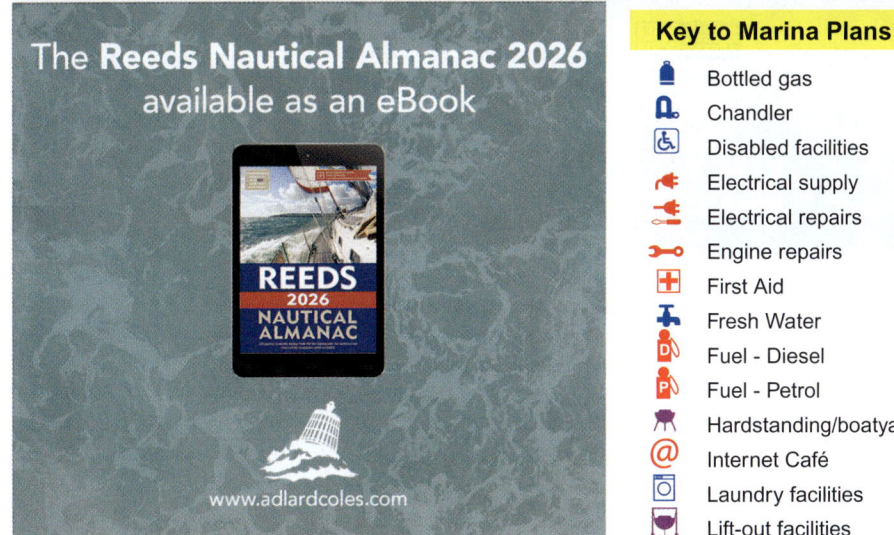

Key to Marina Plans symbols

- Bottled gas
- Chandler
- Disabled facilities
- Electrical supply
- Electrical repairs
- Engine repairs
- First Aid
- Fresh Water
- Fuel - Diesel
- Fuel - Petrol
- Hardstanding/boatyard
- Internet Café
- Laundry facilities
- Lift-out facilities
- Parking
- Pub/Restaurant
- Pump out
- Rigging service
- Sail repairs
- Shipwright
- Shop/Supermarket
- Showers
- Slipway
- Toilets
- Telephone
- Trolleys
- Visitors berths
- Wi-Fi

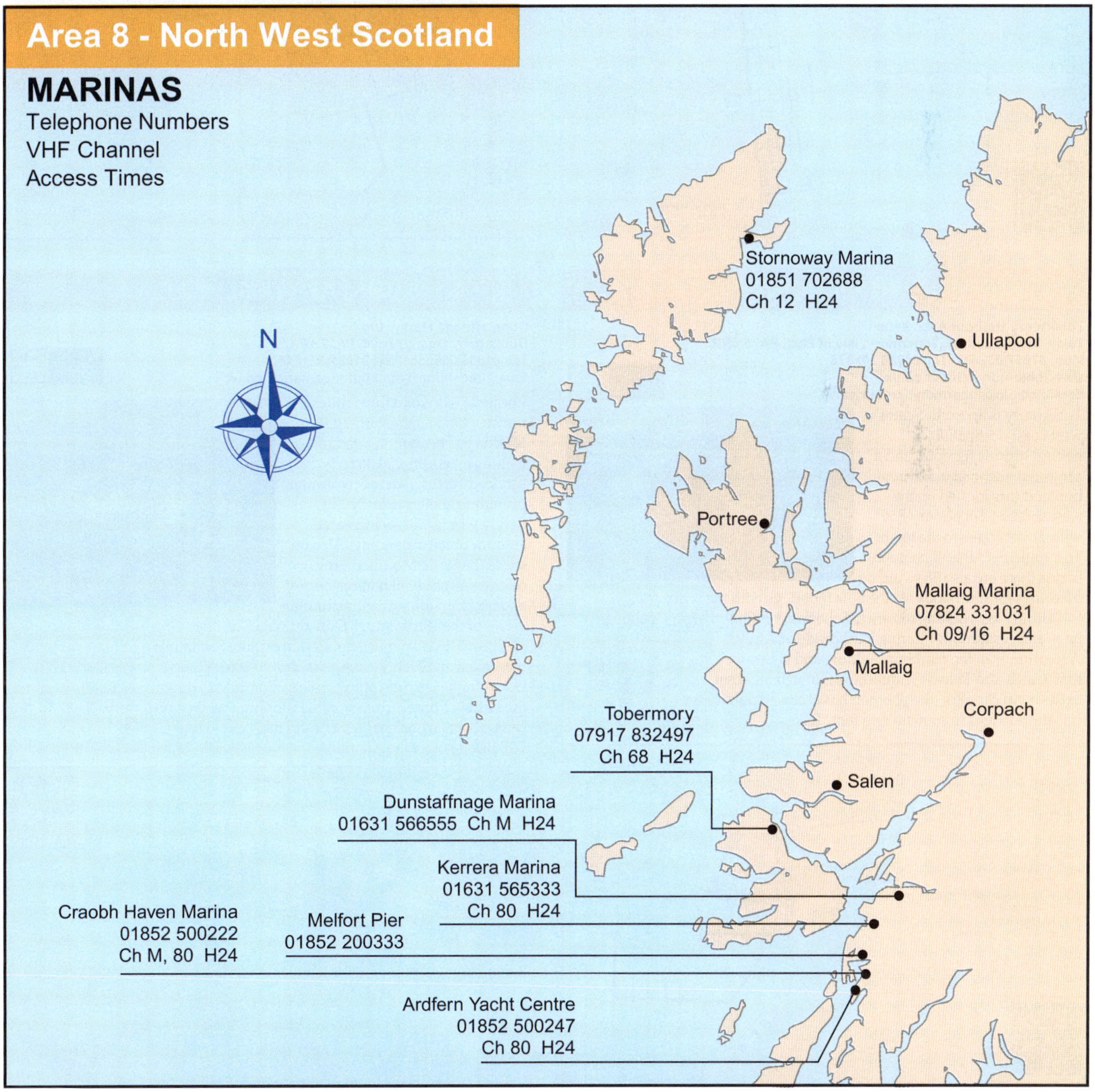

Area 8 - North West Scotland

MARINAS
Telephone Numbers
VHF Channel
Access Times

Stornoway Marina
01851 702688
Ch 12 H24

Ullapool

Portree

Mallaig Marina
07824 331031
Ch 09/16 H24

Mallaig

Corpach

Tobermory
07917 832497
Ch 68 H24

Salen

Dunstaffnage Marina
01631 566555 Ch M H24

Kerrera Marina
01631 565333
Ch 80 H24

Craobh Haven Marina
01852 500222
Ch M, 80 H24

Melfort Pier
01852 200333

Ardfern Yacht Centre
01852 500247
Ch 80 H24

MARINA GUIDE 2026   63

MARINAS & SERVICES

STORNOWAY MARINA

Stornoway Port Authority
Amity House, Esplanade Quay,
Stornoway, Isle of Lewis, HS1 2XS
Tel: 01851 702688
Email: info@stornowayport.com

VHF Ch 12
ACCESS HW24

Stornoway Marina is sheltered and has easy access at all states of the tide and weather conditions. Vessels up to 24 metres in length and 3 metres draft can be accommodated.

The 80-berth marina provides a safe haven for island hoppers and days sailors. The marina is particularly popular as it is located right in the heart of the bustling town centre. Fresh water, electricity, wi-fi, toilet, shower and laundry facilities are available quayside for all visitors.

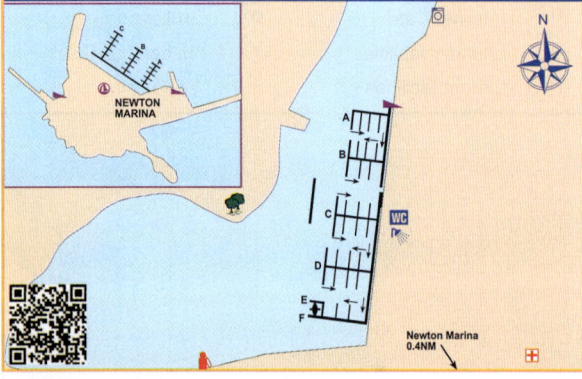

MALLAIG MARINA

Mallaig Marina
East Bay, Mallaig, Inverness-shire, PH41 4QS
Tel: 07824 331031
Email: info@mallaigharbourauthority.com

VHF Ch 09, 16
ACCESS H24

Mallaig Marina, part funded by the EU Sail West project, provides the ideal location for exploring the magnificent West Coast of Scotland. This 50-berth marina includes 6 visitor moorings, set in a working harbour, an easy walk to all local facilities.

The village itself offers a range of options for the discerning diner, shopper or tourist. Fuel is available in cans from the local petrol station. As well as the local fishing fleet, there is regular activity from the many ferries servicing Skye, Knoydart, the Small Isles and the Western Isles. Ferry traffic has right of way when entering or exiting the Harbour. The village also welcomes the Jacobite Steam Train twice daily throughout the summer months.

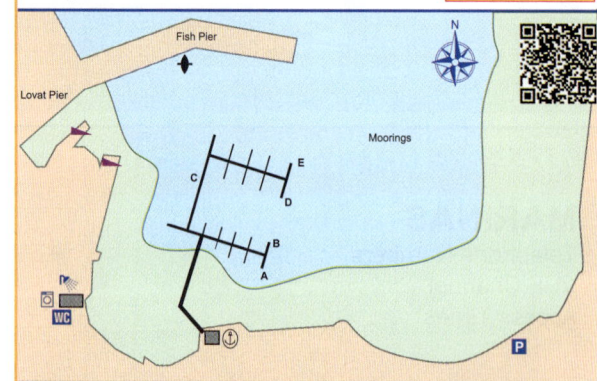

TOBERMORY

Tobermory Harbour Association
Taigh Solais, Ledaig, Tobermory, Isle of Mull, PA75 6NR
Mob: 07917 832497   Tel: 01688 302876
www.tobermoryharbour.co.uk
Email: admin@tobermoryharbour.co.uk

VHF Ch 68
ACCESS H24

Tobermory is an iconic Scottish west coast destination, a natural historic harbour, and a protected anchorage. Harbour pontoons are located on the west shore of Tobermory Bay with direct access to the town. To supplement the 58 pontoon berths there are also 38 swinging moorings for hire – look for the blue moorings with the white top.

Within easy walking distance, Tobermory offers an array of shops, bars, and restaurants offering local produce. Mull Aquarium is in the Harbour Building and is Europe's first 'Catch and Release' Aquarium. Situated adjacent to the main car park, the pontoon has access to public transport to and from mainland ferry links.

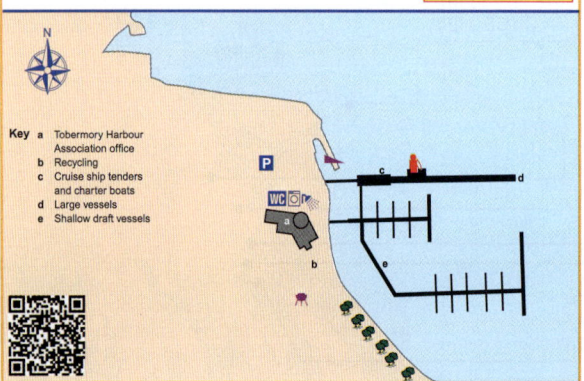

DUNSTAFFNAGE MARINA

Dunstaffnage Marina Ltd
Dunbeg, by Oban, Argyll, PA37 1PX
Tel: 01631 566555   Fax: 01631 571044
Email: reception@dunstaffnagemarina.co.uk

VHF Ch M
ACCESS H24

Located just two to three miles north of Oban, Dunstaffnage Marina has been renovated to include an additional 36 fully serviced berths, a new breakwater providing shelter from NE'ly to E'ly winds and an increased amount of hard standing. Also on site is the Wide Mouthed Frog, offering a convivial bar, restaurant and accommodation with stunning views of the 13th century Dunstaffnage Castle.

The marina is perfectly placed to explore Scotland's west coast and Hebridean Islands. Only 10M NE up Loch Linnhe is Port Appin, while sailing 15M S, down the Firth of Lorne, brings you to Puldohran where you can walk to an ancient hostelry situated next to the C18 Bridge Over the Atlantic.

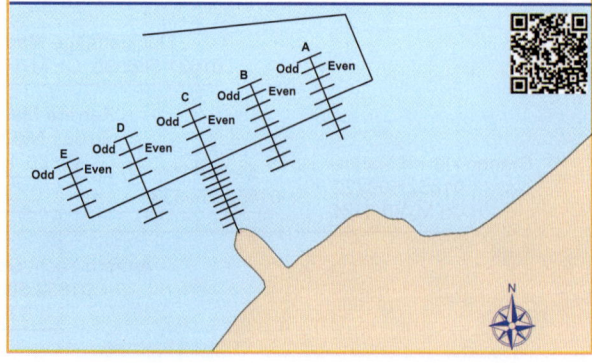

MARINA GUIDE 2026

NORTH WEST SCOTLAND

AREA 8

KERRERA MARINA

Kerrera Marina
Isle of Kerrera, Oban, Argyll, PA34 4SX
Tel: 01631 565333
Email: office@kerreramarina.com www.kerreramarina.com

VHF Ch 80
ACCESS H24

A warm welcome awaits at Kerrera Marina. Access all tides, 70 pontoon berths, 30 moorings along with winter storage & full boat yard services with 50T hoist. Shore base facilities are extensive - gas, diesel, water, showers, laundry, wi-fi and a cosy lounge with TV & library. We offer a pre-booked ferry service into Oban, please see our website.

Kerrera is a magical place to explore, full of amazing wildlife, beautiful beaches & wonderful views. Our bar and restaurant overlooks the sheltered bay of Ardantrive serving delicious local produce. The island also has a tearoom, two farm shops and a castle steeped in history.

FACILITIES AT A GLANCE

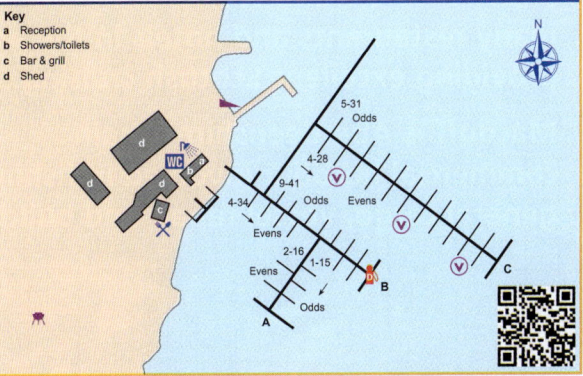

Key
a Reception
b Showers/toilets
c Bar & grill
d Shed

MELFORT PIER AND HARBOUR

Melfort Pier and Harbour
Kilmelford, by Oban, Argyll
Tel: 01852 200333
Email: melharbour@aol.com www.mellowmelfort.com

VHF
ACCESS

Melfort Pier & Harbour is situated on the shores of Loch Melfort, one of the most peaceful lochs on the south west coast of Scotland. Overlooked by the Pass of Melfort and the Braes of Lorn, it lies approximately 18 miles north of Lochgilphead and 16 miles south of Oban. Its onsite facilities include showers, laundry, free Wi-Fi access and parking – pets welcome. Fuel, power and water are available at nearby Kilmelford Yacht Haven.

For those who want a few nights on dry land, Melfort Pier & Harbour offers lochside houses, each one equipped with a sauna, spa bath and balcony offering stunning views over the loch - available per night.

FACILITIES AT A GLANCE

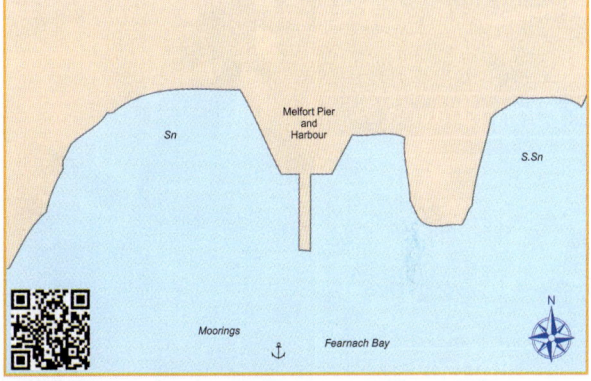

CRAOBH MARINA

Craobh Marina
By Lochgilphead, Argyll, Scotland, PA31 8UA
Tel: 01852 500222 Fax: 01852 500252
Out of hours: 07702 517038
Email: info@craobhmarina.co.uk www.craobhmarina.co.uk

VHF Ch 80
ACCESS H24

Craobh Marina is idyllically situated in the heart of Scotland's most sought after cruising grounds. Not only does Craobh offer ready access to a wonderful choice of scenic cruising throughout the western isles, the marina is conveniently close to Glasgow and its international transport hub.

Craobh Marina has been developed from a near perfect natural harbour, offering secure and sheltered berthing for up to 250 vessels to 40m LOA and with a draft of 4m. With an unusually deep and wide entrance Craobh Marina provides shelter and a warm welcome for all types of craft.

FACILITIES AT A GLANCE

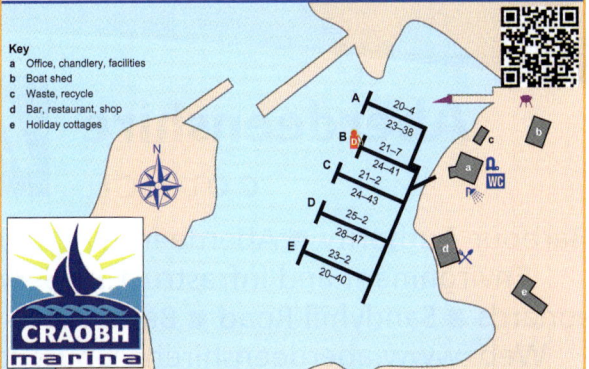

Key
a Office, chandlery, facilities
b Boat shed
c Waste, recycle
d Bar, restaurant, shop
e Holiday cottages

ARDFERN YACHT CENTRE

Ardfern Yacht Centre
Ardfern, by Lochgilphead, Argyll, PA31 8QN
Tel: 01852 500247 Fax: 01852 500624
www.ardfernyacht.co.uk Email: office@ardfernyacht.co.uk

VHF Ch 80
ACCESS H24

Developed around an old pier once frequented by steamers, Ardfern Yacht Centre lies at the head of Loch Craignish, one of Scotland's most sheltered and picturesque sea lochs. With several islands and protected anchorages nearby, Ardfern is an ideal place from which to cruise the west coast of Scotland and the Outer Hebrides.

The Yacht Centre comprises pontoon berths and swinging moorings as well as a workshop, boat storage and well-stocked chandlery, while a grocery store and eating places can be found in the village. Among the onshore activities available locally are horse riding, cycling, and walking.

FACILITIES AT A GLANCE

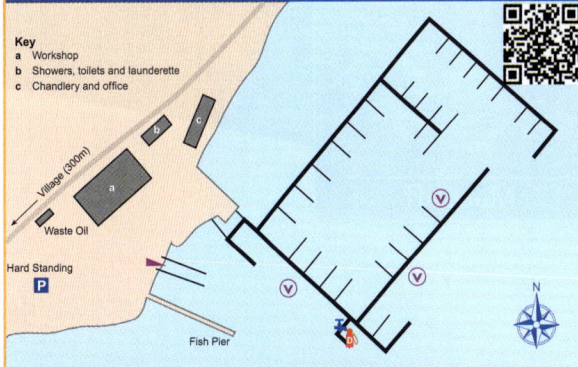

Key
a Workshop
b Showers, toilets and launderette
c Chandlery and office

MARINA GUIDE 2026

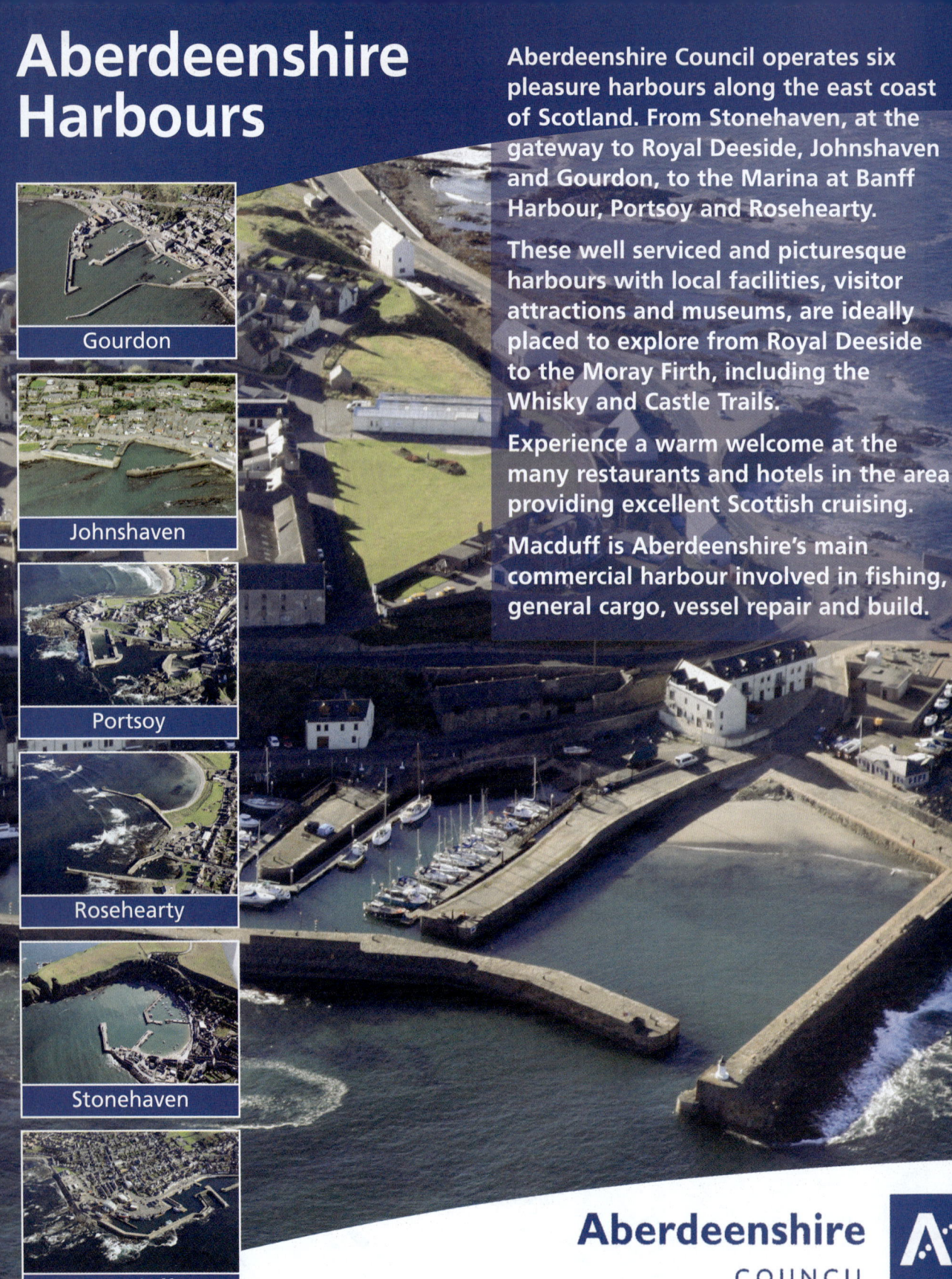

Aberdeenshire Harbours

Aberdeenshire Council operates six pleasure harbours along the east coast of Scotland. From Stonehaven, at the gateway to Royal Deeside, Johnshaven and Gourdon, to the Marina at Banff Harbour, Portsoy and Rosehearty.

These well serviced and picturesque harbours with local facilities, visitor attractions and museums, are ideally placed to explore from Royal Deeside to the Moray Firth, including the Whisky and Castle Trails.

Experience a warm welcome at the many restaurants and hotels in the area providing excellent Scottish cruising.

Macduff is Aberdeenshire's main commercial harbour involved in fishing, general cargo, vessel repair and build.

- Gourdon
- Johnshaven
- Portsoy
- Rosehearty
- Stonehaven
- Macduff

Aberdeenshire COUNCIL

Harbour Authority ■ Aberdeenshire Council
Environment and Infrastructure Service
St Leonards ■ Sandyhill Road ■ Banff AB45 1SD
Web: www.aberdeenshireharbours.co.uk
Email: harboursadmin@aberdeenshire.gov.uk

AREA 9

SOUTH WEST SCOTLAND – Crinan Canal to Mull of Galloway

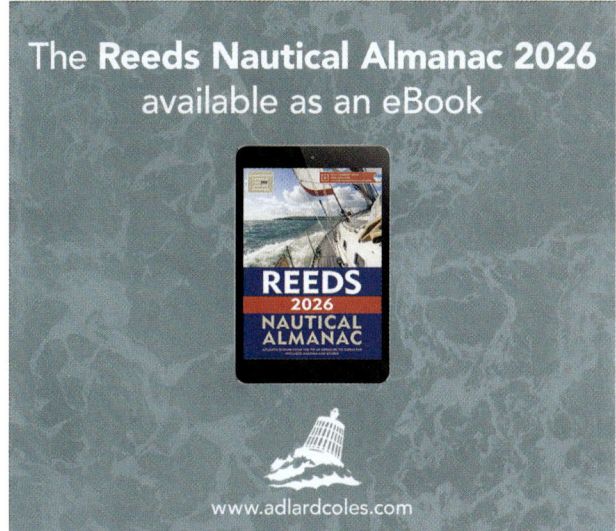

Key to Marina Plans symbols

- Bottled gas
- Chandler
- Disabled facilities
- Electrical supply
- Electrical repairs
- Engine repairs
- First Aid
- Fresh Water
- Fuel - Diesel
- Fuel - Petrol
- Hardstanding/boatyard
- Internet Café
- Laundry facilities
- Lift-out facilities
- Parking
- Pub/Restaurant
- Pump out
- Rigging service
- Sail repairs
- Shipwright
- Shop/Supermarket
- Showers
- Slipway
- Toilets
- Telephone
- Trolleys
- Visitors berths
- Wi-Fi

Area 9 - South West Scotland

MARINAS
Telephone Numbers
VHF Channel
Access Times

- Holy Loch Marina 01369 701800 Ch 80 H24
- Portavadie Marina 01700 811075 Ch 80 H24
- Rhu Marina 01436 820238 Ch M, 80 H24
- Sandpoint Marina 01389 762396 Ch M HW±3
- Crinan Boatyard 01546 830232 Ch 12, 16 H24
- Ardrishaig
- Tarbert Harbour 01880 820344 Ch 14 H24
- Rhu
- Kip Marina 01475 521485 Ch 80 H24
- James Watt Dock Marina 01475 729838 H24
- Port Ellen 07464 151200
- Ardrossan
- Largs Yacht Haven 01475 675333 Ch M, 80 H24
- Port Bannatyne Marina 01700 503116 CH M H24
- Lamlash
- Troon
- Clyde Marina 01294 607077 Ch 80 H24
- Campbeltown Marina 07798 524821 Ch 13 H24
- Troon Yacht Haven 01292 315553 Ch M, 80 H24
- Maryport Marina 01900 814431 Ch 12 HW±2½
- Stranraer Marina 01776 706565 Ch 14 H24
- Kirkcudbright Marina 01557 331135 Ch 13 HW±2½
- Portpatrick
- Maryport

Explore the enchanting islands of Scotland with this **absorbing and beautiful guide**

www.adlardcoles.com

MARINA GUIDE 2026

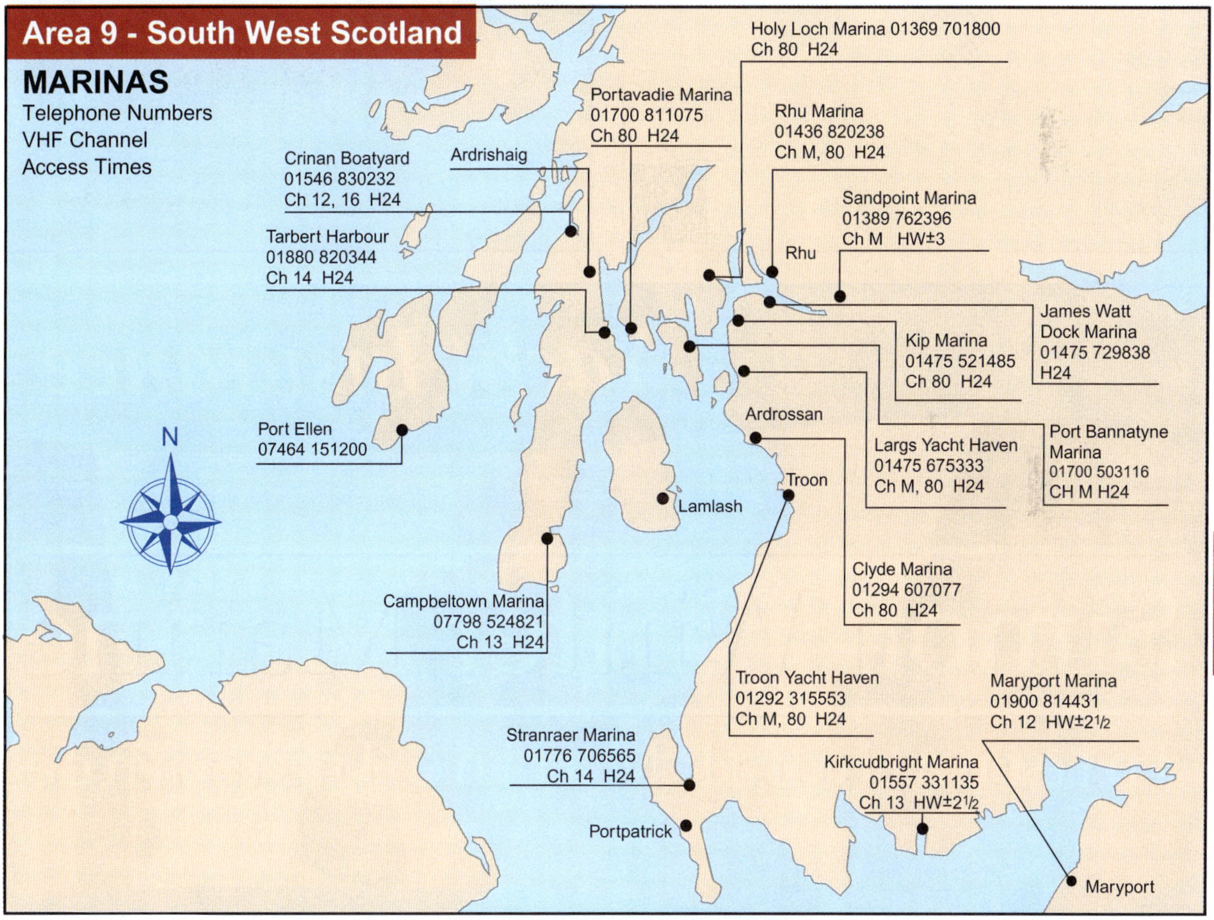

MARINAS & SERVICES

PORT ELLEN MARINA

Port Ellen Marina
Port Ellen, Islay, Argyll, PA42 7DB
Tel: 07464 151200 www.portellenmarina.co.uk
Email: portellenmarina@outlook.com

VHF
ACCESS H24

A safe and relaxed mooring superbly located in the quaint village of Port Ellen, making it an ideal stopping off point whether planning to sail north or south. Islay is world-renowned for its many malt whisky distilleries, nine at the last count and one to reopen shortly.

Meeting guests and short term storage is trouble free with the excellent air and ferry services to the mainland and Glasgow. Once on Islay you will be tempted to extend your stay so be warned, check www.portellenmarina.com for the many reasons to visit.

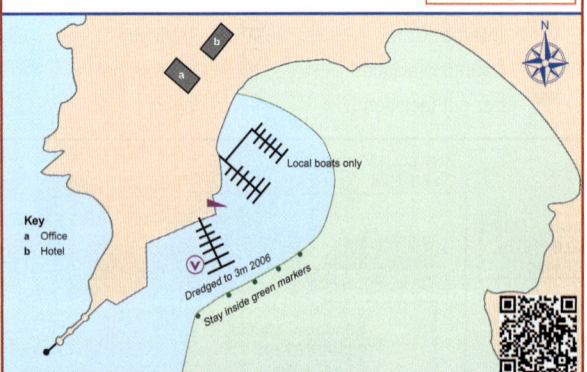

CRINAN BOATYARD

Crinan Boatyard Ltd
Crinan, Lochgilphead, Argyll, PA31 8SW
Tel: 01546 830232 Fax: 01546 830281
Email: info@crinanboatyard.co.uk
www.crinanboatyard.co.uk

VHF Ch 12, 16
ACCESS H24

Situated at the westerly entrance of the scenic Crinan Canal, Crinan Boatyard offers swinging moorings nightly or longer term, a fuelling/loading berth, a well stocked Chandlery, heads, showers, laundry and an experienced work force for repair work all on site. A hotel and coffee shop, just a short walk away at the Canal basin, great walking and the historic Kilmartin Glen close by are some of the attractions on shore.

The nearby town of Lochgilphead 7 miles away offers shopping and good travel links to Glasgow (85 miles) and its International Airport.

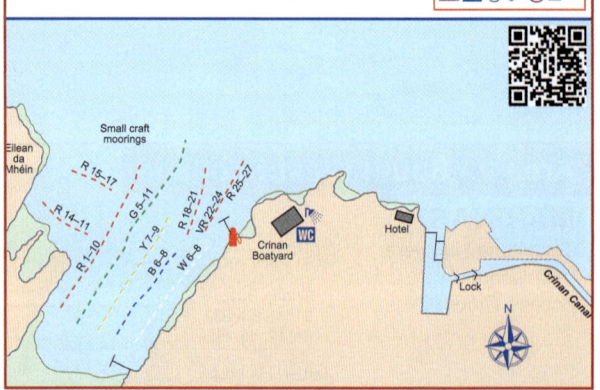

Yacht Insurance

Simon Winter Marine
International Marine Insurance

For a quotation please call **0344 545 6132**

www.simonwintermarine.co.uk

Simon Winter Marine Limited is an Appointed Representative of Winter & Co (Marine) Ltd Winter & Co (Marine) Ltd is authorised and regulated by The Financial Conduct Authority

SOUTH WEST SCOTLAND — AREA 9

TARBERT HARBOUR

Tarbert Harbour Authority
Harbour Office, Garval Road, Tarbert, Argyll, PA29 6TR
Tel: 01880 820344
Email: info@tarbertharbour.co.uk

VHF Ch 14
ACCESS H24

East Loch Tarbert is situated on the western shores of Loch Fyne. The naturally sheltered harbour is accessible through an easily navigated narrow entrance, and is a prefect stopping point for those heading north to the Crinan Canal.

The pontoons can accommodate up to 100 visiting vessels of various sizes, with fresh water, electricity and wi-fi available FOC. Toilet, shower and laundry facilities are accessible 24/7, and the unique recreation area and community marquee are available to use - perfect for families, gatherings and musters. The marina pontoons are situated at the heart of the heritage village of Tarbert, which boasts a busy festival calendar and offers a wide range of amenities.

FACILITIES AT A GLANCE

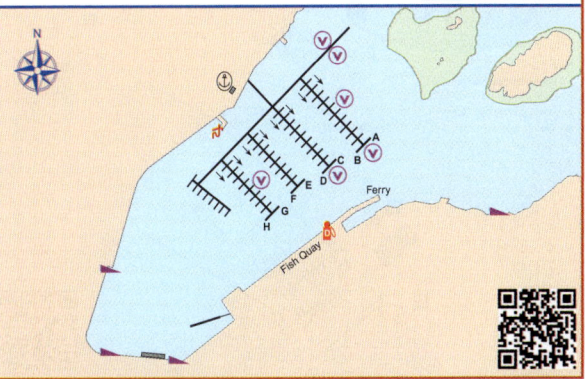

Tarbert Harbour — THE HEART OF THE HERITAGE VILLAGE

STEP ASHORE!

Tarbert is a picturesque fishing village on Loch Fyne. Step ashore to enjoy scenic walks, fresh seafood, gift shops, restaurants and galleries.

Our renowned fun events include the Scottish Series Yacht Race, the Traditional Boat Festival and more!

Tarbert is also where the CALMAC ferry operates its service between Portavadie.

Plan your visit at:
Tel: 01880 820 344
Tarbert Harbour, Loch Fyne, Argyll, Scotland, PA29 6TR
www.tarbertharbour.co.uk

PORT BANNATYNE MARINA

Port Bannatyne Marina
Marine Road, Port Bannatyne, PA20 0LT
Tel: 01700 503116 Mobile: 07711 319992
Email: office@portbannatynemarina.co.uk

VHF Ch M1
ACCESS H24

Nestled in the bay at Port Bannatyne on the Isle of Bute, the marina is set in breathtakingly beautiful surroundings. The shore facilities include toilets and showers, lifting and winter storage and all boat repairs. Free wi-fi is available throughout the marina. Protected by a breakwater and accessible H24 the marina is dredged to –2.4m CD.

The village of Port Bannatyne offers a Post Office for essential groceries. There are frequent bus services to both Rothesay and Ettrick Bay where a walk along a beautiful beach with amazing views can be completed with either a meal or tea and cake at the beach side restaurant.

FACILITIES AT A GLANCE

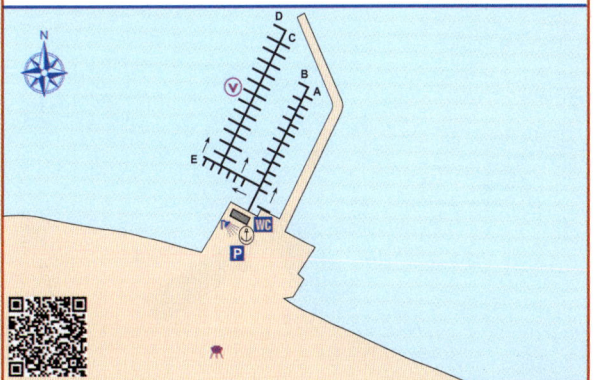

PORTAVADIE MARINA

Portavadie Marina
Portavadie, Loch Fyne, Argyll, PA21 2DA
Tel: 01700 811075 Fax: 01700 811074
Email: info@portavadiemarina.com

VHF Ch 80
ACCESS H24

Portavadie Marina offers deep and sheltered berthing to residential and visiting boats in an area renowned for its superb cruising waters. Situated on the east side of Loch Fyne in close proximity to several islands and the famous Kyles of Bute, Portavadie is within easy sailing distance of the Crinan Canal, giving access to the Inner and Outer Hebrides.

The marina has 230 berths 40 of which are reserved for visitors, plus comprehensive on shore facilities, including a restaurant/bar, leisure/spa complex with pools and self catering accommodation. There is also a shop and small chandlery overlooking the marina, a dedicated fuel berth for petrol and diesel and bike hire. This unspoiled area of Argyll which is less than two hours by road from Glasgow offers an ideal base for boat owners looking for a safe and secure haven.

FACILITIES AT A GLANCE

Key
a Reception, offices, conference room, open deck viewing platform
b Bar & restaurant
c WC, Showers & laundry
d Luxury self-catering apartments
e Leisure complex

Berthing
A-H pontoons
Odd numbers on the north side
Even numbers on the south side
Numbers start at the inner end

Visitor S pontoon
Mostly alongside with just S46 to S60 at the access bridge remaining

Visitor N pontoon
Runs from N1 at the north end to N19 at the access bridge

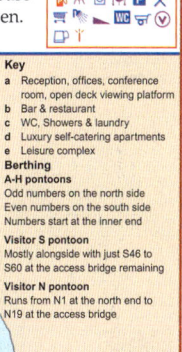

MARINA GUIDE 2026

MARINAS & SERVICES

CAMPBELTOWN MARINA

Campbeltown Marina Ltd
Dubh Artach, Roading, Campbeltown, PA28 6LU
Tel: 07798 524821
Email: campbeltownmarina@btinternet.com

VHF Ch 13
ACCESS H24

Campbeltown Marina is a brand new facility opened in June 2015 and is situated in the town centre at the head of the deep, sheltered waters of Campbeltown Loch on the SE aspect of the Kintyre Peninsula. It is within easy reach of the Antrim Coast, Ayrshire and the Upper Clyde. Diesel is available at the Old Quay and gas is across the road. Petrol can be bought a 5-minute walk away and a well stocked chandlery is situated in the town centre.

Campbeltown is the perfect getaway destination with plenty to offer the whole family. Golf, cycling and walking routes, modern swimming pool and horse riding are some of the activities on offer. Situated directly in the town centre there is a wide choice of shops, cafes, bars, restaurants and supermarkets within easy walking distance.

FACILITIES AT A GLANCE

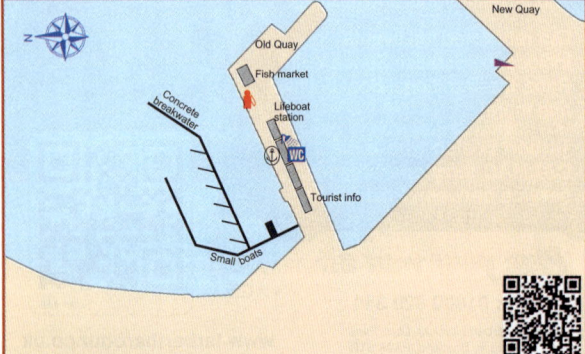

HOLY LOCH MARINA

Holy Loch Marina
Rankin's Brae, Sandbank, Dunoon, PA23 8FE
Tel: 01369 701800
Email: info@holylochmarina.co.uk www.holylochmarina.co.uk

VHF Ch 80
ACCESS H24

Holy Loch Marina, the marine gateway to Loch Lomond and the Trossachs National Park, lies on the south shore of the loch, roughly half a mile west of Lazaretto Point. Holy Loch is among the Clyde's most beautiful natural harbours and, besides being a peaceful location, offers an abundance of wildlife, places of local historical interest as well as excellent walking and cycling through the Argyll Forest Park. The marina can be entered in all weather conditions and is within easy sailing distance of Loch Long and Upper Firth.

FACILITIES AT A GLANCE

Key
a Office/Harbourmaster
b Boat storage
c Holy Loch Sailing Club
d Pier

RHU MARINA

Rhu Marina
Boatfolk Marinas Ltd, Pier Road, Rhu, G84 8LH
Tel: 01436 820238
Email: rhu@boatfolk.co.uk
www.boatfolk.co.uk/rhumarina

VHF Ch M, 80
ACCESS H24

Located on the north shore of the Clyde Estuary, Rhu Marina is accessible at all states of the tide and can accommodate yachts up to 24m in length. It also operates 40 swinging moorings in the bay adjacent to the marina, with a ferry service provided.

Within easy walking distance of the marina is Rhu village, a conservation village incorporating a few shops, a pub and the beautiful Glenarn Gardens as well as the Royal Northern & Clyde Yacht Club. A mile or two to the east lies the holiday town of Helensburgh, renowned for its attractive architecture and elegant parks and gardens, while Glasgow city is just 25 miles away and can be easily reached by train.

FACILITIES AT A GLANCE

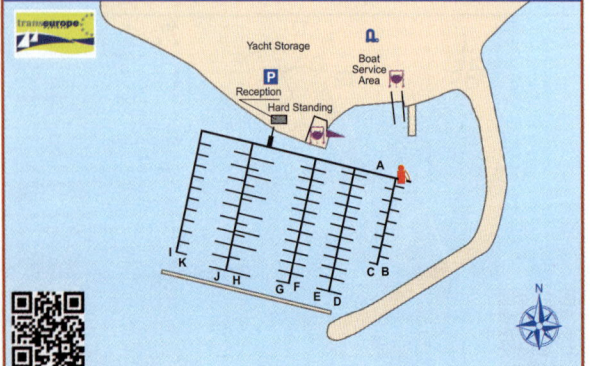

SANDPOINT MARINA

Sandpoint Marina Ltd
Sandpoint, Woodyard Road, Dumbarton, G82 4BG
Tel: 01389 762396 Fax: 01389 732605
Email: sales@sandpoint-marina.co.uk
www.sandpoint-marina.co.uk

VHF
ACCESS HW±3

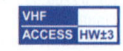

Lying on the north bank of the Clyde estuary on the opposite side of the River Leven from Dumbarton Castle, Sandpoint Marina provides easy access to some of the most stunning cruising grounds in the United Kingdom. It is an independently run marina, offering a professional yet personal service to every boat owner. Among the facilities to hand are an on site chandlery, storage areas, a 40 ton travel hoist and 20 individual workshop units.

Within a 20-minute drive of Glasgow city centre, the marina is situated close to the shores of Loch Lomond, the largest fresh water loch in Britain.

FACILITIES AT A GLANCE

Key
a Marina office
b Workshops
c Undercover storage shed

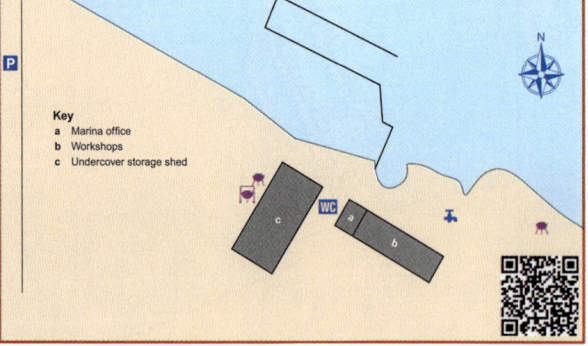

MARINA GUIDE 2026

SOUTH WEST SCOTLAND — AREA 9

KIP MARINA

Kip Marina, The Yacht Harbour
Inverkip, Renfrewshire, Scotland, PA16 0AS
Tel: 01475 521485
www.kipmarina.co.uk Email: info@kipmarina.co.uk

VHF Ch 80
ACCESS H24

Inverkip is a small village which lies on the south shores of the River Kip as it enters the Firth of Clyde. Once established for fishing, smuggling and, in the 17th century, witch-hunts, it became a seaside resort in the 1860s as a result of the installation of the railway. Today it is a yachting centre, boasting a state-of-the-art marina with over 600 berths and full boatyard facilities. With the capacity to accommodate yachts of up to 23m LOA, Kip Marina offers direct road and rail access to Glasgow and its international airport, therefore making it an ideal location for either a winter lay up or crew changeover.

FACILITIES AT A GLANCE

Key
a Reception and chandlery
b Workshop and contractors
c Chartroom bar and restaurant

JAMES WATT DOCK MARINA

James Watt Dock Marina
East Hamilton Street
Greenock, Renfrewshire, PA15 2TD
Tel: 01475 729838
www.jwdmarina.co.uk Email: info@jwdmarina.co.uk

VHF 80
ACCESS H24

James Watt Dock Marina offers around 170 berths alongside or on finger pontoons for craft ranging in size from 7m to 100+m within a historic dock setting. With excellent motorway and public transport connections and easy access to some of the best sailing waters at all states of tide, James Watt Dock Marina provides unbeatable opportunities for boaters

The marina is a short distance from Greenock's cinema, pool, ice rink, restaurants and shops, and with nearby transport connections, the marina will be a great location for both visitors and regular berthers.

FACILITIES AT A GLANCE

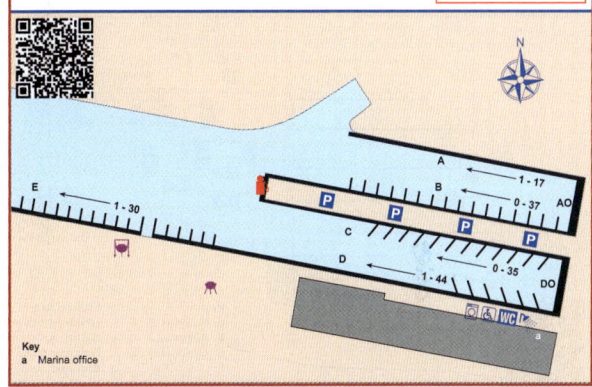

Key
a Marina office

Wherever you want to go, the legendary Jimmy Cornell's books will help you get there

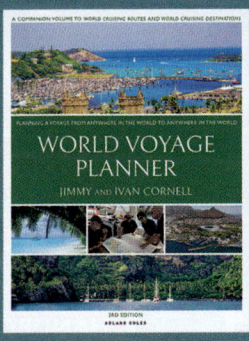
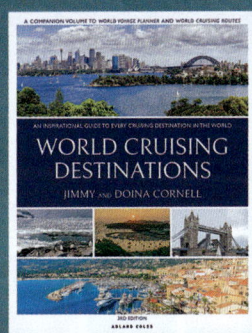
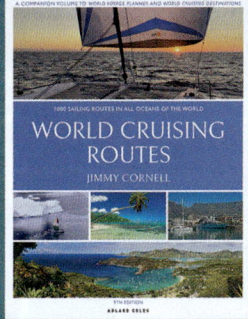

'The bible of cruising sailors … the definitive reference book for long distance navigators'

YACHTING LIFE

www.adlardcoles.com

MARINA GUIDE 2026

MARINAS & SERVICES

LARGS YACHT HAVEN

Largs Yacht Haven Ltd
Irvine Road, Largs, Ayrshire, KA30 8EZ
Tel: 01475 675333
Email: largs@yachthavens.com www.yachthavens.com

VHF Ch M, 80
ACCESS H24

Largs Yacht Haven offers a superb location among lochs and islands, with numerous fishing villages and harbours nearby. Sheltered cruising can be enjoyed in the inner Clyde, while the west coast and Ireland are only a day's sail away. With a stunning backdrop of the Scottish mountains, Largs incorporates 700 fully serviced berths and provides a range of on site facilities including chandlers, sailmakers, engineers, shops, restaurants and club.

A 20-minute coastal walk brings you to the town of Largs, which has all the usual amenities as well as excellent road and rail connections to Glasgow.

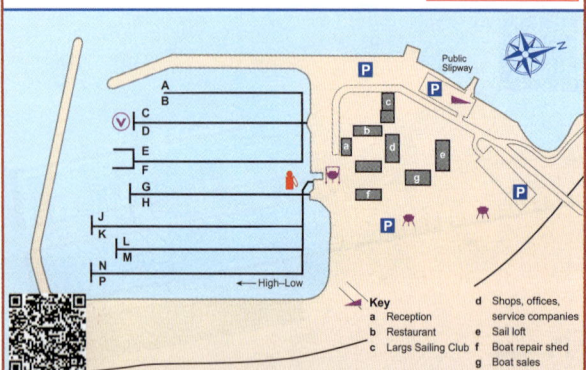

CLYDE MARINA

Clyde Marina Ltd
The Harbour, Ardrossan, Ayrshire, KA22 8DB
Tel: 01294 607077 Fax: 01294 607076
www.clydemarina.com Email: info@clydemarina.com

VHF Ch 80
ACCESS H24

Situated on the Clyde Coast between Irvine and Largs, Clyde Marina is Scotland's third largest marina and boatyard. It is set in a landscaped environment boasting a 50T hoist and active boat sales. A deep draft marina berthing vessels up to 30m LOA, draft up to 5m. Peviously accommodated vessels include tall ships and Whitbread 60s plus a variety of sail and power craft. Fully serviced pontoons plus all the yard facilities you would expect from a leading marina including boatyard and boatshed for repairs or storage. Good road and rail connections and only 30 minutes from Glasgow and Prestwick airports.

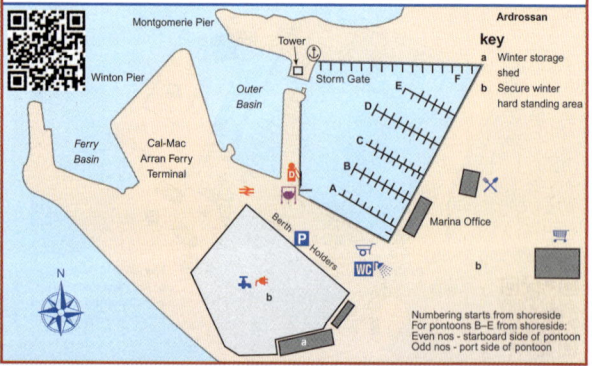

Your **essential pocket references** to everything you need to know onboard

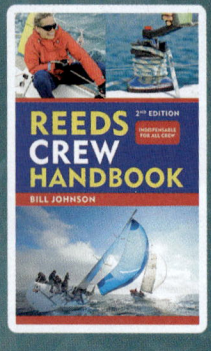 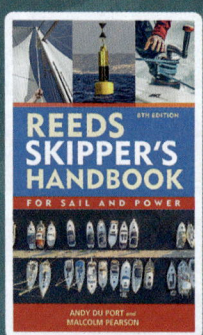 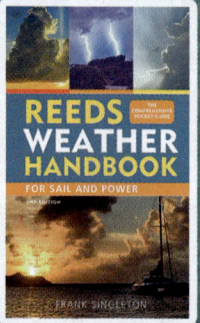 

www.adlardcoles.com

72 MARINA GUIDE 2026

SOUTH WEST SCOTLAND

AREA 9

TROON YACHT HAVEN

Troon Yacht Haven Ltd
The Harbour, Troon, Ayrshire, KA10 6DJ
Tel: 01292 315553
Email: troon@yachthavens.com
www.yachthavens.com

VHF Ch 80
ACCESS H24

Troon Yacht Haven, situated on the Southern Clyde Estuary, benefits from deep water at all states of the tide. Tucked away in the harbour of Troon, it is well sheltered and within easy access of the town centre.

There are plenty of cruising opportunities to be had from here, whether it be hopping across to the Isle of Arran, with its peaceful anchorages and mountain walks, sailing round the Mull or through the Crinan Canal to the Western Isles, or heading for the sheltered waters of the Clyde.

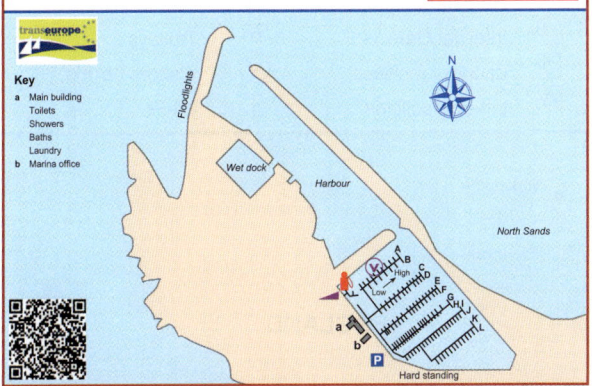

STRANRAER MARINA

Stranraer Marina
West Pier, Market Street, Stranraer, DG9 7RE
Tel: 01776 706565 Mob: 07734 073421
Email: lesley.smith@dumgal.gov.uk

VHF Ch 14
ACCESS H24

Stranraer Marina is at the southern end of beautiful Loch Ryan with 24H access and modern facilities with a 30T boat crane, transporter and hardstanding available. The visitor berths are those immediately adjacent to the breakwater. Craft over 12m are advised to call ahead for availability.

Stranraer town centre is only a short walk from the marina. Berthing rates are available at www.dumgal.gov.uk/harbours. It should be noted that the marina is exposed in strong N winds. Two ferry terminals are located on the E side of the loch approximately 6M N of the marina and extra care should be taken in this area.

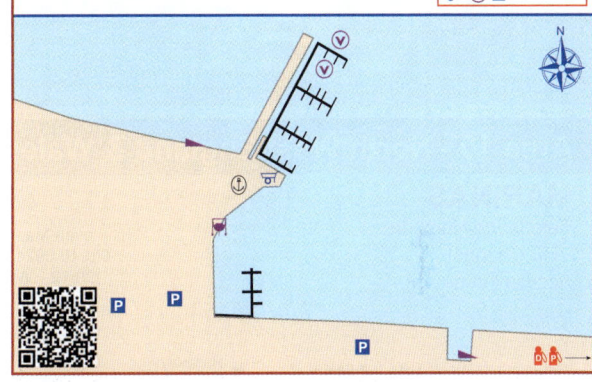

KIRKCUDBRIGHT MARINA

Kirkcudbright Marina
HM Office, Harbour Square, Kirkcudbright, DG6 4HY
Tel: 01557 331135 Mob: 07709 479663
Email: robbie.garside@dumgal.gov.uk

VHF Ch 16, 73
ACCESS HW±2.5

A very well sheltered picturesque marina accessed HW+/-2.5 hrs via a 3.5 mile long, narrow channel that is well marked and lit, contact should be made with Range Safety vessel 'Gallovidian' prior to approach. Limited visitors berths so vessels should contact the harbour master in advance.

The marina is only 250m from the centre of Kirkcudbright, an historic 'artist's' town where visitors may enjoy a wide range of facilities and tourist attractions including castle, museum, tollbooth, art galleries and traditional shops. There is a superb programme of summer festivities.

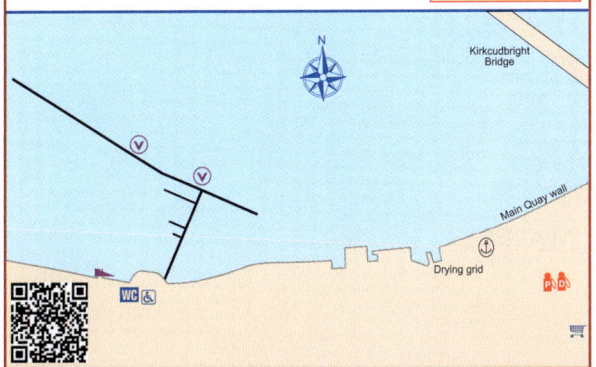

MARYPORT MARINA

Maryport Harbour and Marina Ltd
Marine Road, Maryport, Cumbria, CA15 8AY
Tel: 01900 814431
www.maryportmarina.com
Email: enquiries@maryportmarina.com

VHF Ch 12,16
ACCESS HW±2.5

Maryport Marina is located in the historic Senhouse Dock, which was originally built for sailing clippers in the late 19th century. The old stone harbour walls provide good shelter to the 190 berths from the prevailing south westerlies.

Maryport town centre and its shops, pubs and other amenities is within easy walking distance from the marina. Maryport a perfect location from which to explore the west coast of Scotland as well as the Isle of Man and the Galloway Coast. For those who wish to venture inland, then the Lake District is only seven miles away.

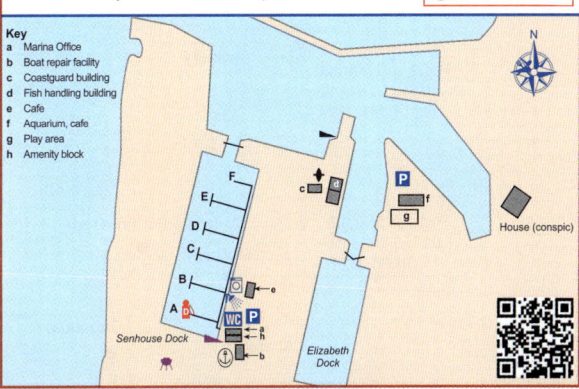

MARINAS & SERVICES

NW ENGLAND, ISLE OF MAN & N WALES – Mull of Galloway to Bardsey Is

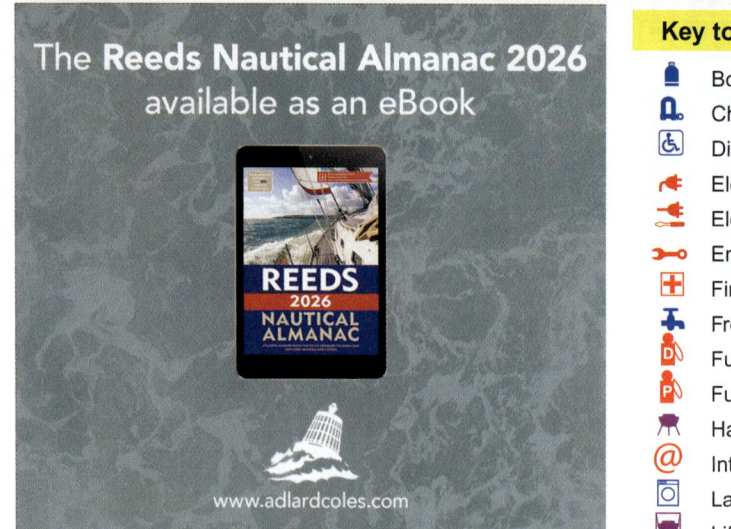

Key to Marina Plans symbols

- Bottled gas
- Chandler
- Disabled facilities
- Electrical supply
- Electrical repairs
- Engine repairs
- First Aid
- Fresh Water
- Fuel - Diesel
- Fuel - Petrol
- Hardstanding/boatyard
- Internet Café
- Laundry facilities
- Lift-out facilities
- Parking
- Pub/Restaurant
- Pump out
- Rigging service
- Sail repairs
- Shipwright
- Shop/Supermarket
- Showers
- Slipway
- Toilets
- Telephone
- Trolleys
- Visitors berths
- Wi-Fi

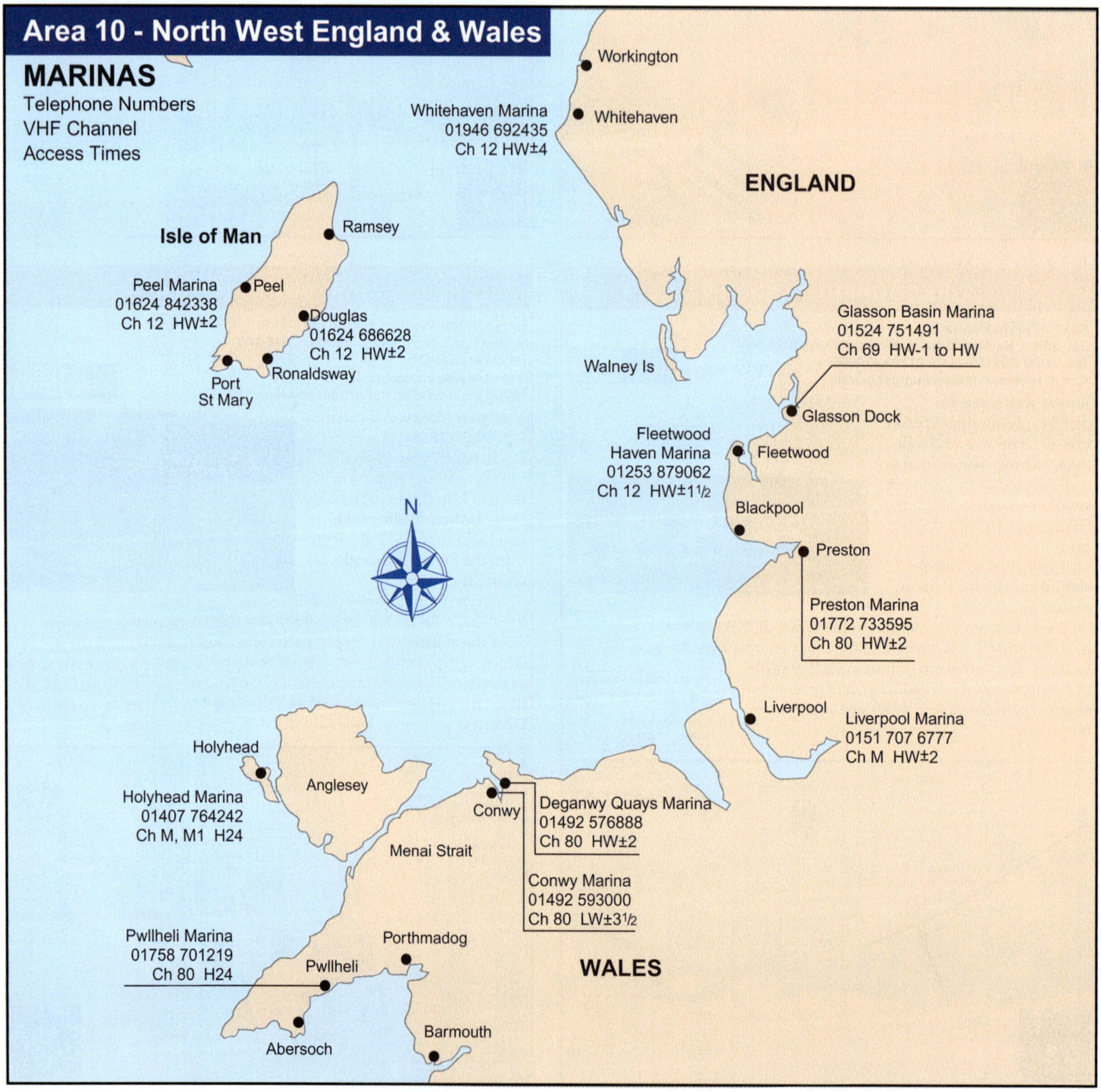

Area 10 - North West England & Wales

MARINAS
Telephone Numbers
VHF Channel
Access Times

ENGLAND

Workington

Whitehaven Marina
01946 692435
Ch 12 HW±4

Whitehaven

Isle of Man

Ramsey

Peel Marina
01624 842338
Ch 12 HW±2

Peel

Douglas
01624 686628
Ch 12 HW±2

Port St Mary   Ronaldsway

Walney Is

Glasson Basin Marina
01524 751491
Ch 69 HW-1 to HW

Glasson Dock

Fleetwood Haven Marina
01253 879062
Ch 12 HW±1½

Fleetwood

Blackpool

Preston

Preston Marina
01772 733595
Ch 80 HW±2

Liverpool

Liverpool Marina
0151 707 6777
Ch M HW±2

Holyhead

Holyhead Marina
01407 764242
Ch M, M1 H24

Anglesey

Conwy

Deganwy Quays Marina
01492 576888
Ch 80 HW±2

Menai Strait

Conwy Marina
01492 593000
Ch 80 LW±3½

Pwllheli Marina
01758 701219
Ch 80 H24

Pwllheli   Porthmadog

Abersoch   Barmouth

WALES

NORTH WEST ENGLAND AND NORTH WALES — AREA 10

WHITEHAVEN MARINA

Whitehaven Marina Ltd
Harbour Office, Bulwark Quay, Whitehaven, Cumbria, CA28 7HS
Tel: 01946 692345
Email: enquiries@whitehavenmarina.com
www.whitehavenmarina.com

VHF Ch 12
ACCESS HW±4

Whitehaven Marina can be found at the south-western entrance to the Solway Firth, providing a strategic departure point for those yachts heading for the Isle of Man, Ireland or Southern Scotland. The harbour is one of the more accessible ports of refuge in NW England, affording a safe entry in most weathers. The approach channel across the outer harbour is dredged to about 1.0m above chart datum, allowing entry into the inner harbour via a sea lock at around HW±4. Over 100 new walk ashore berths were installed in 2013.

Conveniently situated for visiting the Lake District, Whitehaven is an attractive Georgian town, renowned in the C18 for its rum and slave imports.

FACILITIES AT A GLANCE

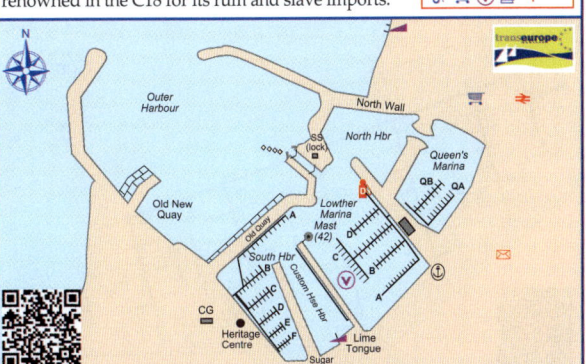

GLASSON WATERSIDE & MARINA

Glasson Waterside & Marina
School Lane, Glasson Dock, Lancaster, LA2 0AW
Tel: 01524 751491 Fax: 01524 752626
Email: glasson@aquavista.com
www.aquavista.com

VHF Ch 69
ACCESS HW-1 to HW

Glasson Basin Marina lies on the River Lune, west of Sunderland Point. Access is via the outer dock which opens 45 minutes before HW. Liverpool and thence via BWB lock into the inner basin. It is recommended to leave Lune No. 1 Buoy approx 1.5 hrs before HW. Contact the dock on Channel 69. The Marina can only be contacted by telephone. All the necessary requirements can be found either on site or within easy reach of Glasson Dock, including boat, rigging and sail repair services as well as a launderette, ablution facilities, shops and restaurants.

FACILITIES AT A GLANCE

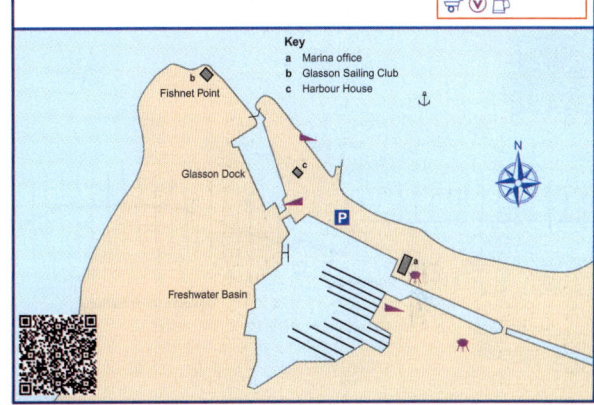

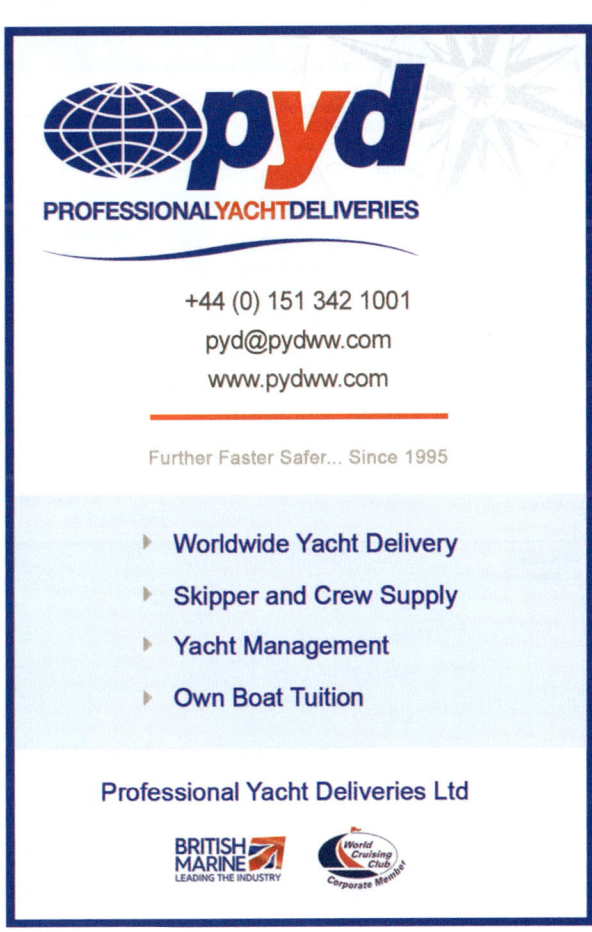

MARINA GUIDE 2026

DOUGLAS MARINA

Douglas Marina
Sea Terminal Building, Douglas, IM1 2RF
Tel: 01624 686628
www.gov.im/harbours/
Email: harbours@gov.im

VHF Ch 12, 16
ACCESS HW±2

Douglas Marina is accessible HW±2 with 2.5m retained at LW. The depth of water inside the marina can vary so please advise draft. The maximum length accommodated on pontoons is 15m. Wall berths are also available. Douglas Marina Operations Centre requires clearance for entrance to the outer harbour due to commercial traffic. Please inform arrival on VHF Ch 12 10 minutes before port entry.

The marina has many facilities including electricity, fresh water, diesel, lift out, drying pad, gas, chandlery and showers/toilet facilities.

Douglas Marina is in the heart of the Isle of Man's capital so all local amenities and transport links such as the Steam Railway just a short walk.

FACILITIES AT A GLANCE

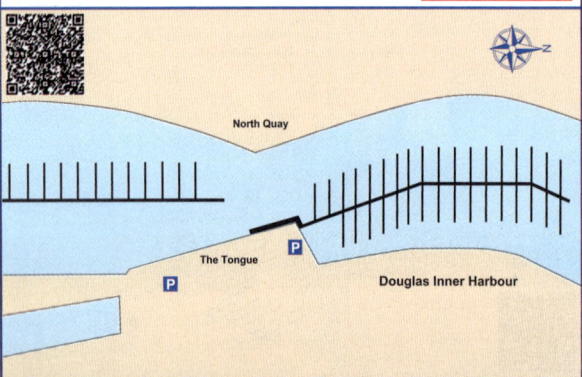

PEEL MARINA

Peel Marina
The Harbour Office, East Quay, Peel, IM5 1AR
Tel: 01624 842338 Fax: 01624 843610
www.gov.im/harbours/
Email: harbours@gov.im

VHF Ch 12
ACCESS HW±2

The Inner harbour has provision on pontoons for visiting vessels up 15m with rafting also available on the harbour walls. Access is available HW±2hrs with a maximum draft of 2.5m retained at low water but this does vary so please advise vessel dimensions on approach via VHF Ch 12.

Fresh water and electricity are available on all pontoon and some wall berths. Diesel fuel is available at the quayside with petrol sourced from a local forecourt in Peel.

Peel is a lovely active fishing port with many local amenities and a beautiful castle overlooking the harbour.

FACILITIES AT A GLANCE

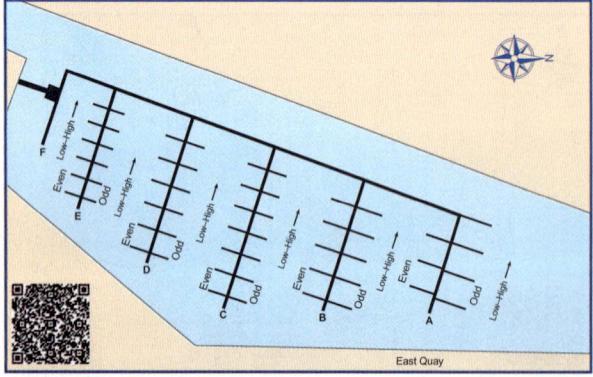

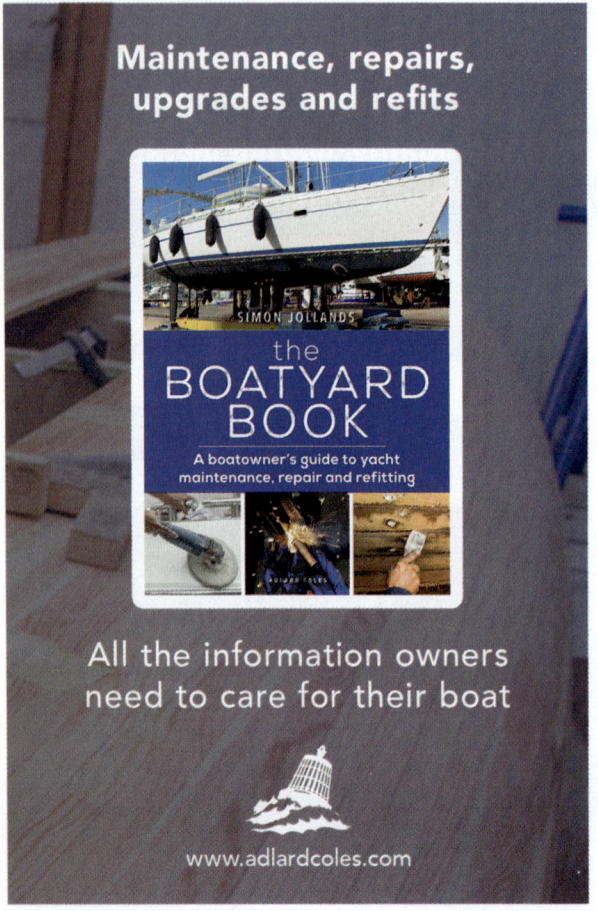

FLEETWOOD BEACON MARINA

Fleetwood Haven Marina
c/o ABP, Port & Marina Office, Fleetwood, FY7 8BP
Tel: 01253 879062 Fax: 01253 879063
Email: fleetwoodhaven@abports.co.uk

VHF Ch 12
ACCESS HW±1.5

Fleetwood Haven Marina provides a good location from which to cruise Morecambe Bay and the Irish Sea. To the north west is the Isle of Man, the north is the Solway Firth and the Clyde Estuary, while to the south west is Conwy, the Menai Straits and Holyhead.

Tucked away in a protected dock which dates to 1835, the marina has 182 full service berths and offers extensive facilities including a 75-tonne boat hoist, laundry and a first class shower/bathroom block.

Call Fleetwood Dock Radio on VHF Channel 12 (Tel 01253 872351) for permission to enter the dock channel.

FACILITIES AT A GLANCE

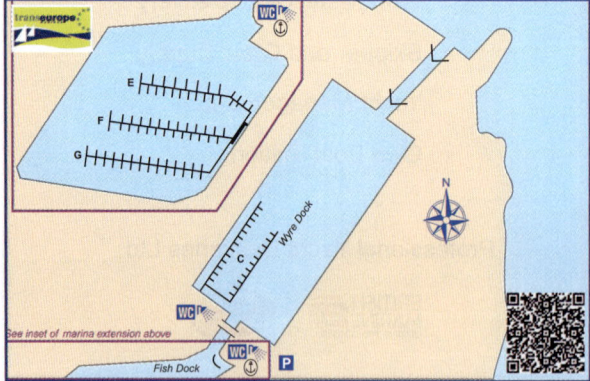

PRESTON MARINA

Preston Marine Services Ltd
The Boathouse, Navigation Way, Preston, PR2 2YP
Tel: 01772 733595
Email: info@prestonmarina.co.uk   www.prestonmarina.co.uk

VHF Ch 80
ACCESS HW±2

Preston Marina forms part of the comprehensive Riversway Docklands development, meeting all the demands of modern day boat owners. With the docks' history dating back over 100 years, today the marina comprises 40 acres of fully serviced pontoon berths sheltered behind the lock gates.

Lying 15 miles up the River Ribble, which itself is an interesting cruising ground with an abundance of wildlife, Preston is well placed for sailing to parts of Scotland, Ireland or Wales. The Docklands development includes a wide choice of restaurants, shops and cinemas as well as being in easy reach of all the cultural and leisure facilities provided by a large town.

FACILITIES AT A GLANCE

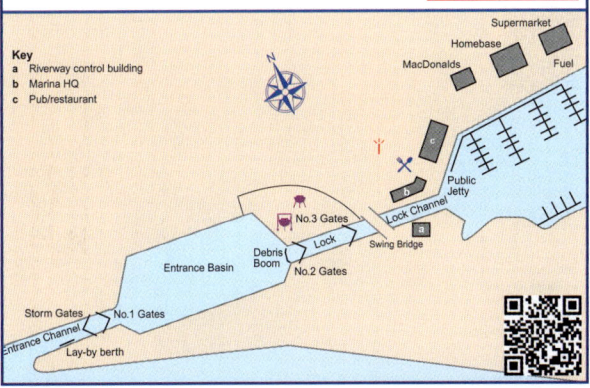

'It would be hard to imagine a more thoughtful, intelligent and companionable person to go to sea with than Paul Heiney'

— BILL BRYSON

www.adlardcoles.com

LIVERPOOL MARINA

Liverpool Marina
Coburg Wharf, Sefton Street, Liverpool, L3 4BP
Tel: 0151 707 6777   Fax: 0151 707 6770
Email: mail@liverpoolmarina.co.uk

VHF Ch M
ACCESS HW±2

Liverpool Marina is ideally situated for yachtsmen wishing to cruise the Irish Sea. Access is through a computerised lock that opens two and a half hours either side of high water between 0600 and 2200 daily. Once in the marina, you can enjoy the benefits of the facilities on offer, including a first class club bar and restaurant.

Liverpool is a thriving cosmopolitan city, with attractions ranging from numerous bars and restaurants to museums, art galleries and the Beatles Story.

FACILITIES AT A GLANCE

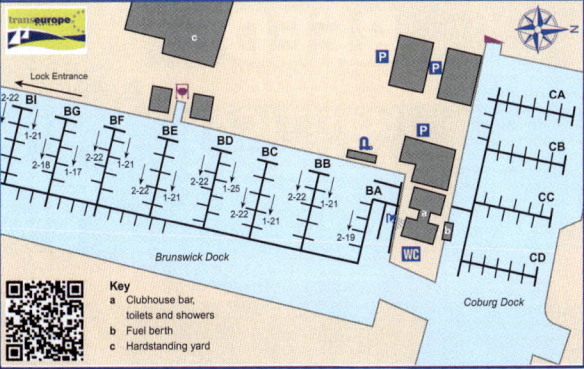

CONWY MARINA

Conwy Marina
Conwy, LL32 8EP
Tel: 01492 593000
Email: conwy@boatfolk.co.uk
www.boatfolk.co.uk/conwymarina

VHF Ch 80
ACCESS LW±3.5

Situated in an area of outstanding natural beauty, with the Mountains of Snowdonia National Park providing a stunning backdrop, Conwy is the first purpose-built marina to be developed on the north coast of Wales. Enjoying a unique site next to the 13th century Conwy Castle, the third of Edward I's great castles, it provides a convenient base from which to explore the cruising grounds of the North Wales coast. The unspoilt coves of Anglesey and the beautiful Menai Straits prove a popular destination, while further afield are the Llyn Peninsula and the Islands of Bardsey and Tudwells. The marina incorporates about 500 fully serviced berths which are accessible through a barrier gate at half tide.

FACILITIES AT A GLANCE

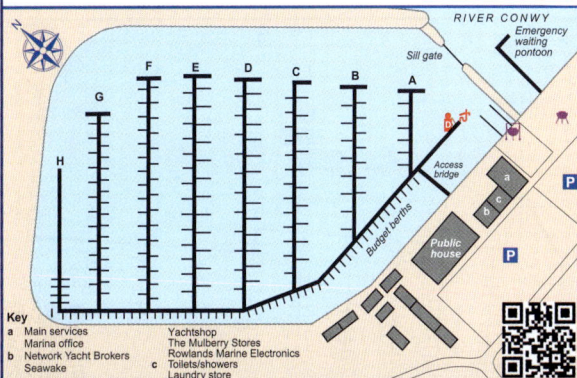

MARINAS & SERVICES

DEGANWY MARINA

Deganwy Marina
Deganwy, Conwy, LL31 9DJ
Tel: 01492 576888 Fax: 01492 580366
Email: enquiries@deganwymarina.co.uk
www.deganwymarina.co.uk

VHF	Ch 80
ACCESS	HW±3

Deganwy Marina is located in the centre of the north Wales coastline on the estuary of the Conwy River and sits between the river and the small town of Deganwy with the beautiful backdrop of the Vardre hills. The views from the marina across the Conwy River are truly outstanding with the medieval walled town and Castle of Conwy outlined against the foothills of the Snowdonia National Park.

Deganwy Marina has 165 fully serviced berths, which are accessed via a tidal gate between half tide and high water.

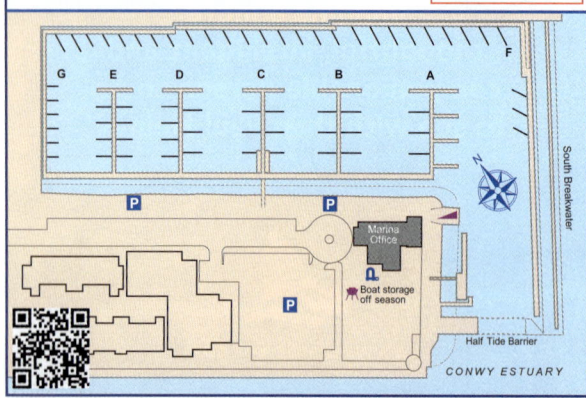

HOLYHEAD MARINA

Holyhead Marina Ltd
Newry Beach, Holyhead, Gwynedd, LL65 1YA
Tel: 01407 764242 Fax: 01407 769152
Email: info@holyheadmarina.co.uk

VHF	Ch M
ACCESS	H24

One of the few natural deep water harbours on the Welsh coast, Anglesey is conveniently placed as a first port of call if heading to N Wales from the N, S or W. The marina, destroyed in 2018 by Storm Emma, provides limited berthing on a single jetty and a number of mooring buoys. The Mountains and breakwaters give shelter from E through NW but N-NE'ly winds give rise to uncomfortable swell. The re-build has been delayed by competing plans for waterside development. Call ahead for berth/mooring which are in high demand.

Anglesey boasts numerous picturesque anchorages and beaches in addition to striking views over Snowdonia, while only a tide or two away are the Isle of Man and Eire.

PWLLHELI MARINA

Pwllheli Marina
Glan Don, Pwllheli, North Wales, LL53 5YT
Tel: 01758 701219
Email: hafanpwllheli@gwynedd.llwy.cymru

VHF	Ch 80
ACCESS	

Pwllheli is an old Welsh market town providing the gateway to the Llyn Peninsula, which stretches out as far as Bardsey Island to form an 'Area of Outstanding Natural Beauty'. Enjoying the spectacular backdrop of the Snowdonia Mountains, Pwllheli's numerous attractions include an open-air market every Wednesday, 'Neuadd Dwyfor', offering a mix of live theatre and latest films, and beautiful beaches.

Pwllheli Marina is situated on the south side of the Llyn Peninsula. One of Wales' finest marinas and sailing centres, it has over 400 pontoon berths and excellent onshore facilities.

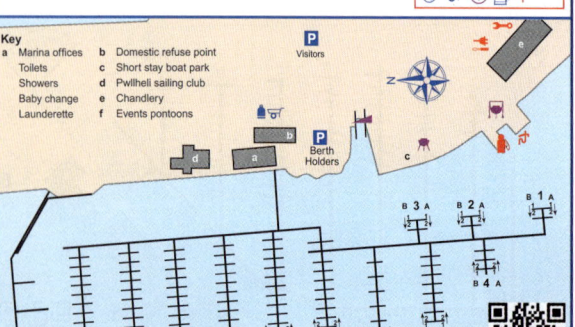

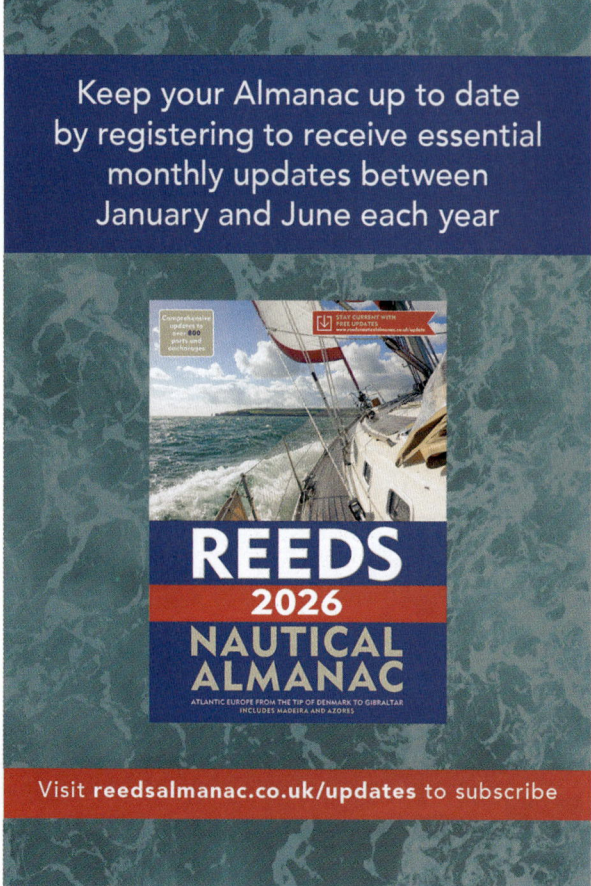

Keep your Almanac up to date by registering to receive essential monthly updates between January and June each year

Visit **reedsalmanac.co.uk/updates** to subscribe

AREA 11

SOUTH WALES & BRISTOL CHANNEL – Bardsey Island to Land's End

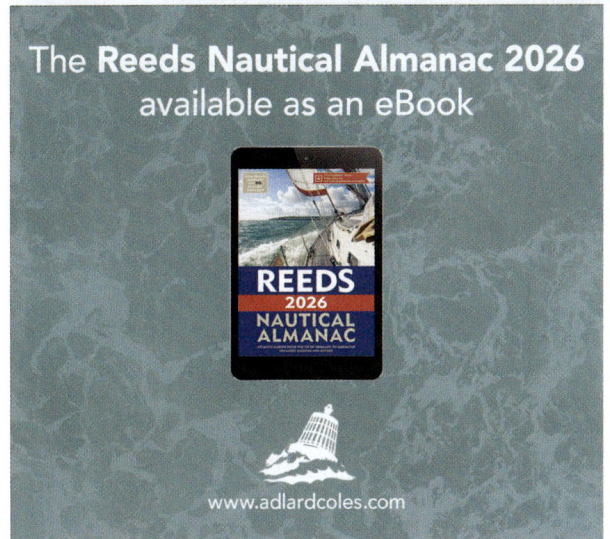

The **Reeds Nautical Almanac 2026** available as an eBook

www.adlardcoles.com

Key to Marina Plans symbols

	Bottled gas	P	Parking
	Chandler		Pub/Restaurant
	Disabled facilities		Pump out
	Electrical supply		Rigging service
	Electrical repairs		Sail repairs
	Engine repairs		Shipwright
	First Aid		Shop/Supermarket
	Fresh Water		Showers
D	Fuel - Diesel		Slipway
P	Fuel - Petrol	WC	Toilets
	Hardstanding/boatyard		Telephone
@	Internet Café		Trolleys
	Laundry facilities	V	Visitors berths
	Lift-out facilities		Wi-Fi

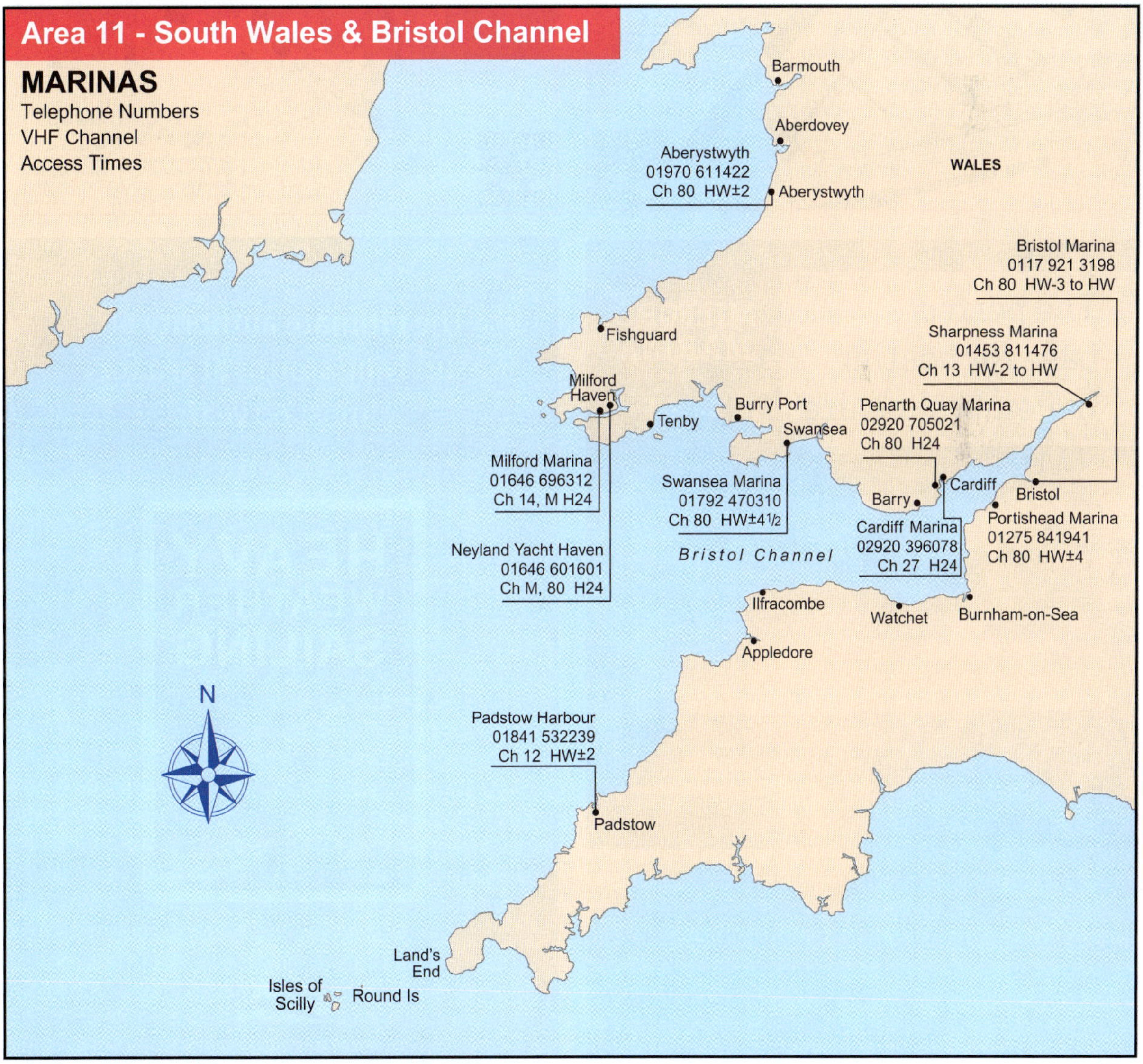

Area 11 - South Wales & Bristol Channel

MARINAS
Telephone Numbers
VHF Channel
Access Times

WALES

Barmouth

Aberdovey

Aberystwyth
01970 611422
Ch 80 HW±2
• Aberystwyth

• Fishguard

Milford Haven

Milford Marina
01646 696312
Ch 14, M H24

Neyland Yacht Haven
01646 601601
Ch M, 80 H24

Tenby

Burry Port

Swansea Marina
01792 470310
Ch 80 HW±4½

Swansea

Bristol Channel

Bristol Marina
0117 921 3198
Ch 80 HW-3 to HW

Sharpness Marina
01453 811476
Ch 13 HW-2 to HW

Penarth Quay Marina
02920 705021
Ch 80 H24

Cardiff

Barry

Cardiff Marina
02920 396078
Ch 27 H24

Bristol

Portishead Marina
01275 841941
Ch 80 HW±4

Ilfracombe

Watchet

Burnham-on-Sea

Appledore

Padstow Harbour
01841 532239
Ch 12 HW±2

Padstow

Land's End

Isles of Scilly

Round Is

MARINA GUIDE 2026

79

MARINAS & SERVICES

ABERYSTWYTH MARINA

Aberystwyth Marina
Trefechan, Aberystwyth, Ceredigion, SY23 1AS
Tel: 01970 611422
Email: info@westernmarinas.co.uk

VHF Ch 80
ACCESS HW±2

Aberystwyth Marina offers 165 first class berths providing safe, secure and sheltered moorings for motor boats and yachts.

The onsite chandlery has a selection of clothing, safety equipment, ropes, maintenance, navigation and electrical equipment. The brokerage has a range of motor boats and yachts for sale. In addition, the marina offers a range of boatyard and engine servicing. Other facilities include a slipway and 10t hoist.

Aberystwyth has a range of cafes, seaside fish and chip shops, restaurants, pubs and bars, many a short walk from the marina. The seafront, Promenade and pier is a great location for a walk and to look out over the Irish Sea.

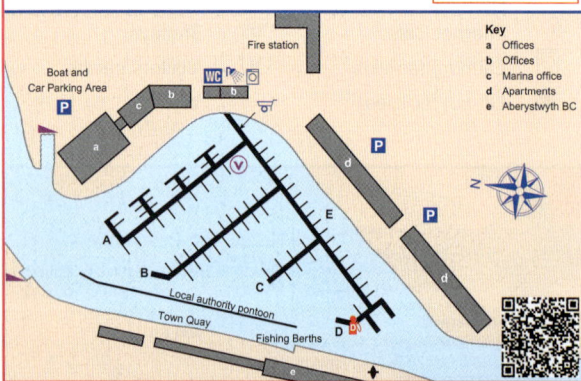

Key
a Offices
b Offices
c Marina office
d Apartments
e Aberystwyth BC

MILFORD MARINA

Milford Marina
Milford Docks, Milford Haven, Pembrokeshire, SA73 3AF
Tel: 01646 696312 Fax: 01646 696314
Email: enquiries@milfordmarina.com www.milfordmarina.com

VHF Ch 14
ACCESS H24

Set within one of the deepest natural harbours in the world, Milford Marina is situated in a non-tidal basin within the UK's only coastal National Park, the ideal base for discovering the fabulous coastline in Pembrokeshire, Wales and Ireland. Continued investment has meant that the marina provides safe, secure and sheltered boat berths with a full range of shoreside facilities in the heart of SW Wales.

Accessed via an entrance lock (with waiting pontoons both inside and outside the lock), the marina is perfect for exploring the picturesque upper reaches of the River Cleddau or cruising out beyond St Ann's Head to the unspoilt islands of Skomer, Skokholm and Grassholm.

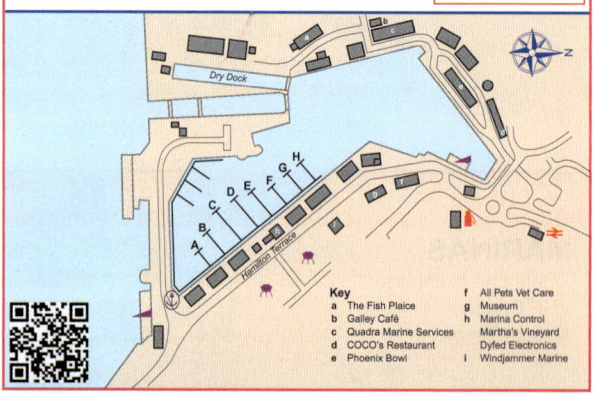

Key
a The Fish Plaice
b Galley Café
c Quadra Marine Services
d COCO's Restaurant
e Phoenix Bowl
f All Pets Vet Care
g Museum
h Marina Control
Martha's Vineyard
Dyfed Electronics
i Windjammer Marine

The perfect base for boating in Pembrokeshire

MILFORD MARINA
Berthing | Boatyard | Services

- Annual berthing
- Visitor berthing
- Short stay berths
- Fuel facilities

Call us today on 01646 696312
or visit www.milfordmarina.com

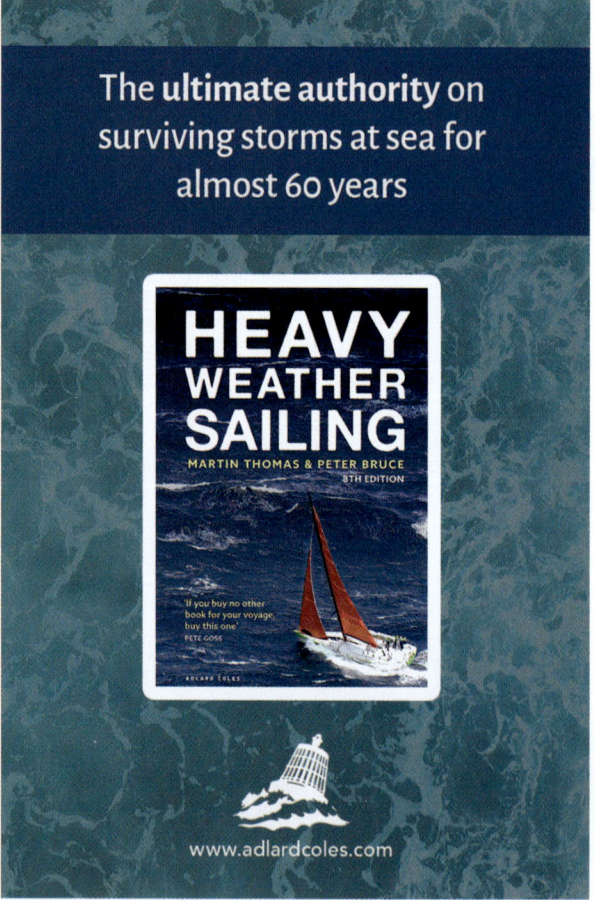

The **ultimate authority** on surviving storms at sea for almost 60 years

HEAVY WEATHER SAILING
MARTIN THOMAS & PETER BRUCE
8TH EDITION

'If you buy no other book for your voyage, buy this one'
PETE GOSS

www.adlardcoles.com

SOUTH WALES AND BRISTOL CHANNEL — AREA 11

NEYLAND YACHT HAVEN

Neyland Yacht Haven Ltd
Brunel Quay, Neyland, Pembrokeshire, SA73 1PY
Tel: 01646 601601
Email: neyland@yachthavens.com   www.yachthavens.com

VHF Ch M, 80
ACCESS H24

Approximately 10 miles from the entrance to Milford Haven lies Neyland Yacht Haven. Tucked away in a well protected inlet just before the Cleddau Bridge, this marina has 450 berths and can accommodate yachts up to 20m LOA with draughts of up to 2.0m. The marina is divided into two basins, with the lower one enjoying full tidal access, while entry to the upper one is restricted by a tidal sill. Visitor and annual berthing enquiries welcome.

Offering a comprehensive range of services, Neyland Yacht Haven is within a five minute walk of the town centre where the various shops and takeaways cater for most everyday needs; bicycle hire is also available. The Yacht Haven is a member of the TransEurope Group.

FACILITIES AT A GLANCE

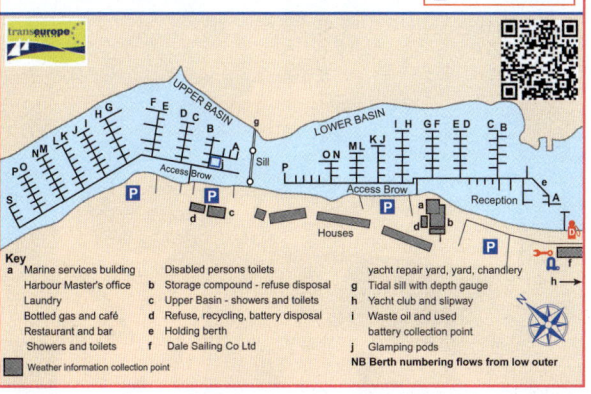

Key
a Marine services building
   Harbour Master's office
   Laundry
   Bottled gas and café
   Restaurant and bar
   Showers and toilets
b Disabled persons toilets
c Storage compound - refuse disposal
   Upper Basin - showers and toilets
d Refuse, recycling, battery disposal
e Holding berth
f Dale Sailing Co Ltd
   Weather information collection point
g yacht repair yard, yard, chandlery
   Tidal sill with depth gauge
h Yacht club and slipway
i Waste oil and used battery collection point
j Glamping pods
NB Berth numbering flows from low outer

NEYLAND Marine Services Ltd
Electronic & Electrical Engineers

We provide unequalled sales and service to the pleasure boating, fishing and shipping industry.

Your complete repair and supply service for electrical and electronic equipment, engineering installations and components.

Supply, service and dealers for most manufacturers.

Tel: 01646 600358
email: info@neylandmarine.co.uk
www.neylandmarine.co.uk

Unit 52 Honeyborough Business Park,
Neyland, Pembrokeshire SA73 1SE

SWANSEA MARINA

Swansea Marina
Lockside, Maritime Quarter, Swansea, SA1 1WG
Tel: 01792 470310   Fax: 01792 463948
www.swansea.gov.uk/swanseamarina
Email: swanmar@swansea.gov.uk

VHF Ch 80
ACCESS HW±4.5

At the hub of the city's redeveloped and award winning Maritime Quarter, Swansea Marina can be accessed HW±4½ hrs via a lock. Surrounded by a plethora of shops, restaurants and marine businesses to cater for most yachtsmen's needs, the marina is in close proximity to the picturesque Gower coast, where there is no shortage of quiet sandy beaches off which to anchor. It also provides the perfect starting point for cruising to Ilfracombe, Lundy Island, the North Cornish coast or West Wales.

Within easy walking distance of the marina is the city centre, boasting a covered shopping centre and market. For those who prefer walking or cycling, take the long promenade to the Mumbles fishing village from where there are plenty of coastal walks.

FACILITIES AT A GLANCE

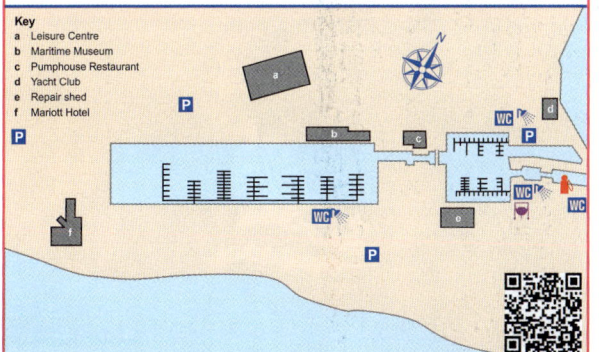

Key
a Leisure Centre
b Maritime Museum
c Pumphouse Restaurant
d Yacht Club
e Repair shed
f Mariott Hotel

CARDIFF MARINA

Cardiff Marina
Watkiss Way, Cardiff, CF11 0SY
Tel: 02920 396078
Email: info@westernmarinas.co.uk
www.westernmarinas.co.uk

VHF Ch M
ACCESS H24

A sheltered haven on the River Ely, Cardiff Marina offers 350 fully serviced berths within Cardiff Bay. Adjacent to Cardiff Marina, the waterside setting of Bayscape, a new mixed-use development of 115 apartments, is also home to the brand-new marina management suite, laundry and washrooms. The south facing terrace of the lounge bar, is a great location for berth holders to relax and unwind. Marina facilities also include a 50t Sealift, platform crane for mast work and brokerage. In addition, Cardiff Marine Village is home to Cardiff Marine Services, Wales' leading boatyard and refit and repair centre. The 3-acre site also has ample space for hard standing storage.

FACILITIES AT A GLANCE

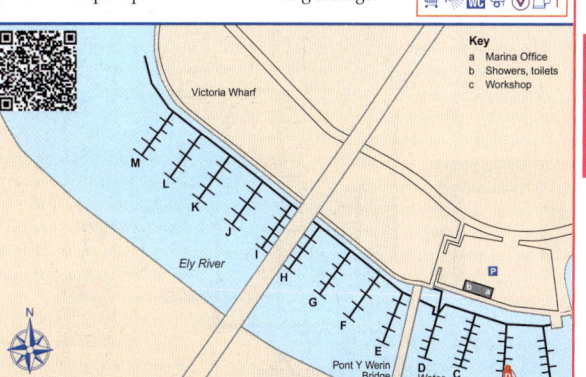

Key
a Marina Office
b Showers, toilets
c Workshop

MARINA GUIDE 2026

MARINAS & SERVICES

PENARTH MARINA

Penarth Marina
Penarth, Vale of Glamorgan, CF64 1TQ
Tel: 02920 705021
Email: penarth@boatfolk.co.uk
www.boatfolk.co.uk/penarthmarina

VHF Ch 80
ACCESS H24

Penarth Marina has been established in the historic basins of Penarth Docks for over 20 years and is the premier boating facility in the region. The marina is Cardiff Bay's only 5 Gold Anchor marina and provides an ideal base for those using the Bay and the Bristol Channel.

With 24hr access there is always water available for boating. Penarth and Cardiff boast an extensive range of leisure facilities, shops and restaurants making this marina an ideal base or destination. The marina has a blue flag and is a member of the TransEurope Group.

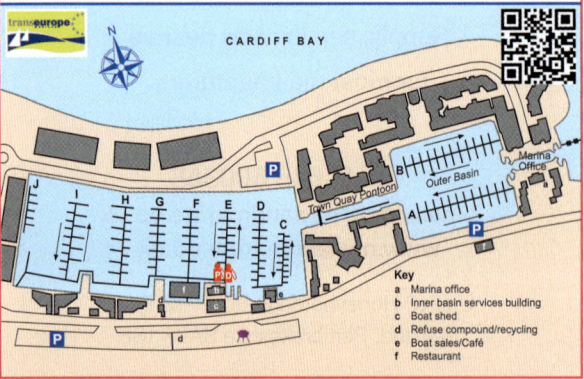

Key
a Marina office
b Inner basin services building
c Boat shed
d Refuse compound/recycling
e Boat sales/Café
f Restaurant

BRISTOL MARINA

Bristol Marina Ltd
Hanover Place, Bristol, BS1 6UH
Tel: 0117 921 3198
Email: info@bristolmarina.co.uk

VHF Ch 80
ACCESS HW-3 to HW

Situated in the heart of the city, Bristol is a fully serviced marina providing over 100 pontoon berths for vessels up to 20m LOA. Among the facilities are a new fuelling berth and pump out station as well as an on site chandler and sailmaker. It is situated on the south side of the Floating Harbour, about eight miles from the mouth of the River Avon. Accessible from seaward via the Cumberland Basin, passing through both Entrance Lock and Junction Lock, it can be reached approximately three hours before HW.

Shops, restaurants, theatres and cinemas are all within easy reach of the marina, while local attractions include the SS *Great Britain*, designed by Isambard Kingdom Brunel, and the famous Clifton Suspension Bridge, which has an excellent visitors' centre depicting its fascinating story.

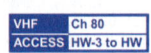

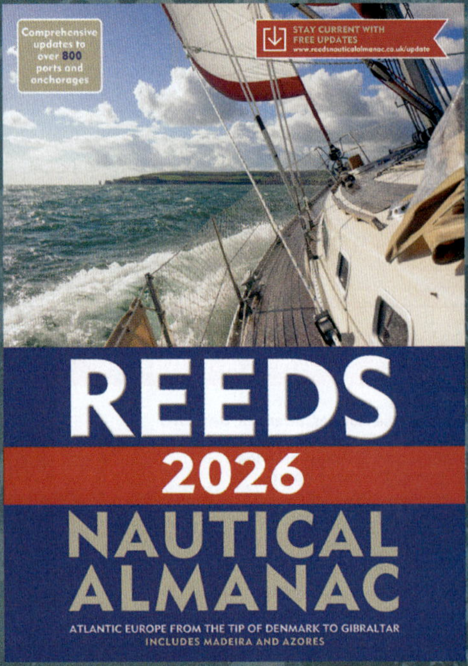

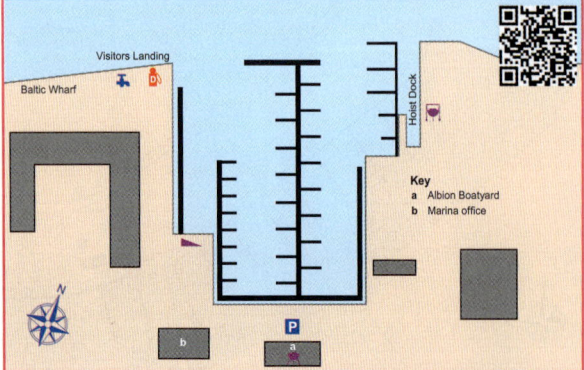

Key
a Albion Boatyard
b Marina office

SOUTH WALES AND BRISTOL CHANNEL — AREA 11

PORTISHEAD MARINA

Portishead Marina
Newfoundland Way, Portishead, North Somerset, BS20 7DF
Tel: 01275 841941
Email: portishead@boatfolk.co.uk
www.boatfolk.co.uk/portisheadmarina

VHF Ch 80
ACCESS HW±3.5

Portishead Marina is a popular destination for cruising in the Bristol Channel. Providing an excellent link between the inland waterways at Bristol and Sharpness and offering access to the open water and marinas down channel. The entrance to the marina is via a lock, with a minimum access of HW+/-3.5hrs. Contact the marina on Ch 80 ahead of time for next available lock. The marina provides 320 fully serviced berths and can accommodate vessels up to 40m LOA, draft up to 5.5m. The marina has a 35 tonnes boat hoist and the boatyard offers all the facilities you would expect from a boatfolk site.

FACILITIES AT A GLANCE

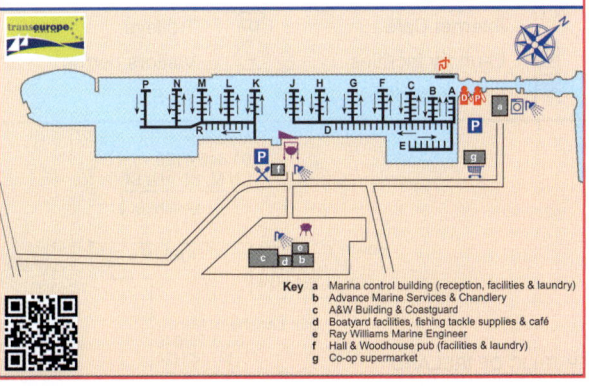

Key
a Marina control building (reception, facilities & laundry)
b Advance Marine Services & Chandlery
c A&W Building & Coastguard
d Boatyard facilities, fishing tackle supplies & café
e Ray Williams Marine Engineer
f Hall & Woodhouse pub (facilities & laundry)
g Co-op supermarket

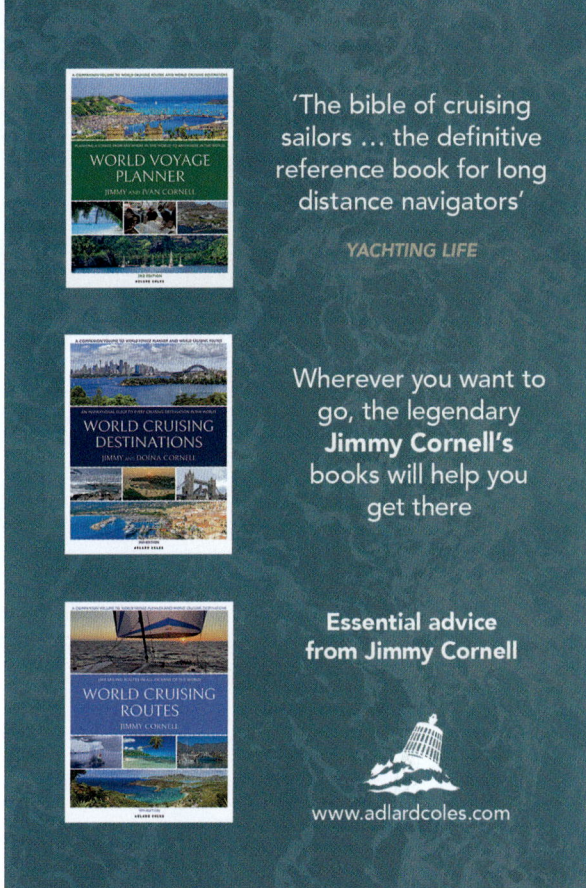

'The bible of cruising sailors ... the definitive reference book for long distance navigators'
YACHTING LIFE

Wherever you want to go, the legendary **Jimmy Cornell's** books will help you get there

Essential advice from Jimmy Cornell

www.adlardcoles.com

PADSTOW HARBOUR

Padstow Harbour Commissioners
The Harbour Office, Padstow, Cornwall, PL28 8AQ
Tel: 01841 532239
Email: padstowharbour@btconnect.com
www.padstow-harbour.co.uk

VHF Ch 12, 16
ACCESS HW±2

Padstow is a small commercial port with a rich history situated 1.5 miles from the sea within the estuary of the River Camel. The inner harbour is serviced by a tidal gate – part of the 1988–1990 flood defence scheme, which is open approximately two hours either side of high water. A minimum of 3m of water is maintained in the inner harbour at all times. Onshore facilities are excellent, please enquire at the Harbour Office.

This is a thriving fishing port, so perhaps it wasn't surprising that celebrity chefs like Rick Stein and Paul Ainsworth would set up shop in the town. This is a great resting point for everything Cornish from surf and coastal walks to fish and chips and cream teas.

FACILITIES AT A GLANCE

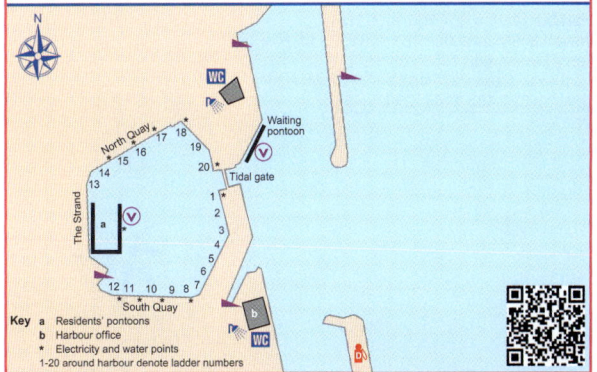

Key
a Residents' pontoons
b Harbour office
• Electricity and water points
1–20 around harbour denote ladder numbers

Padstow Harbour Commissoners

Contact Us

📍 The Harbour Office, Padstow, Cornwall, PL28 8AQ
📞 01841 532239
🌐 www.padstow-harbour.co.uk
✉ padstow.harbour@padstow-harbour.co.uk

Services include:
- Toilets, Laundry, Fuel, Water, Electric & CCTV Security
- Free WiFi access
- Inner harbour controlled by tidal gate, HW ± 2 hours
- Minimum depth in the Inner Harbour is 3 metres

MARINAS & SERVICES

SOUTH IRELAND – Malahide, clockwise to Liscannor Bay

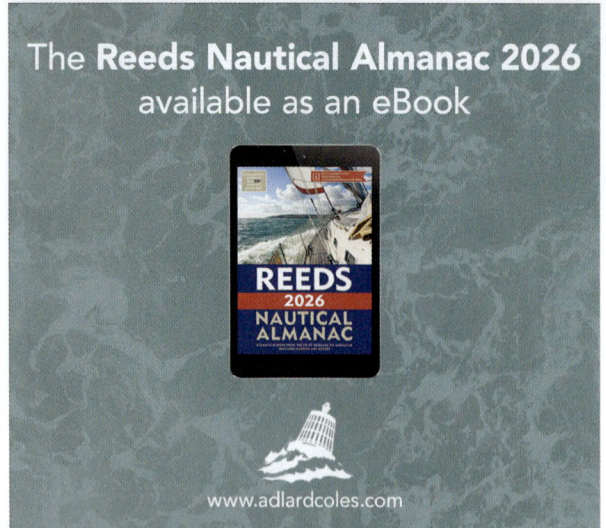

The Reeds Nautical Almanac 2026 available as an eBook

www.adlardcoles.com

Key to Marina Plans symbols

- Bottled gas
- Chandler
- Disabled facilities
- Electrical supply
- Electrical repairs
- Engine repairs
- First Aid
- Fresh Water
- Fuel - Diesel
- Fuel - Petrol
- Hardstanding/boatyard
- Internet Café
- Laundry facilities
- Lift-out facilities
- Parking
- Pub/Restaurant
- Pump out
- Rigging service
- Sail repairs
- Shipwright
- Shop/Supermarket
- Showers
- Slipway
- Toilets
- Telephone
- Trolleys
- Visitors berths
- Wi-Fi

Area 12 - South Ireland

MARINAS
Telephone Numbers
VHF Channel
Access Times

REPUBLIC OF IRELAND

Malahide
01 845 4129
Ch M, 80 HW±4

Howth YC Marina
01 839 2777
Ch M, 80 H24

Dun Laoghaire Marina
01202 0040
Ch M, 16 H24

Arklow Marina
087 237 5189 H24

New Ross Marina
086 388 9652
H24

Waterford City Marina
087 238 4944
H24

Kilmore Quay
053 912 9955
Ch 09, 16 H24

Cork Harbour Marina 087 366 9009 H24
Crosshaven BY Marina 021 483 1161 Ch M H24
East Ferry Marina 086 735 7785 H24
Royal Cork YC Marina 021 483 1023 Ch M H24
Salve Marine 021 483 1145 Ch M H24

Kinsale YC Marina
087 678 7377 Ch M H24
Castlepark Marina
021 477 4959 Ch 06 H24

Lawrence Cove
027 75044
Ch 16 H24

Bantry Harbour Marina
027 53277
Ch 14 H24

Cahersiveen Marina
066 947 2777
Ch M H24

Fenit Marina 066 713 6231 Ch M H24

Dingle Marina
087 925 4115
Ch M H24

Kilrush
065 905 2072
Ch 80 H24

SOUTH IRELAND — AREA 12

MALAHIDE MARINA

Malahide Marina
Malahide, Co. Dublin
Tel: +353 1 845 4129 Fax: +353 1 845 4255
Email: info@malahidemarina.net
www.malahidemarina.net

VHF: Ch M, 80
ACCESS: HW±4

Malahide Marina is a premier, fully serviced marina just 10 minutes from Dublin Airport and 20 minutes from Dublin's city centre. It accommodates up to 350 yachts, with the capacity to handle vessels up to 50m in length.

The marina boasts first-class facilities, including a boatyard with hard standing for approximately 170 boats and a 40-ton mobile hoist. In addition to berthing, there are comprehensive boat repair and maintenance services, including hull cleaning, antifouling, engine servicing, electrical repairs, fiberglass and gel coat repairs, rigging inspections, and general upkeep.

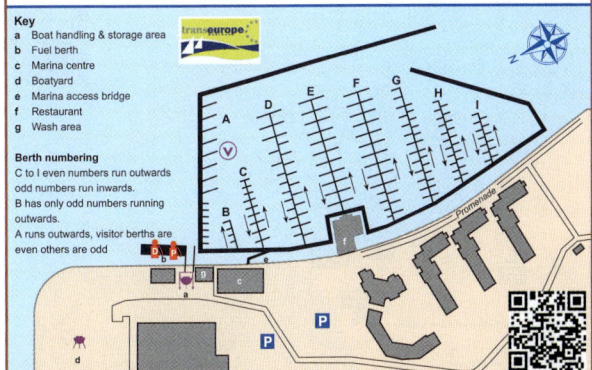

HOWTH MARINA

Howth Marina
Howth Marina, Harbour Road, Howth, Co. Dublin
Tel: +353 1 8392777 Fax: +353 1 8392430
Email: marina@hyc.ie
www.hyc.ie

VHF: Ch M, 80
ACCESS: H24

Based on the north coast of the rugged peninsula that forms the northern side of Dublin Bay, Howth Marina is ideally situated for north or south-bound traffic in the Irish Sea. Well sheltered in all winds, it can be entered at any state of the tide. Overlooking the marina is Howth Yacht Club, which has in recent years been expanded and is now said to be the largest yacht club in Ireland. With good road and rail links, Howth is in easy reach of Dublin's airport and ferry terminal, making it an obvious choice for crew changeovers.

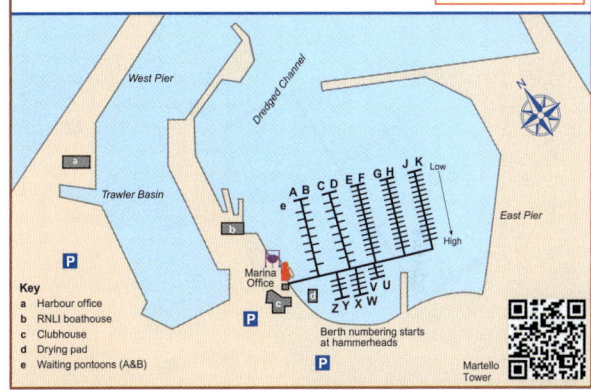

DUN LAOGHAIRE MARINA

Dun Laoghaire Marina
Harbour Road, Dun Laoghaire, Co Dublin, Ireland
Tel: +353 1 202 0040
Email: info@dlmarina.com   www.dlmarina.com

VHF: Ch M, 16
ACCESS: H24

Dun Laoghaire Marina – Gateway to Dublin and the first marina in the Republic of Ireland to be awarded five Gold anchors by THYA and also achieved the ICOMIA 'Clean Marina' accreditation – is the largest marina in Ireland. 24 hour access in all weather conditions. The town centre is located within 400m. Serviced berthing for 820 boats from 6m to 23m with visitors mainly on the hammerheads.

Larger vessels up to 46m and 160 tonnes can be berthed alongside breakwater pontoons. Minimum draft is 4.0m LWS. Three phase power is available. With Dublin rail station 12km and airport 35km, this is an ideal base for Irish culture and entertainment, as well as crew changes etc. Easy access to Dublin Bay, home to the biennial Dun Laoghaire Regatta.

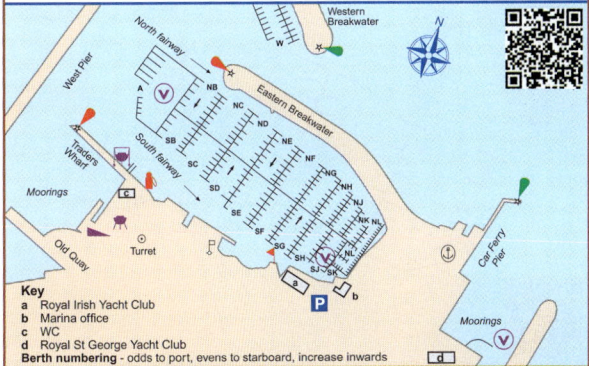

ARKLOW MARINA

Arklow Marina
North Quay, Arklow, Co. Wicklow, Ireland
Mobiles: +353 87 2375189 or + 353 87 2588078
Email: niallotoole61@gmail.com
www.arklowmarina.com

VHF:
ACCESS: H24

Arklow is a popular fishing port and seaside town situated at the mouth of the River Avoca, 16 miles S of Wicklow and 11 miles NE of Gorey. The town is ideally situated for visiting the many beauty spots of Co Wicklow including, Avondale, Glendalough, Glenmalure and Avoca. Activities suitable for children nearby include Clara Lara Fun Park and Avondale Beyond the Trees. There are bus and train services within walking distance, along with shops, restaurants and bars.

Arklow Marina is on the north bank of the river just upstream of the commercial quays, with 4 berths in an inner harbour and 30 berths on pontoons outside the marina entrance. Vessels over 14m LOA should moor on the river pontoons.

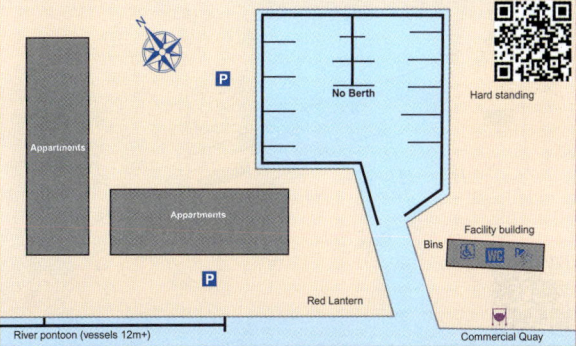

MARINA GUIDE 2026

MARINAS & SERVICES

NEW ROSS MARINA

New Ross Marina
The Tholsel, Quay Street, New Ross, Co Wexford, Y34 CF64
Tel: +353 87 9083456
www.newrossmarina.com
Email: newrossmarina@wexfordcoco.ie

VHF Ch 14
ACCESS H24

Situated on the River Barrow, the New Ross Marina is an ideal base for those sailing the south and east of Ireland. A 60-berth marina located 18M from Hook Head, New Ross is a short hop from Kilmore Quay, Dunmore East and Waterford City Marinas.

The River Barrow is the second longest river in Ireland and an important link to the Inland Waterways Network throughout the island, connecting New Ross to Dublin, Limerick, Carrick on Shannon, Enniskillen and the NW. The replica famine ship Dunbrody is a stroll up the quays, and the Kennedy Homestead just a few miles down the road.

FACILITIES AT A GLANCE

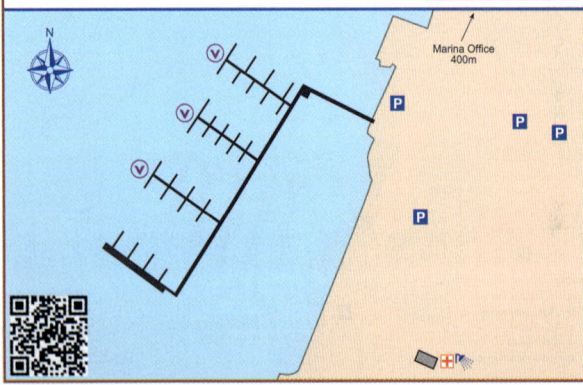

KILMORE QUAY

Kilmore Quay
Wexford, Ireland
Tel: +353 53 9129955 www.kilmorequaymarina.com
Email: assistant.marineofficer@wexfordcoco.ie

VHF Ch 09, 16
ACCESS H24

Located in the SE corner of Ireland, Kilmore Quay is a small rural fishing village situated approximately 14 miles from the town of Wexford and 12 miles from Rosslare ferry port.

Its 55-berthed marina, offering shelter from the elements as well as various on shore facilities, including diesel available 24/7, has become a regular port of call for many cruising yachtsmen. With several nearby areas of either historical or natural significance accessible using local bike hire, Kilmore is renowned for its 'green' approach to the environment.

FACILITIES AT A GLANCE

Key
a Harbour master's office - onshore facilities
b Lifeboat station
c Information board
d Stella Maris - community centre

WATERFORD CITY MARINA

Waterford City Marina
Waterford, Ireland
Tel: +353 87 2384944
Email: jcodd@waterfordcouncil.ie

VHF
ACCESS H24

Famous for its connections with Waterford Crystal, manufactured in the city centre, Waterford is the capital of the SE region of Ireland. As a major city, it benefits from good rail links with Dublin, and Limerick, a regional airport with daily flights to Britain and an extensive bus service to surrounding towns and villages. The marina is found on the banks of the River Suir, in the heart of this historic Viking city dating back to the ninth century. Yachtsmen can make the most of Waterford's wide range of shops, restaurants and bars without having to walk too far from their boats. With 100 fully serviced berths and first rate security, Waterford City Marina now provides shower, toilet and laundry facilities in its new reception building.

FACILITIES AT A GLANCE

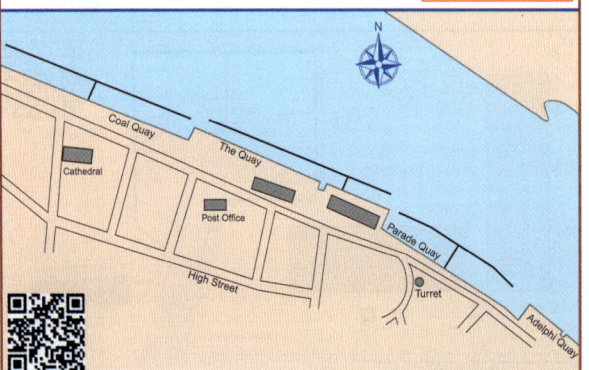

CROSSHAVEN BOATYARD MARINA

Crosshaven Boatyard Marina
Crosshaven, Co Cork, Ireland
Tel: +353 214 831161 Fax: +353 214 831603
Email: info@crosshavenboatyard.com

VHF Ch M
ACCESS H24

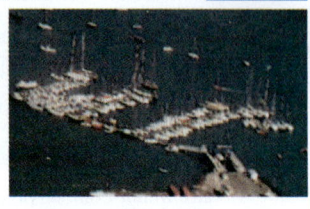

One of three marinas at Crosshaven, Crosshaven Boatyard was founded in 1950 and originally made its name from the construction of some of the most world-renowned yachts, including *Gypsy Moth* and Denis Doyle's *Moonduster*. Nowadays, however, the yard has diversified to provide a wide range of services to both the marine leisure and professional industries. Situated on a safe and sheltered river only 12 miles from Cork City Centre, the marina boasts 100 fully-serviced berths along with the capacity to accommodate yachts up to 35m LOA with a 4m draught. In addition, it is ideally situated for cruising the stunning south west coast of Ireland.

FACILITIES AT A GLANCE

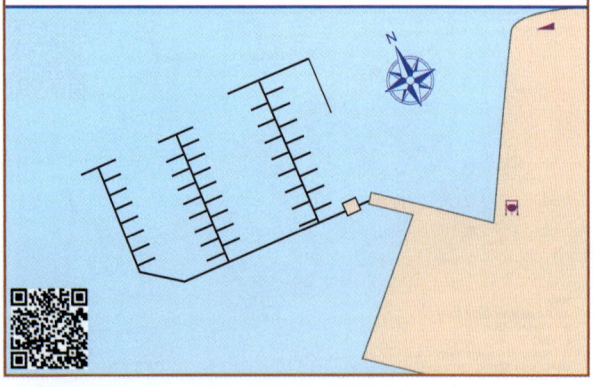

MARINA GUIDE 2026

SOUTH IRELAND — AREA 12

SALVE MARINE

Salve Marine
Crosshaven, Co Cork, Ireland
Tel: +353 21 483 1145 Fax: +353 21 483 1747
Email: salvemarineltd@gmail.com

VHF Ch M
ACCESS H24

Crosshaven is a picturesque seaside resort providing a gateway to Ireland's south and south west coasts. Offering a variety of activities to suit all types, its rocky coves and quiet sandy beaches stretch from Graball to Church Bay and from Fennell's Bay to nearby Myrtleville. Besides a selection of craft shops selling locally produced arts and crafts, there are plenty of pubs, restaurants and takeaways to suit even the most discerning of tastes. Lying within a few hundred metres of the village centre is Salve Marine, accommodating yachts up to 43m LOA with draughts of up to 4m. Its comprehensive services range from engineering and welding facilities to hull and rigging repairs.

FACILITIES AT A GLANCE

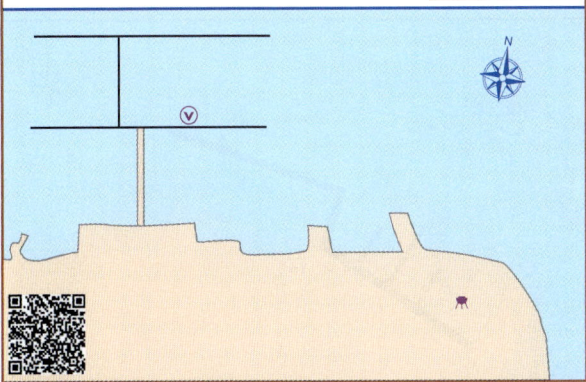

CORK HARBOUR MARINA

Cork Harbour Marina
Monkstown, Co Cork, Ireland
Tel: +353 87 366 9009
Email: info@corkharbourmarina.ie www.corkharbourmarina.ie

VHF
ACCESS H24

Located in the picturesque town of Monkstown, Cork Harbour Marina is in the heart of Cork Harbour. The marina can cater for all boat types with a draft of up to 7m and the marina is accessible at all phases of the tide.

Within strolling distance from the marina is the 'Bosun' restaurant and 'Napoli', an Italian delicatessen. There is also a sailing club, tennis club and golf club located nearby. Monkstown is just a short riverside walk from Passage West, with all the amenities one might require.

There is a frequent bus service from the marina gates to Cork City. Cork Harbour Marina is 15km from Cork International Airport.

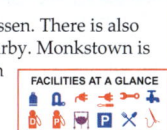

FACILITIES AT A GLANCE

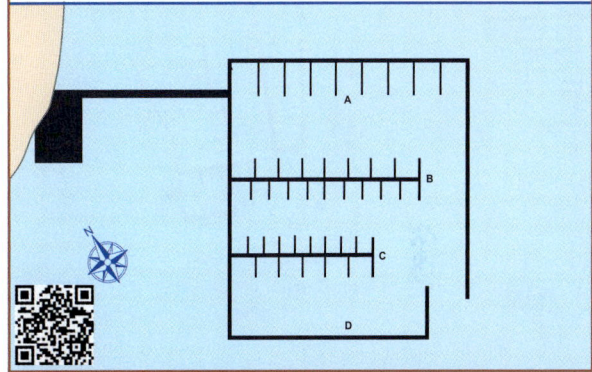

ROYAL CORK YACHT CLUB

Royal Cork Yacht Club Marina
Crosshaven, Co Cork, Ireland
Tel: +353 21 483 1023 Fax: +353 21 483 2657
Email: mark@royalcork.com   www.royalcork.com

VHF Ch M
ACCESS H24

Founded in 1720, the Royal Cork Yacht Club is the oldest and one of the most prominent yacht clubs in the world. Organising, among many other events, the prestigious biennial Volvo Cork Week, it boasts a number of World, European and national sailors among its membership.

The Yacht Club's marina is situated at Crosshaven, on the hillside at the mouth of the Owenabue River, just inside the entrance to Cork Harbour. The harbour is popular with yachtsmen as it is accessible and well sheltered in all weather conditions. It also benefits from the Gulf Stream producing a temperate climate practically all year round.

FACILITIES AT A GLANCE

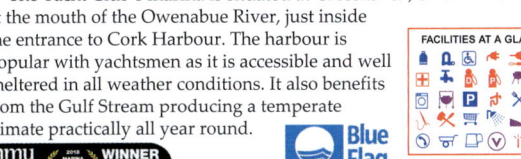

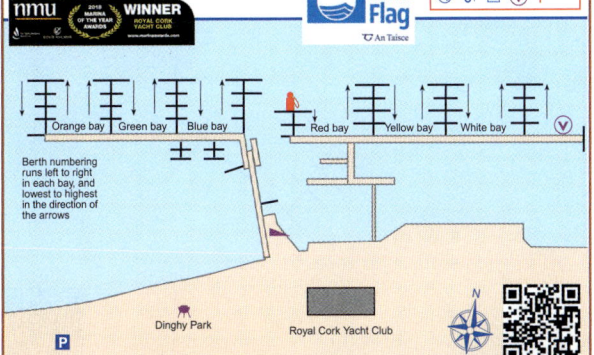

Your essential pocket references to everything you need to know onboard

www.adlardcoles.com

MARINA GUIDE 2026

MARINAS & SERVICES

KINSALE YACHT CLUB MARINA

Kinsale Yacht Club Marina
Kinsale, Co Cork, Ireland
Tel: +353 876 787377
Email: kyc@iol.ie

VHF Ch M
ACCESS H24

Kinsale is a natural, virtually land-locked harbour on the estuary of the Bandon River, approximately 12 miles south west of Cork harbour entrance. Home to a thriving fishing fleet as well as frequented by commercial shipping, it boasts two fully serviced marinas, with the Kinsale Yacht Club & Marina being the closest to the town. Visitors to this marina automatically become temporary members of the club and are therefore entitled to make full use of the facilities, which include a fully licensed bar and restaurant serving evening meals on Wednesdays, Thursdays and Saturdays. Fuel, water and repair services are also available.

FACILITIES AT A GLANCE

Pontoon Numbering
A Inner (odds) 1-55
A Outer (evens) 2-40
B Inner (odds) 1-49
B Outer (evens) 2-46
C Inner (odds) 1-47
C Outer (evens) 2-36
D Inner 1-19
E 3-29
F 1-17
G Visitors

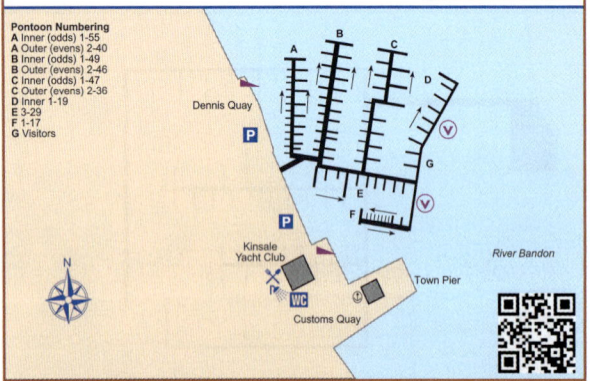

BANTRY HARBOUR MARINA

Bantry Harbour Marina
Wolfe Tone Square, Bantry, Co Cork, Ireland
Tel: +353 2753277
Email: harbourmaster@bantrybayport.com

VHF Ch 14
ACCESS H24

Bantry Harbour Marina is situated on the eastern most corner of Bantry Bay. Lying off Bantry town in Co. Cork on the southwest coast of Ireland the marina offers straightforward access on any state of the tide, The northern route round Whiddy Island is the preferred route with a deep-water channel marked by large lit navigational buoys.

The facilities at the Marina include toilets, EHU and rubbish/recycling disposal, you will also find a Petrol/Diesel garage with shop essentials 2 minutes away or it is only a 10min walk to the larger SuperValu supermarket, the main Bantry town is just a 5-minute walk away.

FACILITIES AT A GLANCE

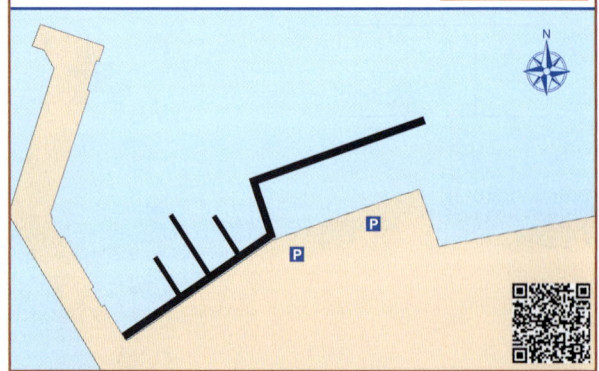

CASTLEPARK MARINA

Castlepark Marina Centre
Kinsale, Co Cork, Ireland
Tel: +353 21 4774959
Email: info@castleparkmarina.com

VHF Ch 16, 14
ACCESS H24

Situated on the south side of Kinsale Harbour, Castlepark is a small marina with deep water pontoon berths that are accessible at all states of the tide. Surrounded by rolling hills, it boasts its own beach as well as being in close proximity to the parklands of James Fort and a traditional Irish pub. The attractive town of Kinsale, with its narrow streets and slate-clad houses, lies just 1.5 miles away by road or five minutes away by ferry. Known as Ireland's 'fine food centre', it incorporates a number of gourmet food shops and high quality restaurants as well as a wine museum.

FACILITIES AT A GLANCE

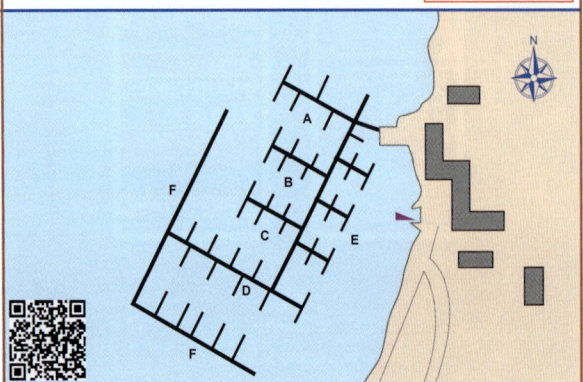

LAWRENCE COVE MARINA

Lawrence Cove Marina
Lawrence Cove, Bere Island, Co Cork, Ireland
Tel: +353 27 75044 mob: +353 879 125930
Email: rachelsherig@gmail.com
www.lawrencecovemarina.ie

VHF Ch 16
ACCESS H24

Lawrence Cove enjoys a peaceful location on an island at the entrance to Bantry Bay. Privately owned and run, it offers sheltered and secluded waters as well as excellent facilities and fully serviced pontoon berths. A few hundred yards from the marina you will find a shop, pub and restaurant, while the mainland, with its various attractions, can be easily reached by ferry. Lawrence Cove lies at the heart of the wonderful cruising grounds of Ireland's south west coast and, just two hours from Cork airport, is an ideal place to leave your boat for long or short periods.

FACILITIES AT A GLANCE

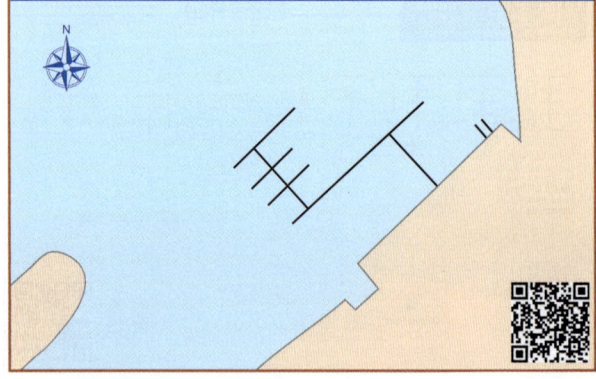

MARINA GUIDE 2026

SOUTH IRELAND — AREA 12

CAHERSIVEEN MARINA

Cahersiveen Marina
The Pier, Cahersiveen, Co. Kerry, Ireland
Tel: +353 66 9472777
Email: acardsiveen@gmail.com
www.cahersiveenmarina.ie

VHF Ch M, 80
ACCESS H24

Situated two miles up Valentia River from Valentia Harbour, Cahersiveen Marina is well protected in all wind directions and is convenient for sailing to Valentia Island and Dingle Bay as well as for visiting some of the spectacular uninhabited islands in the surrounding area. Boasting a host of sheltered sandy beaches, the region is renowned for salt and fresh water fishing as well as being good for scuba diving.

Within easy walking distance of the marina lies the historic town of Cahersiveen, incorporating an array of convivial pubs and restaurants.

FACILITIES AT A GLANCE

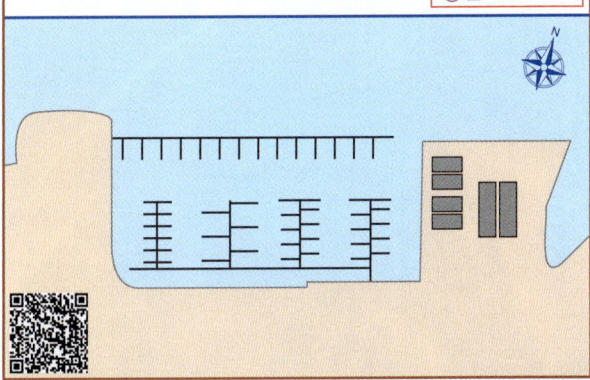

DINGLE MARINA

Dingle Marina
c/o Dingle Fishery Harbour Centre, Strand Street, Dingle, Co Kerry, Ireland
Tel: +353 (0)87 925 4115 Fax: +353 (0)69 5152546
Email: dingleharbour@agriculture.gov.ie
www.dinglemarina.ie

VHF Ch 14
ACCESS H24

Dingle is Ireland's most westerly marina, lying at the heart of the sheltered Dingle Harbour, and is easily reached both day and night via a well buoyed approach channel. The surrounding area is an interesting and unfrequented cruising ground, with several islands, bays and beaches for the yachtsman to explore.

The marina lies in the heart of the old market town, renowned for its hospitality and traditional Irish pub music. Besides enjoying the excellent seafood restaurants and 52 pubs, other recreational pastimes include horse riding, golf, climbing and diving.

FACILITIES AT A GLANCE

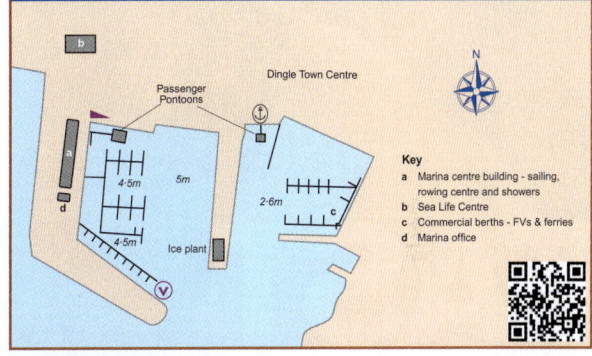

Key
a Marina centre building – sailing, rowing centre and showers
b Sea Life Centre
c Commercial berths – FVs & ferries
d Marina office

FENIT HARBOUR MARINA

Fenit Harbour & Marina
Fenit, Tralee, Co. Kerry, Republic of Ireland
Tel: +353 66 7136231 Fax: +353 66 7136473
Email: fenit.harbour@kerrycoco.ie www.kerrycoco.ie

VHF Ch M
ACCESS H24

Fenit Harbour Marina is tucked away in Tralee Bay, not far south of the Shannon Estuary. Besides offering a superb cruising ground, being within a day's sail of Dingle and Kilrush, the marina also provides a convenient base from which to visit inland attractions such as the picturesque tourist towns of Tralee and Killarney. This 120-berth marina accommodates boats up to 15m LOA and benefits from deep water at all states of the tide.

The small village of Fenit incorporates a grocery shop as well a several pubs and restaurants, while among the local activities are horse riding, swimming from one of the nearby sandy beaches and golfing.

FACILITIES AT A GLANCE

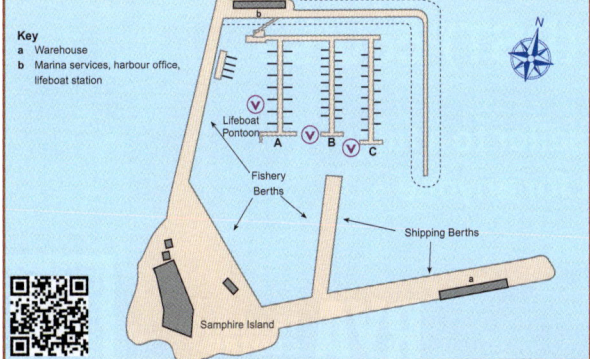

Key
a Warehouse
b Marina services, harbour office, lifeboat station

KILRUSH MARINA

Kilrush Marina Ltd
Kilrush, Co. Clare, Ireland
Tel: +353 65 9052072 Mobile: +353 87 3712656
Email: info@kilrushmarina.ie

VHF Ch 80
ACCESS H24

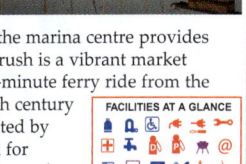

Kilrush Marina and boatyard is well placed for exploring the unspoilt west coast of Ireland, including Galway Bay, Dingle, W Cork and Kerry. It also provides a gateway to over 150 miles of cruising on Lough Derg, the R Shannon and the Irish canal system. Accessed via lock gates, the marina lies at one end of the main street in Kilrush, the marina centre provides all the facilities for the visiting sailor. Kilrush is a vibrant market town with a long maritime history. A 15-minute ferry ride from the marina takes you to Scattery Is, once a 6th century monastic settlement but now only inhabited by wildlife. The Shannon Estuary is reputed for being the country's first marine Special Area of Conservation (SAC) and is home to Ireland's only known resident group of bottlenose dolphins.

FACILITIES AT A GLANCE

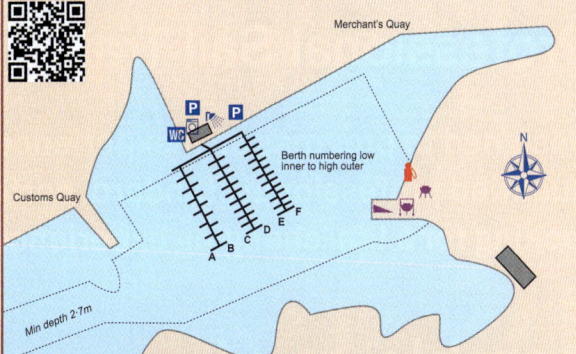

MARINA GUIDE 2026

HAMBLE SCHOOL OF YACHTING

Hannah Brewis
Race Skipper
Clipper 2023-24 Race

Fast Track training skipper
Professional Sail Training

FAST TRACK SAIL TRAINING

GO PROFESSIONAL
Professional Sail Training (PST) course

Designed to progress an inexperienced sailor to a fully qualified professional standard, perfect for anyone looking for a life-changing experience.

hamble.co.uk

RYA TRAINING CENTRE

AREA 13

NORTH IRELAND – Liscannor Bay, clockwise to Lambay Island

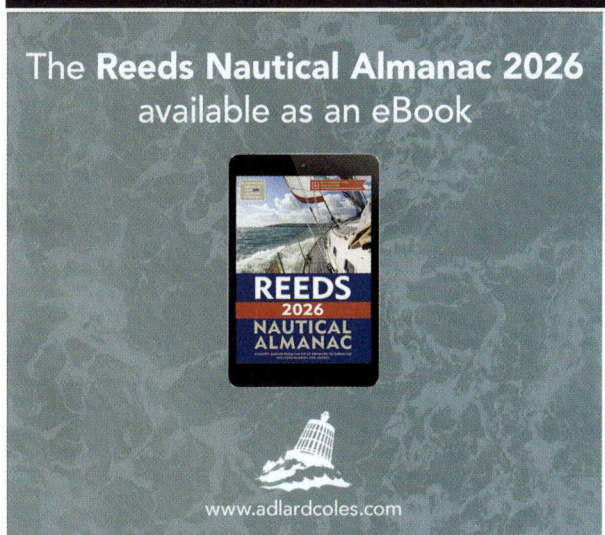

Key to Marina Plans symbols

	Bottled gas	P	Parking
	Chandler		Pub/Restaurant
	Disabled facilities		Pump out
	Electrical supply		Rigging service
	Electrical repairs		Sail repairs
	Engine repairs		Shipwright
	First Aid		Shop/Supermarket
	Fresh Water		Showers
D	Fuel - Diesel		Slipway
P	Fuel - Petrol	WC	Toilets
	Hardstanding/boatyard		Telephone
@	Internet Café		Trolleys
	Laundry facilities	V	Visitors berths
	Lift-out facilities		Wi-Fi

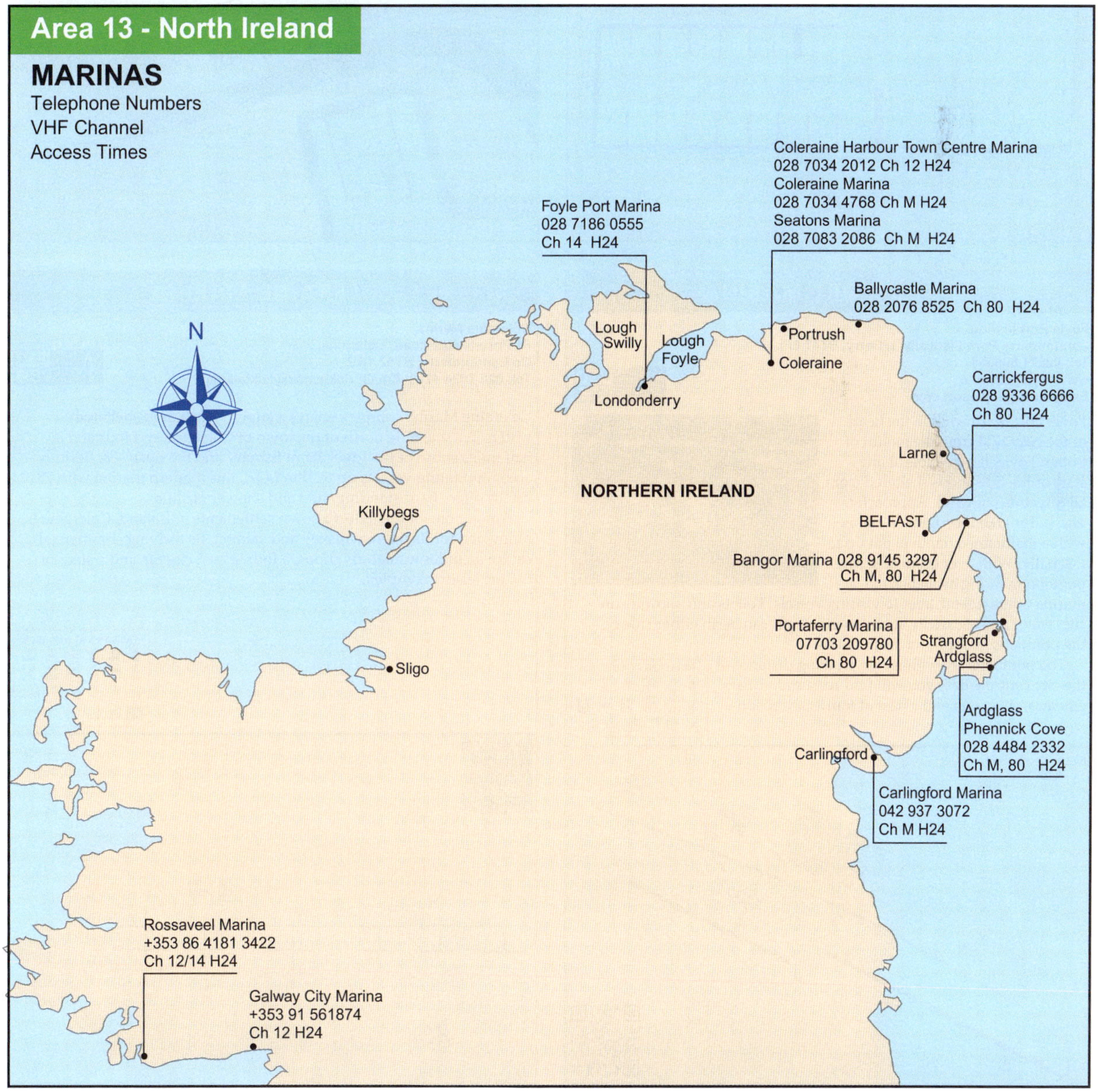

Area 13 - North Ireland

MARINAS
Telephone Numbers
VHF Channel
Access Times

Coleraine Harbour Town Centre Marina
028 7034 2012 Ch 12 H24
Coleraine Marina
028 7034 4768 Ch M H24
Seatons Marina
028 7083 2086 Ch M H24

Foyle Port Marina
028 7186 0555
Ch 14 H24

Ballycastle Marina
028 2076 8525 Ch 80 H24

Carrickfergus
028 9336 6666
Ch 80 H24

Bangor Marina 028 9145 3297
Ch M, 80 H24

Portaferry Marina
07703 209780
Ch 80 H24

Ardglass
Phennick Cove
028 4484 2332
Ch M, 80 H24

Carlingford Marina
042 937 3072
Ch M H24

Rossaveel Marina
+353 86 4181 3422
Ch 12/14 H24

Galway City Marina
+353 91 561874
Ch 12 H24

MARINA GUIDE 2026

MARINAS & SERVICES

GALWAY CITY MARINA

Galway City Marina
Galway Harbour Co, Harbour Office, Galway, Ireland
Tel: +353 91 561874 Fax: +353 91 563738
Email: info@theportofgalway.com

VHF	Ch 12
ACCESS	HW-2 to HW

The Galway harbour Company operates a small marina in the confines of Galway Harbour with an additional 60m of pontoon-walkway. Freshwater and electrical power is available at the pontoons. Power cars can be purchased from the harbour office during the day. A number of visitors pontoons are available for hire during the summer and for winter layup. Sailors intending to call to Galway Harbour should first make contact with the Harbour office to determine if a berth is available — advisable as demand is high in this quiet and beautiful part of Ireland.

FACILITIES AT A GLANCE

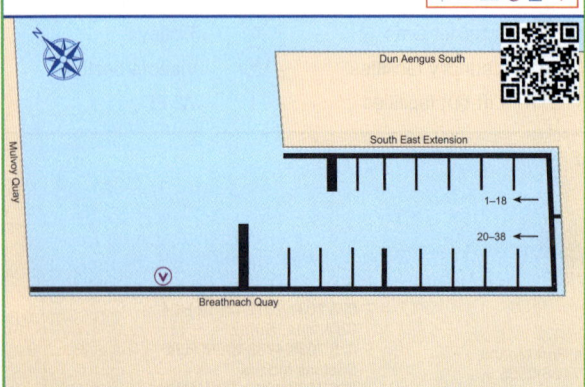

ROSSAVEEL MARINA

Rossaveel Marina
Ros An Mhil, Galway, Ireland
Tel: +353 87 9212014
Email: ciaran.seoighe@agriculture.gov.ie

VHF	Ch 12
ACCESS	H24

Nestled on the north coast of Galway Bay, the Rossaveel marinas (North and South) are a relatively new development in a busy working port and fishing harbour. The North Marina has a minimum depth of 2.6m for 166, although planning is underway for a further 60. The South Marina has 2m water for 44 vessels. All berths are serviced with water and electricity and fuel can be bought locally. Two slips are available for both tidal work and trailer launching.

Rossaveel has all the usual conveniences of a small town and from here ferries can be taken to the Aran Islands.

FACILITIES AT A GLANCE

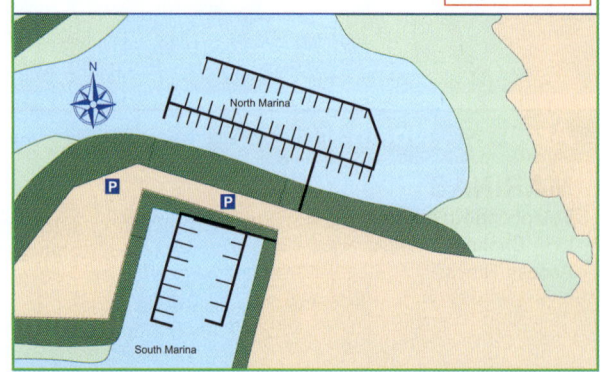

FOYLE PORT MARINA

Foyle Port Marina
Londonderry Port, Lisahally, L'Derry, BT47 6FL
Tel: 02871 860555
www.foyleport.com
Email: info@foyleport.com

VHF	Ch 14
ACCESS	H24

Foyle Port Marina lies in the heart of the city, 17M from the mouth of Lough Foyle, is accessible at any state of the tide and is sheltered from all directions of wind. Approach is via well-marked navigation channel with a maintained depth of 8m up to Lisahally. With over 680m of secure pontoon mooring available, the marina offers full facilities to visiting vessels. Toilets and showers on site, water and electricity at each berth. Craft can berth either side of the pontoons in depths of 5–7m at LW.

The pontoons are within easy walking distance of the city centre where you will find restaurants, bars, cinemas, shopping and a host of tourist attractions.

FACILITIES AT A GLANCE

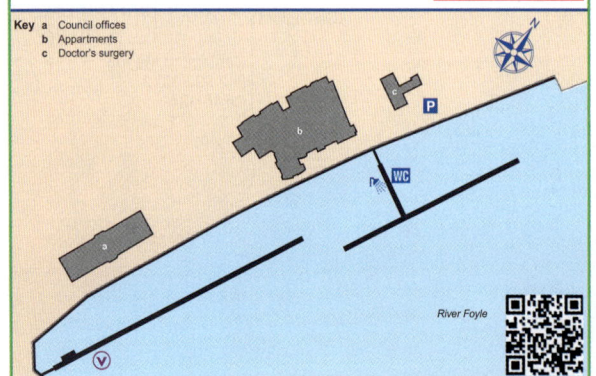

COLERAINE MARINA

Coleraine Marina
64 Portstewart Road, Coleraine,
Co Londonderry, BT52 1RR
Tel: 028 7034 4768 Email: rickiemac@talktalk.net

VHF	Ch M
ACCESS	H24

Coleraine Marina complex enjoys a superb location in sheltered waters just one mile north of the town of Coleraine and four and a half miles south of the River Bann Estuary and the open sea. Besides accommodating vessels up to 18m LOA, this modern marina with 78 berths offers hard standing, fuel and shower facilities.

Among one of the oldest known settlements in Ireland, Coleraine is renowned for its linen, whiskey and salmon. Its thriving commercial centre includes numerous shops, a four-screen cinema and a state-of-the-art leisure complex.

FACILITIES AT A GLANCE

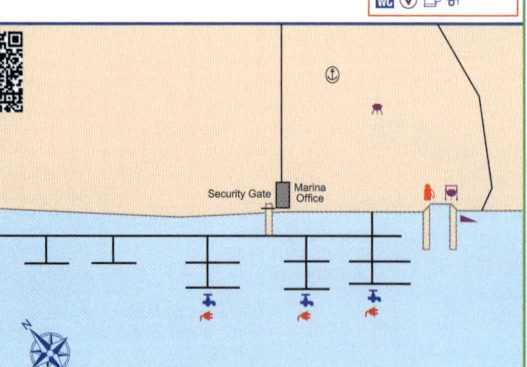

NORTH IRELAND

AREA 13

SEATONS MARINA

Seatons Marina
Drumslade Rd, Coleraine, Londonderry, BT52 1SE
Tel: 028 7083 2086 Mobile 07718 883099
Email: jill@seatonsmarina.co.uk   www.seatonsmarina.co.uk

VHF
ACCESS H24

Seatons Marina is a privately owned business on the north coast of Ireland, which was established by Eric Seaton in 1962. It lies on the east bank of the River Bann, approximately two miles downstream from Coleraine and three miles from the sea. Long term pontoon berths are available for yachts up to 11.5 with a maximum draft of 2.4m; fore and aft moorings are available for larger vessels. Lift out and mast stepping facilities are provided by a 12 tonne trailer hoist.

FACILITIES AT A GLANCE

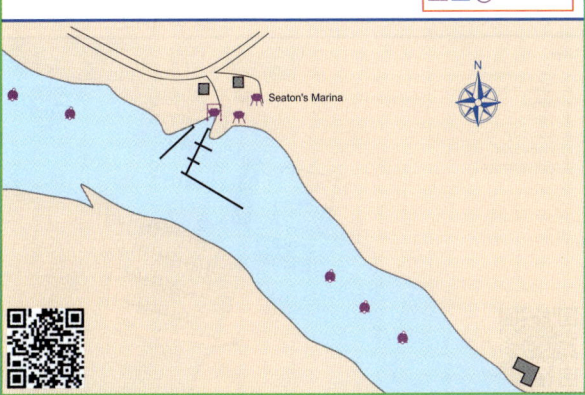

COLERAINE HARBOUR MARINA

Coleraine Harbour Town Centre Marina
Coleraine Harbour Office, 4 Riversdale Road, Coleraine, BT52 1XA
Tel: 028 7034 2012 Mobile: 07742 242788
Email: info@coleraineharbour.com
www.coleraineharbour.com

VHF Ch 12
ACCESS H24

The Marina lies upstream about five miles from the sea. Ideally situated in a sheltered location in the centre of the town, just a few minutes stroll from a selection of shops, cafes, restaurants and bars. It is the ideal location for a short or long stay.

In addition to the pontoon berths there is a 40 tonne Roodberg slipway launch/recovery trailer. Hard standing and covered storage are available.

FACILITIES AT A GLANCE

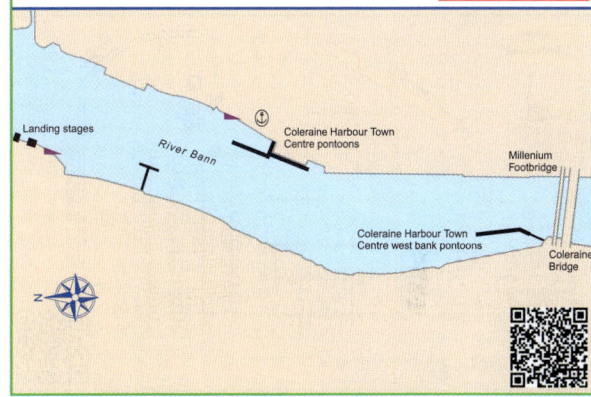

BALLYCASTLE MARINA

Ballycastle Marina
Bayview Road, Ballycastle, Northern Ireland
Tel: 028 2076 8525/07803 505084 Fax: 028 2076 6215
Email: info@moyle-council.org

VHF Ch 80
ACCESS H24

Ballycastle is a traditional seaside town situated on Northern Ireland's North Antrim coast. The 74-berthed, sheltered marina provides a perfect base from which to explore the well known local attractions such as the Giant's Causeway world heritage site, the spectacular Nine Glens of Antrim, and Rathlin, the only inhabited island in Northern Ireland. The most northern coastal marina in Ireland, Ballycastle is accessible at all states of the tide, although yachts are required to contact the marina on VHF Ch 80 before entering the harbour. Along the seafront are a selection of restaurants, bars and shops, while the town centre is only about a five minute walk away.

FACILITIES AT A GLANCE

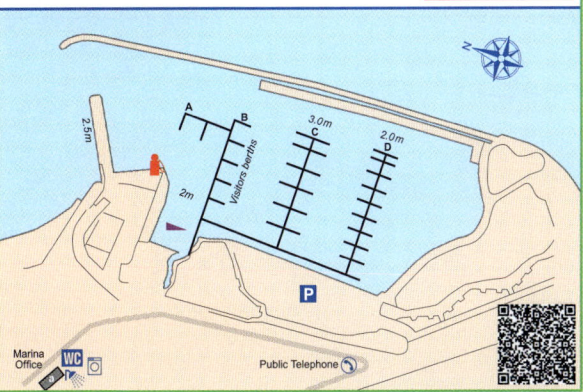

CARRICKFERGUS MARINA

Carrickferus Marina
3 Quayside, Carrickfergus, Co. Antrim, BT38 8BJ
Tel: 028 9336 6666 www.midandeastantrim.gov.uk
marina.reception@midandeastantrim.gov.uk
harbour.master@midandeastantrim.gov.uk

VHF Ch 80
ACCESS H24

Carrickfergus Marina is situated on the north shore of Belfast Lough overlooked by the town's medieval 12th century Norman Castle. Known as the gateway to the Causeway Coastal Route, Carrickfergus is also well connected to main arterial routes headed to Belfast (7 miles) and further afield.

Our 300-berth, fully serviced marina has earned the prestigious 5 Gold Anchor Award and European Blue Flag status. No detail is overlooked in our exclusive berth holder facilities. From immaculately presented showers and personal laundry service, together with bespoke marine services, these are just some of the facilities available during a stay.

FACILITIES AT A GLANCE

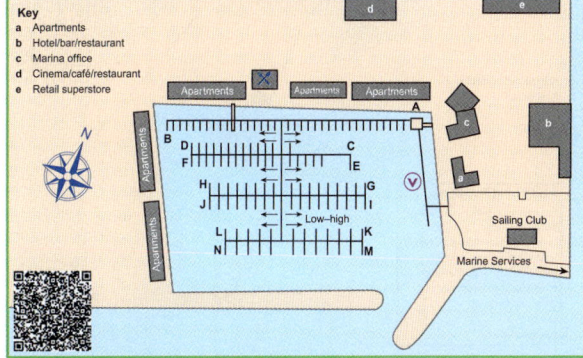

MARINA GUIDE 2026

MARINAS & SERVICES

BANGOR MARINA

Bangor Marina
Bangor, Co. Down, BT20 5ED
Tel: 028 9145 3297
Email: bangor@boatfolk.co.uk
www.boatfolk.co.uk/bangormarina

⚓⚓⚓⚓
VHF Ch 11, 80
ACCESS H24

Situated on the south shore of Belfast Lough, Bangor is located close to the Irish Sea cruising routes. The marina is right at the town's centre, within walking distance of shops, restaurants, hotels and bars. The Tourist information centre is across the road from marina reception and there are numerous visitors' attractions in the Borough. The Royal Ulster Yacht Club and the Ballyholme Yacht Club are both nearby and welcome visitors.

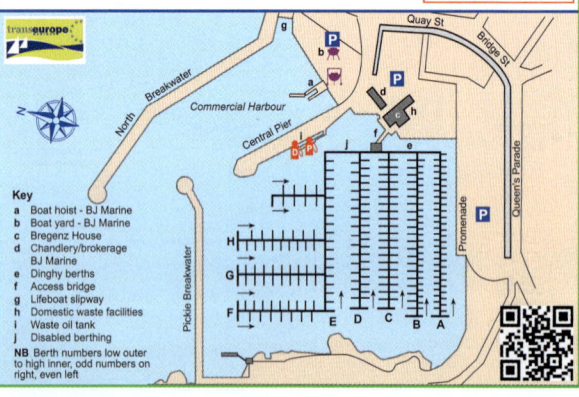

Key
a Boat hoist - BJ Marine
b Boat yard - BJ Marine
c Bregenz House
d Chandlery/brokerage BJ Marine
e Dinghy berths
f Access bridge
g Lifeboat slipway
h Domestic waste facilities
i Waste oil tank
j Disabled berthing

NB Berth numbers low outer to high inner, odd numbers on right, even left

CARLINGFORD MARINA

Carlingford Marina
Co. Louth, Ireland
Tel: +353 (0)42 937 3072   Fax: +353 (0)42 937 3075
Email: info@carlingfordmarina.ie
www.carlingfordmarina.ie

VHF Ch M
ACCESS H24

Carlingford Lough is an eight-mile sheltered haven between the Cooley Mountains to the south and the Mourne Mountains to the north. The marina is situated on the southern shore, about four miles from Haulbowline Lighthouse, and can be easily reached via a deep water shipping channel. Among the most attractive destinations in the Irish Sea, Carlingford is only 60 miles from the Isle of Man and within a day's sail from Strangford Lough and Ardglass. Full facilities in the marina include a first class bar and restaurant offering superb views across the water.

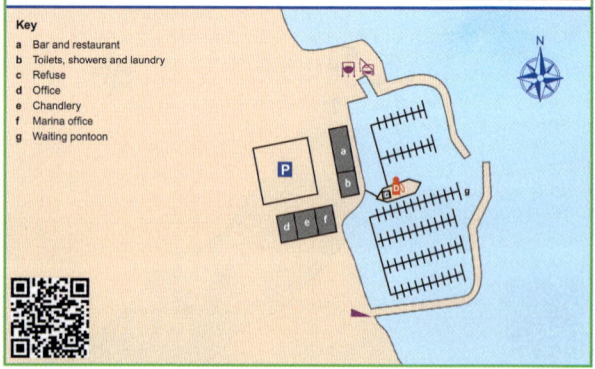

Key
a Bar and restaurant
b Toilets, showers and laundry
c Refuse
d Office
e Chandlery
f Marina office
g Waiting pontoon

ARDGLASS MARINA

Ardglass Marina
19 Quay Street, Ardglass, BT30 7SA
Tel: 028 4484 2332
Email: infoardglassmarina@gmail.com
www.ardglassmarina.co.uk

VHF Ch M, 80
ACCESS H24

Situated just south of Strangford, Ardglass has the capacity to accommodate up to 22 yachts as well as space for small craft. Despite being relatively small in size, the marina boasts an extensive array of facilities, either on site or close at hand. Recent access improvements have been made for wheelchair users in the shower/WC and reception. Grocery stores, a post office, chemist and off-licence, are all within a five-minute walk from the marina. Among the local onshore activities are golf, mountain climbing in Newcastle, which is 18 miles south, as well as scenic walks at Ardglass and Delamont Park.

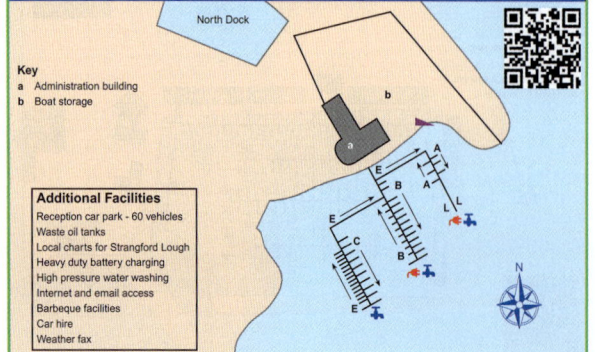

Key
a Administration building
b Boat storage

Additional Facilities
Reception car park - 60 vehicles
Waste oil tanks
Local charts for Strangford Lough
Heavy duty battery charging
High pressure water washing
Internet and email access
Barbeque facilities
Car hire
Weather fax

PORTAFERRY MARINA

Portaferry Marina
1 Mill View, Portaferry, BT22 1LQ
Mobile: 07703 209780 Fax: 028 4272 9784
Email: info@portaferrymarina.co.uk

VHF Ch 80
ACCESS H24

Portaferry Marina lies on the east shore of the Narrows, the gateway to Strangford Lough on the north east coast of Ireland. A marine nature reserve of outstanding natural beauty, the Lough offers plenty of recreational activities. The marina, which caters for draughts of up to 2.5m, is fairly small, accommodating around 30 yachts. The office is situated about 200m from the marina itself, where you will find ablution facilities along with a launderette.

Portaferry incorporates several pubs and restaurants as well as a few convenience stores, while one of its prime attractions is the Exploris Aquarium. Places of historic interest in the vicinity include Castleward, an 18th century mansion in Strangford, and Mount Stewart House & Garden in Newtownards.

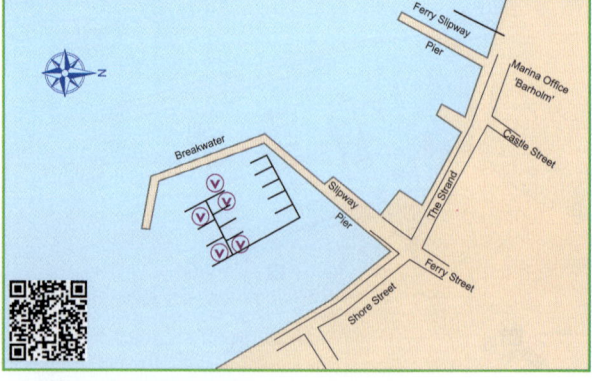

MARINA GUIDE 2026

AREA 14

CHANNEL ISLANDS – Guernsey & Jersey

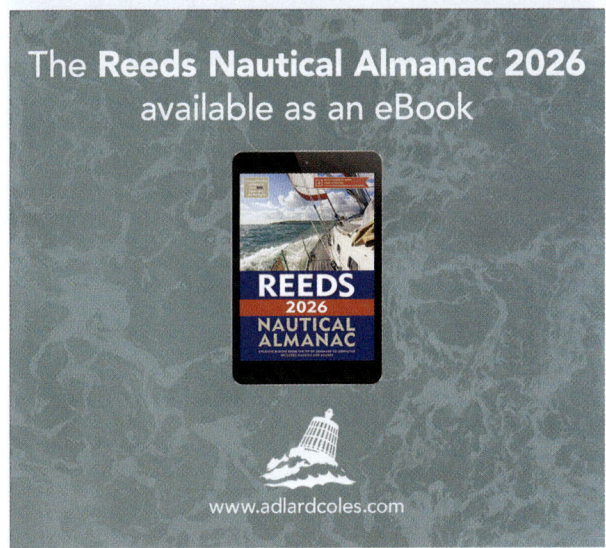

The Reeds Nautical Almanac 2026 available as an eBook

www.adlardcoles.com

Key to Marina Plans symbols

	Bottled gas	P	Parking
	Chandler		Pub/Restaurant
	Disabled facilities		Pump out
	Electrical supply		Rigging service
	Electrical repairs		Sail repairs
	Engine repairs	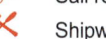	Shipwright
	First Aid		Shop/Supermarket
	Fresh Water		Showers
	Fuel - Diesel		Slipway
	Fuel - Petrol	WC	Toilets
	Hardstanding/boatyard		Telephone
@	Internet Café		Trolleys
	Laundry facilities		Visitors berths
	Lift-out facilities	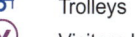	Wi-Fi

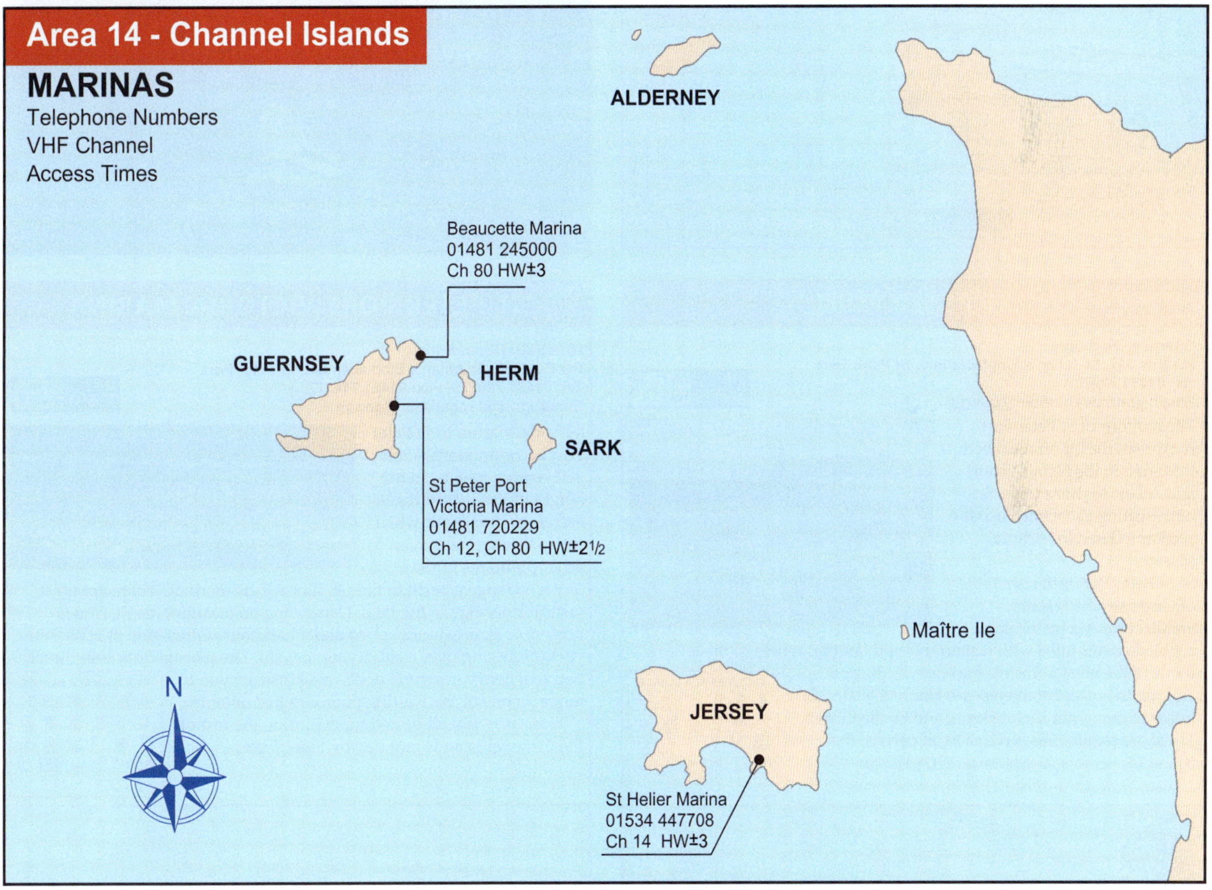

Area 14 - Channel Islands

MARINAS
Telephone Numbers
VHF Channel
Access Times

ALDERNEY

Beaucette Marina
01481 245000
Ch 80 HW±3

GUERNSEY

HERM

SARK

St Peter Port
Victoria Marina
01481 720229
Ch 12, Ch 80 HW±2½

Maître Ile

JERSEY

St Helier Marina
01534 447708
Ch 14 HW±3

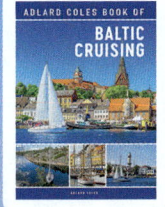

Lavishly illustrated with **gorgeous photography**

As inspirational as it is practical, this guide covers all the best destinations to explore

www.adlardcoles.com

MARINA GUIDE 2026

BEAUCETTE MARINA

Beaucette Marina
Vale, Guernsey, GY3 5BQ
Tel: 01481 245000 Fax: 01481 247071
Mobile: 07781 102302
Email: info@beaucettemarina.com

VHF Ch 80
ACCESS HW±3

Situated on the north east tip of Guernsey, Beaucette enjoys a peaceful, rural setting in contrast to the more vibrant atmosphere of Victoria Marina. Now owned by a private individual and offering a high standard of service, the site was originally formed from an old quarry.

There is a general store close by, while the bustling town of St Peter Port is only 20 minutes away by bus.

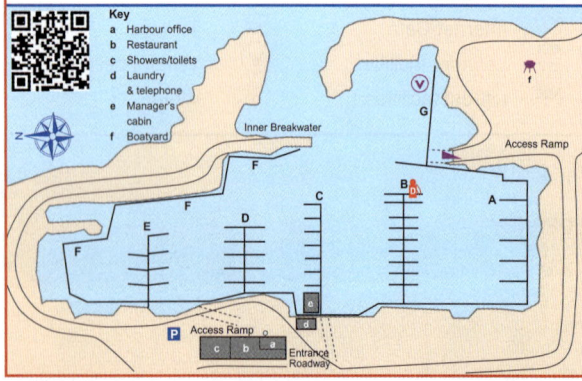

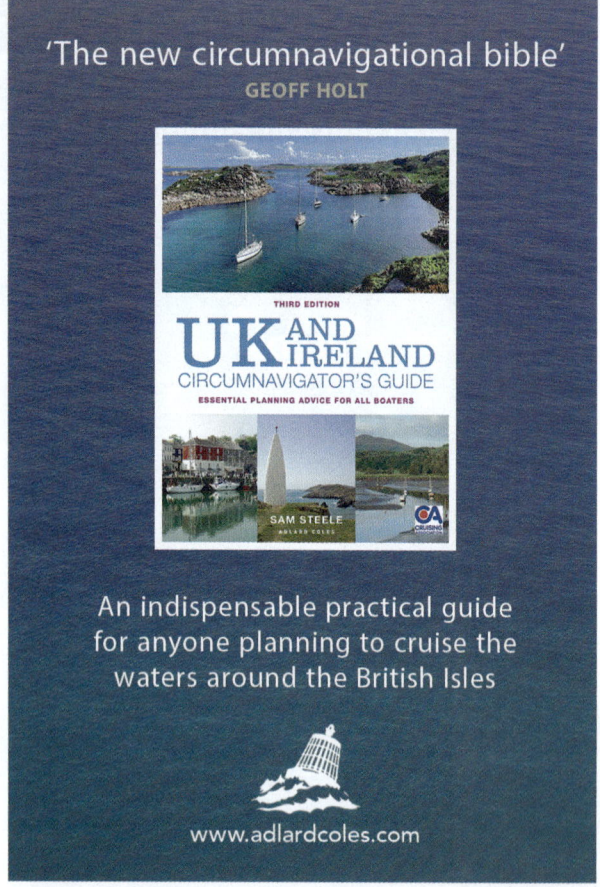

'The new circumnavigational bible'
GEOFF HOLT

UK AND IRELAND CIRCUMNAVIGATOR'S GUIDE
THIRD EDITION
ESSENTIAL PLANNING ADVICE FOR ALL BOATERS
SAM STEELE

An indispensable practical guide for anyone planning to cruise the waters around the British Isles

www.adlardcoles.com

ST PETER PORT

Guernsey Harbours
PO Box 631, St Julian's Emplacement, St Peter Port
Tel: 01481 720229
Email: guernsey.harbour@gov.gg

VHF Ch 12, 80
ACCESS HW±2.5

The harbour of St Peter Port comprises the Queen Elizabeth II Marina to the N and Victoria and Albert Marinas to the S, with visiting yachtsmen usually accommodated in Victoria Marina.

St Peter Port is the capital of Guernsey. Its regency architecture and picturesque cobbled streets filled with restaurants and boutiques help to make it one of the most attractive harbours in Europe. Among the places of interest are Hauteville House, home of the writer Victor Hugo, and Castle Cornet. There are regular bus services to all parts of the island for visitors to explore a rich heritage.

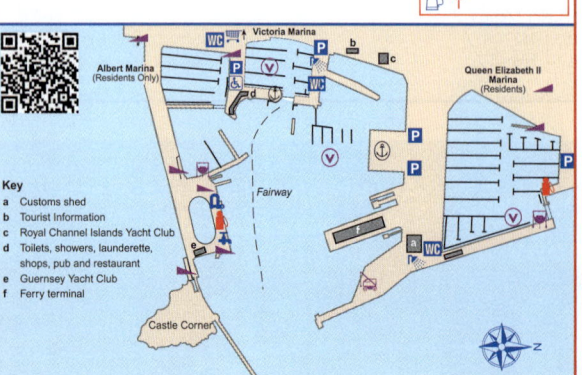

ST PETER PORT VICTORIA MARINA

Guernsey Harbours
PO Box 631, St Julian's Emplacement, St Peter Port
Tel: 01481 720229 Fax: 01481 714177
Email: guernsey.harbour@gov.gg

VHF Ch 80
ACCESS HW±2.5

Victoria Marina in St Peter Port accommodates some 300 visiting yachts. In the height of the season it gets extremely busy, but when full visitors can berth on 5 other pontoons in the Pool or pre-arrange a berth in the QE II or Albert marinas. There are no visitor moorings in the Pool. Depending on draught, the marina is accessible approximately two and a half hours either side of HW, with yachts crossing over a sill drying to 4.2m. The marina dory will direct you to a berth on arrival or else will instruct you to moor on one of the waiting pontoons just outside.

Guernsey is well placed for exploring the rest of the Channel Islands and nearby French ports.

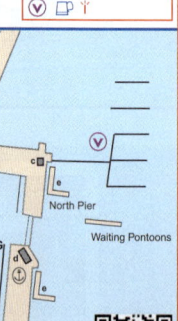

Indispensable guides that could save your life

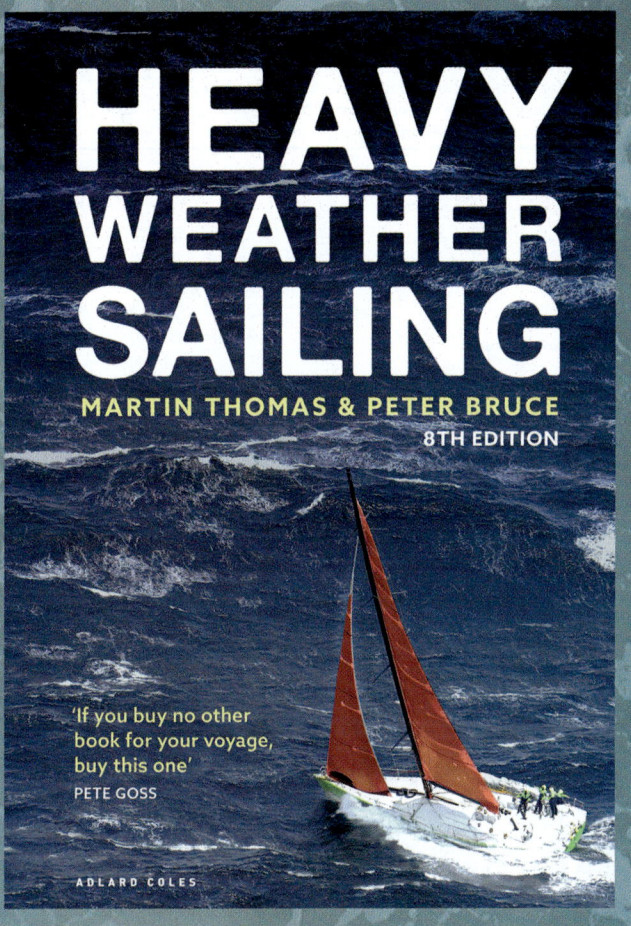

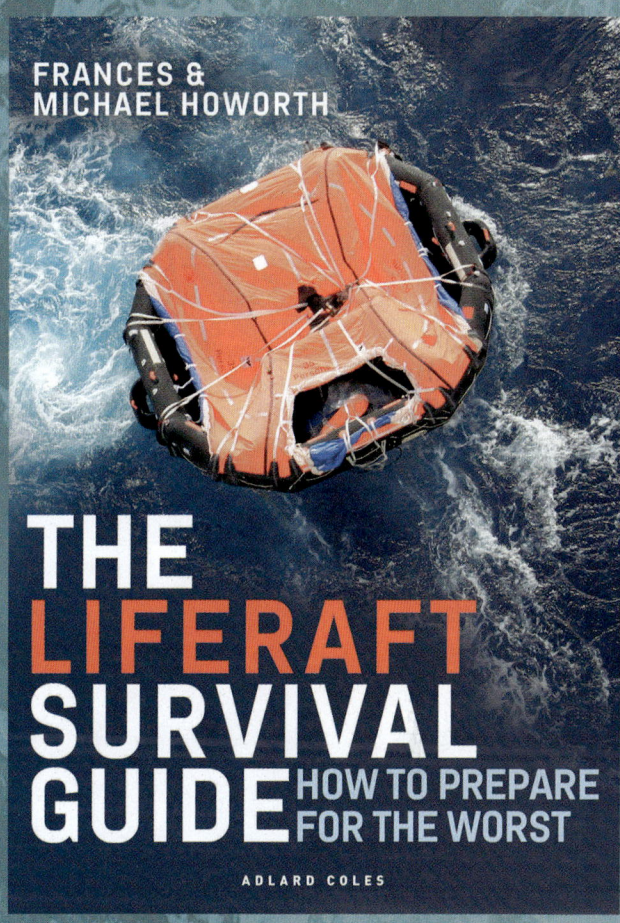

Prepare for the worst and ensure your crew's survival

www.adlardcoles.com

MARINAS & SERVICES

WE'VE GOT IT...
AUTO MARINE
📍 COMMERCIAL BUILDINGS

- Deck shoes
- Helly Hansen Clothing
- Wetsuits
- Fishing equipment
- Rope, chain & anchors
- Fenders
- Charts & books
- Electric outboard motors
- Watersports
- Souvenirs & gifts
- Kayaks
- Chandlery
- Dinghies
- Paint & antifouling
- Life jackets
- Trailer parts
- Electronic plotters
- BBQ's & cookers
- Lobster pots
- Compasses
- Bilge pumps & hose
- Dry bags & gloves
- Boat care products
- Outboard oils
- Flags
- Marine & leisure batteries
- SEALEY tools
- ...and lots more!

WHERE TO FIND US AT COMMERCIAL BUILDINGS

| HEAVY BUILDING MATERIALS | HIRE | BUILDING CENTRE | HEAD OFFICE | TIMBER | AUTO MARINE | TRADE CENTRE |

AUTO MARINE
tel 01534 883377
normans.je

ST HELIER HARBOUR

St Helier Harbour
Maritime House, La Route du Port Elizabeth
St Helier, Jersey, JE1 1HB
Tel: 01534 447708
www.portofjersey.je   Email: marinas@ports.je

VHF Ch 80
ACCESS HW±3

Set in the Norman Breton Gulf, Jersey is the most southerly of the Channel Islands, offering over 200 visitor berths on a flexible daily, weekly or monthly basis. With its close proximity to the adjacent French coast and with sheltered bays and anchorages there are plenty of opportunities to explore new cruising areas, making Jersey an ideal base. Jersey airport is only 15 minutes away from St Helier Marina by bus or car.

Visiting craft are directed into St Helier Marina which is located in the town with access is HW±3. Alternatively, there is a holding pontoon just outside of the marina entrance providing full services and walk ashore access. Visiting vessels of up to 20m may be directed into Elizabeth Marina by prior arrangement.

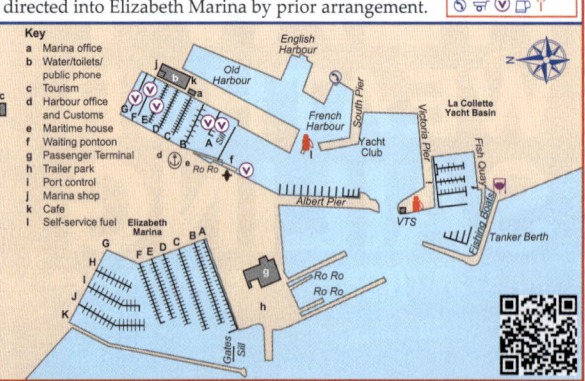

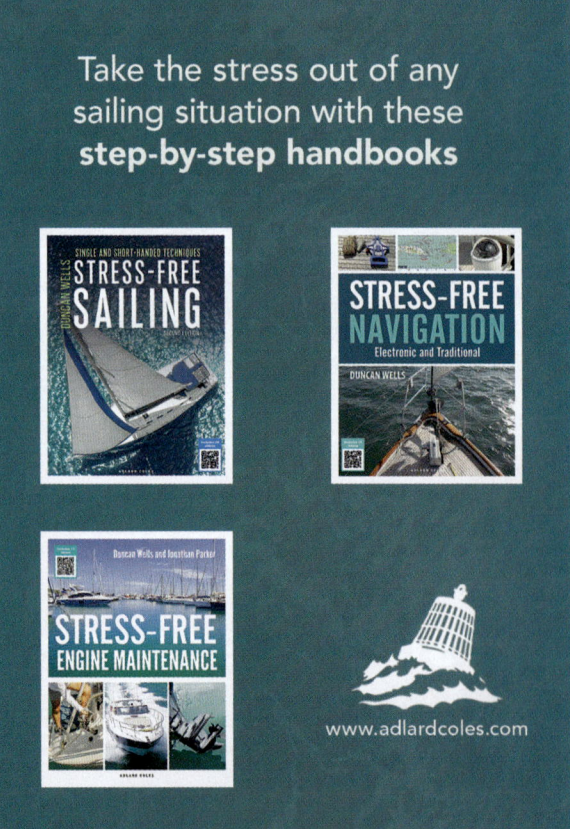

Take the stress out of any sailing situation with these **step-by-step handbooks**

www.adlardcoles.com

SECTION 2
MARINE SUPPLIES AND SERVICES GUIDE

Adhesives 100	Electronic Devices & Equipment 109	Safety Equipment 118
Associations................................. 100	Engines & Accessories 110	Sailmakers & Repairs 119
Berths & Moorings..................... 100	Foul Weather Gear............................... 111	Solar Power 120
Boatbuilders & Repairs 100	General Marine Equipment & Spares. 111	Sprayhoods & Dodgers....................... 120
Boatyard Services & Supplies ... 101	Harbour Masters 111	Surveyors & Naval Architects 120
Boat Deliveries & Storage 103	Harbours 113	Tape Technology.................................. 121
Books & Charts/Publishers 104	Insurance & Finance 113	Transport/Yacht Deliveries 121
Bow Thrusters 104	Liferaft & Inflatables........................... 113	Tuition/Sailing Schools 121
Breakdown 104	Marinas 113	Waterside Accommodation &
Chandlers..................................... 104	Marine Engineers................................. 115	Restaurants... 123
Chart Agents 108	Masts/Spars & Rigging 117	Weather Info 123
Clothing 108	Navigational Equipment - General..... 117	Wood Fittings....................................... 123
Code of Practice Examiners...... 108	Paint & Osmosis 118	Yacht Brokers....................................... 123
Computers & Software.............. 108	Propellers & Sterngear/Repairs.......... 118	Yacht Charters & Holidays 124
Deck Equipment......................... 108	Radio Courses/Schools 118	Yacht Clubs... 124
Diesel Marine & Fuel Additives 108	Reefing Systems................................... 118	Yacht Designers 128
Divers.. 108	Repair Materials & Accessories......... 118	Yacht Management 128
Electrical & Electronic Engineers...... 109	Rope & Wire 118	Yacht Valeting...................................... 128

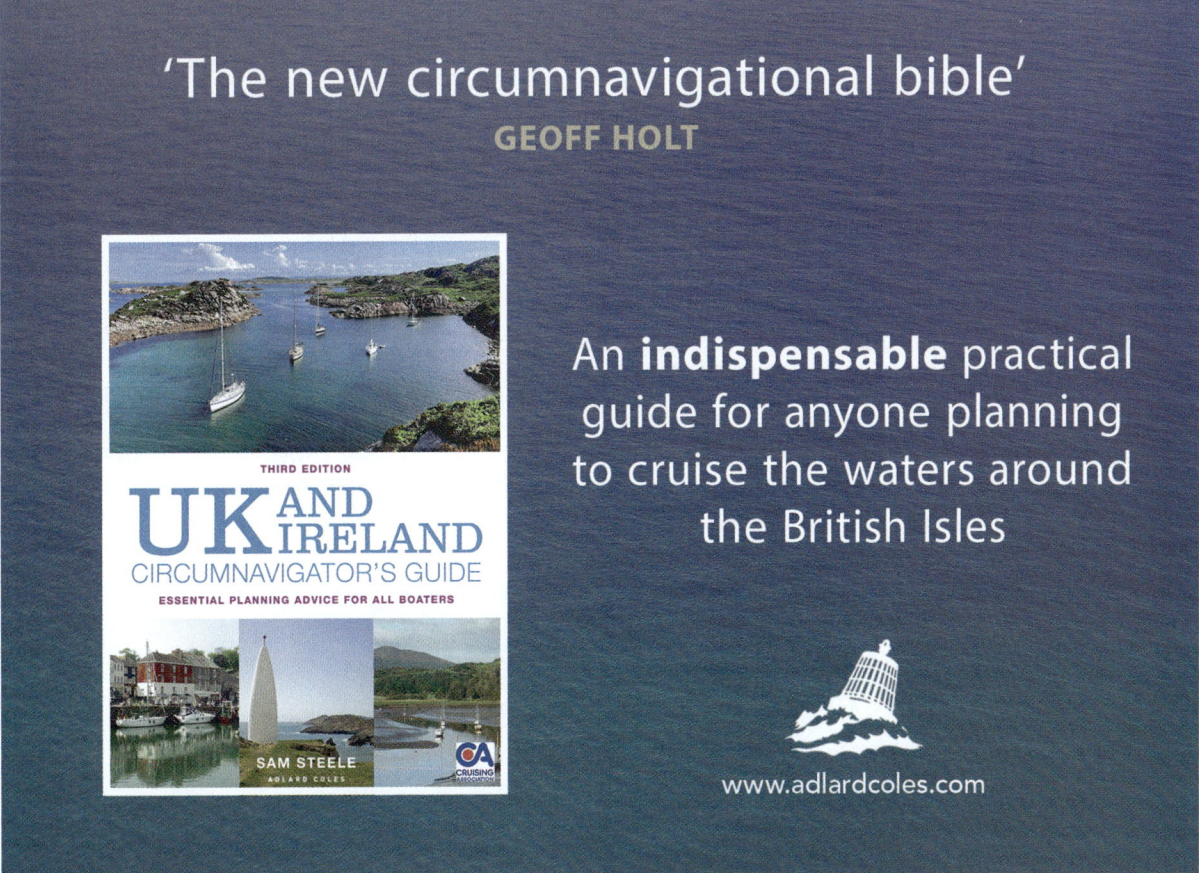

'The new circumnavigational bible'
GEOFF HOLT

An **indispensable** practical guide for anyone planning to cruise the waters around the British Isles

THIRD EDITION
UK AND IRELAND CIRCUMNAVIGATOR'S GUIDE
ESSENTIAL PLANNING ADVICE FOR ALL BOATERS
SAM STEELE
ADLARD COLES

www.adlardcoles.com

ADHESIVES – BOATYARD SERVICES & SUPPLIES

ADHESIVES

Casco Adhesives
Darwen 07710 546899

CC Marine Services Ltd
West Mersea 07751 734510

Industrial Self Adhesives Ltd
Nottingham 0115 9681895

Sika Ltd Garden City 01707 394444

Technix Rubber & Plastics Ltd
Southampton 01489 789944

Tiflex Liskeard 01579 320808

Trade Grade Products Ltd
Poole 01202 820177

UK Epoxy Resins
Burscough 01704 892364

Wessex Resins & Adhesives Ltd
Romsey 01794 521111

3M United Kingdom plc
Bracknell 01344 858315

ASSOCIATIONS/ AGENCIES

Cruising Association
London 020 7537 2828

Fishermans Mutual Association (Eyemouth) Ltd
Eyemouth 01890 750373

Maritime and Coastguard Agency
Southampton 0870 6006505

Royal Institute of Navigation
London 020 7591 3130

Royal National Lifeboat Institution
Poole 01202 663000

Royal Yachting Association (RYA) Southampton 0845 345 0400

BERTHS & MOORINGS

ABC Powermarine
Beaumaris 01248 811413

Aqua Bell Ltd Norwich 01603 713013

Ardfern Yacht Centre
Lochgilphead 01852 500247/500636

Ardmair Boat Centre
Ullapool 01854 612054

Arisaig Marine Ltd
Inverness-shire 01687 450224

Bristol Boat Ltd Bristol 01225 872032

British Waterways
Argyll 01546 603210

Burgh Castle Marine
Norfolk 01493 780331

Cambrian Marine Services Ltd
Cardiff 029 2034 3459

Chelsea Harbour Ltd
London 020 7225 9108

Clapson & Son (Shipbuilders) Ltd
Barton-on-Humber 01652 635620

Crinan Boatyard, Crinan 01546 830232

Dartside Quay Brixham 01803 845445

Douglas Marine
Preston 01772 812462

Dublin City Moorings
Dublin +353 1 8183300

Emsworth Yacht Harbour
Emsworth 01243 377727

Exeter Ship Canal 01392 274306

Hafan Pwllheli 01758 701219

Highway Marine
Sandwich 01304 613925

Iron Wharf Boatyard
Faversham 01795 536296

Jalsea Marine Services Ltd
Northwich 01606 77870

Jersey Harbours
St Helier 01534 447788

Jones (Boatbuilders), David
Chester 01244 390363

Lawrenny Yacht Station
Kilgetty 01646 651212

MacFarlane & Son
Glasgow 01360 870214

Neptune Marina Ltd
Ipswich 01473 215204

Orkney Marinas Ltd
Kirkwall 07810 465835

V Marine
Shoreham-by-Sea 01273 461491

Sutton Harbour Marina
Plymouth 01752 204186

WicorMarine Fareham 01329 237112

Winters Marine Ltd
Salcombe 01548 843580

Yarmouth Marine Service
Yarmouth 01983 760521

Youngboats
Faversham 01795 536176

BOAT BUILDERS & REPAIRS

ABC Hayling Island 023 9246 1968

ABC Powermarine
Beaumaris 01248 811413

Advance Yacht Systems
Southampton 023 8033 7722

Aqua-Star Ltd
St Sampsons 01481 244550

ArdoFran Marine
Oban 01631 566123

Baumbach Bros Boatbuilders
Hayle 01736 753228

Beacon Boatyard
Rochester 01634 841320

Bedwell & Co
Walton on the Naze 01255 675873

Blackwell, Craig
Co Meath +353 87 677 9605

Boyd Boat Building
Falmouth 07885 436722

Boatcraft
Ardrossan 01294 603047

B+ St Peter Port 01481 726071

Brennan, John
Dun Laoghaire +353 1 280 5308

Burghead Boat Centre
Findhorn 01309 690099

Carrick Marine Projects
Co Antrim 02893 355884

Chapman & Hewitt Boatbuilders
Wadebridge 01208 813487

Chicks Marine Ltd
Guernsey 01481 723716

Clarence Boatyard
East Cowes 01983 294243

Cooks Maritime Craftsmen - Poliglow
Lymington 01590 675521

Creekside Boatyard (Old Mill Creek)
Dartmouth 01803 832649

CTC Marine & Leisure
Middlesbrough 01642 372600

Davies Marine Services
Ramsgate 01843 586172

Dickie International
Bangor 01248 363400

Dickie International
Pwllheli 01758 701828

East Llanion Marine Ltd
Pembroke Dock 01646 686866

Emblem Enterprises
East Cowes 01983 294243

Fairlie Quay Fairlie 01475 568267

Fairweather Marine
Fareham 01329 283500

Lavishly illustrated with **gorgeous photography**

As inspirational as it is practical, this guide covers all the best destinations to explore

www.adlardcoles.com

MARINA GUIDE 2026

MARINA SUPPLIES AND SERVICES GUIDE

Farrow & Chambers Yacht Builders
Humberston
www.farrowandchambers.co.uk
Fast Tack Plymouth 01752 255171
Fergulsea Engineering
Ayr 01292 262978
Ferrypoint Boat Co
Youghal +353 24 94232
Floetree Ltd (Loch Lomond Marina)
Balloch 01389 752069
Freshwater Boatyard
Truro 01326 270443
Frogmore Boatyard
Kingsbridge 01548 531257
Furniss Boat Building
Falmouth 01326 311766
Gallichan Marine Ltd
Jersey 01534 746387
Garvel Clyde
Greenock 01475 725372
Goodchild Marine Services
Great Yarmouth 01493 782301
Gosport Boatyard
Gosport 023 9252 6534
Gweek Quay Boatyard
Helston 01326 221657
Halls
Walton on the Naze 01255 675596
Harris Pye Marine
Barry 01446 720066
Haven Boatyard
Lymington 01590 677073
Hayling Yacht Company
Hayling Island 023 9246 3592
Hoare Ltd, Bob
Poole 01202 736704
Holyhead Boatyard
Holyhead 01407 760111
Jackson Marine
Lowestoft 01502 539772
Jackson Yacht Services
Jersey 01534 743819
JEP Marine
Canterbury 01227 710102
JWS Marine Services
Southsea 023 9275 5155
Kimelford Yacht Haven
Oban 01852 200248
Kingfisher Marine
Weymouth 01305 766595
Kingfisher Ultraclean UK Ltd
Tarporley 0800 085 7039
King's Boatyard
Pin Mill 01473 780258
Kinsale Boatyard
Kinsale +353 21477 4774
Kippford Slipway Ltd
Dalbeattie 01556 620249

Lawrenny Yacht Station
Lawrenny 01646 651212
Lencraft Boats Ltd
Dungarvan +353 58 682220
Mackay Boatbuilders
Arbroath 01241 872879
Marine Blast
Holy Loch 01369 705394
Marine Services
Norwich 01692 582239
Mashford Brothers
Torpoint 01752 822232
Mayor & Co Ltd, J
Preston 01772 812250
Mears, HJ Axmouth 01297 23344
Mill, Dan, Galway +353 86 337 9304
Miller Marine
Tyne & Wear 01207 542149
Morrison, A
Killyleagh 028 44828215
Moss (Boatbuilders), David
Thornton-Cleveleys 01253 893830
Multi Marine Composites Ltd
Torpoint 01752 823513
Newing, Roy E
Canterbury 01227 860345
Noble and Sons, Alexander
Girvan 01465 712223
Northney Marine Services
Hayling Island 023 9246 9246
Northshore Sport & Leisure
King's Lynn 01485 210236
O'Sullivans Marine Ltd
Tralee +353 66 7124957
Pachol, Terry
Brighton 01273 682724
Partington Marine Ltd, William
Pwllheli 01758 612808
Pasco's Boatyard
Truro 01326 270269
Penrhos Marine
Aberdovey 01654 767478
Penzance Marine Services
Penzance 01736 361081
PJ Bespoke Boat Fitters Ltd
Crewe 01270 812244
Preston Marine Services Ltd
Preston 01772 733595
Red Bay Boats Ltd
Cushendall 028 2177 1331
Reliance Marine Wirral 0151 625 5219
Reever, Adrian
Maldon 07548 744090
Retreat Boatyard Ltd
Exeter 01392 874720/875934
Richardson Boatbuilders, Ian
Stromness 01856 850321

Richardson Yacht Services Ltd
Newport 01983 821095
Roberts Marine Ltd, S
Liverpool 0151 707 8300
Rothman Pantall & Co
Fareham 01329 280221
Rustler Yachts
Falmouth 01326 310210
Salterns Boatyard
Poole 01202 707391
Sea & Shore Ship Chandler
Dundee 01382 450666
Seamark-Nunn & Co
Felixstowe 01394 275327
Seapower
Woolverstone 01473 780090
Slipway Cooperative Ltd
Bristol 0117 907 9938
Small, Donal
Galway +353 83 1831057
Smith, GB, & Sons
Rock 01208 862815
Spicer Boatbuilder, Nick
Weymouth Marina 01305 767118
Squadron Marine Ltd
Poole 01202 674531
Storrar Marine Store
Newcastle upon Tyne 0191 266 1037
TT Marine Ashwell 01462 742449
Waterfront Marine
Bangor 01248 352513
Way, A&R, Boat Building
Tarbert, Loch Fyne 01546 606657
WestCoast Marine
Troon 01292 318121
Western Marine
Dublin +353 1 280 0321
Wigmore Wright Marine Services
Penarth 029 2070 9983
Williams, Peter
Fowey 01726 870987
WQI Ltd
Bournemouth 01202 771292
Yarmouth Marine Service
01983 760521
Youngboats
Faversham 01795 536176

BOATYARD SERVICES & SUPPLIES

ABC Marine
Hayling Island 023 9246 1968
Abersoch Boatyard Services Ltd
Abersoch 01758 713900
Amble Boat Co Ltd
Amble 01665 710267
Amsbrisbeg Ltd
Port Bannatyne 01700 831215

BOATYARD SERVICES & SUPPLIES – BOAT DELIVERIES & STORAGE

Ardmair Boat Centre
Ullapool 01854 612054

Ardmaleish Boat Building Co Rothesay
01700 502007

www.ardoran.co.uk
W coast Scotland. All marine facilities.

Ardrishaig Boatyard
Lochgilphead 01546 603280

Arklow Slipway
Arklow +353 402 33233

Baltic Wharf Boatyard
Totnes 01803 867922

Baltimore Boatyard
Baltimore +353 28 20444

Bates, Declan
Kilmore Quay +353 87 252 9936

Bedwell and Co
Walton-on-the-Naze 01255 675873

Berthon Boat Co
Lymington 01590 673312

Birdham Shipyard
Chichester 01243 512310

BJ Marine Ltd Bangor 028 91271434

Blagdon, A
Plymouth 01752 561830

Boatcraft Ardrossan 01294 603047

Boatworks + Ltd
St Peter Port 01481 726071

Brennan, John
Dun Laoghaire +353 1 280 5308

Brighton Marina Boatyard
Brighton 01273 819919

Bristol Marina (Yard)
Bristol 0117 921 3198

Buckie Shipyard Ltd
Buckie 01542 831245

Bucklers Hard Boat Builders Ltd
Brockenhurst 01590 616214

C & J Marine Services
Newcastle Upon Tyne 0191 295 0072

Caley Marina Inverness 01463 236539

Cambrian Boat Centre
Swansea 01792 655925

Cambrian Marine Services Ltd
Cardiff 029 2034 3459

Cantell and Son Ltd
Newhaven 01273 514118

Canvey Yacht Builders Ltd
Canvey Island 01268 696094

Carroll's Ballyhack Boatyard
New Ross +353 51 389164

Castlepoint Boatyard
Crosshaven +353 21 4832154

Chabot, Gary
Newhaven 07702 006767

Chapman & Hewitt Boatbuilders
Wadebridge 01208 813487

Chippendale Craft Rye 01797 227707

Clapson & Son (Shipbuilders) Ltd
Barton on Humber 01652 635620

Clarence Boatyard
East Cowes 01983 294243

Coastal Marine Boatbuilders
Eyemouth 01890 750328

Coastcraft Mount Ltd
Cockenzie 01875 812150

Coates Marine Ltd
Whitby 01947 604486

Connor, Richard
Coleraine 07712 115751

Coombes, AA
Bembridge 01983 872296

Corpach Boatbuilding Company
Fort William 01397 772861

Craobh Marina
By Lochgilphead 01852 500222

Creekside Boatyard (Old Mill Creek)
Dartmouth 01803 832649

Crinan Boatyard
By Lochgilphead 01546 830232

Crosshaven Boatyard Co Ltd
Crosshaven +353 21 831161

Dale Sailing Co Ltd
Neyland 01646 603110

Darthaven Marina
Kingswear 01803 752242

Dartside Quay
Brixham 01803 845445

Dauntless Boatyard Ltd
Canvey Island 01268 793782

Davis's Boatyard Poole 01202 674349

Dinas Boat Yard Ltd
Y Felinheli 01248 671642

Dorset Lake Shipyard Ltd
Poole 01202 674531

Dorset Yachts Co Ltd
Poole 01202 674531

Douglas Boatyard
Preston 01772 812462

Dover Yacht Co Dover 01304 201073

Dun Laoghaire Marina
Dun Laoghaire +353 1 2020040

Elephant Boatyard
Southampton 023 8040 3268

Elton Boatbuilding Ltd
Kirkcudbright 01557 330177

Felixstowe Ferry Boatyard
Felixstowe 01394 282173

Ferguson Engineering
Wexford +353 6568 66822133

Ferry Marine South
Queensferry 0131 331 1233

Findhorn Boatyard
Findhorn 01309 690099

Firmhelm Ltd Pwllheli 01758 612251

Fowey Boatyard
Fowey 01726 832194

Fox's Marina Ipswich 01473 689111

Frank Halls & Son
Walton on the Naze 01255 675596

Freeport Marine
Jersey 01534 888100

Furniss Boat Building
Falmouth 01326 311766

Garval Clyde
Greenock 01475 725372

Goodchild Marine Services
Great Yarmouth 01493 782301

Gosport Boatyard
Gosport 023 9252 6534

Gweek Quay Boatyard
Helston 01326 221657

Haines Boatyard
Chichester 01243 512228

Harbour Marine
Plymouth 01752 204691

Harbour Marine Services Ltd
Southwold 01502 724721

Harris Pye Marine Barry 01446 720066

Hartlepool Marine Engineering
Hartlepool 01429 867883

Hayles, Harold
Yarmouth, IoW 01983 760373

Henderson, J Shiskine 01770 860259

Heron Marine
Whitstable 01227 361255

Hewitt, George
Binham 01328 830078

Holyhead Marina & Trinity Marine Ltd
Holyhead 01407 764242

Instow Marine Services
Bideford 01271 861081

Ipswich Haven Marina
Ipswich 01473 236644

Iron Wharf Boatyard
Faversham 01795 536296

Island Boat Services
Port of St Mary 01624 832073

Isle of Skye Yachts
Ardvasar 01471 844216

Jalsea Marine Services Ltd Weaver
Shipyard, Northwich 01606 77870

JBS Group
Peterhead 01779 475395

J B Timber Ltd
North Ferriby 01482 631765

Jersey Harbours Dept
St Helier 01534 885588

Kilnsale Boatyard
Kinsale +353 21 4774774

Kingfisher Ultraclean UK Ltd
Tarporley 01928 787878

Kilrush Marina Boatyard
Kilrush +35 87 7990091

Kinsale Boatyard +353 21477 4774

KPB Beaucette 07781 152581

Lake Yard Poole 01202 674531

Lallow, C Isle of Wight 01983 292112

MARINA SUPPLIES AND SERVICES GUIDE

Latham's Boatyard
Poole 01202 748029

Laxey Towing
Douglas, Isle of Man 07624 493592

Leonard Marine, Peter
Newhaven 01273 515987

Lincombe Marine
Salcombe 01548 843580

Lomax Boatbuilders
Cliffony +353 71 66124

Lymington Yt Haven 01590 677071

MacDougalls Marine Services
Isle of Mull 01681 700294

Macduff Shipyard Ltd
Macduff 01261 832234

Madog Boatyard
Porthmadog 01766 514205/513435

Mainbrayce Marine
Alderney 01481 822772

Malakoff and Moore
Lerwick 01595 695544

Mallaig Boat Building and Engineering
Mallaig 01687 462304

Maramarine
Helensburgh 01436 810971

Marindus Engineering
Kilmore Quay +353 53 29794

Mariners Farm Boatyard
Gillingham 01634 233179

Marvig Boatyard
Marvig, Lewis 07771 763662

McGruar and Co Ltd
Helensburgh 01436 831313

Mevagh Boatyard
Mulroy Bay +353 74 915 4470

Mill, Dan, Galway +353 86 337 9304

Mitchell's Boatyard
Poole 01202 747857

Mooney Boats
Killybegs +353 73 31152/31388

Moore & Son, J
St Austell 01726 842964

Morrison, A Killyleagh 028 44828215

Moss (Boatbuilders), David
Thornton-Cleveleys 01253 893830

Mustang Marine
Milford Haven 01646 696320

New Horizons Rhu 01436 821555

Noble and Sons, Alexander
Girvan 01465 712223

North Pier (Oban)
Oban 01631 562892

North Wales Boat Centre
Conwy 01492 580370

Northam Marine
Brightlingsea 01206 302003

Northshore Yacht Yard
Chichester 01243 512611

Oban Yachts and Marine Services
By Oban 01631 565333

Pearn and Co, Norman
Looe 01503 262244

Penrhos Marine
Aberdovey 01654 767478

Penzance Dry Dock and Engineering Co Ltd Penzance 01736 363838

Philip & Son Dartmouth 01803 833351

Phillips, HJ Rye 01797 223234

Pierce-Purcell
Galway +353 87 279 3821

Ponsharden Boatyard
Penryn 01326 372215

Powersail and Island Chandlers Ltd
East Cowes Marina 01983 299800

Priors Boatyard
Burnham-on-Crouch 01621 782160

R K Marine Ltd
Swanwick 01489 583572

Rat Island Sailboat Company (Yard) St Mary's 01720 423399

Rennison, Russell
Gosport 07734 688819

Retreat Boatyard Ltd
Exeter 01392 874720/875934

Rice and Cole Ltd
Burnham-on-Crouch 01621 782063

Richardson Boatbuilders, Ian Stromness 01856 850321

Richardsons Boatbuilders
Binfield 01983 821095

Riverside Yard
Shoreham Beach 01273 592456

River Yar Boatyard
Yarmouth, IoW 01983 761000

Robertsons Boatyard
Woodbridge 01394 382305

Rossbrin Boatyard
Balldehob +353 28 37352

Rossiter Yachts Ltd
Christchurch 01202 483250

Rossreagh Boatyard
Rathmullan +353 74 9150182

Rudders Boatyard & Moorings
Milford Haven 01646 600288

Ryan & Roberts Marine Services
Askeaton +353 61 392198

Rye Harbour Marina Rye
01797 227667

Rynn Engineering, Pat
Galway +353 91 562568

Salterns Boatyard Poole 01202 707391

Sandbanks Yacht Company
Poole 01202 611262

Scarborough Marine Engineering Ltd
Scarborough 01723 375199

Severn Valley Cruisers Ltd (Boatyard)
Stourport-on-Severn 01299 871165

Shepards Wharf Boatyard Ltd
Cowes 01983 297821

Shipshape
King's Lynn 01553 764058

Shotley Marina Ltd
Ipswich 01473 788982

Shotley Marine Services Ltd
Ipswich 01473 788913

Silvers Marina Ltd
Helensburgh 01436 831222

Skinners Boat Yard
Baltimore +353 28 20114

Smith, GB, & Sons
Rock 01208 862815

Smith & Gibbs
Eastbourne 07802 582009

Sparkes Boatyard
Hayling Island 023 92463572

Spencer Sailing Services, Jim
Brightlingsea 01206 302911

Standard House Boatyard
Wells-next-the-Sea 01328 710593

Storrar Marine Store
Newcastle upon Tyne 0191 266 1037

Strand Shipyard Rye 01797 222070

Surry Boatyard
Shoreham-by-Sea 01273 461491

The Shipyard
Littlehampton 01903 713327

Titchmarsh Marina
Walton-on-the-Naze 01255 672185

Tollesbury Marina
Tollesbury 01621 869202

T J Rigging Conwy 07780 972411

Toms and Son Ltd, C
Polruan 01726 870232

Tony's Marine Service
Coleraine 028 7035 6422

Torquay Marina
Torquay 01803 200210

Trinity Marine & Holyhead Marina
Holyhead 01407 763855

Trouts Boatyard (River Exe)
Topsham 01392 873044

Upson and Co, RF
Aldeburgh 01728 453047

Versatility Workboats
Rye 01797 224422

Weir Quay Boatyard
Bere Alston 01822 840474

West Solent Boatbuilders
Lymington 01590 642080

WicorMarine Fareham 01329 237112

Woodrolfe Boatyard
Maldon 01621 869202

Yarmouth Marine Services
Yarmouth, IoW 01983 760521

BOAT DELIVERIES & STORAGE

ABC Marine
Hayling Island 023 9246 1968

Abersoch Boatyard Services Ltd
Pwllheli 01758 713900

Ambrisbeg Ltd
Port Bannatyne 01700 502719

BOAT DELIVERIES & STORAGE – CHANDLERS

Arisaig Marine
Inverness-shire   01687 450224
Bedwell and Co
Walton-on-the-Naze   01255 675873
Berthon Boat Company
Lymington   01590 673312
Boat Shifters
             07733 344018/01326 210548
C & J Marine Services
Newcastle upon Tyne   0191 295 0072
Caley Marine
Inverness   01463 233437
Carrick Marine Projects
Co Antrim   02893 355884
Challenger Marine
Penryn   01326 377222
Coates Marine Ltd
Whitby   01947 604486
Convoi Exceptionnel Ltd
Hamble   023 8045 3045
**Creekside Boatyard (Old Mill
Creek)** Dartmouth   01803 832649
Crinan Boatyard Ltd
Crinan   01546 830232
Dale Sailing Co Ltd
Neyland   01646 603110
Dart Marina Ltd
Dartmouth   01803 833351
Dartside Quay
Brixham   01803 845445
Dauntless Boatyard Ltd
Canvey Island   01268 793782
Debbage Yachting
Ipswich   01473 601169
Douglas Marine Preston 01772 812462
East & Co, Robin
Kingsbridge   01548 531257
East Coast Offshore Yachting
                         01480 861381
Emsworth Yacht Harbour
Emsworth   01243 377727
Exeter Ship Canal   01392 274306
Exmouth Marina   01395 269314
Firmhelm Ltd Pwllheli   01758 612244
Forrest Marine Ltd
Exeter   08452 308335
Fowey Boatyard
Fowey   01726 832194
Freshwater Boatyard
Truro   01326 270443
Hafan Pwllheli Pwllheli 01758 701219
Houghton Boat Transport
Tewkesbury   07831 486710
Gweek Quay Boatyard
Helston   01326 221657
Iron Wharf Boatyard
Faversham   01795 536296
Jalsea Marine Services Ltd
Northwich   01606 77870
KG McColl Oban   01852 200248
Latham's Boatyard
Poole   01202 748029

Lincombe Boat Yard
Salcombe   01548 843580
Marine Blast Holy Loch 01369 705394
Marine Resource Centre Ltd
Oban   01631 720291
Marine & General Engineers
Guernsey   01481 245808
Milford Marina
Milford Haven   01646 696312/3
Moonfleet Sailing Poole 01202 682269
Murphy Marine Services
Cahersiveen   +353 66 9476365
Southerly Chichester   01243 512611
Pasco's Boatyard Truro 01326 270269
Pearn and Co, Norman
Looe   01503 262244
Performance Yachting
Plymouth   01752 565023
Peters & May Ltd
Southampton   023 8048 0480
Ponsharden Boatyard
Penryn   01326 372215
Portsmouth Marine Engineering
Fareham   01329 232854
Priors Boatyard
Burnham-on-Crouch   01621 782160
Reeder School of Seamanship, Mike
Lymington   01590 674560
Rossiter Yachts
Christchurch   01202 483250
Sealand Boat Deliveries Ltd
Liverpool   01254 705225
Shearwater Sailing
Southampton   01962 775213
**Shepards Wharf Boatyard
Cowes Harbour Commission**
Cowes   01983 297821
Silvers Marina Ltd
Helensburgh   01436 831222
Southcoasting Navigators
Devon   01626 335626
Waterfront Marine
Bangor   01248 352513
West Country Boat Transport
                         01566 785651
WicorMarine Fareham   01329 237112
Winters Marine Ltd
Salcombe   01548 843580
Wolff, David   07659 550131 **Yacht
Solutions Ltd**
Portsmouth   023 9275 5155
Yarmouth Marine Service
Yarmouth, IoW   01983 760521
Youngboats
Faversham   01795 536176

BOOKS, CHARTS & PUBLISHERS

Adlard Coles Nautical
London   020 7631 5600

Brown Son & Ferguson Ltd
Glasgow   0141 429 1234
Cooke & Son Ltd, B
Hull   01482 223454
Dubois Phillips & McCallum Ltd
Liverpool   0151 236 2776
Imray, Laurie, Norie & Wilson
Huntingdon   01480 462114
Kelvin Hughes
Southampton   023 8063 4911
Lilley & Gillie Ltd, John 0191 257 2217
Marine Chart Services
Wellingborough   01933 441629
Price & Co Ltd, WF
Bristol   0117 929 2229
QPC
Fareham   01329 287880
Stanford Charts
Bristol   0117 929 9966
Stanford Charts
London   020 7836 1321
Stanford Charts   0845 880 3730
Manchester   0870 890 3730
Wiley Nautical
Chichester   01243 779777

BOW THRUSTERS

ARS Anglian Diesels Ltd
Wakefield   01924 332492
Buckler's Hard Boat Builders Ltd
Beaulieu   01590 616214
JS Mouldings International
Bursledon   023 8063 4400

BREAKDOWN

BJ Marine Ltd
Bangor, Ireland   028 9127 1434
Seastart
National   0800 885500

CHANDLERS

ABC Powermarine
Beaumaris   01248 811413
Admiral Marine Supplies
Bootle   01469 575909
Allgadgets.co.uk
Exmouth   01395 227727
Alpine Room & Yacht Equipment
Chelmsford   01245 223563
Aquatogs Cowes   01983 295071
Arbroath Fishermen's Association
Arbroath   01241 873132
Ardfern Yacht Centre Ltd
Argyll   01852 500247
Ardoran Marine
Oban   01631 566123
Arthurs Chandlery
Gosport   023 9252 6522

MARINA SUPPLIES AND SERVICES GUIDE

Arun Canvas and Rigging Ltd
Littlehampton   01903 732561

Aruncraft Chandlers
Littlehampton   01903 713327

ASAP Supplies – Equipment & Spares Worldwide
Beccles   0845 1300870

Auto Marine Southsea   02392 825601

Bayside Marine
Brixham   01803 856771

Bedwell and Co
Walton on the Naze   01255 675873

BJ Marine Ltd Bangor   028 9127 1434

Bluecastle Chandlers
Portland   01305 822298

Blue Water Marine Ltd
Pwllheli   01758 614600

Boatacs
Westcliffe on Sea   01702 475057

Boathouse, The
Penryn   01326 374177

Booley Galway   +353 91 562869

Boston Marina   01205 364420

Bosun's Locker, The
Falmouth   01326 312212

Bosun's Locker, The
Ramsgate   01843 597158

Bosuns Locker, The
South Queensferry 0131 331 3875/4496

B+ St Peter Port   01481 726071

Bridger Marine, John
Exeter   01392 250970

Bristol Boat Ltd Bristol   01225 872032

Brixham Yacht Supplies Ltd
Brixham   01803 882290

Brunel Chandlery Ltd
Neyland   01646 601667

Buccaneer Ltd
Macduff   01261 835199

Bucklers Hard Boat Builders
Beaulieu   01590 616214

Burghead Boat Centre
Findhorn   01309 690099

Bussell & Co, WL
Weymouth   01305 785633

Buzzard Marine
Yarmouth   01983 760707

C & M Marine
Bridlington   01262 672212

Cabin Yacht Stores
Rochester   01634 718020

Caley Marina Inverness   01463 236539

Cambrian Boat Centre
Swansea   01792 655925

Cantell & Son Ltd
Newhaven   01273 514118

Captain Watts Plymouth 01752 927067

Carne (Sales) Ltd, David
Penryn   01326 374177

Carrickcraft
Malahide   +353 1 845 5438

Caters Carrick Ltd
Carrickfergus   028 93351919

CH Marine (Cork)   +353 21 4315700

CH Marine Skibbereen +353 28 23190

Charity & Taylor Ltd
Lowestoft   01502 581529

Chertsey Marine Ltd
Penton Hook Marina   01932 565195

Chicks Marine Ltd
Guernsey   01481 740771

Christchurch Boat Shop
Christchurch   01202 482751

Clancy Hardware
Kilrush   +35 65 905 1085

Clapson & Son (Shipbuilders) Ltd South Ferriby Marina   01652 635620

Clarke, Albert, Marine
Newtownards   028 9187 2325

Clyde Chandlers
Ardrossan   01294 607077

CMC Campbeltown   01586 551441

Coastal Marine Boatbuilders Ltd
(Dunbar) Eyemouth   01890 750328

Coates Marine Ltd
Whitby   01947 604486

Collins Marine
St Helier   01534 732415

Compass Marine
Lancing   01903 761773

Cosalt International Ltd
Aberdeen   01224 588327

Cosalt International Ltd
Southampton   023 8063 2824

Cotter, Kieran
Baltimore   +353 28 20106

Cox Yacht Charter Ltd, Nick
Lymington   01590 673489

C Q Chandlers Ltd Poole 01202 682095

Crinan Boats Ltd
Lochgilphead   01546 830232

CTC Marine & Leisure
Middlesbrough   01642 372600

Dale Sailing Co Ltd
Milford Haven   01646 603110

Danson Marine
Sidcup   0208 304 5678

Dartmouth Chandlery
Dartmouth   01803 839292

Dartside Quay
Brixham   01803 845445

Dauntless Boatyard Ltd
Canvey Island   01268 793782

Davis's Yacht Chandler
Littlehampton   01903 722778

Denney & Son, EL
Redcar   01642 483507

Deva Marine Conwy   01492 572777

Dickie & Sons Ltd, AM
Bangor   01248 363400

Dickie & Sons Ltd, AM
Pwllheli   01758 701828

Dinghy Supplies Ltd/Sutton Marine Ltd
Sutton   +353 1 832 2312

Diverse Yacht Services
Hamble   023 80453399

Dixon Chandlery, Peter
Exmouth   01395 273248

Doling & Son, GW
Barrow In Furness   01229 823708

Dovey Marine
Aberdovey   01654 767581

Down Marine Co Ltd
Belfast   028 9048 0247

Douglas Marine Preston 01772 812462

Dubois Phillips & McCallum Ltd
Liverpool   0151 236 2776

Duncan Ltd, JS Wick   01955 602689

Duncan Yacht Chandlers
Ely   01353 663095

East Anglian Sea School
Ipswich   01473 659992

Eccles Marine Co
Middlesbrough   01642 372600

Ely Boat Chandlers
Hayling Island   023 9246 1968

Emsworth Chandlery
Emsworth   01243 375500

Force 4 Chandlery
Stroud   0845 1300710

Exe Leisure Exeter   01392 879055

Express Marine Services
Chichester   01243 773788

Fairways Chandlery
Burnham-on-Crouch   01621 782659

Fairweather Marine
Fareham   01329 283500

Fal Chandlers
Falmouth Marina   01326 212411

Ferrypoint Boat Co
Youghal   +353 24 94232

Findhorn Marina & Boatyard
Findhorn   01309 690099

Firmhelm Ltd P
wllheli   01758 612244

Fisherman's Mutual Asssociation (Eyemouth) Ltd
Eyemouth   01890 750373

Floetree Ltd (Loch Lomond Marina)
Balloch   01389 752069

Force 4 (Deacons)
Bursledon   023 8040 2182

Force 4 Chichester   01243 773788

Force 4 Chandlery
Mail order   0845 1300710

Force 4 Chandlery
Plymouth   01752 252489

Force 4 (Hamble Point)
Southampton   023 80455 058

Force 4 (Mercury)
Southampton   023 8045 4849

CHANDLERS

Force 4 (Port Hamble) Southampton	023 8045 4858	
Force 4 (Shamrock) Southampton	023 8063 2725	
Force 4 (Swanwick) Swanwick	01489 881825	
Freeport Marine Jersey	01534 888100	
French Marine Motors Ltd Brightlingsea	01206 302133	
Furneaux Riddall & Co Ltd Portsmouth	023 9266 8621	
Gael Force Glasgow	0141 941 1211	
Gael Force Stornoway	01851 705540	
Gallichan Marine Ltd Jersey	01534 746387	
Galway Maritime Galway	+353 91 566568	
GB Attfield & Company Dursley	01453 547185	
Gibbons Ship Chandlers Ltd Sunderland	0191 567 2101	
Goodwick Marine Fishguard	01348 873955	
Gorleston Marine Ltd Great Yarmouth	01493 661883	
GP Barnes Ltd Shoreham	01273 591705/596680	
Great Outdoors Clarenbridge, Galway	+353 87 2793821	
Green Marine, Jimmy Fore St Beer	01297 20744	
Grimsby Rigging Services Ltd Grimsby	01472 362758	
Gunn Navigation Services, Thomas Aberdeen	01224 595045	
Hale Marine, Ron Portsmouth	023 92732985	
Harbour Marine Services Ltd (HMS) Southwold	01502 724721	
Hardware & Marine Supplies Wexford	+353 53 29791	
Hartlepool Marine Supplies Hartlepool	01429 862932	
Harwoods Yarmouth	01983 760258	
Hawkins Marine Shipstores, John Rochester	01634 840812	
Hayles, Harold Yarmouth	01983 760373	
Herm Seaway Marine Ltd St Peter Port	01481 726829	
Highway Marine Sandwich	01304 613925	
Hoare Ltd, Bob, Poole	01202 736704	
Hodges, T Coleraine	028 7035 6422	
Iron Stores Marine St Helier	01534 877455	
Isles of Scilly Steamship Co St Mary's	01720 422710	
Jackson Yacht Services Jersey	01534 743819	
Jamison and Green Ltd Belfast	028 9032 2444	
Jeckells and Son Ltd Lowestoft	01502 565007	
JF Marine Chandlery Rhu	01436 820584	
JNW Services Aberdeen	01224 594050	
JNW Services Peterhead	01779 477346	
JSB Ltd Tarbert, Loch Fyne	01880 820180	
Johnston Brothers Mallaig	01687 462215	
Johnstons Marine Stores Lamlash	01770 600333	
Kearon Ltd, George Arklow	+353 402 32319	
Kelvin Hughes Ltd Southampton	023 80634911	
Kildale Marine Hull	01482 227464	
Kingfisher Marine Weymouth	01305 766595	
Kings Lock Chandlery Middlewich	01606 737564	
Kip Chandlery Inverkip Greenock	01475 521485	
Kirkcudbright Scallop Gear Ltd Kirkcudbright	01557 330399	
Kyle Chandlers Troon	01292 311880	
Lady Bee Chandlery Southwick	01273 591705	
Landon Marine Truro	01872 272668	
Largs Chandlers Largs	01475 686026	
Lencraft Boats Ltd Dungarvan	+353 58 68220	
Lincoln Marina Lincoln	01522 526896	
Looe Chandlery West Looe	01503 264355	
Lynch Ltd, PA Morpeth	01670 512291	
Mackay Boatbuilders (Arbroath) Ltd Aberdeen	01241 872879	
Mackay Marine Services Aberdeen	01224 575772	
Mailspeed Marine Crawley	01273837823	
Mailspeed Marine Essex Marina	01342 710618	
Mailspeed Marine Warrington	01342 710618	
Mainbrayce Chandlers Braye, Alderney	01481 822772	
Manx Marine Ltd Douglas	01624 674842	
Marine & Leisure Europe Ltd Plymouth	01752 268826	
Marine MegaStore Hamble	023 8045 4400	
Marine MegaStore Morpeth	01670 516151	
Marine Parts Direct Swords, Co Dublin	+353 1 807 5144	
Marine Scene Bridgend	01656 671822	
Marine Scene Cardiff	029 2070 5780	
Marine Services Jersey	01534 626930	
Marine Store Wyatts West Mersea	01206 384745	
Marine Store Maldon	01621 854280	
Marine Store Titchmarsh Marina	01255 679028	
Marine Store Walton on the Naze	01255 679028	
Marine Superstore Port Solent Chandlery Portsmouth	023 9221 9843	
MarineCo Torpoint	01752 816005	
Maryport Harbour and Marina Maryport	01900 814431	
Matthews Ltd, D Cork	+353 214 277633	
McClean Greenock	01475 728234	
McCready Sailboats Ltd Holywood	028 9042 1821	
Moore, Kevin Cowes	01983 289699	
Moore & Son, J Mevagissey	01726 842964	
Morgan & Sons Marine, LH Brightlingsea	01206 302003	
Mount Batten Boathouse Plymouth	01752 482666	
Murphy Marine Services Cahersiveen	+353 66 9476365	
Murphy, Nicholas Dunmore East	+353 51 383259	
MUT Wick	07753 350143	
Mylor Chandlery & Rigging Falmouth	01326 375482	
Nautical World Bangor	028 91460330	
New World Yacht Care Helensburgh	01436 820586	
Newhaven Chandlery Newhaven	01273 612612	
Nifpo Ardglass	028 4484 2144	
Norfolk Marine Great Yarmouth	01692 670272	
Norfolk Marine Chandlery Shop Norwich	01603 783150	
Ocean Leisure Ltd London	020 7930 5050	
One Stop Chandlery Maldon	01621 853558	
O'Sullivans Marine Ltd Tralee	+353 66 7129635	
Partington Marine Ltd, William Pwllheli	01758 612808	
Pascall Atkey & Sons Ltd Isle of Wight	01983 292381	

MARINA SUPPLIES AND SERVICES GUIDE

Pennine Marine Ltd
Skipton 01756 792335
Penrhos Marine
Aberdovey 01654 767478
Penzance Marine Services
Penzance 01736 361081
Perry Marine, Rob
Axminster 01297 631314
Pepe Boatyard
Hayling Island 023 9246 1968
Performance Yachting & Chandlery
Plymouth 01752 565023
Pinnell & Bax
Northampton 01604 592808
Piplers of Poole Poole 01202 673056
Pirate's Cave, The
Rochester 01634 295233
Powersail Island Chandlers Ltd
East Cowes Marina 01983 299800
Preston Marine Services Ltd
Preston 01772 733595
Price & Co Ltd, WF
Bristol 0117 929 2229
PSM Ltd Alderney 07781 106635
Purcell Marine
Galway +353 87 279 3821
Purple Sails & Marine
Walsall 08456 435510
Quay West Marine
Poole 01202 732445
Quayside Marine
Salcombe 01548 844300
R&A Fabrication
Kirkcudbright 01557 330399
Racecourse Yacht Basin (Windsor) Ltd
Windsor 01753 851501
Rat Rigs Water Sports
Cardiff 029 2062 1309
Reliance Marine Wirral 0151 625 5219
Rigmarine Padstow 01841 532657
Riversway Marine
Preston 0844 879 4901
RHP Marine Cowes 01983 290421
RNS Marine Northam 01237 474167
Sail Loft Bideford 01271 860001
Sailaway
St Anthony 01326 231357
Salcombe Boatstore
Salcombe 01548 843708
Salterns Chandlery
Poole 01202 701556
Shipmate Salcombe 01548 844555
Sandrock Marine Rye 01797 222679
Schull Watersports Centre
Schull +353 28 28554
Sea & Shore Ship Chandler
Dundee 01382 450666
Sea Cruisers of Rye 01797 222070

Sea Span Edinburgh 0131 552 2224
Sea Teach Ltd Emsworth 01243 375774
Seafare Tobermory 01688 302277
Seahog Boats Preston 01772 633016
Seamark-Nunn & Co
Felixstowe 01394 451000
Seaquest Marine Ltd
St Peter Port 01481 721773
Seaware Ltd Penryn 01326 377948
Seaway Marine Macduff 01261 832877
Sharp & Enright Dover 01304 206295
Shearwater Engineering Services Ltd
Dunoon 01369 706666
Shipshape Marine
King's Lynn 01553 764058
Ship Shape Ramsgate 01843 597000
Shorewater Sports
Chichester 01243 672315
Simpson Marine Ltd
Newhaven 01273 612612
Simpson Marine Ltd, WA
Dundee 01382 566670
Sketrick Marine Centre
Killinchy 028 9754 1400
Smith AM (Marine) Ltd
London 020 8529 6988
Solent Marine Chandlery Ltd
Gosport 023 9258 4622
South Coast Marine
Christchurch 01202 482695
South Pier Shipyard
St Helier 01534 711000
Southampton Yacht Services Ltd
Southampton 023 803 35266
Sparkes Chandlery
Hayling Island 02392 463572
S Roberts Marine Ltd
Liverpool 0151 707 8300
SSL Marine Eastbourne 01323 47900
Standard House Chandlery
Wells-next-the-Sea 01328 710593
Stornoway Fishermen's Co-op
Stornoway 01851 702563
Sunset Marine & Watersports
Sligo +353 71 9162792
Sussex Marine
St Leonards on Sea 01424 425882
Sussex Yachts Ltd
Shoreham 01273 605482
Sussex Marine Centre
Shoreham 01273 454737
Sutton Marine (Dublin)
Sutton +353 1 832 2312
SW Nets Newlyn 01736 360254
Tarbert Ltd, JSB Tarbert 01880 820180
TCS Chandlery
Essex Marina 01702 258094
TCS Chandlery Grays 01375 374702

TCS Chandlery Southend 01702 444423
Thulecraft Ltd Lerwick 01595 693192
Tony's Marine Services
Coleraine 07866 690436
Torbay Boating Centre
Paignton 01803 558760
Torquay Chandlers
Torquay 01803 211854
Trafalgar Yacht Services
Fareham 01329 822445
Trident UK N Shields 0191 490 1736
Union Chandlery Cork +353 21 4554334
Uphill Boat Services
Weston-Super-Mare 01934 418617
Upper Deck Marine and Outriggers
Fowey 01726 832287
V Ships (Isle of Man)
Douglas 01624 688886
V F Marine Rhu 01436 820584
Viking Marine Ltd
Dun Laoghaire +353 1 280 6654
Walker Boat Sales
Deganwy 01492 555706
Waterfront Marine
Bangor 01248 352513
Wayne Maddox Marine
Margate 01843 297157
Western Marine
Dalkey +353 1280 0321
Wetworks, The
Burnham-on-Crouch 01621 786413
Whitstable Marine
Whitstable 01227 274168
Williams Ltd, TJ
Cardiff 029 20 487676
Windjammer Marine
Milford Marina 01646 699070
Yacht & Boat Chandlery
Faversham 01795 531777
Yacht Chandlers Conwy 01492 572777
Yacht Equipment
Chelmsford 01245 223563
Yachtmail Ltd
Lymington 01590 672784
Yachtshop Conwy 01492 338505
Yachtshop Holyhead 01407 760031
You Boat Chandlery
Gosport 02392 522226

CHART AGENTS

Brown Son & Ferguson Ltd
Glasgow 0141 429 1234
Chattan Security Ltd
Edinburgh 0131 554 7527
Cooke & Son Ltd, B Hull 01482 223454
Dubois Phillips & McCallum Ltd
Liverpool 0151 236 2776
Imray Laurie Norie and Wilson Ltd
Huntingdon 01480 462114

MARINA GUIDE 2026

CHART AGENTS – ELECTRONIC DEVICES AND EQUIPMENT

Kelvin Hughes
Southampton 023 8063 4911
Lilley & Gillie Ltd, John
North Shields 0191 257 2217
Marine Chart Services
Wellingborough 01933 441629
Sea Chest Nautical Bookshop
Plymouth 01752 222012
Seath Instruments (1992) Ltd
Lowestoft 01502 573811
Small Craft Deliveries
Woodbridge 01394 382655
Smith (Marine) Ltd, AM
London 020 8529 6988
South Bank Marine Charts Ltd Grimsby
01472 361137
Stanford Charts Bristol 0117 929 9966
Stanford Charts
London 020 7836 1321
Todd Chart Agency Ltd
County Down 028 9146 6640
UK Hydrographics Office
Taunton 01823 337900
Warsash Nautical Bookshop
Warsash 01489 572384

CLOTHING

Absolute
Gorleston on Sea 01493 442259
Aquatogs Cowes 01983 245892
Crew Clothing London 020 8875 2300
Crewsaver Gosport 01329 820000
Douglas Gill
Nottingham 0115 9460844
Fat Face fatface.com
Gul International Ltd
Bodmin 01208 262400
Guy Cotten UK Ltd
Liskeard 01579 347115
Harwoods
Yarmouth 01983 760258
Helly Hansen
Nottingham 0115 979 5997
Henri Lloyd
Manchester 0161 799 1212
Joules 0845 6066871
Mad Cowes Clothing Co
Cowes 0845 456 5158
Matthews Ltd, D
Cork +353 214 277633
Mountain & Marine
Poynton 01625 859863
Musto Ltd Laindon 01268 491555
Purple Sails & Marine
Walsall 0845 6435510
Quba Sails
Lymington 01590 689362
Quba Sails Salcombe 01548 844599
Yacht Parts Plymouth 01752 252489

CODE OF PRACTICE EXAMINERS

Booth Marine Surveys, Graham
Birchington-on-Sea 01843 843793
Cannell & Associates, David M
Wivenhoe 01206 823337

COMPUTERS & SOFTWARE

Dolphin Maritime Software
White Cross 01524 841946
Forum Software Ltd
Nr Haverfordwest 01646 636363
Kelvin Hughes Ltd
Southampton 023 8063 4911
Memory-Map
Aldermaston 0844 8110950
PC Maritime Plymouth 01752 254205

DECK EQUIPMENT

Aries Van Gear Spares
Penryn 01326 377467
Ronstan Gosport 023 9252 5377
Harken UK Lymington 01590 689122
IMP Royston 01763 241300
Kearon Ltd George +353 402 32319
Pro-Boat Ltd
Burnham-on-Crouch 01621 785455
Ryland, Kenneth
Stanton 01386 584270
Timage & Co Ltd
Braintree 01376 343087

DIESEL MARINE/ FUEL ADDITIVES

Corralls Poole 01202 674551
Cotters Marine & General Supplies
Baltimore +353 28 20106
Expresslube
Henfield 01444 254115
Gorey Marine Fuel Supplies
Gorey 07797 742384
Hammond Motorboats
Dover 01304 206809
Iron Wharf Boatyard
Faversham 01795 536296
Lallow, Clare Cowes 01983 760707
Marine Support & Towage
Cowes 01983 200716/07860 297633
McNair, D
Campbeltown 01586 552020
Quayside Fuel
Weymouth 07747 182181
Rossiter Yachts
Christchurch 01202 483250
Sleeman & Hawken
Shaldon 01626 778266

DIVERS

Abco Divers Belfast 028 90610492
Andark Diving
Burseldon 01489 581755
Argonaut Marine
Aberdeen 01224 706526
Baltimore Diving and Watersports Centre West Cork +353 28 20300
C & C Marine Services
Largs 01475 687180
Cardiff Commercial Boat Operators Ltd
Cardiff 029 2037 7872
Clyde Diving Centre
Inverkip 01475 521281
Divetech UK King's Lynn 01485 572323
Diving & Marine Engineering
Barry 01446 721553
Donnelly, R
South Shields 07973 119455
DV Diving 028 9146 4671
Falmouth Divers Ltd
Penryn 01326 374736
Fathoms Ltd Wick 01955 605956
Felixarc Marine Ltd
Lowestoft 01502 509215
Grampian Diving Services
New Deer 01771 644206
Higgins, Noel +353 872027650
Hudson, Dave
Trearddur Bay 01407 860628
Hunt, Kevin Tralee +353 6671 25979
Kaymac Diving Services
Swansea 08431 165523
Keller, Hilary Buncrana +353 77 62146
Kilkee Diving Centre
Kilkee +353 6590 56707
Leask Marine Kirkwall 01856 874725
Looe Divers Hannafore 01503 262727
MacDonald, D Nairn 01667 455661
Medway Diving Contractors Ltd
Gillingham 01634 851902
MMC Diving Services
Lake, Isle of Wight 07966 579965
Mojo Maritime
Penzance 01736 762771
Murray, Alex
Stornoway 01851 704978
New Dawn Dive Centre
Lymington 01590 675656
Northern Divers (Engineering) Ltd
Hull 01482 227276
Offshore Marine Services Ltd
Bembridge 01983 873125
Parkinson (Sinbad Marine Services), J
Killybegs +353 73 31417
Port of London Authority
Gravesend 01474 560311

MARINA SUPPLIES AND SERVICES GUIDE

Purcell, D – Crouch Sailing School
Burnham 01621 784140/0585 33

Salvesen UK Ltd
Liverpool 0151 933 6038

Sea-Lift Diving Dover 01304 829956

Southern Cylinder Services
Fareham 01329 221125

Sub Aqua Services
North Ormesby 01642 230209

Teign Diving Centre
Teignmouth 01626 773965

Tuskar Rock Marine
Rosslare +353 53 33376

Underwater Services
Dyffryn Arbwy 01341 247702

Wilson Alan c/o Portrush Yacht Club
Portrush 028 2076 2225

Woolford, William
Bridlington 01262 671710

ELECTRICAL AND ELECTRONIC ENGINEERS

AAS Marine
Aberystwyth 01970 631090

Allworth Riverside Services, Adrian
Chelsea Harbour Marina
 07831 574774

ASL Auto Services
Boston 01205 761560

Auto Marine Electrics
Holy Loch 01369 701555

Baker, Keith Brentford 07792 937790

Belson Design Ltd, Nick
Southampton 077 6835 1330

Biggs, John Weymouth Marina,
Weymouth 01305 778445

BJ Marine Ltd Bangor 028 9127 1434

BM Electrical
Kirkcudbright 07584 657192

Boat Electrics Troon 01292 315355

BT Marine Falmouth 07977 0265269

Buccaneer Ltd Macduff 01261 835199

Calibra Marine
Dartmouth 01803 833094

Campbell & McHardy Lossiemouth
Marina, Lossiemouth 01343 812137

CES Sandown Sparkes Marina,
Hayling Island 023 9246 6005

Colin Coady Marine
Malahide +353 87 265 6496

Contact Electrical
Arbroath 01241 874528

DDZ Marine Ardossan 01294 607077

Dean & Young
Bantry +353 275 0864

Dobson, Chris
Whitehaven 07986 086641

EC Leisure Craft
Essex Marina 01702 568482

Energy Solutions
Rochester 01634 290772

Enterprise Marine Electronic & Technical Services Ltd
Aberdeen 01224 593281

Eurotek Marine
Eastbourne 01323 479144

Evans, Lyndon
Brentford 07795 218704

Floetree Ltd (Loch Lomond Marina)
Balloch 01389 752069

Hall, Simon, SCH Marine
Fleetwood 07850 738303

Hamble Marine Hamble 02380 001088

HNP Engineers (Lerwick) Ltd
Lerwick 01595 692493

Jackson Yacht Services
Jersey 01534 743819

Jedynak, A Salcombe 01548 843321

Kippford Slipway Ltd
Dalbeattie 01556 620249

Lynch Ltd, PA Morpeth 01670 512291

Lynch, John Tralee +353 87 992 3102

Mackay Boatbuilders (Arbroath) Ltd
Aberdeen 01241 872879

Marine, AW Gosport 023 9250 1207

Marine Electrical Repair Service
London 020 7228 1336

Maxfield Electrical
Doncaster 07976 825349

MB Marine Troon 01292 311944

McMillan, Peter
Kilrush +35 86 8388617

MES Falmouth Marina,
Falmouth 01326 378497

Mount Batten Boathouse
Plymouth 01752 482666

New World Yacht Care
Rhu 01436 820586

Neyland Marine Services Ltd
Milford Haven 01646 600358

Powell, Martin Shamrock Quay,
Southampton 023 8033 2123

PR Systems
Plymouth 01752 936145

Radio & Electronic Services Beaucette Marina,
Guernsey 01481 728837

RHP Marine Cowes 01983 290421

Rothwell, Chris
Torquay Marina 01803 850960

Ruddy Marine
Galway +353 87 742 7439

Rutherford, Jeff Largs 01475 568026

SCH Marine, Simon Hall
Fleetwood 07850 738303

SM International
Plymouth 01752 662129

Sussex Fishing Services
Rye 01797 223895

Sussex Fishing Services
Rye 01797 223895

Sweetenham, Peter
Skibbereen +353 86 3386054

Ultra Marine Systems
Mayflower International Marina,
Plymouth 07989 941020

Upham, Roger
Chichester 01243 514511

Volspec Ipswich 01473 780144

Weyland Marine Services
Milford Haven 01646 600358

ELECTRONIC DEVICES AND EQUIPMENT

Anchorwatch UK
Edinburgh 0131 447 5057

Aquascan International Ltd
Newport 01633 841117

Atlantis Marine Power Ltd
Plymouth 01752 208810

Autosound Marine
Bradford 01274 688990

B&G Romsey 01794 518448

Brookes & Gatehouse
Romsey 01794 518448

Boat Electrics & Electronics Ltd
Troon 01292 315355

Cactus Navigation & Communication
London 020 7833 3435

CDL Aberdeen 01224 706655

Charity & Taylor Ltd
Lowestoft 01502 581529

Diverse Yacht Services
Hamble 023 8045 3399

Dyfed Electronics Ltd
Milford Haven 01646 694572

Echopilot Marine Electronics Ltd
Ringwood 01425 476211

Enterprise Marine
Aberdeen 01224 593281

Euronav Portsmouth 023 9298 8806

Exposure Lights
Pulborough 01798 83930

Furuno UK
Fraserburgh 01346 518300
Havant 023 9244 1000

Garmin (Europe) Ltd
Romsey 0870 850 1242

Golden Arrow Marine Ltd
Southampton 023 8071 0371

ELECTRONIC DEVICES AND EQUIPMENT – HARBOUR MASTERS

Greenham Regis Marine Electronics
Lymington 01590 671144

Greenham Regis Marine Electronics
Poole 01202 676363

Greenham Regis Marine Electronics
Southampton 023 8063 6555

ICS Electronics Arundel 01903 731101

JG Technologies Ltd
Weymouth 0845 458 9616

KM Electronics
Lowestoft 01502 569079

Kongsberg Simrad Ltd
Aberdeen 01224 226500

Kongsberg Simrad Ltd
Wick 01955 603606

Landau UK Ltd Hamble 02380 454040

Enterprise Marine
Aberdeen 01224 593281

Marathon Leisure
Hayling Island 023 9263 7711

Marine Instruments
Falmouth 01326 375483

MB Marine Troon 01292 311944

Microcustom Ltd Ipswich 01473 215777

Nasa Marine Instruments
Stevenage 01438 354033

Navionics UK Plymouth 01752 204735

Ocean Leisure Ltd
London 020 7930 5050

Plymouth Marine Electronics
Plymouth 01752 227711

Radio & Electronic Services Ltd
St Peter Port 01481 728837

Raymarine Ltd
Portsmouth 02392 714700

Redfish Car Company
Stockton-on-Tees 01642 633638

Robertson, MK Oban 01631 563836

Satcom Distribution Ltd
Salisbury 01722 410800

Seaquest Marine Ltd
Guernsey 01481 721773

Seatronics Aberdeen 01224 853100

Selex Communications
Aberdeen 01224 890316

Selex Communications
Bristol 0117 931 3550

Selex Communications
Brixham 01803 882716

Selex Communications
Fraserburgh 01346 518187

Selex Communications
Glasgow 0141 882 6909

Selex Communications
Hull 01482 326144

Selex Communications
Kilkeel 028 4176 9009

Selex Communications
Liverpool 01268 823400

Selex Communications
Lowestoft 01502 572365

Selex Communications
Newcastle upon Tyne 0191 265 0374

Selex Communications
Newlyn 01736 361320

Selex Communications
Penryn 01326 378031

Selex Communications
Plymouth 01752 222878

Selex Communications
Rosyth 01383 419606

Selex Communications
Southampton 023 8051 1868

Silva Ltd Livingston 01506 419555

SM International
Plymouth 01752 662129

Sperry Marine Ltd
Peterhead 01779 473475

Stenmar Ltd Aberdeen 01224 827288

Transas Nautic
Portsmouth 023 9267 4016

Veripos Precise Navigation
Aberdeen 01224 965800

Wema (UK) Honiton 01404 881810

Wilson & Co Ltd, DB
Glasgow 0141 647 0161

Woodsons of Aberdeen Ltd
Aberdeen 01224 722884

ENGINES AND ACCESSORIES

Airylea Motors
Aberdeen 01224 872891

Amble Boat Co Ltd
Amble 01665 710267

Anchor Marine Products
Benfleet 01268 566666

Aquafac Ltd Luton 01582 568700

Barrus Ltd, EP Bicester 01869 363636

British Polar Engines Ltd
Glasgow 0141 445 2455

Bukh Diesel UK Ltd
Poole 01202 668840

CJ Marine Mechanical
Troon 01292 313400

Cleghorn Waring Ltd
Letchworth 01462 480380

Cook's Diesel Service Ltd
Faversham 01795 538553

Southern Shipwright (SSL)
Brighton 01273 601779

Southern Shipwright (SSL)
Eastbourne 01323 479000

Fender-Fix
Maidstone 01622 751518

Fettes & Rankine Engineering
Aberdeen 01224 573343

Fleetwood & Sons Ltd, Henry
Lossiemouth 01343 813015

Gorleston Marine Ltd
Great Yarmouth 01493 661883

Halyard Salisbury 01722 710922

Interseals (Guernsey) Ltd
Guernsey 01481 246364

Kelpie Boats
Pembroke Dock 01646 683661

Keypart Watford 01923 330570

Lancing Marine Brighton 01273 410025

Lencraft Boats Ltd
Dungarvan +353 58 68220

Lewmar Ltd Havant 023 9247 1841

Liverpool Power Boats
Bootle 0151 944 1163

Lynch Ltd, PA
Morpeth 01670 512291

MacDonald & Co Ltd, JN
Glasgow 0141 810 3400

Mariners Weigh
Shaldon 01626 873698

MMS Ardrossan 01294 604831

Mooring Mate Ltd
Bournemouth 01202 421199

Murphy Marine Services
Cahersiveen +353 66 9476365

Newens Marine, Chas
Putney 020 8788 4587

Ocean Safety
Southampton 023 8072 0800

RK Marine Ltd
Hamble 01489 583585
Swanwick 01489 583572

Sillette Sonic Ltd
Sutton 020 8337 7543

Sowester Simpson-Lawrence Ltd
Poole 01202 667700

Timage & Co Ltd
Braintree 01376 343087

Thorne Boat Services
Thorne 01405 814197

Vetus Den Ouden Ltd
Totton 023 8045 4507

Western Marine
Dublin +353 1 280 0321

Whitstable Marine
Whitstable 01227 262525

Yates Marine, Martin
Galgate 01524 751750

Ynys Marine Cardigan 01239 613179

FOUL-WEATHER GEAR

Aquatogs Cowes 01983 295071

Crew Clothing London 020 8875 2300

MARINA SUPPLIES AND SERVICES GUIDE

Century Finchampstead		0118 9731616
Crewsaver Gosport		01329 820000
Douglas Gill Nottingham		0115 946 0844
FBI Leeds		0113 270 7000
Gul International Ltd Bodmin		01208 262400
Helly Hansen Nottingham		0115 979 5997
Henri Lloyd Manchester		0161 799 1212
Musto Ltd Laindon		01268 491555
Pro Rainer Windsor		07752 903882

GENERAL MARINE EQUIPMENT & SPARES

Ampair Ringwood	01425 480780
Aries Vane Gear Spares Penryn	01326 377467
Arthurs Chandlery, R Gosport	023 9252 6522
Atlantis Marine Power Ltd Plymouth	01752 208810
Barden UK Ltd Fareham	01489 570770
Calibra Marine International Ltd Southampton	08702 400358
CH Marine (Cork)	+353 21 4315700
Chris Hornsey (Chandlery) Ltd Southsea	023 9273 4728
Compass Marine (Dartmouth) Dartmouth	01803 835915
Cox Yacht Charter Ltd, Nick Lymington	01590 673489
CTC Marine & Leisure Middlesbrough	01642 372600
Exposure Lights Pulborough	01798 83930
Frederiksen Boat Fittings (UK) Ltd Gosport	023 9252 5377
Furneaux Riddall & Co Ltd Portsmouth	023 9266 8621
Hardware & Marine Supplies Co Wexford	+353 (53) 29791
Index Marine Bournemouth	01202 470149
Kearon Ltd, George Arklow	+353 402 32319
Marathon Leisure Hayling Island	023 9263 7711
Pro-Boat Ltd Burnham-on-Crouch	01621 785455
Pump International Ltd Cornwall	01209 831937
Quay West Marine Poole	01202 732445
Rogers, Angie Bristol	0117 973 8276
Ryland, Kenneth Stanton	01386 584270
Tiflex Liskeard	01579 320808
Vetus Boating Equipment Southampton	02380 454507
Whitstable Marine Whitstable	01227 262525
Yacht Parts Plymouth	01752 252489

HARBOUR MASTERS

Aberaeron	01545 571645
Aberdeen	01224 597000
Aberdovey	01654 767626
Aberystwyth	01970 611433
Alderney & Burhou	01481 822620
Amble	01665 710306
Anstruther (remote)	03451 555555 Extn 461541
Appledore	01237 474569
Arbroath	01241 872166
Ardglass	028 4484 1291
Ardrossan Control Tower	01294 463972
Arinagour Piermaster	01879 230347
Arklow	+353 402 32466
Baltimore	+353 28 22145
Banff	01261 815544
Bantry Bay	+353 27 53277
Barmouth	01341 280671
Barry	01446 732665
Beaucette	01481 245000
Beaulieu River	01590 616200
Belfast Lough	028 90 553012
Belfast River Manager	028 90 328507
Bembridge	01983 872828
Berwick-upon-Tweed	07931 730165
Bideford	01237 346131
Blyth (Port Ops)	01670 357025
Boston	01205 362328
Bridlington	01262 670148/9
Bridport	01308 423222
Brighton	01273 819919
Bristol	0117 926 4797
Brixham	01803 853321
Buckie	01542 831700
Bude	01288 353111
Burghead	01542 831700
Burnham-on-Crouch	01621 783602
Burnham-on-Sea	0300 303 7799
Burtonport	+353 075 42155
Caernarfon	01286 672118
Caernarfon	07786 730865
Caledonian Canal Off. (Inverness)	01463 725500
Camber Berthing Offices – Portsmouth	023 92297395
Campbeltown	01586 552552 07825 732862
Canna	01687 310733
Cardiff	029 20400500
Carnlough Harbour	07703 606763
Castletown Bay	01624 823549
Charlestown	01726 67526
Chichester Harbour	01243 512301
Clovelly	01273 431549 07975 501380
Conwy	01492 596253
Cork	+353 21 4273125
Corpach Canal Sea Lock	01397 772249
Courtmacsherry	+353 8673 94299 +353 23 46311/46600
Coverack	01326 380679
Cowes	01983 293952
Crail	01333 450820
Craobh Haven	01852 502222
Crinan Canal Office	01546 603210
Cromarty Firth	01381 600479
Cromarty Harbour	01381 600493
Crookhaven	+353 28 35319
Cullen	01542 831700
Dingle	+353 66 9151629
Douglas	01624 686628
Dover	01304 240400 Ext 4520
Dublin	+353 1 874871
Dun Laoghaire	+353 1 280 1130/8074
Dunbar	07958 754858
Drogheda	**+353 86 3586672**
Dundee	01382 224121
East Loch Tarbert	01859 502444
Eastbourne	01323 470099
Eigg Harbour	01687 482428
Elie	01333 330051
Estuary Control - Dumbarton	01389 726211
Exe	01392 274306
Exeter	01392 265791
Exmouth	01392 223265 07864 958658
Eyemouth	01890 750223 07885 742505

HARBOUR MASTERS – MARINAS

Felixstowe	07803 476621	Lough Foyle	028 7186 0555	Portsmouth Harbour Control	023 92723694
Findochty	01542 831700	Lowestoft	01502 572286	Portsmouth Harbour	023 92723124
Fisherrow	0131 665 5900	Lyme Regis	01297 442137	Preston	01772 726711
Fishguard (Lower Harbour)	01348 874726	Lymington	01590 672014	Pwllheli	01758 701219
		Lyness	01856 791387	Queenborough	01795 662051
Fishguard	01348 404425	Macduff	01261 832236	Queens Garelochloch/Rhu	01436 674321
Fleetwood	01253 872323	Maryport	01900 814431	Ramsey	01624 812245
Flotta	01856 701411	Menai Strait	01248 712312	Ramsgate	01843 572100
Folkestone	01303 715354	Methil	01333 462725	River Bann & Coleraine	028 7034 2012
Fowey	01726 832471/2.	Mevagissey	01726 843305	River Blackwater	01621 856487
Fraserburgh	01346 515858	Milford Haven	01646 696100	River Colne (Brightlingsea)	01206 302200
Galway Bay	+353 91 561874	Minehead (Mon-Fri)	01643 702566	River Dart	01803 832337
Garlieston	01988 600274	Montrose	01674 672302	River Deben	01473 736257
Glasson Dock	07910 315606	Mousehole	01736 731511	River Exe Dockmaster	01392 274306
Gorey Port Control	01534 447788	Mullion Cove	01326 240222	River Humber	01482 327171
Gourdon	01569 762741	Nairn Harbour Office	01667 452453	River Medway	01795 596593
Great Yarmouth	01493 335501	Newhaven Harbour Admin	01273 612872/612926	River Orwell	01473 231010
Grimsby Dockmaster	01472 359181	Newlyn	01736 731897	River Roach	01621 783602
Groomsport Bay	028 91 278040	Newquay	07737 387217	River Stour	01255 243000
Hamble River	01489 576387	Newport Harbour Office	01983 823885	River Tyne/N Shields	0191 257 2080
Hayle	07500 993867	North Berwick	00776 467373	River Yealm	01752 872533
Helford River	01326 732544	Oban	01631 562892	Rivers Alde & Ore	07528 092635
Helmsdale	01431 821692	Padstow	01841 532239	Rosslare Europort	+353 53 915 7921
Holy Island	01289 389217	Peel	01624 842338	Rothesay	01700 503842
Holyhead	01407 763071	Penrhyn Bangor	01248 352525		07799 724225
Hopeman	01542 831700	Penzance	01736 366113	Ryde	01983 613903
Howth	+353 1 832 2252	Peterhead	01779 483630	Salcombe	01548 843791
Ilfracombe	01271 862108	Pierowall	01857 677216	Sark	01481 832323
Inverness	01463 715715	Pittenweem	01333 312591	Scalloway	01595 880574
Ipswich	01473 211771	Plockton	01599 534589	Schull	+353 27 28136
Irvine	01294 487286	Polperro	01503 272634	Scarborough	01723 373530
Johnshaven	01561 362262		07966 528045	Scrabster	01847 892779
Kettletoft Bay	01857 600227	Poole	01202 440233	Seaham	07786 565205
Killybegs	+353 73 31032	Port Ellen Harbour Association	01496 302458	Sharpness, Gloucester Harbour Trustees	01453 811913
Kilmore Quay	+353 53 912 9955	Port Isaac	01208 880321	Shoreham	01273 598100
Kinlochbervie	01971 521235		07855 429422	Silloth	016973 31358
	07901 514350	Port St Mary	01624 833205	Sligo	+353 91 53819
Kinsale	+353 21 4772503	Porth Dinllaen	01758 720276	Southampton	023 8033 9733
Kirkcudbright	01557 331135	Porthleven	01326 574207	Southend-on-Sea	01702 611889
Kirkwall	01856 872292	Porthmadog	01766 512927	Southwold	01502 724712
Langstone Harbour	023 9246 3419	Portknockie	01542 831700	St Helier	01534 447788
Larne	02828 872100	Portland	01305 824044	St Ives	07793 515460
Lerwick	01595 692991	Portpatrick	01776 810355	St Margaret's Hope	01856 831454
Littlehampton	01903 721215	Portree	01478 612926	St Mary's	01720 422768
Liverpool	0151 949 6134/5	Portrush	028 70822307	St Michael's Mount	07870 400282
Loch Gairloch	01445 712140	Portsmouth Harbour Commercial Docks	023 92297395	St Monans (part-time)	07930 869538
Loch Inver	01571 844267				
	07958 734610				
Looe	01503 262839				
	07918 728955				
Lossiemouth (Marina)	07969 213513				
	07969 213521				

St Peter Port		01481 720229
Stonehaven		01569 762741
Stornoway		01851 702688
Strangford Lough		028 44 881637
Stranraer		07734 073421
Stromness		07810 465825
Stronsay		01857 616317
Sullom Voe		01806 242551
Sunderland		0191 567 2626
Swale		01795 561234
Swansea		01792 653787
Tayport Hbr Trust		01382 553799
Tees & Hartlepool Port Authority		01429 277205
Teignmouth		01626 773165
Tenby		01834 842717
Thames Estuary		01474 562200
Tobermory Moorings Officer		07917 832497
Torquay		01803 292429
Troon		01292 281687
Truro		01872 272130
Ullapool		01854 612091
Waldringfield		01394 736291
Walton-on-the-Naze		01255 851899
Watchet		01643 703704
Waterford		+353 87 2224961
Wells-next-the-Sea		01328 711646
West Bay (Bridport)		01308 423222 / 07870 240636
Wexford		+353 53 912 2039
Weymouth		01305 206423
Whitby		01947 602354
Whitehaven		01946 692435
Whitehills		01261 861291
Whitstable		01227 274086
Wick		01955 602030
Wicklow		+353 404 67455
Workington		01900 602301
Yarmouth		01983 760321
Youghal		+353 24 92626 / +353 86 780 0878

HARBOURS

Bristol Harbour	0117 903 1484
Clyde Marina, Ardrossan	01294 607077
Jersey Hbrs St Helier	01534 885588
Maryport Harbour and Marina Maryport	01900 818447/4431
Peterhead Bay Authority Peterhead	01779 474020
Sark Moorings – Channel Islands	01481 832260

INSURANCE/FINANCE

Admiral Marine Ltd Salisbury	01722 416106
Bishop Skinner Boat Insurance London	0800 7838057
Bluefin London	0800 074 5200
Castlemain Ltd St Peter Port	01481 721319
Craven Hodgson Associates Leeds	0113 243 8443
Giles Insurance Brokers Irvine	01294 315481
GJW Direct Liverpool	0151 473 8000
Haven Knox-Johnston West Malling	01732 223600
Lombard Southampton	023 8024 2171
Mercia Marine Malvern	01684 564457
Nautical Insurance Services Ltd Leigh-on-Sea	01702 470811
Navigators & General Brighton	01273 863400
Pantaenius UK Ltd Plymouth	01752 223656
Porthcawl Insurance Consultants Porthcawl	01656 784866
Saga Boat Insurance Folkestone	01303 771135
St Margarets Insurances London	020 8778 6161
Towergate Insurance Shrewsbury	0344 892 1987

LIFERAFTS & INFLATABLES

Adec Marine Ltd Croydon	020 8686 9717
Avon Inflatables Llanelli	01554 882000
Cosalt International Ltd Aberdeen	01224 826662
Glaslyn Marine Supplies Ltd Porthmadog	01766 513545
Hale Marine, Ron Portsmouth	023 9273 2985
Guernsey Yacht Club St Peter Port	01481 722838
KTS Seasafety Kilkeel	028 918 28405
Nationwide Marine Hire Warrington	01925 245788
Norwest Marine Ltd Liverpool	0151 207 2860
Ocean Safety Southampton	023 8072 0800
Polymarine Ltd Conwy	01492 583322
Premium Liferaft Services Burnham-on-Crouch	0800 243673
Ribeye Dartmouth	01803 832060
South Eastern Marine Services Ltd Basildon	01268 534427
Suffolk Marine Safety Ipswich	01473 833010
Whitstable Marine Whitstable	01227 262525

MARINAS

Aberystwyth Marina	01970 611422
Amble Marina	01665 712168
Arbroath Harbour	01241 872166
Ardfern Yacht Centre Ltd	01852 500247
Ardglass Marina	028 44842332
Arklow Marina	+353 87 258 8078
Ballycastle Marina	028 2076 8525
Banff Harbour Marina	01261 832236
Bangor Marina	028 91 453297
Bantry Harbour Marina	+353 275 3277
Beaucette Marina	01481 245000
Bembridge Harbour Authority	01983 872828
Berthon Lymington Marina	01590 647405
Birdham Pool Marina	01243 512310
Blackwater Marina	01621 740264
Boston Gateway Marina	07480 525230
Bradwell Marina	01621 776235
Bray Marina	01628 623654
Brentford Dock Marina	0208 568 5096
Bridgemarsh Marine	01621 740414
Brighton Marina	01273 819919
Bristol Marina	0117 921 3198
Brixham Marina	01803 882929
Buckler's Hard Marina	01590 616200
Burnham Yacht Harbour Marina Ltd	01621 782150
Cahersiveen Marina	+353 66 947 2777
Caley Marina	01463 236539
Campbeltown Marina	07798 524821
Cardiff Marina	02920 396078
Carlingford Marina	+353 42 9373072
Carrickfergus Marina	028 9336 6666
Castlepark Marina	+353 21 477 4959
Chatham Maritime Marina	01634 899200
Chelsea Harbour Marina	07770 542783
Chichester Marina	01243 512731
Clyde Marina Ltd	01294 607077
Cobbs Quay Marina	01202 674299

MARINAS – MARINE ENGINEERS

Coleraine Harbour Marina 028 703 44768
Coleraine Harbour Town Centre Marina 028 7034 2012
Conwy Marina 01492 593000
Cork Harbour Marina +353 87 3669009
Cowes Harbour Shepards Marina 01983 297821
Cowes Yacht Haven 01983 299975
Craobh Marina 01852 500222
Crinan Boatyard 01546 830232
Crosshaven Boatyard Marina +353 21 483 1161
Dart Marina Yacht Harbour 01803 837161
Darthaven Marina 01803 752242
Deacons Marina 02380 402253
Deganwy Marina 01492 576888
Dingle Marina +353 (0)87 925 4115
Dolphin Boatyard 01803 842424
Douglas Marina 01624 686628
Dover Marina 01304 241663
Dun Laoghaire Marina +353 1 202 0040
Dunstaffnage Marina Ltd 01631 566555
East Cowes Marina 01983 293983
Emsworth Yacht Harbour 01243 377727
Essex Marina 01702 258531
Falmouth Haven Marina 01326 310991
Falmouth Marina 01326 316620
Fambridge Yacht Haven 01621 740370
Fambridge Yacht Station 01621 742911
Fenit Harbour & Marina +353 66 7136231
Fleetwood Beacon Marina 01253 879062
Fox's Marina & Boatyard 01473 689111
Foyle Port Marina 02871 860555
Gallions Point Marina 0207 476 7054
Galway Harbour Marina +353 91 561874
Gillingham Marina 01634 280022
Glasson Waterside & Marina 01524 751491
Gosport Marina 023 9252 4811
Hafan Pwllheli 01758 701219
Hamble Point Marina 02380 452464
Harbour of Rye 01797 225225
Hartlepool Marina 01429 865744

Haslar Marina 023 9260 1201
Heybridge Basin 07712 079764
Holy Loch Marina 01369 701800
Holyhead Marina 01407 764242
Howth Marina +353 1839 2777
Hull Waterside & Marina 01482 609960
Humber Cruising Association 01472 268424
Hythe Marina Village 02380 207073
Inverness Marina 01463 220501
Ipswich Beacon Marina 01473 236644
Island Harbour Marina 01983 539994
James Watt Dock Marina 01475 729838
Kemps Quay 023 8063 2323
Kerrera Marina 01631 565333
Kilmore Quay Marina +353 53 91 29955
Kilrush Marina +353 65 9052072
Kinsale Yacht Club Marina +353 876 787377
Kip Marina 01475 521485
Kirkcudbright Marina Dumfries and Galloway Council 01557 331135
Kirkwall Marina 07810 465835
Lady Bee Marina 01273 591705
Lake Yard Marina 01202 674531
Largs Yacht Haven 01475 675333
Lawrence Cove Marina +353 27 75044
Limehouse Waterside & Marina 020 7308 9930
Littlehampton Marina 01903 713553
Liverpool Marina 0151 707 6777
Lossiemouth Marina 01343 813066
Lowestoft Beacon Marina 01502 580300
Lowestoft Cruising Club 07900 446909
Lymington Harbour Commission 01590 672014
Lymington Town Quay 01590 672014
Lymington Yacht Haven 01590 677071
Malahide Marina +353 1 845 4129
Mallaig Marina 01687 462406
Maryport Harbour and Marina Ltd 01900 814431
Mayflower International Marina 01752 556633
Melfort Pier & Harbour 01852 200333
Mercury Yacht Harbour and Holiday Park 023 8045 5994
Milford Marina 01646 696312
Mylor Yacht Harbour 01326 372121

Nairn Marina 01667 456008
Neptune Marina c/o Ipswich Beacon Marina 01473 236644
New Ross Marina +353 87 908 3456
Newhaven Marina 01273 513881
Neyland Yacht Haven 01646 601601
Northney Marina 02392 466321
Noss on Dart Marina 01803 839087
Ocean Village Marina 023 8022 9385
Padstow Harbour 01841 532239
Parkstone Yacht Club Haven 01202 738824
Peel Marina 01624 842338
Penarth Marina 02920 705021
Penton Hook 01932 568681
Peterhead Bay Marina 01779 477868
Plymouth Yacht Haven 01752 404231
Poole Quay Boat Haven 01202 649488
Port Bannatyne Marina 01700 503116
Port Edgar Marina 0131 331 3330
Port Ellen Marina 07464 151200
Port Hamble Marina 023 8045 2741
Port of Poole Marina 01202 649488
Port Pendennis Marina 01326 211211
Port Solent Marina 02392 210765
Port Werburgh 01634 252107
Portaferry Marina 07703 209780
Portavadie Marina 01700 811075
Portishead Marina 01275 841941
Portland Marina 01305 866190
Preston Marina 01772 733595
Queen Anne's Battery 01752 671142
Rhu Marina 01436 820238
Ridge Wharf Yacht Centre 01929 552650
Rossaveel Marina +353 87 9212014
Royal Clarence Marina 02392 523523
Royal Cork Yacht Club Marina +353 21 483 1023
Royal Harbour Marina, Ramsgate 01843 572100
Royal Harwich Yacht Club Marina 01473 780319
Royal Norfolk and Suffolk Yacht Club 01502 566726
Royal Northumberland Yacht Club 01670 353636
Royal Quays Marina 0191 272 8282
Ryde Marina 01983 613879
Salterns Marina Ltd 01202 709971
Salve Engineering Marina +353 21 483 1145

MARINA SUPPLIES AND SERVICES GUIDE

Sandpoint Marina (Dumbarton)	01389 762396	
Saxon Wharf	023 8033 9490	
Seaport Marina	01463 725500	
Seaton's Marina	028 703 832086	
Shamrock Quay	023 8022 9461	
Shotley Marina	01473 788982	
South Dock Marina	020 7252 2244	
South Ferriby Marina	01652 635620	
Southsea Marina	02392 822719	
Sovereign Harbour	01323 470099	
Sparkes Marina	023 92463572	
St Helier Marina	01534 447708	
St Katharine Docks Marina	0207 264 5312	
St Peter Port Marinas	01481 720229	
St Peter's Marina	0191 265 4472	
Stornoway Marina	01851 702688	
Stranraer Marina	01776 706565	
Stromness Marina	07483 366655	
Suffolk Yacht Harbour Ltd	01473 659240	
Sunderland Marina	0191 514 4721	
Sutton Harbour	01752 204702	
Swansea Marina	01792 470310	
Swanwick Marina	01489 884081	
Tarbert Harbour	01880 820344	
Titchmarsh Marina	01255 672185	
Tobermory Harbour Authority	01688 302876	
Tollesbury Marina	01621 869202	
Torquay Marina	01803 200210	
Town Quay Marina	02380 234397	
Troon Yacht Haven	01292 315553	
Universal Marina	01489 574272	
Victoria Marina	01481 725987	
Walton & Frinton Yacht Trust Limited	01255 675873	
Waterford City Marina	+353 87 2384944	
Weymouth Harbour	01305 838423	
Weymouth Marina	01305 767576	
Whitby Marina	01947 602354	
Whitehaven Marina	01946 692435	
Whitehills Marina	01261 861291	
Wick Marina	01955 602030	
Wicor Marine Yacht Haven	01329 237112	
Windsor Marina	01753 853911	
Wisbech Yacht Harbour	01945 588059	
Woolverstone Marina and Lodge Park	01473 780206	
Yarmouth Harbour	01983 760321	

MARINE ENGINEERS

AAS Marine
Aberystwyth 01970 631090

Allerton Engineering
Lowestoft 01502 537870

APAS Engineering Ltd
Southampton 023 8063 2558

Ardmair Boat Centre
Ullapool 01854 612054

Arisaig Marine
Inverness-shire 01687 450224

Arun Craft
Littlehampton 01903 723667

ASL Auto Services
Boston 01205 761560

Atlantis Marine Power Ltd
Plymouth 01752 208810

Attrill & Sons, H
Bembridge 01983 872319

Auto & Marine Services
Botley 07836 507000

Auto Marine
Southsea 023 9282 5601

Baker, Keith
Brentford 07792 937790

BJ Marine Ltd Bangor 028 9127 1434

Brevik Marine Service Ltd
Stornoway 07876 721154

Bristol Boat Ltd Bristol 01225 872032

Browne, Jimmy
Tralee +353 87 262 7158

Buccaneer Ltd
Macduff 01261 835199

Buzzard Marine Engineering
Yarmouth 01983 760707

C & B Marine Ltd
Chichester Marina 01243 511273

Caddy, Simon
Falmouth Marina 01326 372682

Caledonian Marine
Rhu Marina 01436 821184

Cardigan Outboards
Cardigan 01239 613966

Channel Islands Marine Ltd
Guernsey 01481 716880

Channel Islands Marine Ltd
Jersey 01534 767595

Cook's Diesel Service Ltd
Faversham 01795 538553

Cox, Andrew Falmouth 07974 250533

Cragie Engineering
Kirkwall 01856 874680

Crinan Boatyard Ltd
Crinan 01546 830232

Cronin Commercials
Dunmanway +353 23 8845498

Cutler Marine Engineering, John
Emsworth 01243 375014

Dale Sailing Co Ltd
Milford Haven 01646 603110

Davis Marine Services
Ramsgate 01843 586172

Denney & Son, EL
Redcar 01642 483507

DH Marine (Shetland) Ltd
Shetland 01595 690618

Dobson, Chris
Whitehaven 07986 086641

Emark Marine Ltd
Emsworth 01243 375383

Evans, Lyndon
Brentford 07795 218704

Evans Marine Engineering, Tony
Pwllheli 01758 703070

Ferrypoint Boat Co
Youghal +353 24 94232

Fettes & Rankine Engineering
Aberdeen 01224 573343

Floetree Ltd Loch Lomond Marina
Balloch 01389 752069

Fowey Harbour Marine Engineers
Fowey 01726 832806

Fox Marine Services Ltd
Jersey 01534 721312

Fleetwood Marine 07508 807290

Freeport Marine Jersey 01534 888100

French Marine Motors Ltd
Colchester 01206 302133

French Marine Motors Ltd
Titchmarsh Marina 01255 850303

GH Douglas Marine Services
Fleetwood 01253 877200

Golden Arrow Marine
Southampton 023 8071 0371

Goodchild Marine Services
Great Yarmouth 01493 782301

Goodwick Marine
Fishguard 01348 873955

Gordon Diesel Services
Stornoway 01851 702122

Gosport Marina 023 9252 4811

Griffins Garage Dingle Marina,
Co Kerry +353 66 91 51178

Hale Marine Portsmouth 023 9273 2985

Hamilton Brothers
Campbeltown 01586 553031

Hamnavoe Engineering
Stromness 01856 850576

MARINE ENGINEERS – NAVIGATION EQUIPMENT

Harbour Engineering
Itchenor 01243 513454

Hartlepool Marine Engineering
Hartlepool 01429 867883

Hayles, Harold Yarmouth 01983 760373

Herm Seaway Marine Ltd
St Peter Port 01481 726829

HNP Engineers (Lerwick Ltd)
Lerwick 01595 692493

Hodges, T Coleraine 028 7035 6422

Home Marine Emsworth Yacht Harbour, Emsworth 01243 374125

Hook Marine Ltd Troon 01292 679500

Humphrey, Chris
Teignmouth 01626 772324

Instow Marine Services
Bideford 01271 861081

Jones (Boatbuilders), David
Chester 01244 390363

Keating Marine Engineering Ltd, Bill
Jersey 01534 733977

Kingston Marine Services
Cowes 01983 299385

Kippford Slipway Ltd
Dalbeattie 01556 620249

L&A Marine
Campbeltown 01586 554479

Lansdale Pannell Marine
Chichester 01243 550042

Lencraft Boats Ltd
Dungarvan +353 58 68220

Llyn Marine Services
Pwllheli 01758 612606

Lynx Engineering
St Helens, Isle of Wight 01983 873711

M&G Marine Services
Mayflower International Marina, Plymouth 01752 563445

MacDonald & Co Ltd, JN
Glasgow 0141 810 3400

Mackay Marine Services
Aberdeen 01224 575772

Macmillan Engineering Ltd
Goat Is, Stornoway 001851 704411

Mainbrayce Marine
Alderney 01481 722772

Malakoff and Moore
Lerwick 01595 695544

Marine Blast Holy Loch 01369 705394

Mallaig Boat Building and Engineering
Mallaig 01687 462304

Marindus Engineering
Kilmore Quay +353 53 29794

Marine Engineering Looe
Brixham 01803 844777

Marine Engineering Looe 01503 263009

Marine Engineering Services
Port Dinorwic 01248 671215

Marine General Engineers Beaucette Marina, Guernsey 01481 245808

Marine Propulsion
Hayling Island 07836 737488

Marine & General Engineers
St. Sampsons Harbour, Guernsey
01481 245808

Marine Servicing
Eastbourne 07932 318414

Marine-Trak Engineering
Mylor Yacht Harbour 01326 376588

Marine Warehouse
Gosport 023 9258 0420

Marlec Marine
Ramsgate 01843 592176

Martin Outboards
Galgate 01524 751750

McKenzie, D
Campbeltown 07799 651637

McQueen, Michael
Kilrush +35 87 2574623

Meiher, Denis Fenit +353 87 958 4744

MES Marine Greenock 01475 744655

MMS Ardrossan 01294 604831/ 07836 342332

Mobile Marine Engineering
Liverpool Marina 01565 733553

Mobile Marine Maintenance
Poole 07931 776482

Mount's Bay Engineering
Newlyn 01736 363095

MP Marine Maryport 01900 810299

Murphy Marine Services
Cahersiveen +353 66 9476365

New World Yacht Care
Helensburgh 01436 820586

North Western Automarine Engineers
Largs 01475 687139

Noss Marine Services Dart Marina, Dartmouth 01803 833343

Owen Marine, Robert
Porthmadog 01766 513435

Pace, Andy Newhaven 01273 516010

Penzance Dry Dock and Engineering Co Ltd Penzance 01736 363838

Pirie & Co, John S
Fraserburgh 01346 513314

Portavon Marine
Keynsham 01225 424301

Power Afloat, Elkins Boatyard
Christchurch 01202 489555

Powerplus Marine Cowes Yacht Haven, Cowes 01983 290421

Pro-Marine Queen Anne's Battery Marina, Plymouth 01752 267984

PT Marine Engineering
Hayling Island 023 9246 9332

R & M Marine
Portsmouth 023 9273 7555

R & S Engineering
Dingle Marina +353 66 915 1189

Reddish Marine
Salcombe 01548 844094

RHP Marine
Cowes 01983 290421

RK Marine Ltd
Hamble 01489 583585

RK Marine Ltd
Swanwick 01489 583572

Rossiter Yachts Ltd
Christchurch 01202 483250

Ryan & Roberts Marine Services
Askeaton +353 61 392198

Salve Marine Ltd
Crosshaven +353 21 4831145

Seamark-Nunn & Co
Felixstowe 01394 275327

Seapower
Ipswich 01473 780090

Seaward Engineering
Glasgow 0141 632 4910

Seaway Marine
Gosport 023 9260 2722

Shearwater Engineering Services Ltd
Dunoon 01369 706666

Silvers Marina Ltd
Helensburgh 01436 831222

Starey Marine
Salcombe 01548 843655

Swordfish Marine Engineering
Holy Loch 01369 701905

Tarbert Marine
Arbroath 01241 872879

Thorne Boat Services
Thorne 01405 814197

Tollesbury Marine Engineering
Tollesbury Marina 01621 869919

MARINA SUPPLIES AND SERVICES GUIDE

Tony's Marine Services Coleraine		07866 690436
TOR (Gerald Hales) Stornoway		01851 871025
Vasey Marine Engineering, Gordon Fareham		07798 638625
Volspec Ltd Tollesbury		01621 869756
Wallis, Peter Torquay Marina, Torquay		01803 844777
Wartsila Havant		023 9240 0121
WB Marine Chichester		01243 512857
West Coast Marine Troon		01292 318121
West Marine, Brighton		01273 626656
Weymouth Marina Mechanical Services Weymouth		01305 779379
Whittington, G Lady Bee Marine, Shoreham		01273 593801
Whitewater Marine Malahide		+353 1 816 8473
Wigmore Wright Marine Services Penarth Marina		029 2070 9983
Wright, M Manaccan		01326 231502
Wyko Industrial Services Aberdeen		01224 246560
Ynys Marine Cardigan		01239 613179
Youngboats Faversham		01795 536176
1° West Marine Ltd Portsmouth		023 9283 8335

MASTS, SPARS & RIGGING

JWS Marine Services Portsmouth 02392 755155
A2 Rigging Falmouth 01326 312233
Allspars Plymouth 01752 266766
Amble Boat Co Ltd Morpeth 01665 710267
Arun Canvas & Rigging Littlehampton 01903 732561
B+ St Peter Port 01481 726071
Briggs, Nick Fleetwood 07513 403831
Buchanan, Keith St Mary's 01720 422037
Bussell & Co, WL Weymouth 01305 785633
Carbospars Ltd Hamble 023 8045 6736
Cable & Rope Works Bexhill-on-Sea 01424 220112
Clarke Rigging, Niall Coleraine 07916 083858
Clyde Rigging Ardrossan 07773 244821
Coates Marine Ltd Whitby 01947 604486
Cunliffe, Alistair Fleetwood 07555 798310
Dauntless Boatyard Ltd Canvey Island 01268 793782
Davies Marine Services Ramsgate 01843 586172
Eurospars Ltd Plymouth 01752 550550
Exe Leisure Exeter 01392 879055
Fox's Marine Ipswich Ltd Ipswich 01473 689111
Freeland Yacht Spars Ltd Dorchester on Thames 01865 341277
Gordon, AD Portland 01305 821569
Hamble Custom Rigging Centre Hamble 023 8045 2000
Harris Rigging Totnes 01803 840160
Hemisphere Rigging Services Plymouth 01752 403574
Heyn Engineering Belfast 028 9035 0022
Holman Rigging Chichester 01243 514000
Irish Spars and Rigging Malahide +353 86 209 5996
JWS Marine Services Portsmouth 02392 755155
Kildale Marine Hull 01482 227464
Kilrush Marina Boatyard Kilrush +35 87 7990091
Lowestoft Yacht Services Lowestoft 01502 585535
Laverty, Billy Galway +353 86 3892614
Leitch, WB Tarbert, Loch Fyne 01880 820287
Lewis, Harry, Kinsale +353 87 266 7127
LR Rigging Noss on Dart 01803 840160
Marine Resource Centre Oban 01631 720291
Martin Leaning Masts & Rigging Hayling 023 9237 1152
Mast & Rigging Crosshaven +353 21 483 3878
Mast & Rigging Dublin +353 41 988 0389
Mast & Rigging Services Largs 01475 670110
Mast & Rigging Services Inverkip 01475 522700
MP Marine Maryport 01900 810299
Ocean Rigging Lymington 01590 676292
Owen Sails Oban 01631 720485
Pro Rig S Ireland +353 87 298 3333
Ratsey, Stephen Milford Haven 01646 601561
RigIt Ardrossan 07593 220213
Rig Magic Ipswich 01473 655089
Rig Shop Southampton 023 8033 8341
Ronstan Gosport 023 9252 5377
Salcombe Boatstore Salcombe 01548 843708
Seldén Mast Ltd Gosport 01329 504000
Silvers Marina Ltd Helensburgh 01436 831222
Silverwood Yacht Services Ltd Portsmouth 023 9232 7067
Spencer Rigging Cowes 01983 292022
Storrar Marine Store Newcastle upon Tyne 0191 266 1037
Tedfords Rigging & Rafts Belfast 028 9032 6763
TJ Rigging Conwy 07780 972411
TS Rigging Maldon 01621 874861
Windjammer Marine Milford Marina 01646 699070
Yacht Rigging Services Plymouth 01752 226609
Z Spars UK Hadleigh 01473 822130

NAVIGATION EQUIPMENT – GENERAL

Belson Design Ltd, Nick Southampton 077 6835 1330
Brown Son & Ferguson Ltd Glasgow 0141 429 1234
Cooke & Son Ltd, B Hull 01482 223454
Diverse Yacht Services Hamble 023 8045 3399
Dolphin Maritime Software Ltd Lancaster 01524 841946
Dubois Phillips & McCallum Ltd Liverpool 0151 236 2776
Garmin Southampton 02380 524000

NAVIGATION EQUIPMENT – SAILMAKERS & REPAIRS

Geonav UK Ltd
Poole 0870 240 4575

Imray Laurie Norie and Wilson Ltd
St Ives, Cambs 01480 462114

Kelvin Hughes
Southampton 023 8063 4911

Lilley & Gillie Ltd, John
North Shields 0191 257 2217

Marine Chart Services
Wellingborough 01933 441629

Navico UK
Romsey 01794 510010

PC Maritime
Plymouth 01752 254205

Price & Co, WF Bristol 0117 929 2229

Raymarine Ltd
Portsmouth 023 9269 3611

Royal Institute of Navigation
London 020 7591 3130

Sea Chest Nautical Bookshop
Plymouth 01752 222012

Seath Instruments (1992) Ltd
Lowestoft 01502 573811

Smith (Marine) Ltd, AM
London 020 8529 6988

South Bank Marine Charts Ltd
Grimsby 01472 361137

Southcoasting Navigators
Devon 01626 335626

Stanford Charts
Bristol 0117 929 9966
London 020 7836 1321
Manchester 0870 890 3730

Todd Chart Agency Ltd
County Down 028 9146 6640

UK Hydrographic Office
Taunton 01823 337900

Warsash Nautical Bookshop
Warsash 01489 572384

Yachting Instruments Ltd
Sturminster Newton 01258 817662

PAINT & OSMOSIS

Advanced Blast Cleaning Paint
Tavistock 01822 617192
07970 407911

Herm Seaway Marine Ltd
St Peter Port 01481 726829

Gillingham Marina 01634 280022

Hempel Paints
Southampton 02380 232000

International Coatings Ltd
Southampton 023 8022 6722

Marineware Ltd
Southampton 023 8033 0208

NLB Marine
Ardrossan 01563 521509

Pro-Boat Ltd
Burnham on Crouch 01621 785455

Rustbuster Ltd
Peterborough 01775 761222

SP Systems, I of Wight 01983 828000

PROPELLERS & STERGEAR/REPAIRS

CJR Propulsion Ltd
Southampton 023 8063 9366

Darglow Engineering Ltd
Wareham 01929 556512

Propeller Revolutions
Poole 01202 671226

Sillette – Sonic Ltd
Sutton 020 8337 7543

Vetus Den Ouden Ltd
Southampton 02380 454507

RADIO COURSES / SCHOOLS

Bisham Abbey Sailing & Navigation School Bisham 01628 474960

**East Coast Offshore Yachting –
Les Rant** Perry 01480 861381

Hamble School of Yachting
Hamble 023 8045 6687

Pembrokeshire Cruising
Neyland 01646 602500

Plymouth Sailing School
Plymouth 01752 493377

Start Point Sailing
Kingsbridge 01548 810917

REEFING SYSTEMS

Atlantic Spars Ltd
Brixham 01803 843322

Calibra Marine International Ltd
Southampton 08702 400358

Eurospars Ltd
Plymouth 01752 550550

Holman Rigging
Chichester 01243 514000

Sea Teach Ltd Emsworth 01243 375774

Southern Spar Services
Northam 023 8033 1714

Wragg, Chris Lymington 01590 677052

Z Spars UK Hadleigh 01473 822130

REPAIR MATERIALS & ACCESSORIES

Akeron Ltd
Southend on Sea 01702 297101

Howells & Son, KJ Poole 01202 665724

JB Timber Ltd
North Ferriby 01482 631765

Robbins Timber
Bristol 0117 9633136

Sika Ltd
Welwyn Garden City 01707 394444

Solent Composite Systems
East Cowes 01983 292602

Technix Rubber & Plastics Ltd
Southampton 01489 789944

Tiflex Liskeard 01579 320808

Timage & Co Ltd
Braintree 01376 343087

Trade Grade Products Ltd
Poole 01202 820177

Wessex Resins & Adhesives Ltd
Romsey 01794 521111

ROPE & WIRE

Cable & Rope Works
Bexhill-on-Sea 01424 220112

Euro Rope Ltd
Scunthorpe 01724 280480

Marlow Ropes
Hailsham 01323 444444

Mr Splice Leicester 0800 1697178

Spinlock Ltd Cowes 01983 295555

TJ Rigging Conwy 07780 972411

SAFETY EQUIPMENT

AB Marine Ltd
St Peter Port 01481 722378

Adec Marine Ltd
Croydon 020 8686 9717

Anchorwatch UK
Edinburgh 0131 447 5057

Avon Inflatables
Llanelli 01554 882000

Cosalt International Ltd
Aberdeen 01224 588327

Crewsaver Gosport 01329 820000

Glaslyn Marine Supplies Ltd
Porthmadog 01766 513545

Exposure Lights
Pulborough 01798 839300

MARINA SUPPLIES AND SERVICES GUIDE

Guardian Fire Protection		
Manchester	0800 358 7522	
Hale Marine, Ron		
Portsmouth	023 9273 2985	
Herm Seaway Marine Ltd		
St Peter Port	01481 722838	
KTS Seasafety Kilkeel	028 41762655	
McMurdo Pains Wessex		
Portsmouth	023 9262 3900	
Met Office Exeter	0870 900 0100	
Nationwide Marine Hire		
Warrington	01925 245788	
Norwest Marine Ltd		
Liverpool	0151 207 2860	
Ocean Safety		
Southampton	023 8072 0800	
Polymarine Ltd Conwy	01492 583322	
Premium Liferaft Services		
Burnham-on-Crouch	0800 243673	
Ribeye Dartmouth	01803 832060	
South Eastern Marine Services Ltd		
Basildon	01268 534427	
Suffolk Sailing		
Ipswich	01473 604678	
Whitstable Marine		
Whitstable	01227 262525	
Winters Marine Ltd		
Salcombe	01548 843580	

SAILMAKERS & REPAIRS

A2 Rigging Falmouth	01326 312233
Alsop Sailmakers, John Salcombe	01548 843702
AM Trimming Windsor	01932 821090
Arun Canvas & Rigging Littlehampton	01903 732561
Barrett, Katy St Peter Port	07781 404299
Batt Sails Bosham	01243 575505
Bissett and Ross Aberdeen	01224 580659
Boatshed, The Felinheli, Bangor	01248 679939
Breaksea Sails Barry	01446 730785
Bristol Sails Bristol	0117 922 5080
Buchanan, Keith St Mary's	01720 422037
C&J Marine Ltd Chichester	01243 785485
Calibra Sails Dartmouth	01803 833094
Clarke Rigging, Niall Coleraine	07916 083858
Coastal Covers Portsmouth	023 9252 0200
Covercare Fareham	01329 311878
Covers + Stuff Douglas, Isle of Man	07624 400037
Crawford, Margaret Kirkwall	01856 875692
Crusader Sails Poole	01202 670580
Crystal Covers Portsmouth	023 9238 0143
Cullen Sailmakers Galway	+353 91 771991
Dolphin Sails Harwich	01255 243366
Doyle Sails Southampton	023 8033 2622
Downer International Sails & Chandlery Dun Laoghaire	+353 1 280 0231
Duthie Marine Safety, Arthur Glasgow	0141 429 4553
Dynamic Sails Emsworth	01243 374495
Flew Sailmakers Portchester	01329 822676
Fylde Coast Sailmaking Co Fleetwood	01253 873476
Freeman Sails Padstow	07771 610053
Garland Sails Bristol	01275 393473
Goacher Sails Bowness, Cumbria	01539 488686
Gowen Ocean Sailmakers West Mersea	01206 384412
Green Sailmakers, Paul Plymouth	01752 660317
Henderson Sails & Covers Southsea	023 9229 4700
Holman Rigging Chichester	01243 514000
Hood Sailmakers UK Wareham	0844 209 4789
Hooper, A Plymouth	01752 830411
Hyde Sails Southampton	0845 543 8945
Jackson Yacht Services Jersey	01534 743819
Jeckells and Son Ltd (Wroxham) Wroxham	01603 782223
Jessail Ardrossan	01294 467311
JKA Sailmakers Pwllheli	01758 613266
Kemp Sails Ltd Wareham	01929 554308/554378
Kildale Marine Hull	01482 227464
Lawrence Sailmakers, J Brightlingsea	01206 302863
Leitch, WB Tarbert, Loch Fyne	01880 820287
Leith UK Berwick on Tweed	01289 307264
Le Monnier, Yannick Galway	+353 87 628 9854
Lodey Sails Newlyn	01736 719359
Lossie Sails Lossiemouth	07989 956698
Lucas Sails Portchester	023 9237 3699
Malakoff and Moore Lerwick	01595 695544
McCready and Co Ltd, J Belfast	028 90232842
McKillop Sails, John Kingsbridge	01548 852343
McNamara Sails, Michael Great Yarmouth	01692 584186
McWilliam Sailmaker (Crosshaven) Crosshaven	+353 21 4831505
Sail Shape Fowey	01726 833731
Montrose Rope and Sails Montrose	01674 672657
Mountfield Sails Hayling Island	023 9246 3720
Mouse Sails Holyhead	01407 763636
Nicholson Hughes Sails Rosneath	01436 831356
North Sails Cork	+353 21 206 1769
North Sea Sails Tollesbury	01621 869367
North West Sails Keighley	01535 652949
Northrop Sails Ramsgate	01843 851665
O'Mahony Sailmakers Kinsale	+353 86 326 0018
O'Sullivans Marine Ltd Tralee	+353 66 7129635
Owen Sails Benderloch	01631 720485
Parker & Kay Sailmakers – East Ipswich	01473 659878
Parker & Kay Sailmakers – South Hamble	023 8045 8213
Penrose Sailmakers Falmouth	01326 312705
Pinnell & Bax Northampton	01604 592808
Pollard Marine Port St Mary	01624 835831

SAILMAKERS & REPAIRS – TUITION/SAILING SCHOOLS

Quantum Sails
Ipswich Haven Marina　01473 659878

Quantum-Parker & Kay Sailmakers
Hamble　023 8045 8213

Quay Sails (Poole) Ltd
Poole　01202 681128

Ratsey & Lapthorn
Isle of Wight　01983 294051

Ratsey Sailmakers, Stephen
Milford Haven　01646 601561

Relling One Design
Portland　01305 826555

SO31 Bags
Southampton　023 8045 5106

Rig Shop, The
Southampton　023 8033 8341

Rockall Sails Chichester　01243 573185

Sail Locker
Woolverstone Marina　01473 780206

Sail Style
Hayling Island　023 9246 3720

Sails & Canvas Exeter　01392 877527
Sail Register Ulceby　01469 589444
Saltern Sail Co Cowes　01983 280014

Saltern Sail Company
Yarmouth　01983 760120

Sanders Sails
Lymington　01590 673981

Saturn Sails Largs　01475 689933

Scott & Co, Graham
St Peter Port　01481 259380

Shore Sailmakers
Swanwick　01489 589450

SKB Sails Falmouth　01326 372107

Sketrick Sailmakers Ltd
Killinchy　028 9754 1400

Solo Sails Penzance　01736 366004

Storrar Marine Store
Newcastle upon Tyne　0191 266 1037

Suffolk Sails
Woodbridge　01394 386323

Sunset Sails Sligo　+353 71 62792

Torquay Marina Sails and Canvas
Exeter　01392 877527

Trident UK Gateshead　0191 490 1736

Sailcare (UK) Ltd Cowes　01983 248589

W Sails Leigh-on-Sea　01702 714550

Warren Hall Beaucette　07781 444280
Watson Sails Dublin　+353 1 846 2206

WB Leitch and Son
Tarbert　01880 820287

Westaway Sails
Plymouth Yacht Haven　01752 892560

Westsails.ie Kilrush　+35 876289854

Wilkinson Sails
Burnham-on-Crouch　01621 786770

Wilkinson Sails
Teynham　01795 521503

Yacht Shop, The
Fleetwood　01253 879238

SOLAR POWER

Ampair Ringwood　01425 480780
Barden UK Ltd Fareham　01489 570770

Marlec Engineering Co Ltd
Corby　01536 201588

SPRAYHOODS & DODGERS

A & B Textiles
Gillingham　01634 579686

Allison–Gray Dundee　01382 505888

Arton, Charles
Milford-on-Sea　01590 644682

Arun Canvas and Rigging Ltd
Littlehampton　01903 732561

Boatshed, The
Felinheli, Bangor　01248 679939

Buchanan, Keith
St Mary's　01720 422037

C & J Marine Textiles
Chichester　01243 785485

Covercare, Fareham　01329 311878

Covercraft
Southampton　023 8033 8286

Crystal Covers
Portsmouth　023 9238 0143

Forth Marine Textiles
Holy Loch　01383 622444

Jeckells and Son Ltd
Wroxham　01603 782223

Jessail Ardrossan　01294 467311

Lomond Boat Covers
Alexandria　01389 602734

Lucas Sails Portchester　023 9237 3699

Poole Canvas Co Ltd
Poole　01202 677477

Sail Register Ulceby　01469 589444

Saundersfoot Auto Marine
Saundersfoot　01834 812115

Trident UK Gateshead　0191 490 1736

SURVEYORS AND NAVAL ARCHITECTS

Amble Boat Company Ltd
Amble　01665 710267

Ark Surveys
East Anglia/South Coast
　01621 857065/01794 521957

Atkin & Associates
Lymington　01590 688633

Barbican Yacht Agency Ltd
Plymouth　01752 228855

Battick, Lee St Helier　01534 611143

Booth Marine Surveys, Graham
Birchington-on-Sea　01843 843793

Byrde & Associates
Kimmeridge　01929 480064

Bureau Maritime Ltd
Maldon　01621 859181

Byrde & Associates
Kimmeridge　01929 480064

Cannell & Associates, David M
Wivenhoe　01206 823337

Cardiff Commercial Boat Operators Ltd
Cardiff　029 2037 7872

Clarke Designs LLP, Owen
Dartmouth　01803 770495

Connor, Richard
Coleraine　07712 115751

Cox, David Penryn　01326 340808

Davies, Peter N
Wivenhoe　01206 823289

Down Marine Co Ltd
Belfast　028 90480247

Evans, Martin
Kirby le Soken　07887 724055

Goodall, JL Whitby　01947 604791

Green, James Plymouth　01752 660516

Greening Naval Architect Ltd, David
Salcombe　01548 842000

Hansing & Associates
North Wales/Midlands　01248 671291

JP Services – Marine Safety & Training
Chichester　01243 537552

MacGregor, WA
Felixstowe　01394 676034

Mahoney & Co, KPO
Co Cork　+353 21 477 6150

MARINA GUIDE 2026

MARINA SUPPLIES AND SERVICES GUIDE

Marinte Surveys UK
Emsworth 07798 554535
Marintec Lymington 01590 683414
Norwood Marine
Margate 01843 835711
Quay Consultants Ltd
West Wittering 01243 673056
Scott Marine Surveyors & Consultants
Conwy 01492 573001
S Roberts Marine Ltd
Liverpool 0151 707 8300
Staton-Bevan, Tony
Lymington 01590 645755/
07850 315744
Thomas, Stephen
Southampton 023 8048 6273
Towler, Perrin
Lymington 01590 718087
Victoria Yacht Surveys 0800 083 2113
Ward & McKenzie
Woodbridge 01394 383222
Ward & McKenzie (North East)
Pocklington 01759 304322
YDSA Yacht Designers & Surveyors Association Bordon 0845 0900162

TAPE TECHNOLOGY

CC Marine Services (Rubbaweld) Ltd
London 020 7402 4009
Trade Grade Products Ltd
Poole 01202 820177
UK Epoxy Resins
Burscough 01704 892364
3M United Kingdom plc
Bracknell 0870 5360036

TRANSPORT/YACHT DELIVERIES

Boat Shifters
07733 344018/01326 210548
Convoi Exceptionnel Ltd
Hamble 023 8045 3045
Debbage Yachting
Ipswich 01473 601169
East Coast Offshore Yachting
01480 861381
Hainsworth's UK and Continental
Bingley 01274 565925
Houghton Boat Transport
Tewkesbury 07831 486710
MCL Transboat 08455 201900
MJS Boat Transport
Alexandria, Scotland 01389 755047

Moonfleet Sailing
Poole 01202 682269
Performance Yachting
Plymouth 01752 565023
Peters & May Ltd
Southampton 023 8048 0480
Reeder School of Seamanship, Mike
Lymington 01590 674560
Seafix Boat Transfer 01766 514507
Sealand Boat Deliveries Ltd
Liverpool 01254 705225
Shearwater Sailing
Southampton 01962 775213
Southcoasting Navigators
Devon 01626 335626
West Country Boat Transport
01566 785651
Wolff, David 07659 550131

TUITION/SAILING SCHOOLS

Association of Scottish Yacht Charterers Argyll 07787 363562
01852 200258
Bisham Abbey Sailing & Navigation School Bisham 01628 474960
Blue Baker Yachts
Ipswich 01473 780008
British Offshore Sailing School
Hamble 023 8045 7733
Coastal Sea School
Weymouth 0870 321 3271
Dart Harbour Sea School 01803 839339
Dartmouth Sailing 01803 833399
Drake Sailing School
Plymouth 01635 253009
East Anglian Sea School
Ipswich 01473 659992
East Coast Offshore Yachting – Les Rant Perry 01480 861381
Gibraltar Sailing Centre +350 78554
Glenans Irish Sailing School
Baltimore +353 28 20154
Hamble School of Yachting
Hamble 023 8045 6687
Haslar Sea School
Gosport 023 9260 2708
Hobo Yachting
Southampton 023 8033 4574
Hoylake Sailing School
Wirral 0151 632 4664
Ibiza Sailing School
07092 235 853

International Yachtmaster Academy
Southampton 0800 515439
JP Services – Marine Safety & Training
Chichester 01243 537552
Lymington Cruising School
Lymington 01590 677478
Marine Leisure Association (MLA)
Southampton 023 8029 3822
Menorca Cruising School 01995 679240
Moonfleet Sailing Poole 01202 682269
National Marine Correspondence School Macclesfield 01625 262365
Pembrokeshire Cruising
Neyland 01646 602500
Performance Yachting & Chandlery
Plymouth 01752 565023
Plain Sailing
Dartmouth 01803 853843
Plymouth Sailing School
Plymouth 01752 493377
Port Edgar Marina & Sailing School
Port Edgar 0131 331 3330
Portsmouth Outdoor Centre
Portsmouth 023 9266 3873
Portugal Sail & Power 01473 833001
Safe Water Training Sea School Ltd
Wirral 0151 630 0466
Sail East Felixstowe 01255 502887
Sail East
River Crouch 07860 271954
Sail East
River Medway 07932 157027
Sail East Harwich 01473 689344
Sally Water Training
East Cowes 01983 299033
Sea-N-Shore Salcombe 01548 842276
Seafever
East Grinstead 01342 316293
Solaris Mediterranean Sea School
01925 642909
Solent School of Yachting
Southampton 023 8045 7733
Southcoasting Navigators
Devon 01626 335626
Southern Sailing
Southampton 01489 575511
Start Point Sailing
Dartmouth 01548 810917
Sunsail
Port Solent/Largs 0870 770 6314
Team Sailing Gosport 023 9252 4370
Workman Marine School
Portishead 01275 845844

WORLD CLASS SKIPPERS WANTED

NO PRESSURE

Sir Robin Knox-Johnston
Founder of the Clipper Round the World Yacht Race

Join the elite and take on the world's longest yacht race, crewed exclusively by novice crew embarking on the race of their lives.

Clipper Race Skippers are exceptional. These men and women have the fortitude to take on the toughest of mental challenges, and the physical endurance to successfully lead a team through Mother Nature's extreme environments on a 40,000 mile lap around the globe.

We are recruiting experienced professional Skippers for the next edition of the Clipper Race. To qualify you must hold a valid Yachtmaster Ocean certificate [commercial endorsed] or International Yacht Training Master of Yachts.

↘ APPLY NOW

clipperroundtheworld.com/careers
raceskipper@clipper-ventures.com
+44 (0) 2392 526000

MARINA SUPPLIES AND SERVICES GUIDE

Wride School of Sailing, Bob
North Ferriby 01482 635623

WATERSIDE ACCOMMODATION & RESTAURANTS

51st State Bar & Grill
Dunoon 01369 703595

Abbey, The Penzance 01736 366906

Al Porto
Hull Marina 01482 238889

Arun View Inn, The
Littlehampton 01903 722335

Baywatch on the Beach
Bembridge 01983 873259

Beaucette Marina Restaurant
Guernsey 01481 247066

Bella Napoli
Brighton Marina 01273 818577

Bembridge Coast Hotel
Bembridge 01983 873931

Budock Vean Hotel
Porth Navas Creek 01326 252100

Café Mozart Cowes 01983 293681

Caffé Uno Port Solent 023 9237 5227

Chandlers Bar & Bistro
Queen Anne's Battery Marina
Plymouth 01752 257772

Cruzzo Malahide Marina
Co Dublin +353 1 845 0599

Cullins Yard Bistro
Dover 01304 211666

Custom House, The
Poole 01202 676767

Dart Marina River Lounge
Dartmouth 01803 832580

Doghouse Swanwick Marina,
Hamble 01489 571602

Dolphin Restaurant
Gorey 01534 853370

Doune Knoydart 01687 462667

El Puertos
Penarth Marina 029 2070 5551

**Falmouth Marina
Marine Bar and Restaurant**
Falmouth 01326 313481

Ferry Boat Inn West Wick Marina
Nr Chelmsford 01621 740208

Ferry Inn, The (restaurant)
Pembroke Dock 01646 682947

Fisherman's Wharf
Sandwich 01304 613636

Folly Inn Cowes 01983 297171

Gaffs Restaurant
Fenit, County Kerry +353 66 71 36666

Godleys Hotel Fenit
County Kerry +353 66 71 36108

Harbour Lights Restaurant
Walton on the Naze 01255 851887

Haven Bar and Bistro, The
Lymington Yacht Haven 01590 679971

Haven Hotel Poole 08453 371550

HMS Ganges Restaurant
Mylor Yacht Harbour 01326 374320

Holy Loch Inn 01369 706903

Hunters Bar & Grill
Holy Loch 01369 707772

Jolly Sailor, The
Bursledon 023 8040 5557

Kames Hotel Argyll 01700 811489

Ketch Rigger, The Hamble Point
Marina Hamble 023 8045 5601

Kings Arms Stoborough 01929 552705

Kota Restaurant
Porthleven 01326 562407

La Cala Lady Bee Marina
Shoreham 01273 597422

La Cantina Restaurant
Dunoon 01369 703595

Lake Yard Ltd
Poole 01202 676953

Le Nautique
St Peter Port 01481 721714

Lighter Inn, The
Topsham 01392 875439

Mariners Bistro Sparkes Marina,
Hayling Island 023 9246 9459

Mary Mouse II Haslar Marina,
Gosport 023 9252 5200

Martha's Vineyard
Milford Haven 01646 697083

Master Builder's House Hotel
Buckler's Hard 01590 616253

Millstream Hotel
Bosham 01243 573234

Montagu Arms Hotel
Beaulieu 01590 612324

Oyster Quay, Mercury Yacht Harbour,
Hamble 023 8045 7220

Paris Hotel Coverack 01326 280258

Pebble Beach, The
Gosport 023 9251 0789

Philip Leisure Group
Dartmouth 01803 833351

Priory Bay Hotel
Seaview, Isle of Wight 01983 613146

QC's Cahersiveen +353 66 9472244

Quay Bar Galway +353 91 568347

Quayside Hotel Brixham 01803 855751

Queen's Hotel Kirkwall 01856 872200

Sails Dartmouth 01803 839281

Shell Bay Seafood Restaurant
Poole Harbour 01929 450363

Simply Italian Sovereign Harbour,
Eastbourne 01323 470911

Spit Sand Fort
The Solent 01329 242077

Steamboat Inn
Lossiemouth 01343 812066

Tayvallich Inn, The
Argyll 01546 870282

Villa Adriana Newhaven Marina
Newhaven 01273 513976

Warehouse Brasserie, The
Poole 01202 677238

36 on the Quay
Emsworth 01243 375592

WEATHER INFORMATION

Met Office Exeter 0870 900 0100

WOOD FITTINGS

Howells & Son, KJ
Poole 01202 665724

Onward Trading Co Ltd
Southampton 01489 885250

Robbins Timber
Bristol 0117 963 3136

Sheraton Marine Cabinet
Witney 01993 868275

YACHT BROKERS

ABC Powermarine
Beaumaris 01248 811413

**ABYA Association of
Brokers & Yacht Agents**
Bordon 0845 0900162

Adur Boat Sales
Southwick 01273 596680

Ancasta International Boat Sales
Southampton 023 8045 0000

Anglia Yacht Brokerage
Bury St Edmunds 01359 271747

Ardmair Boat Centre
Ullapool 01854 612054

Barbican Yacht Agency, The
Plymouth 01752 228855

Bates Wharf Marine Sales Ltd
  01932 571141

BJ Marine Bangor 028 9127 1434

Boatworks + Ltd
St Peter Port 01481 726071

Caley Marina Inverness 01463 236539

Calibra Marine International Ltd
Southampton 08702 400358

Camper & Nicholsons International
London 020 7009 1950

Clarke & Carter Interyacht Ltd
Ipswich/Burnham on Crouch
  01473 659681/01621 785600

Coastal Leisure Ltd
Southampton 023 8033 2222

Dale Sailing Brokerage
Neyland 01646 603105

WATERSIDE ACCOMMODATION & RESTAURANTS – YACHT CLUBS

Deacons Southampton	023 8040 2253	
Exe Leisure Topsham	001392 879055	
Ferrypoint Boat Co Youghal	+353 24 94232	
Gweek Quay Boatyard	01326 221657	
International Barge & Yacht Brokers Southampton	023 8045 5205	
Iron Wharf Boatyard Faversham	01795 536296	
Jackson Yacht Services Jersey	01534 743819	
Kings Yacht Agency Beaulieu	01590 616316	
Kippford Slipway Ltd Dalbeattie	01556 620249	
Lencraft Boats Ltd Dungarvan	+353 58 68220	
Liberty Yachts Ltd Plymouth	01752 227911	
Lucas Yachting, Mike Torquay	01803 212840	
Network Yacht Brokers Dartmouth	01803 834864	
Network Yacht Brokers Plymouth	01752 605377	
New Horizon Yacht Agency Guernsey	01481 726335	
Oyster Brokerage Ltd Southampton	02380 831011	
Pearn and Co, Norman (Looe Boatyard) Looe	01503 262244	
Performance Boat Company Maidenhead	07768 464717	
Peters Chandlery Chichester	01243 511033	
Portavon Marina Keynsham	0117 986 1626	
Retreat BY Topsham	01392 874720	
SD Marine Ltd Southampton	023 8045 7278	
Sea & Shore Ship Chandler Dundee	01382 202666	
South Pier Shipyard St Helier	01534 711000	
South West Yacht Brokers Group Plymouth	01752 401421	
Sunbird Marine Services Fareham	01329 842613	
Swordfish Marine Brokerage Holy Loch	01369 701905	
Trafalgar Yacht Services Fareham	01329 823577	
Transworld Yachts Hamble	023 8045 7704	
Walker Boat Sales Deganwy	01492 555706	
Walton Marine Sales Brighton	01273 670707	
Portishead	01275 840132	
Wroxham	01603 781178	
Watson Marine, Charles Hamble	023 8045 6505	
Western Marine Dublin	+353 1280 0321	
Woodrolfe Brokerage Maldon	01621 868494	
Youngboats Faversham	01795 536176	

YACHT CHARTERS & HOLIDAYS

Ardmair Boat Centre Ullapool	01854 612054
Association of Scottish Yacht Charterers Argyll	01880 820012
Camper & Nicholsons International London	020 7009 1950
Coastal Leisure Ltd Southampton	023 8033 2222
Crusader Yachting Turkey	01732 867321
Dartmouth Sailing	01803 833399
Dartmouth Yacht Charters Kingswear	01803 883501
Doune Marine Mallaig	01687 462667
Four Seasons Yacht Charter Gosport	023 9251 1789
Golden Black Sailing Cornwall	01209 715757
Hamble Point Yacht Charters Hamble	023 8045 7110
Haslar Marina & Victory Yacht Charters Gosport	023 9252 0099
Indulgence Yacht Charters Padstow	01841 719090
Liberty Yachts West Country, Greece, Mallorca & Italy	01752 227911
Nautilus Yachting Mediterranean & Caribbean	01732 867445
On Deck Sailing Southampton	023 8063 9997
Patriot Charters & Sail School Milford Haven	01437 741202
West Country Yachts Plymouth	01752 606999
Falmouth	01326 212320
Puffin Yachts Port Solent	01483 420728
Sailing Holidays Ltd Mediterranean	020 8459 8787
Sailing Holidays in Ireland Kinsale	+353 21 477 2927
Setsail Holidays Greece, Turkey, Croatia, Majorca	01787 310445
Shannon Sailing Ltd Tipperary	+353 67 24499
Sleat Marine Services Isle of Skye	01471 844216
Smart Yachts Mediterranean	01425 614804
South West Marine Training Dartmouth	01803 853843
Sovereign Sailingl Kinsale	+353 87 6172555
Sunsail Worldwide	0870 770 0102
Templecraft Yacht Charters Lewes	01273 812333
TJ Sailing Gosport	07803 499691
Top Yacht Sailing Ltd Havant	02392 347655
Victory Yacht Charters Gosport	023 9252 0099
West Wales Yacht Charter Pwllheli	07748 634869
39 North (Mediterranean) Kingskerwell	07071 393939

YACHT CLUBS

Aberaeron YC Aberdovey	01545 570077
Aberdeen and Stonehaven SC Nr Inverurie	01569 764006
Aberdour BC	01383 860029
Abersoch Power BC Abersoch	01758 712027
Aberystwyth BC Aberystwyth	01970 624575
Aldeburgh YC	01728 452562
Alderney SC	01481 822959
Alexandra YC Southend-on-Sea	01702 340363
Arklow SC	+353 402 33100
Arun YC Littlehampton	01903 716016
Axe YC Axemouth	01297 20043
Ayr Yacht and CC	01292 476034
Ballyholme YC Bangor	028 91271467
Baltimore SC	+353 28 20426
Banff SC	01464 820308
Bantry Bay SC	+353 27 51724
Barry YC	01446 735511
Beaulieu River SC Brockenhurst	01590 616273

MARINA SUPPLIES AND SERVICES GUIDE

Bembridge SC
Isle of Wight   01983 872237
Benfleet YC
Canvey Island   01268 792278
Blackpool and Fleetwood YC   01253 884205
Blackwater SC Maldon   01621 853923
Blundellsands SC   0151 929 2101
Bosham SC Chichester   01243 572341
Brading Haven YC
Isle of Wight   01983 872289
Bradwell CC   01621 892970
Bradwell Quay YC
Wickford   01268 890173
Brancaster Staithe SC   01485 210249
Brandy Hole YC
Hullbridge   01702 230320
Brightlingsea SC   01206 303275
Brighton Marina YC
Peacehaven   01273 818711
Bristol Avon SC   01225 873472
Bristol Channel YC
Swansea   01792 366000
Bristol Corinthian YC
Axbridge   01934 732033
Brixham YC   01803 853332
Burnham Overy Staithe SC   01328 730961
Burnham-on-Crouch SC   01621 782812
Burnham-on-Sea SC
Bridgwater   01278 792911
Burry Port YC   01554 833635
Cabot CC   01275 855207
Caernarfon SC (Menai Strait)
Caernarfon   01286 672861
Campbeltown SC   01586 552488
Island YC Canvey Island   01702 510360
Cardiff YC   029 2046 3697
Cardiff Bay YC   029 20226575
Carlingford Lough YC
Rostrevor   028 4173 8604
Carrickfergus SC
Whitehead   028 93 351402
Castle Cove SC
Weymouth   01305 783708
Castlegate Marine Club
Stockton on Tees   01642 583299
Chanonry SC Fortrose   01463 221415
Chichester Cruiser and Racing Club
                    01483 770391
Chichester YC   01243 512918
Christchurch SC   01202 483150

Clyde CC Glasgow   0141 221 2774
Co Antrim YC
Carrickfergus   028 9337 2322
Cobnor Activities Centre Trust
                    01243 572791
Coleraine YC   028 703 44503
Colne YC Brightlingsea   01206 302594
Conwy YC Deganwy   01492 583690
Coquet YC   01665 710367
Corrib Rowing & YC
Galway City   +353 91 564560
Cowes Combined Clubs   01983 295744
Cowes Corinthian YC
Isle of Wight   01983 296333
Cowes Yachting   01983 280770
Cramond BC   0131 336 1356
Creeksea SC
Burnham-on-Crouch   01245 320578
Crookhaven SC   +353 87 2379997
Crouch YC
Burnham-on-Crouch   01621 782252
Dale YC   01646 636362
Dartmouth YC   01803 832305
Deben YC Woodbridge   01394 384440
Dell Quay SC Chichester   01243 514639
Dingle SC   +353 66 51984
Douglas Bay YC   01624 673965
Dovey YC
Aberdovey   01213 600008
Dun Laoghaire MYC   +353 1 288 938
Dunbar SC
Cockburnspath   01368 86287
East Antrim BC   028 28 277204
East Belfast YC   028 9065 6283
East Cowes SC   01983 531687
East Dorset SC Poole   01202 706111
East Lothian YC   01620 892698
Eastney Cruising Association
Portsmouth   023 92734103
Eling SC   023 80863987
Emsworth SC   01243 372850
Emsworth Slipper SC   01243 372523
Essex YC Southend   01702 478404
Exe SC (River Exe)
Exmouth   01395 264607
Eyott SC Mayland   01245 320703
Fairlie YC   01294 213940
Falmouth Town SC   01326 373915
Falmouth Watersports Association
Falmouth   01326 211223

Fareham Sailing & Motor BC
Fareham   01329 280738
Felixstowe Ferry SC   01394 283785
Findhorn YC Findhorn   01309 690247
Fishguard Bay YC
Lower Fishguard   01348 872866
Flushing SC Falmouth   01326 374043
Folkestone Yacht and Motor BC
Folkestone   01303 251574
Forth Corinthian YC
Haddington   0131 552 5939
Forth YCs Association
Edinburgh   0131 552 3006
Fowey Gallants SC   01726 832335
Foynes YC Foynes   +353 69 91201
Galway Bay SC   +353 91 794527
Glasson SC Lancaster   01524 751089
Gosport CC Gosport   02392 586838
Gravesend SC   07538 326623
Greenwich YC London   020 8858 7339
Grimsby and Cleethorpes YC
Grimsby   01472 356678
Guernsey YC
St Peter Port   01481 725342
Hamble River SC
Southampton   023 80452070
Hampton Pier YC
Herne Bay   01227 364749
Hardway SC Gosport   023 9258 1875
Hartlepool YC   01429 233423
Harwich Town SC   01255 503200
Hastings and St Leonards YC
Hastings   01424 420656
Haven Ports YC
Woodbridge   01473 659658
Hayling Ferry SC; Locks SC
Hayling Island   07870 367571
Hayling Island SC   023 92463768
Helensburgh SC Rhu   01436 672778
Helensburgh   01436 821234
Helford River SC   01326 231006
Herne Bay SC   01227 375650
Highcliffe SC
Christchurch   01425 274874
Holyhead SC   01407 762526
Holywood YC   028 90423355
Hoo Ness YC Sidcup   01634 250052
Hornet SC Gosport   023 9258 0403
Howth YC   +353 1 832 2141
Hoylake SC Wirral   0151 632 2616
Hullbridge YC   01702 231797
Humber Yawl Club   01482 667224
Hundred of Hoo SC   01634 250102

MARINA GUIDE 2026

YACHT CLUBS

Hurlingham YC London	020 8788 5547
Hurst Castle SC	01590 645589
Hythe SC Southampton	02380 846563
Hythe & Saltwood SC	01303 265178
Ilfracombe YC	01271 863969
Iniscealtra SC Limerick	+353 61 338347
Invergordon BC	01349 893772
Irish CC	+353 214870031
Island CC Salcombe	01548 844631
Island SC Isle of Wight	01983 296621
Island YC Canvey Island	01268 510360
Isle of Bute SC Rothesay	01700 502819
Isle of Man YC Port St Mary	01624 832088
Itchenor SC Chichester	01243 512400
Keyhaven YC	01590 642165
Killyleagh YC	028 4482 8250
Kircubbin SC	028 4273 8422
Kirkcudbright SC	01557 331727
Langstone SC Havant	023 9248 4577
Largs SC Largs	01475 670000
Larne Rowing & SC	028 2827 4573
Lawrenny YC	01646 651212
Leigh-on-Sea SC	01702 476788
Lerwick BC	01595 696954
Lilliput SC Poole	01202 740319
Littlehampton Yacht Club Littlehampton	01903 713990
Loch Ryan SC Stranraer	01776 706322
Lochaber YC Fort William	01397 772361
Locks SC Portsmouth	07980 856267
Looe SC	01503 262559
Lossiemouth CC Fochabers	01348 812121
Lough Swilly YC Fahn	+353 74 22377
Lowestoft CC	07810 522515
Lyme Regis Power BC	01297 443788
Lyme Regis SC	01297 442373
Lymington Town SC	0159 674514
Lympstone SC Exeter	01395 278792
Madoc YC Porthmadog	01766 512976
Malahide YC	+353 1 845 3372
Maldon Little Ship Club	01621 854139
Manx Sailing & CC Ramsey	01624 813494
Marchwood YC	023 80666141
Margate YC	01843 292602
Marina BC Pwllheli	01758 612271
Maryport YC	01228 560865
Mayflower SC Plymouth	01752 662526
Mayo SC (Rosmoney)	+353 98 27772
Medway YC Rochester	01634 718399
Menai Bridge BC Beaumaris	01248 810583
Mengham Rythe SC Hayling Island	023 92463337
Merioneth YC Barmouth	01341 280000
Monkstone Cruising and SC Swansea	01792 812229
Montrose SC Montrose	01674 672554
Mumbles YC Swansea	01792 369321
Mylor YC Falmouth	01326 374391
Nairn SC	01667 453897
National YC Dun Laoghaire	+353 1 280 5725
Netley SC Netley	023 80454272
New Quay YC Aberdovey	01545 560516
Newhaven & Seaford SC Seaford	01323 890077
Newport and Uskmouth SC Cardiff	01633 271417
Newtownards SC	028 9181 3426
Neyland YC	01646 600267
North Devon YC Bideford	01271 861390
North Fambridge Yacht Centre	01621 740370
North Haven YC Poole	01202 708830
North of England Yachting Association Kirkwall	01856 872331
North Sunderland Marine Club Sunderland	01665 721231
North Wales CC Conwy	01492 593481
North West Venturers YC (Beaumaris) Beaumaris	0161 2921943
Oban SC Ledaig by Oban	01631 563999
Orford SC Woodbridge	01394 450997
Orkney SC Kirkwall	01856 872331
Orwell YC Ipswich	01473 602288
Oulton Broad Yacht Station	01502 574946
Ouse Amateur SC Kings Lynn	01553 772239
Paignton SC Paignton	01803 525817
Parkstone YC Poole	01202 743610
Peel Sailing and CC Peel	01624 842390
Pembroke Haven YC	01646 684403
Pembrokeshire YC Milford Haven	01646 692799
Penarth YC	029 20708196
Pentland Firth YC Thurso	01847 891803
Penzance YC	01736 364989
Peterhead SC Ellon	01779 75527
Pin Mill SC Woodbridge	01394 780271
Plym YC Plymouth	01752 404991
Poolbeg YC	+353 1 660 4681
Poole YC	01202 672687
Porlock Weir SC Watchet	01643 862702
Port Edgar YC Penicuik	0131 657 2854
Port Navas YC Falmouth	01326 340065
Port of Falmouth Sailing Association Falmouth	01326 372927
Portchester SC	023 9237 6375
Porthcawl Harbour BC Swansea	01656 655935
Porthmadog SC Porthmadog	01766 513546
Portrush YC Portrush	028 7082 3932
Portsmouth SC	02392 820596
Prestwick SC Prestwick	01292 671117
Pwllheli SC Pwllhelli	01758 613343
Queenborough YC	01795 663955
Quoile YC Downpatrick	028 44 612266
River Towy BC Tenby	01267 241755
RAFYC	023 80452208
Redclyffe YC Poole	01929 557227
Restronguet SC Falmouth	01326 374536
Ribble CC Lytham St Anne's	01253 739983
River Wyre YC	01253 811948
RNSA (Plymouth)	01752 55123/83
Rochester CC	01634 841350
Rock Sailing and Water Ski Club Wadebridge	01208 862431
Royal Dart YC Dartmouth	01803 752496
Royal Motor YC Poole	01202 707227
Royal Anglesey YC (Beaumaris) Anglesey	01248 810295

Royal Burnham YC Burnham-on-Crouch 01621 782044	**Royal St George YC** Dun Laoghaire +353 1 280 1811	**Southwold SC** 01986 784225
Royal Channel Islands YC (Guernsey) St Peter Port 01481 725500	**Royal Tay YC** Dundee 01382 477133	**Sovereign Harbour YC** Eastbourne 01323 470888
Royal Channel Islands YC (Jersey) St Aubin 01534 745783	**Royal Temple YC** Ramsgate 01843 591766	**St Helier YC** 01534 721307/32229
Royal Cinque Ports YC Dover 01304 206262	**Royal Torbay YC** Torquay 01803 292006	**St Mawes SC** 01326 270686
Royal Corinthian YC Burnham-on-Crouch 01621 782105	**Royal Ulster YC** Bangor 028 91 270568	**Starcross Fishing & CC (River Exe)** Starcross 01626 891996
Royal Corinthian YC (Cowes) Cowes 01983 293581	**Royal Victoria YC** Fishbourne 01983 882325	**Starcross YC** Exeter 01626 890470
Royal Cork YC Crosshaven +353 214 831023	**Royal Welsh YC (Caernarfon)** Caernarfon 01286 672599	**Stoke SC** Ipswich 01473 624989
Royal Cornwall YC (RCYC) Falmouth 01326 312126	**Royal Welsh YC** Aernarfon 01286 672599	**Stornoway SC** 01851 705412
Royal Dorset YC Weymouth 01305 786258	**Royal Western YC** Plymouth 01752 226299	**Stour SC** 01206 393924
Royal Forth YC Edinburgh 0131 552 3006	**Royal Yacht Squadron** Isle of Wight 01983 292191	**Strangford Lough YC** Newtownards 028 97 541202
Royal Fowey YC Fowey 01726 833573	**Royal Yorkshire YC** Bridlington 01262 672041	**Strangford SC** Downpatrick 028 4488 1404
Royal Gourock YC 01475 632983	**Rye Harbour SC** 01797 223136	**Strood YC** Aylesford 01634 718261
Royal Highland YC Nairn 01667 493855	**Salcombe YC** 01548 842593	**Sunderland YC** 0191 567 5133
Royal Irish YC Dun Laoghaire +353 1 280 9452	**Saltash SC** 01752 845988	**Sunsail** Portsmouth 023 92222224
Royal London YC Isle of Wight 019 83299727	**Scalloway BC** Lerwick 01595 880409	**Sussex YC** Shoreham-by-Sea 01273 464868
Royal Lymington YC 01590 672677	**Scarborough YC** 01723 373821	**Swanage SC** 01929 422987
Royal Mersey YC Birkenhead 0151 645 3204	**Schull SC** +353 28 37352	**Swansea Yacht & Sub-Aqua Club** Swansea 01792 469096
Royal Motor YC Poole 01202 707227	**Scillonian Sailing and BC** St Mary's 01720 277229	**Tamar River SC** Plymouth 01752 362741
Royal Naval Club and Royal Albert YC Portsmouth 023 9282 5924	**Seasalter SC** Whitstable 07773 189943	**Tarbert Lochfyne YC** 01880 820376
Royal Naval Sailing Association Gosport 023 9252 1100	**Seaview YC** Isle of Wight 01983 613268	**Tay Corinthian BC** Dundee 01382 553534
Royal Norfolk & Suffolk YC Lowestoft 01502 566726	**Shoreham SC** Henfield 01273 453078	**Tay YCs Association** 01738 621860
Royal North of Ireland YC 028 90 428041	**Skerries SC** +353 1 849 1233	**Tees & Hartlepool YC** 01429 233423
Royal Northern and Clyde YC Rhu 01436 820322	**Slaughden SC** Duxford 01728 689036	**Tees SC** Aycliffe Village 01429 265400
Royal Northumberland YC Blyth 01670 353636	**Sligo YC** Sligo +353 71 77168	**Teifi BC - Cardigan Bay** Fishguard 01239 613846
Royal Plymouth Corinthian YC Plymouth 01752 664327	**Solva Boat Owners Association** Fishguard 01437 721538	**Teign Corinthian YC** Teignmouth 01626 777699
Royal Scottish Motor YC 0141 881 1024	**Solway YC** Kirkdudbright 01556 620312	**Tenby SC** 01834 842762
Royal Solent YC Yarmouth 01983 760256	**South Caernavonshire YC** Abersoch 01758 712338	**Tenby YC** 01834 842762
Royal Southampton YC Southampton 023 8022 3352	**South Cork SC** +353 28 36383	**Thames Estuary YC** 01702 345967
Royal Southern YC Southampton 023 8045 0300	**South Devon Sailing School** Newton Abbot 01626 52352	**Thorney Island SC** 01243 371731
	South Gare Marine Club - Sail Section Middlesbrough 01642 505630	**Thorpe Bay YC** 01702 587563
	South Shields SC 0191 456 5821	**Thurrock YC** Grays 01375 373720
	South Woodham Ferrers YC Chelmsford 01245 325391	**Tollesbury CC** 01621 869561
	Southampton SC 023 8044 6575	**Topsham SC** 01392 877524
		Torpoint Mosquito SC - Plymouth 01752 812508
		Tralee SC +353 66 7136119
		Troon CC 01292 311190
		Troon YC 01292 315315
		Tudor SC Portsmouth 02392 662002

YACHT CLUBS – YACHT VALETING

Tynemouth SC
Newcastle upon Tyne 0191 2572167
Up River YC
Hullbridge 01702 231654
Upnor SC 01634 718043
Vanguard SC
Workington 01228 674238
Wakering YC
Rochford 01702 530926
Waldringfield SC
Woodbridge 01394 283347
Walls Regatta Club
Lerwick 01595 809273
Walton & Frinton YC
Walton-on-the-Naze 01255 675526
Warrenpoint BC 028 4175 2137
Warsash SC Soton 01489 583575
Watchet Boat Owner Association
Watchet 01984 633736
Waterford Harbour SC
Dunmore East +353 51 383389
Watermouth YC
Watchet 01271 865048
Wear Boating Association
0191 567 5313
Wells SC
Wells-next-the-sea 01328 711190
West Kirby SC 0151 625 5579
West Mersea YC
Colchester 01206 382947
Western Isles YC 01688 302371

Western YC
Kilrush +353 87 2262885
Weston Bay YC
Portishead 07867 966429
Weston CC Soton 02380 466790
Weston SC Soton 02380 452527
Wexford HBC +353 53 22039
Weymouth SC 01305 785481
Whitby YC 07786 289393
Whitstable YC 01227 272942
Wicklow SC +353 404 67526
Witham SC Boston 01205 363598
Wivenhoe SC
Colchester 01206 822132
Woodbridge CC 01394 386737
Wormit BC 01382 553878
Yarmouth SC 01983 760270
Yealm YC
Newton Ferrers 01752 872291
Youghal Sailing Club +353 24 92447

YACHT DESIGNERS

Cannell & Associates, David M
Wivenhoe 01206 823337
Clarke Designs LLP, Owen
Dartmouth 01803 770495
Giles Naval Architects, Laurent
Lymington 01590 641777
Harvey Design, Ray
Barton on Sea 01425 613492
Jones Yacht Design, Stephen
Warsash 01489 576439

Wharram Designs, James
Truro 01872 864792
Wolstenholme Yacht Design
Coltishall 01603 737024

YACHT MANAGEMENT

Barbican Yacht Agency Ltd
Plymouth 01752 228855
Coastal Leisure Ltd
Southampton 023 8033 2222
O'Sullivan Boat Management
Dun Laoghaire +353 86 829 6625
Swanwick Yacht Surveyors
Swanwick 01489 564822
Amble Boat Company Ltd
Amble 01665 710267

YACHT VALETING

Autogleam
Lymington 0800 074 4672
Blackwell, Craig
Co Meath +353 87 677 9605
Bright 'N' Clean
South Coast 01273 604080
Clean It All
Nr Brixham 01803 844564
Kip Marina Inverkip 01475 521485
Mainstay Yacht Maintenance
Dartmouth 01803 839076
Mobile Yacht Maintenance
07900 148806
Shipshape Hayling Is 023 9232 4500

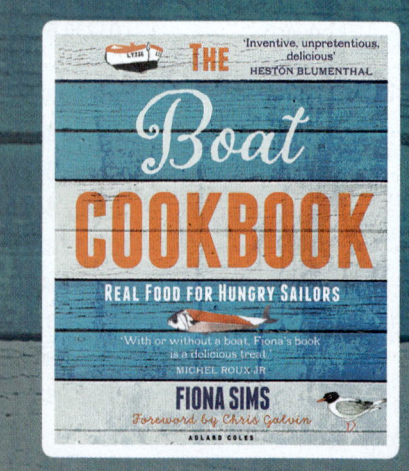

Your shortcut to simple and delicious galley grub – guaranteed to be devoured by hungry crew

www.adlardcoles.com

Minimum fuss but maximum flavour